A HISTORY OF ASTROLOGY DIVINATION AND PROPHECY

A HISTORY OF
ASTROLOGY
DIVINATION
AND PROPHECY

Contents

Ancient practices up to 200 BCE

12	Introduction	42	The Chinese zodiac
14	Written in the entrails Early divination practices	44	Signs and ecstasies Divination in ancient Greece
16	The king will die Celestial omens	48	The Pythia of Delphi
18	Fortunes from the flames Oracle bone divination	50	Revelations in sleep Dream divination
20	Seeking cosmic harmony Cleromancy and the *I Ching*	52	Winged messengers Augury
22	Using the *I Ching*	54	Consulting the dead Necromancy
24	Born under the stars The Babylonian zodiac	56	Signs of the times Mesoamerican astrology
28	Tracking celestial time The Egyptian calendar	60	Fortunes in a dish Greek lecanomancy
30	Ancient Egyptian star charts	62	Sacred signs in the dust Ifá divination
32	Astronomical timekeeping Observing the sky in ancient India	64	The threads of fate Old Norse *seiðr* and divination
34	Wind and water Feng shui	66	Keepers of secret knowledge Druidic seers
36	Practising feng shui	68	A star is born The origins of Hellenistic astrology
38	Earth and sky Chinese astral omenology		
40	Earthly branches The Chinese calendar		

Guided by stars 200 BCE–1100 CE

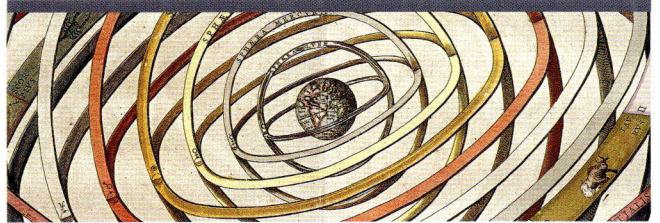

74	Introduction
76	Mapping the skies The first star catalogue
78	Written in the stars Stoic astrology
80	Changing fortunes Hellenistic horoscopes
84	A geocentric universe
86	A causal science Formalizing Hellenistic astrology
90	Signs of the Western zodiac
92	The planets
94	Reading Western birth charts
96	The Magi and the Star of Bethlehem
98	The magic of letters Runes
102	Reading runes
104	Seeds of fate Mesoamerican maize reading
106	Destined for greatness Astrology and politics in imperial Rome
108	Constantine's vision
110	A long and healthy life The birth of Ayurvedic medicine
112	Charting one's fortunes Indian astrology
116	Reading Indian birth charts
118	Notes from above Chinese spirit-writing
120	The way of yin and yang Onmyōdō in Japan
122	Chinese constellations
124	Ideas from afar East Asian horoscopy
126	Heaven on Earth The founding of Baghdad
130	Bridging theory and science Astrology in Abu Ma'shar's treatises
132	A star-studded era Astrology in the Islamic Golden Age
136	Iskandar's nativity chart
138	Lines traced in the sand Arabic geomancy
140	Practising geomancy
142	The power of names Islamic onomancy

Distant and divine 1100–1600

146	Introduction
148	East meets West Translating Arabic astrological texts
150	Divining right from wrong Reviving ancient practices
154	Life or death? Divination in medieval Europe
156	A dismal date in the diary
158	Spheres of influence Jewish and Kabbalistic astrology
160	Evil influence Planetary demons
162	Ways of seeing Mexica obsidian mirrors
164	The right remedy Astro-medicine
168	Divine inspiration Ecstatic visions
170	As above, so below Astrology in Renaissance Europe
174	Fateful prophecy
176	Pocket predictions Astrological almanacs
180	Circling the Sun A heliocentric universe
182	Changing heavens Tycho Brahe's *nova stella*
184	The Great Comet
186	Astral advice Court astrologers
190	The Book of Felicity

Changing fortunes 1600–1900

- **194** Introduction
- **196** Visions of power
  Indigenous American vision quests
- **198** Blending beliefs
  Divination in African syncretic religions
- **202** Messenger of the stars
  Galileo's astrological interests
- **204** Discord and harmony
  Explaining astrology
- **208** Answers for everything
  Prophecy and horary astrology
- **210** Destroyed by fire
- **212** Integrating ideas
  Japanese innovation
- **214** Guidance from the gods
  Polynesian diviner priests
- **216** New beginnings
  Indigenous African astrology
- **220** Tied to fate
  Knot divination
- **222** Revelations and ecstasies
  Millenarianism and prophecy
- **224** Cards containing secrets
  The origins of tarot
- **228** In the hands of fate
  The palm-reading revival
- **230** Roma fortune-telling
- **232** Reading palms
- **234** Seeing through smoke
  Capnomancy and libanomancy
- **236** "Seeing" is believing
  Spiritualism and clairvoyance
- **240** Fields of blood
- **242** Mouthpieces of the gods
  African prophetism
- **244** Fortune in a cup
  Tasseography
- **246** Reading the leaves
- **248** Divine wisdom
  Theosophy and astrology
- **250** The power of one
  Numerology
- **252** Practising numerology

Modern futures 1900 onwards

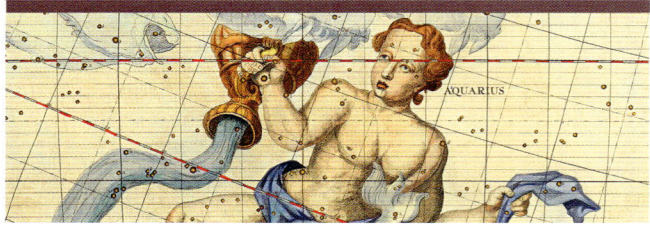

- **256** Introduction
- **258** A classic tarot
  The Rider-Waite deck
- **260** The Major Arcana
- **262** The Minor Arcana
- **264** Tarot-reading
- **266** Divining water
  Dowsing
- **268** Stars and the psyche
  Psychological astrology
- **272** Daily horoscopes
  Sun-sign astrology
- **276** Wartime magic
  Occultism in World War II
- **278** Gazing into the future
  Crystal balls and scrying
- **280** A new epoch dawns
  The Age of Aquarius
- **282** Manifesting the future
  New Age divination
- **284** Animal instincts
  Interpreting animal behaviour
- **286** Journeying to spirit realms
  Shamanism and neoshamanism
- **288** Calls to the other side
  Psychic hotlines
- **290** Astrocartography
- **292** Advice from algorithms
  Digital divination
- **294** The magic of cinema
  Divination in film
- **296** Searching for hidden truths
- **298** Cosmic tools for self-care
  Astrology and wellness culture
- **300** Answers in the stars
  Astrology in the age of uncertainty

Glossary and Index

- **304** Glossary
- **308** Index
- **318** Acknowledgments

Consultant

Nicholas Campion
Nicholas is Associate Professor and director of the Sophia Centre for the Study of Cosmology in Culture at the University of Wales Trinity Saint David, where he is also Programme Director of the MA in Cultural Astronomy and Astrology. His many books include the two-volume *A History of Western Astrology*, *Astrology and Cosmology in the World's Religions*, *Astrology and Popular Religion in the Modern West*, and *The New Age in the Modern West*.

Contributors

Dr Jo Edge
Jo is a historian of late-medieval and early modern medicine, divination, and astrology. She received her undergraduate and postgraduate degrees from the University of London, and is the author of *Onomantic Divination in Late Medieval Britain: Questioning Life, Predicting Death*.

Kim Farnell
A professional astrologer, editor, and writer, Kim has an MA in Cultural Astronomy and Astrology. She is pursuing a PhD at the University of Wales Trinity Saint David on the origins of the modern horoscope column and its relationship to British women's magazines.

Dr Ben Gazur
Ben is a freelance writer with an interest in history, folklore, and popular culture. He contributed to DK's *A History of Ghosts, Spirits and the Supernatural* and is the author of *A Feast of Folklore: The Bizarre Stories Behind British Food*.

Dr Ulla Koch
Ulla is an Assyriologist and a former research fellow at the University of Copenhagen. Her academic work focuses on Mesopotamian divination, religion, and literature. She is the author of *Mesopotamian Astrology: An Introduction to Babylonian and Assyrian Celestial Divination*.

Dr Jeffrey Kotyk
Jeffrey is a postdoctoral scholar at the Max Planck Institute for the History of Science. His work focuses on China's relationship with the world in late Antiquity, and how scientific knowledge (including astronomy and astrology) travelled between East and West.

Mai Lootah
A doctoral candidate at Rice University, Texas, Mai researches 17th-century comets, the "Republic of Letters", and the cosmologies of Ottoman and European writers. She has an MA in Cultural Astronomy from the University of Wales Trinity Saint David.

Dr Cailín Murray
Cailín is an associate professor of anthropology at Ball State University, Indiana. Her research focuses on links between settler colonialism in North America and the anthropology of the supernatural. Cailín contributed to DK's *A History of Ghosts, Spirits and the Supernatural*.

Helen Nde
A Cameroonian-born, Dallas-based writer and artist, Helen is the curator behind the online community Mythological Africans and the author of *The Watkins Book of African Folklore*. She previously contributed to DK's *A History of Ghosts, Spirits and the Supernatural*.

Philip Parker
A writer, historian, and former British diplomat, Philip studied history at Trinity College, Cambridge. He contributed to DK's *A History of Magic, Witchcraft & the Occult* and *A History of Ghosts, Spirits and the Supernatural* and is the author of many critically acclaimed books.

Dr Michelle Pfeffer
Michelle is a historian at Magdalen College, Oxford, researching the history of astrology and its rejection in the early modern world. She co-curates an exhibition at the Bodleian Library on divination and astrology through the ages.

Izabela Podlaska Konkel
An astrologer and teacher at the Warsaw School of Astrology, Izabela has written books on astrology and has translated many works into Polish. She holds a diploma in Cultural Astronomy and Astrology from the University of Wales Trinity Saint David.

Dr Anupam Kumar Suman
Anupam is a cultural astronomer and mathematician with a DPhil in Ancient Astronomy and an MPhil in Classical Indian Religion from the University of Oxford, and an MA in Cultural Astronomy and Astrology from the University of Wales Trinity Saint David.

Preface

Astrology flourishes in the modern world. Most people in the West know their zodiac (or birth) sign and many say that their sign is a good fit for their personality, or that they are like they are because they were born with the planets in one zodiac sign or another. In India, astrology retains its 2,000-year-old tradition, especially in Hindu culture, and notably in the great planet temples of the southern state of Tamil Nadu. These form the heart of a vibrant culture in which astrology can pinpoint auspicious times to perform any action, and so change the future. Today's global connectivity has made the various ancient astrological traditions available to everyone. Western astrology is now taught in China, people in Europe know their Chinese animal signs, and Indian astrologers give consultations over the phone to Americans.

Astrology is the quest for meaning in the heavenly bodies. It has existed in some form in every human culture since ancient times. We have evidence of stargazing from the Stone Age: the so-called Venus of Lausell, a 25,000-year-old carving of a woman holding what seems to be a crescent Moon containing notches, is thought to be a lunar calendar. There is also the Babylonian Venus tablet of Ammisaduqa, which features predictions for the planet Venus dating to c. 1700–1500 BCE. This tablet presents the earliest evidence for a tradition of astrology that continues to flourish in both Western and Indian culture.

The ancient world came up with models for how astrology works that are still relevant today. The Babylonians believed that the movement of the stars and planets was the writing of the gods, and the sky was therefore like a book they could read to find out about affairs on Earth. The 4th-century BCE Greek philosopher Plato thought that consciousness was the foundation of the universe and that the planets embodied the qualities of time. The astrology practised by his later followers was therefore concerned with the nature of the soul and with people's ability to free themselves from fate. Plato's student Aristotle took a different view, proposing that the building blocks of the universe were the four elements – fire, earth, air, and water – and everything, including people and planets, was linked by natural influences. In Indian astrology, seven gods and the seven traditional planets have long been intertwined, and the modern practice retains an overtly religious quality. For millennia, the Chinese have seen the universe as operating according to the flow of energy known as *qi*, and astrology as a means of preserving harmony.

In a traditional sense, astrology is divination when it aims to facilitate contact with divinities, as in India. But divination also applies to the practice of reading patterns in one area to find out what is happening in another. An astral diviner, for instance, looks at patterns in the planets to prophesy their effect on earthly affairs. Sometimes, astrological symbolism is separated from actual planetary movements, as when palm-readers or numerologists apply the meanings of stars or zodiac signs to lines on the hand or significant numbers.

Astrology has become very popular in the modern world for various reasons, the most obvious being that, for those who use it, it is helpful. It allows people to feel connected to the wider cosmos, giving us a framework for thinking about who we are and who we might be. And it also helps us to imagine possible futures.

Nicholas Campion

Planet personified
This depiction of Saturn from the astrological manuscript *Spherae coelestis et planetarum descriptio* (c. 1470) shows the planet in human form, flanked by the zodiac signs of Aquarius and Capricorn, over which Saturn rules.

Ancient practices
up to 200 BCE

Introduction

Two principles guided divination and astrology in the ancient world. The first was that absolutely everything in the universe was interconnected, from the smallest thing to the largest, and from the physical to the psychological, psychic, spiritual, and divine. Gods, stars, planets, people, plants, animals, fish, birds, insects, stones, the air, the wind, fire, flames, water, rain, rivers, thoughts, dreams – literally all things – were seen as part of a single system. The second principle, which follows from the first, was that any one thing could therefore provide information about any other. People could observe the flight patterns of birds, feel the wind, or look at the shapes of stones, and reach a conclusion about how to manage their affairs – political, personal, or otherwise.

Astrology focuses on connections between celestial bodies (mainly the stars and planets) and human lives. The term "astrology" stems from ancient Greek, so was unknown to those studying the skies in ancient Egypt, China, and India. It translates as "the word, or the logic, of the stars".

If astrology is the word of the stars, then the stars are speaking to humans – not in a way people could hear, but in a manner that they could read. This is why American historian Francesca Rochberg refers to Babylonian astrology as "the heavenly writing". The Greek word *logos* is the root of the English word "logic", and ancient peoples found logic in the messages they received from the stars.

The earliest Babylonian omen texts, from ancient Mesopotamia, were structured with an "if" clause and a "then" clause. One tablet reads, "If on the 16th day the Moon and Sun are seen together: [then] one king will send messages of hostility to another." In the event of such doom-laden predictions, all was not lost, however – a difficult forecast could be mitigated by rituals known as *namburbi*, which could change the future. The tablet in question continues: "Let the king perform either a *namburbi* or [some] ritual which is pertinent to it." This serves as a reminder of another feature of astrology – it invariably requires action.

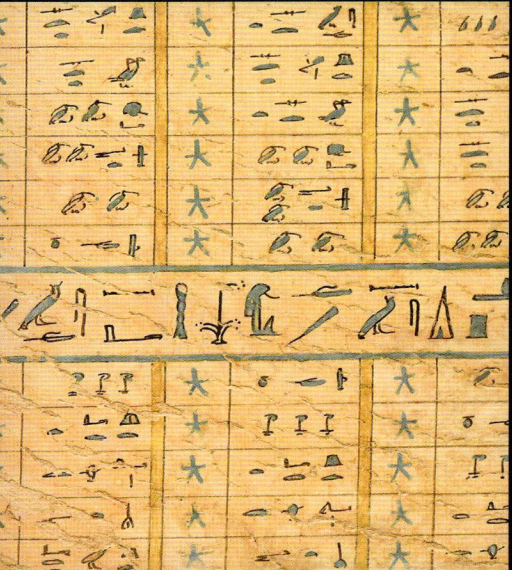

Charting the stars in Egypt *see* p. 30

Year of the dragon *see* p. 42

Examining entrails *see* p. 44

The act of communicating with the stars or other higher beings is known as divination because divinities – gods and goddesses – were often involved. Indeed, in a world in which they were always present, it is difficult to see how they could not be consulted. But the term divination is also employed in a wider sense to describe any activity that uses events or patterns in one part of existence to draw conclusions about developments in another without divine intervention. The ancient Chinese oracle the *I Ching* is a classic example. While the traditional practice of cleromancy requires the diviner to arrange yarrow stalks into patterns, the more usual modern custom is to throw coins and interpret the way they fall. The results are then transposed into hexagrams, consisting of six lines that correspond to riddles written in the *I Ching*. A diviner's task is to interpret these lines and offer advice. The underlying rationale here is not divine intervention, but time. Time is a part of the global mesh of interconnectivity, so if a question is asked of an *I Ching* diviner at a specific moment, the pattern of the yarrow stalks or coins at that moment reveals the answer.

> "Matters of which we have no reliable knowledge are foretold to us by seers who examine fire, the folds of entrails, or the flight of birds..."
>
> **EURIPIDES**, *THE SUPPLIANTS*, 5TH CENTURY BCE

Doom-laden dream *see* p. 50

Bird-watching *see* p. 53

Maya ritual calendar *see* p. 59

On the warpath
This detail of a 9th-century BCE relief from the Northwest Palace of Nimrud shows a scene from an army camp. A *bārû* accompanied the army on campaigns to ask guidance from the gods about tactics and the plans of the enemy.

Written in the entrails
Early divination practices

The gods have long been believed to have access to knowledge hidden from mortals. Although the gods rarely made clear pronouncements, humans sought their guidance, looking for signs they might send (unprovoked divination) and performing rituals to ask specific questions (provoked divination).

Ancient Mesopotamians, who lived from c. 4000 BCE around the rivers Tigris and Euphrates in modern-day Iraq, both looked for unprovoked messages from the gods, in the sky and on Earth, and used provoked forms of divination. Reading the gods' messages required specialist knowledge: *ašipu* (ritual specialists) and *ṭupšarru* (scribes and scholars) were tasked with observing and interpreting unprovoked signs. Provoked methods included seeking answers written in the entrails of animals, in smoke, or in drops of oil on water. These practices were carried out by a *bārû*, or seer.

Ancient ritual
Dating back to the 3rd millennium BCE, extispicy (inspection of the entrails of a sacrificial animal) is the earliest attested form of divination from Mesopotamia. Extispicy developed from sacrifices people made to ensure the success of a particular undertaking and to make sure it was agreeable to the gods. Over the centuries, extispicy evolved into a long and complex ritual, which could be performed for king or commoner to ask the gods about almost anything with a "yes" or "no" answer: Would the enemy attack? Would trade be profitable? Had a witch cast a spell on the asker? Instructions for this ritual were preserved in the *Bārûtu* ("Art of the Diviner"), a manual inscribed on clay tablets, dating from c. 1000 BCE.

The *bārû* would put questions to the divine judges, foremost among them the all-seeing Sun god, Shamash, before slaughtering an animal. The god Nabû, the divine scribe, was believed to write answers to these questions in the animal's entrails, which the *bārû* would then interpret, studying lines, holes, fissures, and other markings on the liver (the "writing tablet of the gods") and other internal organs.

Ignoring these answers could have terrible consequences. One Mesopotamian legend tells of an Akkadian king, Naram-Sin (r. 2254–2218 BCE), who suffered a devastating defeat because he went to war against the will of the gods. He disregarded the negative results of seven extispicies with the words, "What lion undertook divination?"

Reading a liver
In this clay model of a liver from 2000 BCE, the liver is divided into a grid, and the text specifies the meaning of the holes in each square. Models were used by diviners for study and interpretation.

> "If the top of the palace of the middle finger of the lungs is divided and fissured thrice, the vizier of the king will kill him."
>
> FROM AN EXTISPICY MANUAL KNOWN AS *IŠKAR BĀRÛTI* ("THE SERIES OF THE DIVINER'S CRAFT"), 1ST MILLENNIUM BCE

The king will die
Celestial omens

In the ancient civilizations of Mesopotamia, celestial divination was based on close observation of the sky (as opposed to other divinatory forms; see pp. 14–15). The Sumerians, who lived in the region from the 5th to 3rd millennium BCE, watched the heavens, defined constellations, and named stars and planets. They saw the Moon, Sun, and planets as celestial incarnations of deities, but did not, it appears, make astrological predictions.

Their successors, the Babylonians, adopted a lot of Sumerian religious lore. They observed the sky, and kept such meticulous records of the planets' movements that they were able to develop accurate mathematical models for lunar and planetary phenomena. The Babylonians saw the heavenly bodies as both manifestations of the gods themselves and messages from the gods, in the form of signs. The celestial divination they developed did not predict unavoidable fate; they believed they could prevent any ill-omened events by performing the proper rituals.

Spotting signs
The earliest evidence of celestial divination stems from the Old Babylonian period (c. 1894–1595 BCE). This includes the first astrological manuals and records of systematic observation of the movements of the planets, but there are no surviving examples of the actual practice of astrology. On the contrary, ominous phenomena such as eclipses were investigated by asking the gods for guidance via extispicy (see pp. 14–15). Over the next few centuries, however, celestial divination gained importance, written collections of celestial omens grew, and interest in Babylonian astrology spread throughout the ancient Near East.

By the 1st millennium BCE, astrology was so important that the Neo-Assyrian kings (ruling in Mesopotamia from the 9th to 7th century BCE) had close advisors who specialized in celestial divination, as well as observers posted all over the realm to "keep the king's watch". The astrologer's

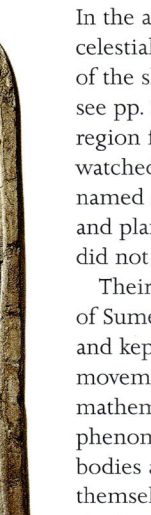

Ruling the heavens
This 9th-century BCE stele of King Shamsi-Adad V contains the symbols of the gods of the Sun (Shamash), storm (Adad), and Moon (Sîn), as well as Aššur, head of the Assyrian pantheon.

Head of a goat-fish, symbolizing Ea (the god of wisdom)

Celestial symbols
This *kudurru*, or boundary stone, from c. 1156–1025 BCE, includes the symbols of Shamash and Venus, identified with Ishtar, goddess of love and war. Together with Sîn, they formed a celestial trinity.

Symbol of Shamash (the Sun god)

Symbol of Venus

Temple symbolizing sky and wind gods

task was to observe the sky and note any potentially significant events. He especially looked for phenomena close to the horizon, for first and last appearances of the planets and the Moon, and for conjunctions between planets (when they appeared close to each other), or between planets and the Moon or fixed stars.

Next, the astrologer would look for relevant omens in the compendia; if the omens were unfavourable, he would seek ways to make the evil bypass the king and country. Evil omens could be averted by rituals such as *namburbû*, which asked the gods to "judge the case" in favour of the person who had received the omen. A total lunar eclipse boded the king's death and demanded a ritual lasting up to several months, where the king went incognito and was addressed as a peasant. Another man assumed the king's title and formal role and was put to death. In this way, the omen came true but the true king survived.

Divine creation

The god of wisdom, Ea, supposedly brought secret knowledge of divination to humans, transmitted in collections of omens. The oldest-known collection, the *Enūma Anu Enlil*, contains more than 7,000 omens, recorded on 70 clay tablets. According to this compendium, the gods Anu and Enlil, together with Ea, established the calendar and made the Sun god, Shamash, ruler of the year, and the Moon god, Sîn, ruler of the month, thereby creating an idealized lunisolar calendar of 360 days. This calendar had a profound influence on later zodiacal astrology.

Warning signs
Omens concerning the movements of the planet Venus are recorded on this 7th-century BCE cuneiform tablet, along with celestial observations from as far back as the Old Babylonian period. These records were also integrated into the *Enūma Anu Enlil*.

"When in the month Ajaru, during the evening watch, the Moon eclipses, the king will die. The sons of the king will vie for the throne of their father…"

FROM THE COMPENDIUM OF OMENS *ENŪMA ANU ENLIL*, TABLET 17

Oracle script
The tortoise shells on which the *jiaguwen* characters are carved were imported from southern China – provided as a tribute by the Qiang people. Inscriptions on the shells reveal the Qiang sent as many as 1,000 at a time.

Fortunes from the flames

Oracle bone divination

When the rulers of China's first historically attested dynasty, the Shang dynasty (c.1600–1046 BCE), wished to know the future, they sought to do so through pyromancy: the divinatory use of fire. They interpreted cracks caused by heating either the shoulder blade (scapula) of an ox – a procedure called scapulimancy – or the underside of a turtle shell (plastron) – a method known as plastromancy. Round incisions were drilled into these "oracle bones", which had been stripped of flesh, then the question being asked of the spirits was carved (or later, painted) onto the surface, and a red-hot poker inserted into the holes. The resulting cracks provided the response of the deities or ancestors.

The spirits addressed included Di (a supreme deity), lesser nature spirits, and the rulers' ancestors. It was considered particularly important to appease this latter group, each of which had an appointed day for sacrifices to be made during the 10-day Shang ritual week. Although some surviving oracle bones bear mundane questions, such as whether an ox should be taken to market, they largely concern matters of importance to the rulers: whether they should go to war, if the harvest would be good, or whether ritual sacrifices were being made correctly. The correct conduct or order of sacrifices is a frequent preoccupation on the oracle bones, though rulers also sought the answers to more personal matters, such as which ancestor had afflicted them with toothache.

Each oracle bone inscription follows a set pattern, with the date of the question, the name of the diviner – often the king, seen as having the most powerful connection with the spirit world – and that of the questioner. The question itself was then inscribed, generally requiring a simple yes or no response (such as "Will the raising of taxes be auspicious?"), along with the answer. Sometimes the actual outcome was recorded to showcase the prophetic power of the king (whose predictions were believed to be nearly always right).

Deciphering "dragon bones"

Such bone inscriptions, the earliest of which date from around 1250 BCE, range from 12 characters to more than 100, and are written in a very early pictographic form of Chinese script known as *jiaguwen*. They were discovered only in 1899 when Wang Yirong, Chancellor of the Imperial Academy, fell ill with malaria. His doctor prescribed ground "dragon bones", but when Wang got some from an apothecary, he found the unground material was actually tortoiseshell carved with ancient characters that he could not decipher. In 1908, their origin was traced to the site of Yin, the ancient Shang capital outside Anyang in Henan province. Around 150,000 oracle bones have since been found, bearing over 6,000 different characters and giving information about the Shang rulers, their families, their calendar, and astronomical events, including the first record of a solar eclipse and a comet.

The use of oracle bones declined towards the end of the Shang dynasty, when inscriptions simply recorded events, rather than questioning the spirits. By the first part of the Zhou dynasty (1046–256 BCE), cleromancy – the use of yarrow stalks and hexagrams – had become China's most common method of divination (see pp.20–23).

Founder king
According to tradition, King Cheng Tang, the founder of the Shang, overthrew the preceding Xia dynasty in fulfilment of a prophecy he read on a turtle shell. He is among the ancestors named on oracle bones.

> "Divination is for resolving doubts. If one does not doubt, why divine?"
>
> SAYING FROM THE *ZUO ZHUAN* C. 300 BCE

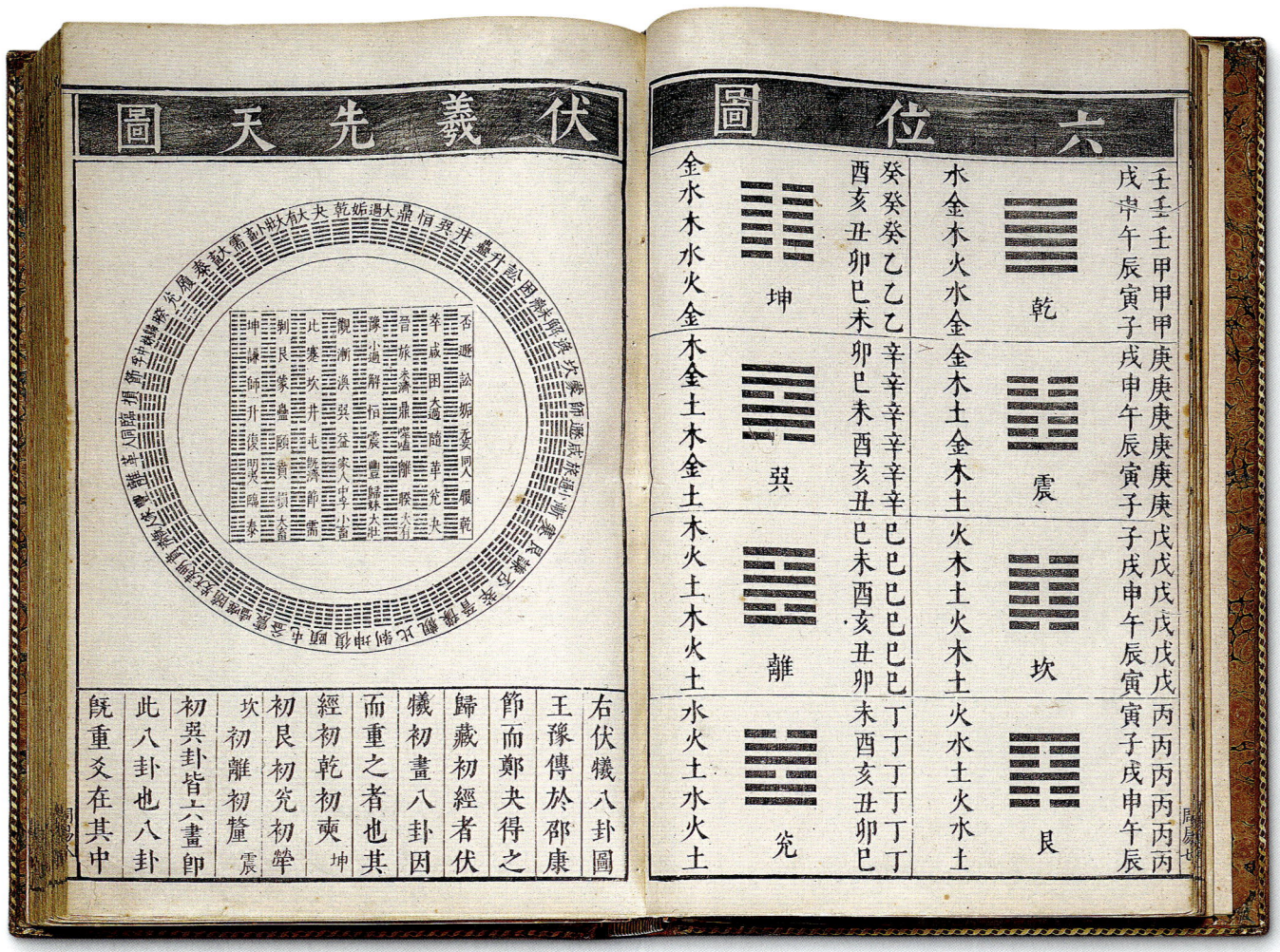

Seeking cosmic harmony
Cleromancy and the *I Ching*

Around the beginning of the Zhou dynasty (1046–256 BCE), the main form of divination in China shifted from the reading of oracle bones (see pp. 18–19) to cleromancy, a form of casting lots that used yarrow stalks to create symbols that foretold the future. This procedure was eventually codified in the *I Ching* (or *Yijing*).

Cleromancy may have developed from the ritual of interpreting the cracks on turtle shells – *zhenzu*, an ancient Chinese term for divination, meaning "reading the crack" – or was possibly linked to *liu bo* ("six rods"), a gambling game where the board featured a schematic representation of the cosmos. The earliest form of Chinese cleromancy involved the random division of 50 yarrow stalks into two heaps and then a complex ritual of sorting to leave a variable number of stalks that was interpreted as either a solid line or a broken one. This was then written down and the procedure repeated three times to create a trigram, with eight possible forms.

Trigram to hexagram
This early 17th-century edition of the *I Ching* shows Emperor Fu Xi's original eight trigrams on the right-hand page (each is doubled to make six lines) and the full arrangement of 64 hexagrams on the left-hand page.

Around 1050 BCE, the number of lines was increased to six, making a hexagram with 64 possible forms (see pp. 22–23). This change was traditionally ascribed to Emperor Wen, whose work the Zhou Yi ("The Judgements") numbered and named the hexagrams, and gave an interpretation for each one. These interpretations grew more complex over time, with the addition of the "Ten Wings", a series of commentaries on the Zhou Yi that were composed during the late Zhou and Han dynasties. In 136 BCE, Emperor Wu of Han ordered all these works to be codified into a definitive form – the I Ching (or "Book of Changes").

All change

By the time of the I Ching, yarrow-stalk divination had acquired a deeper philosophical significance. Confucius added to the existing commentaries, seeking to position the I Ching as a manual for living a virtuous life. The broken–unbroken dichotomy of the hexagram lines was linked to Chinese notions of yin and yang – opposed yet complementary forces that shape the cosmos (with yin being cold, dark, and static, and yang being hot, light, and fluid). The I Ching came to be seen as a manual for understanding underlying truths, a microcosm of the universe, and a reflection of the Daoist belief that supernatural energy, or qi, was in constant flow throughout it.

Mythological origins

Legend has it that the I Ching method of divination was invented by Fu Xi, China's first emperor (who, according to tradition, ruled from 2852 to 2737 BCE). He saw a dragon-horse coming out of the Yellow River and noticed a unique set of markings on its back.

Fu Xi had a revelation that the creature's markings were a reflection of the flow of universal energy – representing heaven, a lake, fire, thunder, wind, water, a mountain, and earth – and they led him to create the "trigrams" that would be used in future divinatory practices.

Fu Xi sits by the Yellow River contemplating the eight trigrams in this 16th-century work by Qiu Ying.

The "changes" the I Ching predicted were seen less as divination and more as a way of understanding the changes that occur in the universe.

The I Ching reached its final form in the 12th century CE, during the Song dynasty, and has since remained a highly influential system of divination in China. Cleromancy was transmitted to the West in the 17th century through Jesuit missionaries (who tried to reinterpret the I Ching, with hexagram numbers said to represent the Trinity), before achieving wider dissemination in New Age writings of the 20th and 21st centuries.

Cleromancer at work
A client poses her question to an I Ching diviner's assistant in this 19th-century engraving. The diviner has a board with the hexagrams laid out and the I Ching on one side to aid his interpretation.

Using the I Ching

Divination using the *I Ching* is based on randomly casting the numbers six, seven, eight, or nine, then turning them into one of 64 hexagrams (sets of six lines). The hexagrams are then cross-referenced to the text of the *I Ching* to find their meaning. One method for obtaining the numbers is to toss three coins six times; the sums of the resulting "heads" or "tails" are drawn as lines, stacked from the bottom up to create a hexagram.

Casting the coins
Heads score 3 and tails score 2. Adding the scores of each toss gives a number between 6 and 9, which is recorded as a line.

Coin combinations	Number	Line
3 heads	9	—⊖—
2 heads, 1 tail	8	— —
1 head, 2 tails	7	———
3 tails	6	—✕—

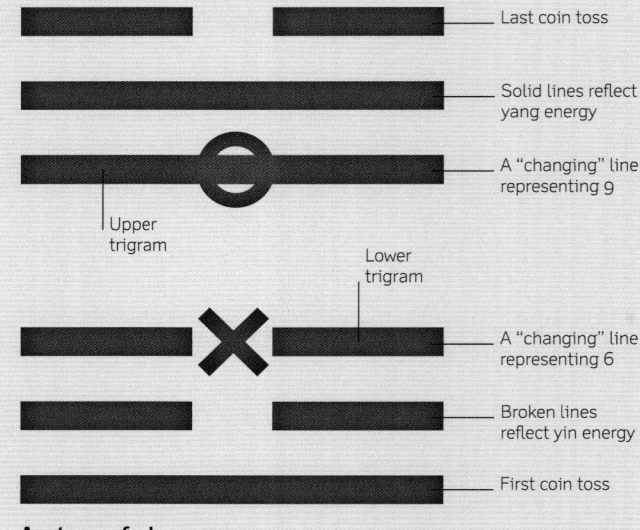

Anatomy of a hexagram
Hexagrams combine the meanings of two trigrams to describe the present situation. Lines formed by the numbers 6 and 9 are "changing". This means that they can be redrawn as their opposites to give a future reading.

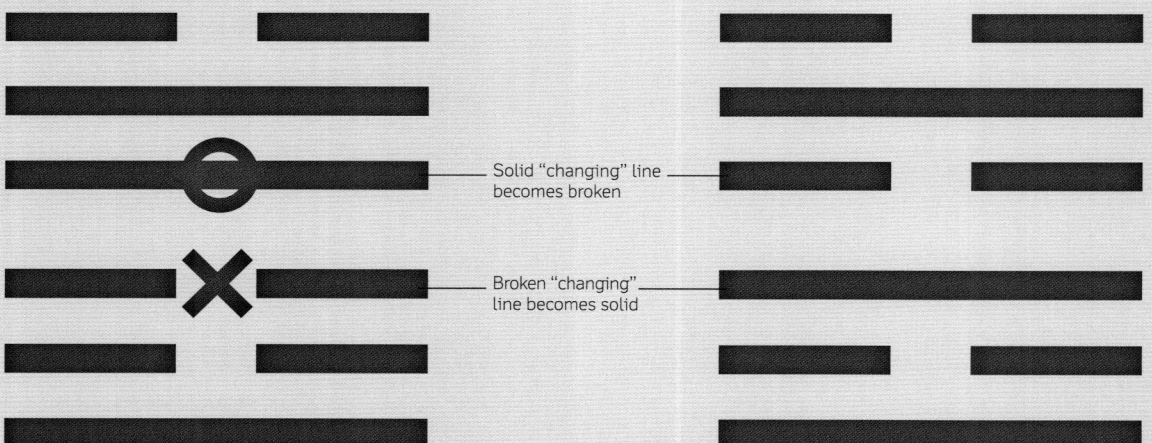

Present hexagram
Here, the upper three lines form the trigram *tui* (joyous, lake); the lower lines create *chen* (arousing, thunder). Together, they form hexagram 17 *sui* (following). Combining a happy tranquil feeling with a desire for action, it suggests going with the flow.

Future hexagram
The upper trigram here is *k'an* (danger, abyss); the lower is *li* (clarity, flame). Combined they form hexagram 63 *chi chi* (after completion). This suggests it may be necessary to take a risk but logical thinking will show the way to success.

Using the *I Ching* 23

Interpreting the hexagrams
Each hexagram number cross-refers to a passage in the *I Ching*, which gives the hexagram name, followed by a detailed interpretation of its meaning.

Finding the upper trigram in the top row and the lower trigram in the left-hand column locates the hexagram

Upper trigram

	1	34	5	26	11	9	14	43
	25	51	3	27	24	42	21	17
	6	40	29	4	7	59	64	47
	33	62	39	52	15	53	56	31
	12	16	8	23	2	20	35	45
	44	32	48	18	46	57	50	28
	13	55	63	22	36	37	30	49
	10	54	60	41	19	61	38	58

Lower trigram

Born under the stars
The Babylonian zodiac

Between c. 2000 and 600 BCE, Babylonian celestial divination concerned matters of public interest such as war, market prices, the weather, the fate of the king, epidemics, and famine or abundance for the country (mundane, or political, astrology). The celestial bodies and their movements were perceived as signs sent by the gods to indicate their support or anger, or warn about impending disaster. Most astrologers were affiliated with the court, and they reported observations and pertinent interpretations directly to the king. The interpretations were derived from large traditional compendia, primarily the *Enūma Anu Enlil* (see pp. 16–17) and the commentary *Šumma Sîn ina tāmartīšū* ("If the Moon god Sîn at his appearance"). The compendia linked celestial phenomena with terrestrial events based on a complicated system of associations, analogies, and word play. Even though a group of astrologers might observe the sky on the same night, they would quote quite different omens from the compendia. Those closest to the king generally cited the more sinister omens – their duty was to "keep the king's watch" and warn him of impending danger.

Celestial hero
This Babylonian cylinder seal dates from c. 1600–1350 BCE. Due to the stars he stands beneath, some scholars believe that the man depicted with water flowing out at each of his shoulders may be an early depiction of the sign of the Giant (Aquarius).

Positions of the planets and the Moon were often given in relation to 17 constellations close to the ecliptic (the path of the Sun as seen from Earth). These constellations were described as "gods who stand in the path of the Moon through whose region the Moon passes and whom he touches in the course of a month". Unlike the later zodiac signs, the "gods on the path of the Moon" did not have special significance in their own right but were simply points of reference.

A developing system

Relatively little is known about the development of astrology and astronomy in the Mesopotamian region, but sources suggest that things began to change in the 7th century BCE. After the fall of Assyria in 612 BCE, astrologers were no longer affiliated with a royal court but were employed by the major temples in the cities of Babylon, Uruk, and Sippar as lamentation priests, administrators, or ritual specialists. However, they continued to practise astrology and make celestial observations, and could hold the title "scribe of *Enūma Anu Enlil*".

At Babylon, a star-watch was kept at the temple to the god Marduk in Esangil, as attested by ephemerides (books of astronomical records, now known as "astronomical diaries"), which contained day-by-day observations. As well as celestial observations, the diaries contained notes on market prices, the water level in the Euphrates River, and significant historical events, such as the death of Alexander the Great in June 323 BCE. From their observations of how long it took a planet to move a certain distance, the Babylonians developed a mathematical means of predicting the movements of celestial bodies.

Delineating the zodiac

By the late 5th century BCE, Babylonian astronomers had invented the zodiacal circle by dividing the ecliptic into 12 equal segments, or signs, named after the closest and most prominent constellations from the "path of the Moon". The 12 signs, called *lumāšu*, were Hireling (Aries), the Bull of Anu/the Stars (Taurus), the Great Twins (Gemini), the Crab (Cancer), the Lion (Leo), the Furrow (Virgo), the Scales (Libra), the Scorpion (Scorpio), Pabilsag (a hippocentaur with a bow and arrow, Sagittarius), the Goat-fish (Capricorn),

Night on record
This planisphere (circular tablet) shows a stylized map of the sky, divided into eight sections, representing the night sky over Nineveh on 3–4 January 650 BCE.

Astral medicine

A typical medical or magical prescription stated that ingredients were to be mixed and left to spend the night "under the stars". Some texts mention specific stars – for instance, the Goat-star (Vega), which was associated with the goddess of healing, Gula. The medication was believed to be irradiated by the stars (gods) and become more effective. Some planets were thought to have a special connection with parts of the human body, such as Jupiter (Marduk) with the spleen and Mars (Nergal) with the kidneys. The idea of correlating parts of the body with the 12 months of the year and particular treatments for illnesses was later seen in the "zodiac man" (see p.179) and was known as *melothesia* in Hellenistic astrology.

Dating from 400–100 BCE, this astral medical tablet bears most of what is known about Babylonian *melothesia*.

the Giant (Aquarius), and the Tails/the Field (Pisces). The *lumāšu* were first used in astronomy but soon came to play an important part in astrology and astral magic and medicine.

Each sign was divided into 12 equal parts, the micro-zodiac, and each part was associated with various religious and therapeutic materials and rituals. These could include cities, cultic events, instructions for performing divination (how to make a god speak that month), materials used for therapeutic remedies (stones, plants, and trees), animals, prescriptions, and taboos.

One collection of cuneiform tablets dating from the Seleucid period (312–64 BCE) contains 12 tablets, each devoted to a zodiac sign, with the sign sometimes accompanied by a planet or the Moon. There are omens concerning lunar eclipses in the corresponding month, and prescriptions for each micro-zodiac sign. Astrologers continued to practise mundane astrology, but refined their approach, which allowed them to make more specific predictions about, for example, war, the marketplace, or the weather.

Natal predictors

The idea that an individual's time of birth – and other phenomena – might predict their fate dated back to the 2nd millennium BCE. For instance, a person's appearance – their hair, face, stature, and so on – was believed to indicate their personality and what could happen to them, and their date of birth could also be interpreted as a sign of what was in store for the newborn. So while the concept of making predictions for the nature or fate of a specific person was not new in itself, it was revived with the development of an entirely new form of astrology, natal astrology or genethlialogy, which was based on predictions pertaining to the time of birth of an individual.

The earliest birth charts, or "horoscopes", date to 410–62 BCE. Around 40 such texts are known. They list the individual's date and time of birth; computed positions of the Sun, the Moon, and the planets in the zodiac; the date of the full Moon and new Moon; the date of solstices; and, if relevant, lunar and solar eclipses. These texts rarely give predictions and do not refer to the interpretative tools used by Hellenistic astrologers from the 1st century BCE, such as houses (see pp. 80–83). Yet the association of attributes with zodiac signs began in a small way, with claims such as "the position of the Bull of Anu means death at war".

Other forms of natal astrology were practised that did not rely on the zodiac but on which stars rose in the east for the first time at sunrise, which planets had first and last visibility, and what the lunar phase was at the time of birth. New omens were written pertaining to the individual, such as: "If a child is born when Venus comes forth and Jupiter has set: his wife will be stronger than him."

Mapping the world
This cuneiform tablet from the 6th century BCE depicts a Babylonian map. The world is encircled by the cosmic waters, or "Bitter River", and Babylon is a rectangle at the top. The text describes how the Sun moves from east to west, then passes through the Underworld to rise again.

> "Capricorn (X): 14 Goat-blood, goat-fat, and goat-hair, you anoint…"
>
> LINE 2 FROM THE EXORCIST-PRIEST IQĪŠÂ'S CALENDAR TEXT, 4TH CENTURY BCE, ON THE THERAPEUTIC MATERIALS ASSOCIATED WITH CAPRICORN

The Babylonian zodiac

Zodiac symbol
This tablet, describing the sign of the Lion (Leo), dates from the Seleucid period (early 2nd century BCE). Leo is depicted standing on the constellation Hydra and facing the planet Jupiter.

Babylonian zodiac

The Babylonian zodiacal circle had 360 UŠ (a unit similar to modern degrees). Like the division of the Babylonian day into 12 *bēru* (double hours), the zodiac was divided into 12 sections or signs, each of 30 UŠ. Each sign corresponded to a constellation close to the ecliptic and the "path of the Moon". In later Hellenistic astrology, the longitudes of the tropical zodiac signs were fixed according to the spring equinox (see p. 89), but the Babylonian zodiacal positions were sidereal – defined in relation to specific bright stars, which the Babylonians also used to calculate the positions of the Sun, Moon, and planets. The stars used as reference points for the Babylonian zodiac were probably alpha Taurus and alpha Scorpio.

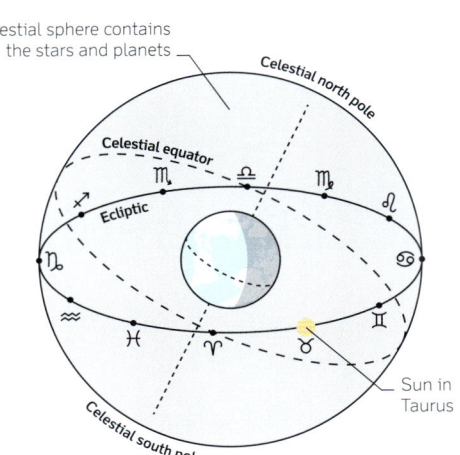

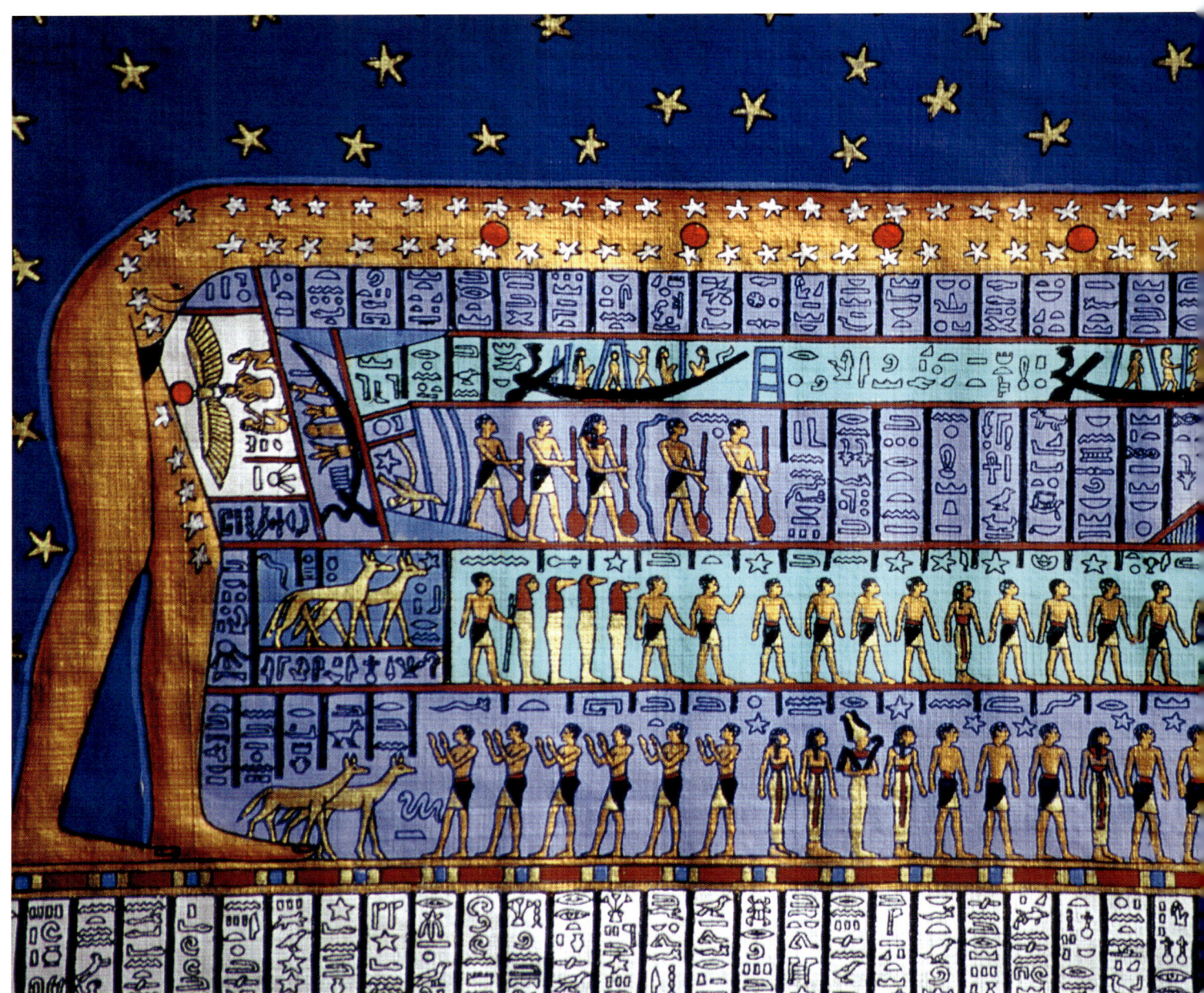

"The Egyptians were the first of all men on Earth to find out the course of the year… and this they found out from the stars."

ANCIENT GREEK WRITER HERODOTUS, *HISTORIES*, II–4

Tracking celestial time
The Egyptian calendar

The ancient Egyptians invented the solar calendar that is still used around the world today. Before then, however, they measured time using a lunar calendar, which was based on observations of the phases of the Moon (associated with Thoth, the Ibis-headed god of writing and learning) and its passage against the background of the stars. The month was counted from the appearance of a new crescent Moon and lasted approximately 29–30 days until the next new Moon appeared, each day representing a stage in the life of Thoth.

A solar year

While the lunar calendar was used for religious purposes, the Egyptians also devised a civil calendar to facilitate the administration of the state, which was more in line with the solar year. Around the time of the Middle Kingdom (c. 1980–630 BCE), they realized that the change of seasons could be predicted in advance, so they correlated the movement of the stars — mainly the Sun, the Moon, and Sopdet (the star of the goddess Isis, later known as Sirius) — with the cycles of nature. The temple priests responsible for keeping time were astronomers who observed celestial phenomena and collected astronomical data.

The priests used three methods to measure the hours of the day and night: water clocks, sundials, and observing the rising of the stars. The year began in July, with Sopdet's heliacal rising (when the star first became visible on the eastern horizon just before sunrise), and was divided into three seasons of four 30-day months: Flood, Growing, and Harvest. The heliacal rising of Sopdet usually coincided with the annual flooding of the River Nile, which was key to irrigating agricultural land and making it fertile with silt, an event still celebrated in Egypt today.

Practical purposes

The civil calendar consisted of 365 days, which included five days added at the end of the year to match the rhythm of the natural seasons and the solar year. Each month contained three 10-day weeks grouped according to the movement of certain stars, called decans (see pp. 30–31). As well as marking the dates of religious festivals and being used in the organization of the state, the calendar indicated lucky and unlucky days for religious, business, private, and state activities according to Egyptian cosmological and mythological beliefs.

Daily cycle
The goddess Nut, as the sky, arches over Earth in this copy of a scene from a temple at Dendera. The Sun god Ra travels along the sky each day by boat before Nut swallows and digests him.

The flow of hours
Clay water clocks (called *clepsydrae*, or "water stealers", by the Greeks) used the flow of water to measure time. This example dates from the reign of Amenhotep (c. 1390–1352 BCE).

Ancient Egyptian star charts

Texts found in the pyramids and coffins of ancient Egypt describe a pharaoh who, after death, becomes a morning star among the infinite stars of past rulers. This belief that the soul could be deified and reborn as a star is reflected in the star charts found on tomb ceilings and coffin lids, drawn to aid the soul's navigation through the heavens.

Egyptian star charts listed the decans, stars or small constellations chosen to mark the passing of the 12 hours of night. The appearance of each decan on the eastern horizon signified the start of the next hour. Every 10 days (representing a week in the Egyptian calendar; see p. 29), a new decan would be the last of the night to rise.

While the calendar was linked to the change of seasons regulated by the Sun god, Ra, the star charts indicated the auspicious hour to perform a rite. They were arranged in grids, with a column for each of the 36 weeks of the year (plus one for the five extra days at the end) and 12 rows, one for each hour of the night. Each decan and the hour it indicated was associated with a different god and a different temple practice. Some charts also included the civil calendar or images of offerings to invoke the gods.

> "Complete darkness, the firmament of the gods, the place from which the birds come."
>
> BOOK OF NUT, A COLLECTION OF ASTRONOMICAL TEXTS

This coffin lid from Assiut, from the early Middle Kingdom (c. 2100 BCE), is decorated with one of the most complete surviving star charts.

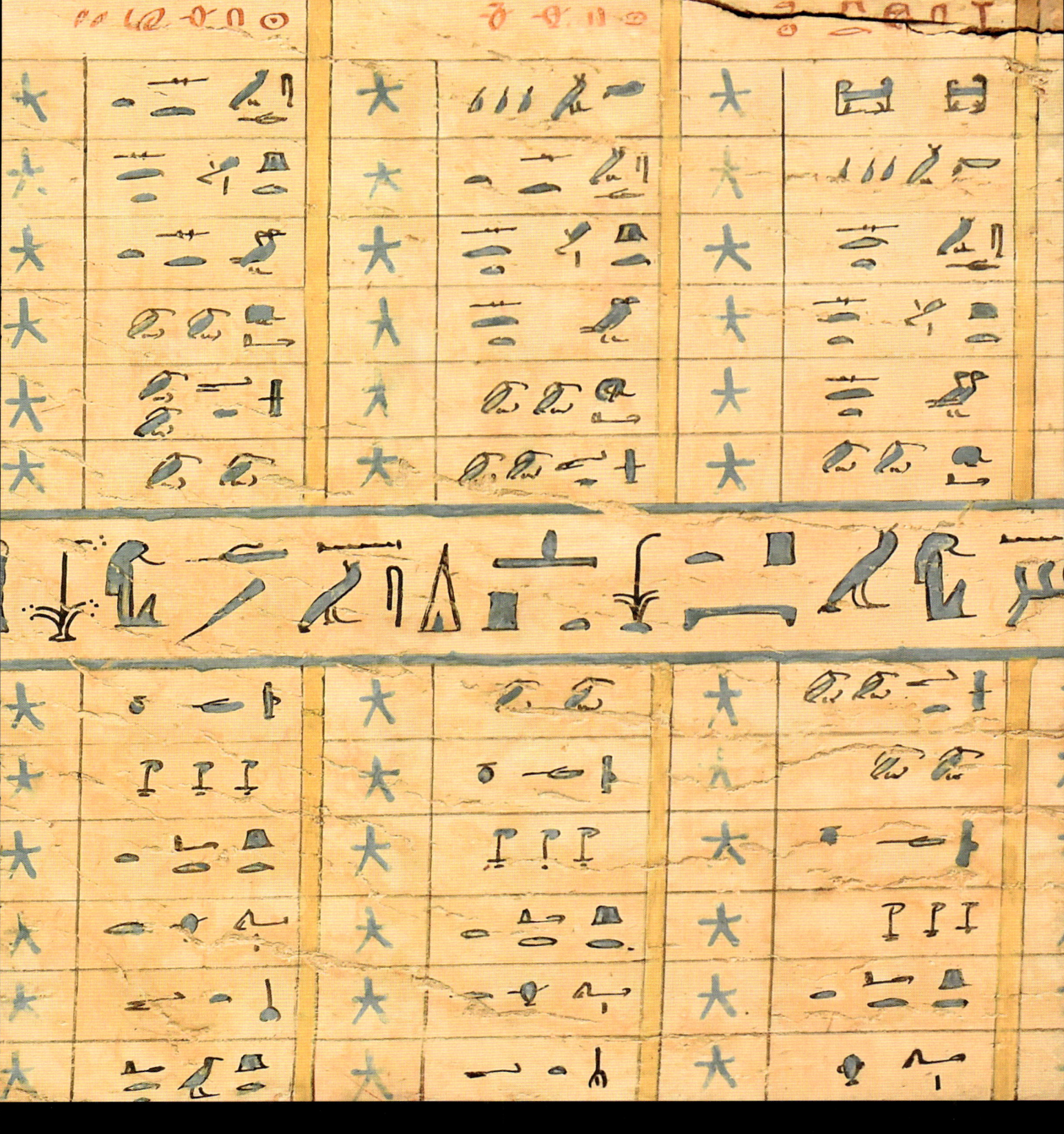

Astronomical timekeeping
Observing the sky in ancient India

For both astronomy and astrology, the people of ancient India used the Sanskrit word *jyotiḥśāstra* (meaning "science of light"). *Jyotiḥśāstra* was an auxiliary limb of the *Vedas* (a set of religious texts composed in the 2nd millennium BCE), required for determining auspicious moments for Vedic sacrifices. However, to begin with (from around 3000 to 1500 BCE), *jyotiḥśāstra* was limited to the observation and worship of astronomical phenomena, and the rituals associated with them.

Worshipping celestial events was probably a continuation of the religious practices of the ancient Harappan civilization of the Indus Valley, as reflected on a seal from the city of Mohenjo-daro, which seems to depict the Pleiades star system. The image on the seal ties in with the description of *Kṛttikā* (the Pleiades) in the Vedic text *Śatapatha Brāhmaṇa*, where the seven visible stars are said to "never swerve from the east". This astronomical observation of Pleiades rising exactly in the east makes it possible to date both seal and description to around 3000 BCE.

In Vedic society, the interplay of the Sun and the Moon – considered to be a cosmic wedding – was deemed the most important celestial relationship.

Seven stars
The seven figures at the bottom of this Harappan seal are thought to depict the constellation *Kṛttikā* (Pleiades). A priest near a *pīpala* tree and a ram are also visible.

The Moon represented the mind of the *puruṣa* ("cosmic man") and the Sun symbolized his eyes. Together, they formed the foundation of timekeeping, astronomical calculations, and astrological correlations. Vedic astronomers knew that the Sun caused day, night, and the tropical seasons, and that the Moon traced a sidereal path (its orbit around Earth as observed in relation to specific distant stars), passing through different segments of the sky, or *nakṣatras* (lunar mansions), on its way. Early Vedic texts list 27 *nakṣatras*, explaining their importance and associated rituals, and including a brief theological description of the ruling deity linked to each one. The lunar mansion *Kṛttikā* – with the fire god Agni as its presiding deity – is at the head of the list.

Cyclical worldview
The Vedic people had an integral world view of Earth, sky, and space. As they saw it, the divine correlation between the microcosm (*adhyātman*) of the individual and the macrocosm (*adhidevātam*) of the sky was intertwined with the various cycles of the seasons, agriculture, regular rituals, planetary movement, and birth and death.

Making the cut
The *Vedāṅga Jyotiṣa*, attributed to Lagadha, is the oldest surviving text on Hindu astrology and timekeeping. This folio is from a 1792 manuscript, and describes how to determine the right time for sacrifices.

This awareness resulted in the establishment of large- and small-scale astronomical time cycles: six-monthly northward (*uttarāyaṇa*) and southward (*dakṣināyaṇa*) Sun transits; a year made up of five seasons, 13 months (including a "leap" month), and 24 half-months; and a day and a night each divided into 15 *muhurta* of 48 minutes. In 1400 BCE, the *Vedāṅga Jyotiṣa* text introduced the concept of *yuga*, an epoch that lasted five years. Apart from a few references to bird omens and dream omens in the *Ṛgveda*, the early Vedic texts give little mention of divination or astrological techniques. Only in the post-Vedic era did *jyotiḥśāstra* develop into three specialized branches: *gaṇita* (astronomy), *saṁhitā* (omens or divination), and *horā* (astrology; see pp. 112–15).

Fire sacrifice
This 19th-century gouache painting shows four Vedic priests performing *yajña* – a fire sacrifice to the god Agni. The timing of Vedic rituals such as this would be dictated by *jyotiḥśāstra*.

34 Ancient practices

Auspicious city
This Ming dynasty (1368–1644 CE) painting shows the Forbidden City and its architect Kuai-Xiang. He designed the palace complex using feng shui principles to ensure the prosperity and safety of the emperor.

Wind and water
Feng shui

Often translated as "geomancy" (see pp. 138–41), feng shui ("wind and water") is a view of the physical environment and natural world that emerged in ancient China before spreading to Korea, Japan, and Southeast Asia. Its origins lie in 1st-millennium BCE divinatory practices for selecting housing and burial sites based on the position of the stars and surrounding landforms. Some elements of the practice may be even older, dating to Neolithic times.

According to feng shui principles, siting buildings and tombs in a landscape is more than an aesthetic decision – their positions will dictate the future prosperity of the families involved. The first authoritative book on feng shui is believed to be the *Zang jing* ("Classic on Burials"), written by Chinese poet and historian Guo Pu during the Jin dynasties (265–420 CE). From this time onwards, the art of feng shui was increasingly studied by state officials and other literate people.

Channelling positive energy
"Wind and water" refer to the natural elements that feng shui practitioners consider when trying to promote a positive flow of *qi* – a kind of energy believed to run through the landscape and all organisms. The flow of *qi* influences all aspects of life and is directed by and expressed in flowing water, the terrain, plants, the weather, minerals, and soils. The art of feng shui attempts to control the movement of *qi* by manipulating both the natural world and human structures. Other influential forces are also considered when trying to optimize *qi*. These include the complementary forces of yin and yang, the five elements (fire, earth, metal, water, and wood), the cardinal directions, the 10 heavenly branches and 12 earthly stems (see pp. 40–41), and the eight trigrams (see pp. 20–21). Many of the features of the *I Ching* divinatory text were absorbed into feng shui. Practitioners use a special magnetic compass (*luo pan*) to determine the flow of *qi* in a given space. In its earliest form, this was a naturally magnetic stone – a lodestone.

All these considerations are designed to bring about harmony that benefits the living and their descendants. It is also important to raise living *qi* and remove dead *qi*. Feng shui distinguishes between yin (dark) practices, used for tombs and cemeteries, and yang (light) practices, which are reserved for households and buildings. Interior and exterior aspects are taken into account, as are individual and community needs.

For centuries, the collective fortunes of cities and nations were shaped by the practice of feng shui, and it was state policy in East Asia from at least the 3rd century CE to use feng shui principles when planning cities. Beijing's Forbidden City, finished in 1420 CE, was constructed on a north-south axis, with the entrance facing south, while in Japan, feng shui guided the location and design of the ancient cities of Kyoto and Nara.

Energetic connections
Feng shui practice considers a cycle of energies that connects yin, yang, and the five elements, influencing the physical world. Each element generates and controls other elements in the cycle.

Fomulas in concentric rings allow complex calculations of energies

Determining energies
Feng shui compasses (*luo pan*), such as this 20th-century example, include information and formulas relating to the constellations, directions, and different forms of energy, which are analysed to gauge the flow of *qi*.

36 Ancient practices

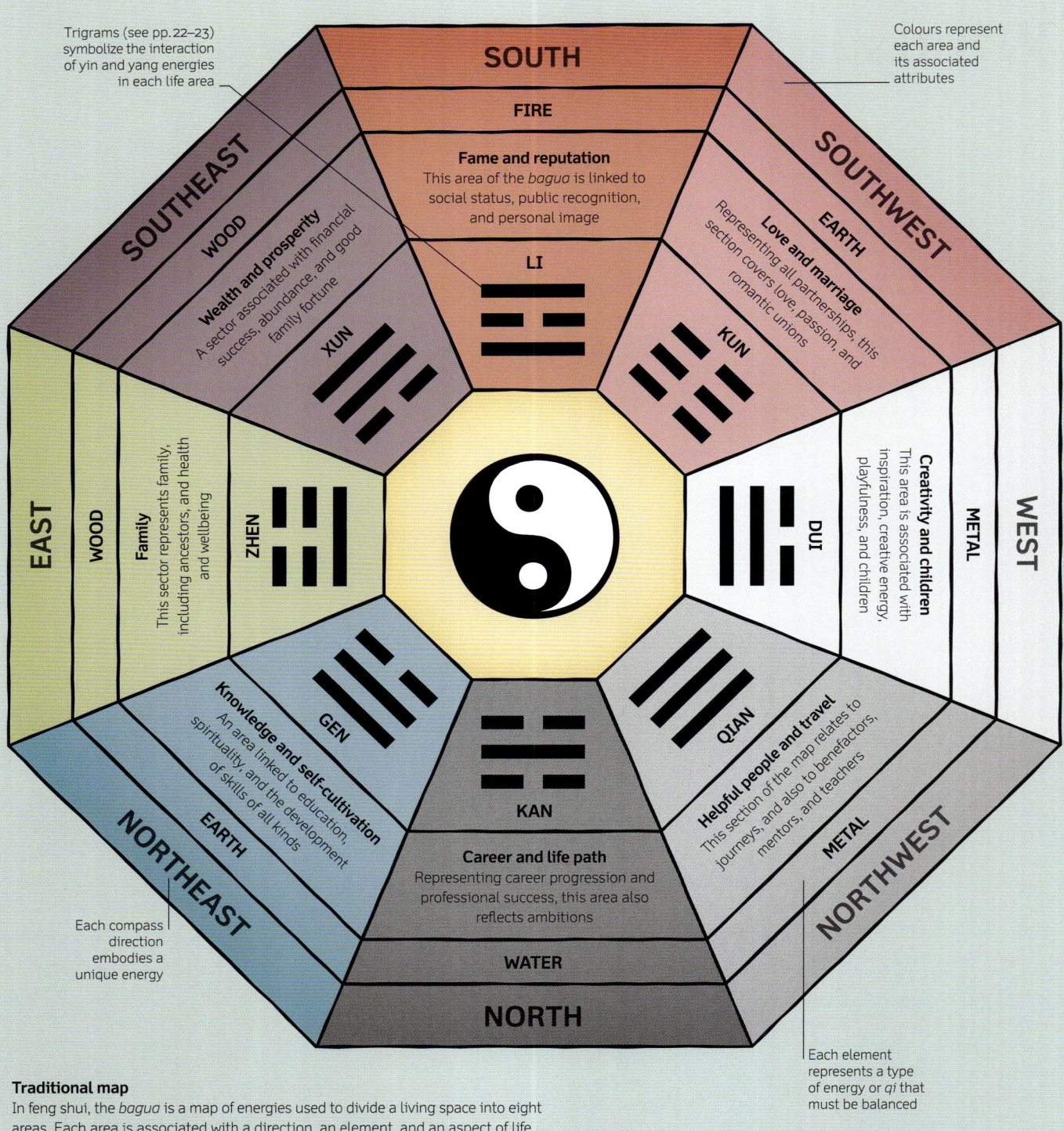

Traditional map
In feng shui, the *bagua* is a map of energies used to divide a living space into eight areas. Each area is associated with a direction, an element, and an aspect of life that embodies different energies. By understanding the location and flow of these energies, appropriate objects and colours can be introduced to achieve harmony.

Practising feng shui

Feng shui is an ancient Chinese practice of orienting and arranging indoor and outdoor spaces to achieve balance and harmony, which manifest as future prosperity. Inside the home, pathways should be decluttered and sightlines cleared to ensure a free flow of energy (*qi*). When selecting and arranging furniture and decorations, it is important to consider their shapes, colours, materials, and positions so that they align with the five elements (wood, fire, earth, metal, and water) believed to influence energy flow. Placing mirrors and plants in optimal positions can also energize the environment. Ideally, entrances and doorways should align with the cardinal directions.

Southeast
South
Southwest
East
Centre
West
Northeast
North
Northwest

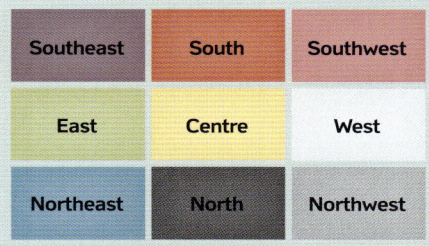

Modern map
In contrast to traditional, octagonal *bagua* maps, modern versions often use a simple grid system.

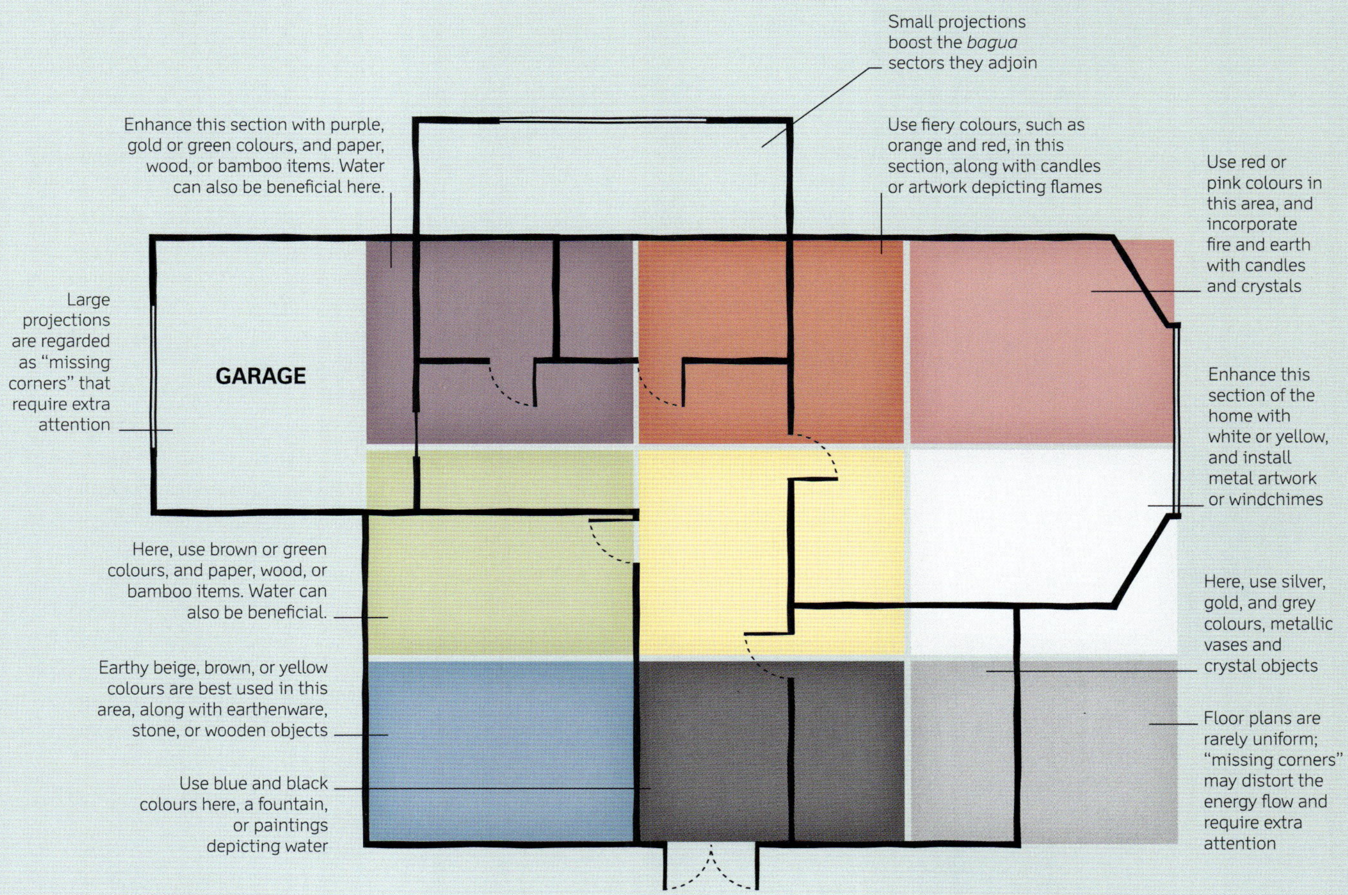

Small projections boost the *bagua* sectors they adjoin
Enhance this section with purple, gold or green colours, and paper, wood, or bamboo items. Water can also be beneficial here.
Use fiery colours, such as orange and red, in this section, along with candles or artwork depicting flames
Use red or pink colours in this area, and incorporate fire and earth with candles and crystals
Large projections are regarded as "missing corners" that require extra attention
GARAGE
Enhance this section of the home with white or yellow, and install metal artwork or windchimes
Here, use brown or green colours, and paper, wood, or bamboo items. Water can also be beneficial.
Here, use silver, gold, and grey colours, metallic vases and crystal objects
Earthy beige, brown, or yellow colours are best used in this area, along with earthenware, stone, or wooden objects
Floor plans are rarely uniform; "missing corners" may distort the energy flow and require extra attention
Use blue and black colours here, a fountain, or paintings depicting water

Applying the *bagua*
Every house is different, but by laying a floor plan over the *bagua* it is possible to see how energy and household areas correspond. Each area of the home, regardless of its usual function, can be enhanced with specific objects and colours that align with the element linked to the *bagua* division.

Earth and sky
Chinese astral omenology

Like other early civilizations, the ancient Chinese believed in the controlling power of the heavens and studied the skies for signs that might portend imminent developments on Earth. However, China's system of astral omenology – the study of celestial omens – evolved differently from practices in ancient Egypt, Mesopotamia, and Greece.

Right to rule
The "Mandate of Heaven" was a uniquely Chinese belief that emerged during the 2nd and 1st millennia BCE. According to this concept, a ruler's legitimacy was sanctioned by Heaven, which was considered to be a divine but impersonal force. If the ruling family behaved virtuously and competently, the mandate to rule was maintained. If, however, the ruling household failed in its duties, signs of divine disapproval were expressed in the form of extraordinary astral occurrences, such as eclipses and inauspicious clusters of planets, or by earthly phenomena, such as floods. These omens were believed to signal the retraction of Heaven's mandate, and its transference to a new ruler and his heirs. After the unification of China under the Qin dynasty (221–207 BCE), the mandate came to mean holding legitimate imperial authority over the whole of China.

Book of portents
This page from a manual on astral omens, commissioned around 1644 CE for use by the imperial court, indicates the long-standing importance of correctly interpreting celestial signs for Chinese rulers.

Sympathetic resonances
Belief in the significance of celestial omens had led Chinese astrologers to create a system of divination based on astral-terrestrial correspondences. Known as "field allocation", this system divided the sky into sections that reflected the traditional regions of ancient China – first the Nine Provinces of antiquity, and later the Twelve States, with the Yellow River corresponding to the Milky Way (foreign states were excluded from this system). Events in the astral realm were believed to manifest or resonate in their corresponding earthly field through the shared presence of qi – a universal energy present in all things (see p. 35).

By the Warring States period (475–221 BCE), comets, planetary conjunctions, and eclipses were being carefully monitored, since their occurrence in a particular astral field might signify impending disasters, revolts, or the death of a ruler in their corresponding terrestrial zone. Conversely, auspicious planetary conjunctions might indicate the bestowal of divine good fortune on a region.

Whether foreboding or favourable, these portents had significant implications for Chinese rulers, leading to field allocation omenology playing an important role in state affairs and political decision-making for centuries. Its use at court waned only in the 17th century, when Chinese astronomers adopted the concept of the spherical Earth, introduced by Jesuits from Europe.

Signs of disaster
Found in a family tomb at the Mawandui archaeological site, Changsha, China, this silk manuscript from the 2nd century BCE describes different types of comets and the various disasters associated with them. Eight comets are shown here, out of a total of 29 illustrated in the document.

Auspicious configuration
Dating from the Han dynasty (206 BCE–220 CE) and unearthed at the Niya Ruins in northwest China in 1995, the embroidered characters on this armband relay an astral omen: "The Five Planets appearing in the east benefit China."

Earthly branches
The Chinese calendar

The origins of Chinese calendrical science can be traced to the ancient Shang Dynasty (c. 1600–1046 BCE), when observations of the cycles of the Moon and the Sun were used for timekeeping. During the 2nd century BCE, the system was refined and these cycles were combined to create a "lunisolar" calendar, in which the cycles of the Moon are adjusted to fit the solar year.

Unlike the Gregorian calendar (used almost universally today), the Chinese calendar is based on lunar phases. The year is divided into 12 lunar months, with the first day of each month falling approximately on the New Moon, and the 15th day on the Full Moon. This gives months of 29 or 30 days (the time it takes for the Moon to orbit Earth) and a year of 354 days. Earth, however, takes 365.24 days to complete one full orbit of the Sun. This disparity means that, over time, the lunar months are out of sync with seasonal markers, such as solstices and equinoxes, which are important for maintaining agricultural schedules. To resolve the problem, the Chinese calendar adds a leap month (a 13th month) every two to three years. The first month of the new year generally begins in late January or early February and each month is traditionally divided into three *xún* – periods of 9 or 10 days. The seven-day week is Western in origin and was not used for official timekeeping in China until modern times.

Yellow Emperor
This 2nd-century CE depiction shows the legendary Yellow Emperor. He is credited with a number of innovations, including the Chinese calendar and the earliest forms of writing.

Long periods of time are calculated in sets of 60 years – a "sexagenary" cycle, representing a full lifetime in dynastic times. A cycle is characterized by 10 heavenly stems and 12 earthly branches – ancient symbols attributed to the mythical Yellow Emperor, Huangdi, around 2700 BCE. When paired, the stems and branches form 60 different combinations, each marking a year of the cycle. Years also have a deeper set of associations. Each heavenly stem is linked to one of the five elements (wood, fire, earth, metal or water) and has either ying or yang attributes. The earthly branches are also associated with one of the 12 animals of the Chinese zodiac (see pp. 42–43).

Auspicious times
The element, zodiac animal, and yin or yang attributes of each year (determined by its heavenly stem and earthly branch combination) are important for predicting fortunes and for determining lucky or unlucky days. Chinese fortune-tellers consult almanacs that detail these factors when suggesting days for marriage, business ventures, funerals, and other important occasions. More specific timings can also be recommended, based on the distinct characteristics of a particular time of day. Because the Sun passes into a new section of the sky every two hours, a system of "double hours" is traditionally used to mark the passage of time in Chinese calendars. These double hours are named after the earthly branches and are each associated with one of the 12 zodiac animals. Noon, for example, is the hour of the horse.

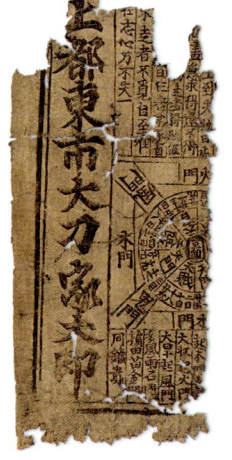

Personal almanac
This 9th-century CE fragment is part of an almanac that was printed and sold at a market in Chang'an, China. Providing guidance on auspicious days and times, such almanacs were popular purchases.

"An inch of time is worth an inch of gold, but an inch of gold cannot buy an inch of time."

CHINESE PROVERB

Calendrical tradition
Produced for Year 23 (1897) of the Reign of the Guangxu Emperor, this almanac page shows the centuries-long tradition of using the Chinese calendar to guide the timing of both personal events and matters of state. The Western calendar was not officially introduced into China until 1912.

The Chinese zodiac

A repeating cycle of 12 animals, each representing a year in the lunar calendar (see pp. 40–41), the Chinese zodiac runs from rat to ox, tiger, rabbit, dragon, snake, horse, sheep, monkey, rooster, dog, pig, then back to rat. Each animal is also related to one of the five elements – earth, wood, fire, water, and metal. This ancient system has been traced back to the Han dynasty (206 BCE – 220 CE), but it may be older. Over time, the zodiac has spread to neighbouring cultures, including those of Japan, Korea, Vietnam, and Tibet.

People born in the year of a given animal are said to have certain characteristics, much like the zodiac attributes of Western astrology. Romantic compatibilities can differ for better or worse between people born under different animals. The ordering of the animals is technically derived from the cycle of the 12 earthly branches used in the Chinese calendar, but various popular legends have emerged to explain the sequence. According to one myth, the Jade Emperor – one of the most revered Daoist gods – called for a race between all animals: the first 12 to win would become part of the zodiac cycle. The rat came in first, followed by the others, determining the zodiac order.

> "'Well done,' said the Jade Emperor to the proud rat. 'The first year of the zodiac will be named after you.'"
>
> TRADITIONAL CHINESE LEGEND

The 12 animals of the Chinese zodiac are depicted with local interpretations of their attributes in this 18th-century calendar from Tibet.

Signs and ecstasies
Divination in ancient Greece

The ancient Greeks continually sought advice from their gods and attempted to understand their will. A wide spectrum of phenomena, from the movement of the stars to the rustling of leaves, were thought to be forms of divine communication – tangible signs that expressed the gods' intentions, or their approval or disapproval of a particular course of action. Specialist interpreters scrutinized these signs to answer questions that ranged from state enquiries about the outcome of a battle to personal concerns, such as whether a proposed marriage would be successful. Direct counsel from gods and spirits was also sought more deliberately through rituals such as incubation. This involved sleeping in a sacred place, such as the shrine of the hero Trophonios at Lebadeia, in the hope of receiving guidance while in a dream state.

Readers of signs

Homer describes study of the flight patterns of birds (*oinoskopeia* or "orthinomancy"), one of the earliest forms of Greek divination, in his 8th-century BCE epic the *Odyssey*. Around 250 years later, the practice was still in widespread use, listed as one of the talents of the prophet Tiresias in *The Phoenician Women* by Euripides (c. 484–406 BCE). Tiresias was also credited with skill in extispicy (*hieroskopeia*), the divinatory art of examining the entrails of sacrificial animals for signs from the gods. It was often performed before military operations, and any abnormalities found were considered a bad omen and suggested lack of divine support.

Known as *manteis*, divinatory ritual specialists like Tiresias combined the roles of prophet and diviner. Some came from families with a long tradition of divination, such as the Branchidai, Telliadai, and Melampodidai, who claimed descent from renowned seers. Other practitioners, the *chresmologoi*, specialized in collecting and relaying oracles – direct messages from the gods. Surviving excerpts from a collection of omens, probably first compiled in the 6th century BCE, and the Greek Magical Papyri, a corpus of spells and rituals assembled in Egypt around 100 CE, are examples of the type of material that formed the everyday work of these divinatory practitioners. Another manual that reveals the divinatory services on offer is the 2nd-century CE *Oneirocritica* ("Interpretation of Dreams") by Artemidoros, a guide to analysing signs delivered to the unconscious.

Some *manteis* were itinerant freelancers, but others were professionals employed by monarchs. The seer Aristander of Telmessos accompanied Alexander the Great on his military campaigns. In one of his most famous predictions, Aristander declared that an eagle hovering above the Macedonian king at the battle of Gaugamela indicated victory against the Persians.

Prophetic insects
This 7th-century BCE gold plaque from Rhodes depicts a bee nymph. According to legend, bee nymphs taught Apollo the art of prophecy, causing bees to be regarded as divine messengers.

Greek prophet
A 5th-century BCE mirror shows Calchas, the leading seer on the Greek side in the Trojan War, studying the liver of a sacrificial animal.

God of divining

The god Apollo was regarded as a deity with particular responsibility for divination. Homer relates that Apollo was already born with prophetic powers, although another story tells how he was taught as a child by the Thriae, three bee nymphs on Mount Olympus, to make prophecies by throwing pebbles. An alternative myth has Pan, god of shepherds and the wilderness, instructing Apollo in the art of divination. Oracular shrines to Apollo were widespread in the Greek world. The most renowned was at Delphi, which attracted thousands of petitioners eager to obtain advice from the god (see pp. 48–49).

Apollo is often shown with a lyre, a gift to him from the god Mercury.

Manteis also operated from oracular shrines – sites where the gods disclosed their will through oracles. The famous shrine of Apollo at Delphi (see pp. 48–49) grew rich on the offerings both of city-states and of private applicants, who paid four *obols* (around £100) for a consultation.

Oracular divination

The role of the *mantis* involved direct communication with the gods through dreams or ecstatic visions. They channelled messages from deities that were particularly associated with divination, such as Zeus, whose shrine at Dodona was regarded as the oldest in Greece, and Apollo (known as *Moiragetes*, "the guide of fate"), but occasionally from others such as Pan, consulted at oracular shrines in Arcadia, and Asclepius, god of healing, said to bring cures in dreams.

The *mantis* might give answers in an ecstatic trance, or as if possessed by the god, but the administration of divinatory activities at oracular temples also involved more mundane tasks. A staff of assistant priests or priestesses performed the rites needed for a successful consultation, translated prophecies into intelligible forms, and supervised applications for advice. At Dodona, petitioners wrote their questions on lead tablets, more than 4,000 of which survive, including one which enquires, "Will it be better for Agelochos if he sets out to be a farmer?"

Varying methods were employed to determine divine will at oracular centres. At Dodona, the Pleiades, the priestesses of Zeus, interpreted the rustling of leaves on a sacred tree, while at the shrine of Hermes Agoraios in Phare, the answer depended on the words of the next person the applicant met. At Delphi, those who could not afford the full fee for the services of the Pythia, Apollo's priestess, could obtain a "yes" or "no" answer to a question by picking black or white beans out of a bag.

The gods could also be consulted using other types of divination, such as hydromancy, the observation of ripples on a body of water, and lecanomancy, a variant in which the spread of oil on a bowl of water was interpreted (see pp. 60–61). Cheiroscopy examined patterns on the palm of the questioner's hand. Less common approaches included teratoscopy, the study of prodigies (such as animals born with two heads), and necromancy, consulting the dead, who were believed to have knowledge denied to the living. Necromancy was considered particularly dangerous and so was rarely used (see pp. 54–55).

Diviner's dice
Sheep's knucklebones such as these were often used for divination. Usually, four or five were thrown by the questioner and the result read off against a list of predetermined responses.

Posing a question
One of thousands of lead tablets from the shrine at Dodona, this is inscribed with a question for the priestesses. On a few tablets, their responses, expressing Zeus's will, are recorded on the reverse.

Games of chance
An amphora (540–530 BCE) shows Greek warriors Achilles and Ajax throwing dice during a lull in the Trojan War. Games of chance acted as a metaphor for fate (both heroes died at Troy).

Everyday approaches
A number of simple practices made divination accessible to all. Methods such as cleromancy (the drawing of lots) or astragalomancy (divination by throwing dice) were akin to game-playing. Greek geographer Pausanias (c.110–180 CE) describes how visitors to the temple of Heracles at Bura in Achaia could put their question to the god, then throw four dice, the result revealing his answer. More exotic means of divination, some based more on folk knowledge and superstition than divinatory skill, included palmomancy, the study of twitches (a shaking right leg meant pain for a slave, profit for a widow, or a scare for a soldier); capnomancy, the study of smoke rising from a sacrificial animal; and even aleuromancy, the reading of patterns in flour. For the Greeks, the gods spoke in many ways.

> "...what is hidden from mortals we should try to find out from the gods by divination: for to him that is in their grace the gods grant a sign."
>
> **XENOPHON**, *MEMORABILIA*, 1.1

The Pythia of Delphi

The most important source of oracles (direct messages from the gods; see pp. 44–47) in the ancient Greek world was the shrine of Apollo at Delphi, established in the 8th century BCE. Petitioners had to offer a sacred cake and sacrifice a goat. If the animal trembled, the ceremony was stopped and the question remained unanswered. The Pythia, Apollo's priestess, who received the oracles, was always a woman over the age of 50. She would only give consultations on the seventh day of the month (Apollo's birthday) and not at all in winter. The Pythia would bathe in a sacred spring and descend into the *adytos*, an underground chamber in the temple. There, she inhaled fumes emanating from a cleft in the rock, after which she delivered the god's response.

Ancient accounts relating to oracles vary: some suggest the messages were unintelligible and interpreted by other priests into hexameter verse; others state that they could be directly understood. The Pythia's answers were notoriously cryptic. Before the Battle of Salamis in 480 BCE, she encouraged the Athenians to "build wooden walls" to fend off the Persians, a response Athenian statesman Themistocles took to mean the construction of a fleet of warships. His strategy proved successful.

> "…of all the oracles in the world [Delphi] had the repute of being the most truthful."
>
> **STRABO**, *GEOGRAPHY*, IX.3

The Pythia speaks to petitioners from her sacred tripod in this 19th-century painting by Camillo Miola.

Revelations in sleep
Dream divination

Ancient Mesopotamian societies saw sleep as an ambiguous state between life and death – a place where the gods could send messages via dreams. Interpreting these dreams (oneiromancy) offered a way to understand divine will and predict the future.

Dreams were regarded as either divinely inspired or, if they were nightmares, tainted by demonic possession. The latter could be banished by an *asipu* (exorcist) through rituals, such as transferring the demonic power to grains of wheat that were then burned. Nightmares were thought to be sent by the god Zaqigu; dreams containing positive signs and messages came from Anzagar or Mamu – who had a temple at Balawat (near Mosul, Iraq). These dreams were referred to as *suttu*, "a divination of the night", or *munattu*, "a waking dream".

Death of a demon
This 8th-century BCE seal depicts a scene from the *Epic of Gilgamesh*, in which Gilgamesh, dagger in hand, and Enkidu, brandishing an axe, apprehend the demon Humbaba. Part of the poem relates Enkidu's dream, in which he is punished for slaying the kneeling demon.

In some cases the divine message was clear — for example, when King Ashurbanipal of Assyria (r. 668–627 BCE) had a dream in which the goddess Ishtar promised him victory in battle. Other dreams were more symbolic, such as that of Gudea, ruler of Lagash in the 21st century BCE, who dreamed of a giant with wings, a woman holding a golden stylus, and a man bearing a tablet made of lapis lazuli. Puzzled, he consulted at the shrine of the goddess Nanse, where he was told the dream meant he should build a temple to Ningirsu, the patron saint of Lagash.

Dreams play a large part in Mesopotamian literature. In the *Epic of Gilgamesh*, the hero's friend, Enkidu, has a dream in which the gods condemn him to die as a punishment for killing the demon Humbaba and he is taken down into the Underworld. When Enkidu awakes, he falls ill and dies, journeying to the afterlife and fulfilling his dream's prediction. In the Sumerian poem *The Dream of Dumuzid*, the mythical god-king Dumuzid sees his own death in a dream in which two reeds are parted. He consults his sister Geshtinanna, the goddess of dream diviners and agriculture, who explains that the two parted reeds mean that Dumuzid will indeed die, forever separating the two siblings.

Consulting the professionals

At shrines, petitioners consulted professional dream interpreters such as the *bārû* (diviner), who also dealt with omens more generally, including those witnessed while awake. The *s'ailu* (questioners), who were often women, specialized in dream interpretation. Occasionally, visitors to the temples would try to provoke a dream message through incubation (sleeping in the god's shrine), but more often they sought an explanation for a dream they had already had.

Interpretations might involve consulting a dream manual, such as the *Iškar Zaqīqu* ("core text of the god Zaqīqu", also known as "The Assyrian Dream Book"), a collection of 11 tablets found in the ruins of Ashurbanipal's palace at Nineveh. It categorized dreams by themes (such as the descent to the Underworld or transformation into an animal) and revealed the meaning of each. As with many ritual texts, or *namburbû*, the interpretation relied on puns or wordplay: if a man dreamed of eating a raven (*arbu*), for instance, he would gain new income (*irbu*). Even in dreams, language exercised power.

Broken dreams
This fragment of a Babylonian clay tablet, dating from around 1900–1600 BCE, contains a series of dream omens. Each line describes an omen seen in a dream and the event it predicted would follow.

> "I had a dream last night.
> Stars of the sky appeared,
> and some kind of meteorite…"
>
> **GILGAMESH TO HIS MOTHER, NINSUN**, *EPIC OF GILGAMESH*, TABLET 1

Winged messengers
Augury

Feathered omens
A 6th-century BCE Greek cup shows a rider accompanied by four water birds. The presence of a winged figure of victory and an eagle are signs the scene is intended to portray good fortune.

The ancient practice of augury, determining the will of the gods by deciphering signs in the sky – especially the behaviour of birds – is conducted by an augur, a type of seer. Babylonian omen collections from the 7th century BCE refer to the interpretation of these signs by a ritual specialist known as a *bārû*. Ornithomancy – a form of divination based entirely on the observation of birds – was practised among the Assyrians by a *dagil issuri* (bird-watcher) at around the same time. Birds were seen as messengers of the gods, their movements determining both private matters, such as whether a marriage was auspicious, and great affairs of state, such as a declaration of war.

Their patterns of flight, behaviour (such as whether they swooped to attack prey), calls, and even whether they ate sacred grain (a Roman divinatory practice) were subject to an augur's scrutiny.

In the early Greek period, ornithomancy or bird augury was first mentioned in Homer's *Iliad* (8th century BCE) when Zeus sends eagles – birds closely associated with him – as signs to the warring mortals; Apollo, the god of prophecy, uses ravens to send his messages; and a black-and-white eagle spied as the Greeks set out for the Trojan War is taken to be an auspicious sign. Tiresias, the most renowned Greek augur, is called the "shepherd of birds", while the Greeks also had the seer Calchas on their side, a specialist in bird augury.

Deciphering bird activity became an established part of Greek culture. An owl, sacred to Athene, reportedly landed amid the Athenian fleet before the Battle of Salamis in 480 BCE. This was said to foreshadow victory against the Persians. In contrast, the dead ravens that dropped out of the sky as Alexander the Great entered Babylon in 323 BCE were believed to signify the military leader's impending death. One 2nd-century BCE papyrus from Faiyum in Egypt features a comprehensive list of bird omens to aid augury; for example, a vulture seen when enquiring about the birth of a child is considered to be an extremely lucky sign.

State bird-watchers

Among the Romans, augury was seen as integral to the state, present from its very foundation (see box). The augurs formed an official college of priests, originally composed of patricians (nobility), but then expanding in 300 BCE to include plebeians from lower social orders. Augurs, elected for life, were present to interpret auguries undertaken ahead of any significant public decision, such as military campaigns or lawsuits. They were also employed to read omens relating to private matters, such as marriages.

Augurs themselves could not call for the taking of an augury – that was the preserve of senior Roman magistrates, such as consuls, who declared the behaviour of the birds to be an augury, which the augur would then interpret. Magistrates could use this power for political ends; for example, they might employ a process known as *servare caelo* (observing the sky for possible omens) to delay elections until a more convenient time. However, not everyone respected auguries. In 249 BCE, the general Publius Clodius Pulcher ordered the sacred chickens on his ship to be thrown into the sea when they would not eat the grain, declaring, "If they will not eat, let them drink." A disastrous defeat against the Carthaginians followed. Ignoring the auguries was evidently fraught with risk.

Feeding hens
This augur is carrying out divination that involves feeding sacred chickens. He bears a *lituus*, a curved staff used to designate the area of sky where the flight of birds is to be observed.

The foundation of Rome

According to legend, augury played a crucial role in the foundation of the city of Rome in 753 BCE. The twin brothers Romulus and Remus argued about who had the right to establish a new city and agreed to employ augury to settle the matter.

The brothers went to separate hills and waited for the appearance of an omen. First, Remus saw six vultures, which he believed gave him precedence. Then Romulus saw 12 vultures – a sign, he claimed, that allowed him to become the new settlement's founder. Romulus proceeded to draw out a *pomerium*, or sacred boundary, for the city on the Palatine Hill. Remus crossed over this, angering his brother so much that Romulus murdered him.

Brothers Romulus and Remus observe the flight of vultures from viewpoints on neighbouring hills.

Fate of Orpheus
Gustave Moreau's 1865 oil painting shows a girl holding Orpheus' head as it rests on his lyre. The poet had descended into the Underworld in search of his wife, but was later beheaded by maenads, female followers of Dionysus.

Consulting the dead
Necromancy

The art of communing with the dead, necromancy is an ancient practice. The first tangible evidence of it may be the plastered skulls at Jericho (Palestine) from c. 7000 BCE that suggest a ritual connected with ancestor worship. The word is derived from the Greek *nekromanteia* (*nekrós* – corpse – and *manteia* – divination). In ancient Greece, *nekya*, or rites to summon ghosts, were only undertaken when the spirits of the deceased were deemed to have special knowledge they could pass on to the living.

Literary ghosts
In Greek literature, the simplest method of communication with the dead was when a ghost spontaneously appeared in a vision or dream. In Homer's epic poem the *Iliad*, for example, Patrocles appears to Achilles, pleading to be properly buried. Another method might be to summon a ghost from the Underworld. In the *Odyssey*, the sorceress Circe instructs Odysseus on how to call up the shade (spirit) of the prophet Tiresias with offerings of milk, honey, wine, and barley. He digs a pit and fills it with the blood of sacrificial rams so the ghosts can drink before they speak. An extreme alternative might be a physical descent to the Underworld. In the legend of Orpheus and Eurydice, the poet journeys to the Underworld in a bid to persuade Hades, lord of the dead, to release his wife.

Belief in necromancy and the ability of the dead to know the fates of the living persisted into classical times, although direct references are rare. In Aeschylus's play *The Persians*, the wife of the dead ruler Darius summons his ghost through hymns and libations.

Communication with the dead was considered possible in locations such as graves, caves, and at four main oracular shrines – the *nekromanteia* at Acheron, Tainaron, Heracleia Ponteia, and Avernus (in Italy) – all of which were believed to be portals to the Underworld. Rites carried out might include luring a spirit into a skull from where it could speak, inscribing questions to the dead on tablets (often made from lead), reanimating corpses, or sleeping in the shrine in the hope of obtaining a dream message.

Underworld shrine
The Greeks believed a *nekromanteion* was a place where communication with the dead was possible. This site at Acheron was thought to be where the dead departed for the Underworld.

A darker art
By Roman times, necromancy was more closely linked to practitioners of magic. Legislation was passed to outlaw it, and accusations of its practice were used to discredit political opponents, sometimes on the grounds of treason. In *Pharsalia*, the poet Lucan describes a scene in which Sextus Pompey, the son of Julius Caesar's opponent, consults a Thessalian witch. She revives a dead soldier, who predicts the death of his father. Her lair contains blood and guts, a depiction of the revulsion which, by then, the thought of necromancy inspired.

Go-between
As goddess of magic and the night, Hecate had the power to cross over from the land of the dead to that of the living and was commonly invoked in necromantic rituals.

Signs of the times
Mesoamerican astrology

Many artefacts left behind by Mesoamerican civilizations (Indigenous cultures in what are now Mexico and Central America) demonstrate the importance they placed on dates and the position of the heavens. Studies of the Olmec, Maya, and Mexica have revealed one of the most complex astrological systems developed independently anywhere in the world.

The Olmec people of Mexico, who flourished from 1200 to 400 BCE, developed two calendars, which were inherited by several Mesoamerican cultures, along with beliefs about the ordering of the universe. The cosmos was believed to be divided into three realms: the sky, where the gods resided; Earth, inhabited by humans; and the Underworld, for the dead. These were linked, and the cycles of the heavens could be read to understand the workings of Earth. By studying the sky and counting days, Mesoamericans could also ordain the correct time for rituals and predict future events.

An apocalyptic prophecy?
This fragment of a Mayan inscription, Tortuguero Monument 6, proved controversial as some believed it predicted the end of the world would occur in 2012, based on calendar cycles.

Counting cycles

The Maya were one of the most influential Mesoamerican cultures. During the Classic Period (c. 250–900 CE), they developed a sophisticated two-calendar system to ensure that earthly events aligned with the cosmic order. The calendars they used could chart long periods of time, such as a *baktun*, 144,000 days (about 394 years), or a *hablatun*, 460,800,000,000 days (about 1.2 billion years).

The *Haab* calendar was used by the Maya as their secular calendar to keep track of days. Lasting for 365 days, it was formed of 18 named "months", each lasting 20 days, plus five days at the end of the year. It was closely tied to Earth. The timings for planting crops and harvesting, and the rituals and festivals associated with these events, were calculated using this calendar. There were also religious connotations to this calendar due to its relationship to the cycle of the heavens. The five extra days at the end of the year were thought to be unlucky; this was when the barrier between Earth and the Underworld was removed and evil forces were unleashed.

The *Tzolk'in* (sacred) calendar was formed of 20 sequential named days and 13 numbers that progress together. If the first day was named 1 *Ben* it would be followed by 2 *Ix*. After the 13th day the number reset to 1, but the name of the day only reset after 20 days. This created a calendar lasting

The Calendar Round

The Maya counted their days using two separate calendars, conceptualized as a pair of wheels that turned together in a process known as the Calendar Round. The religious *Tzolk'in* calendar and the *Haab* civil calendar were different lengths, but both were used to identify a date.

A day that was 10 *Ben* on the *Tzolk'in* calendar and 16 *Sotz'* (month *Sotz'*, day 16) in the *Haab* was called 10 *Ben* 16 *Sotz'*. The same combination of dates would occur after 18,980 days, or about 52 years – a milestone celebrated by the Maya.

The calendar round developed by the Maya was later adopted by the Mexica.

Mesoamerican astrology   57

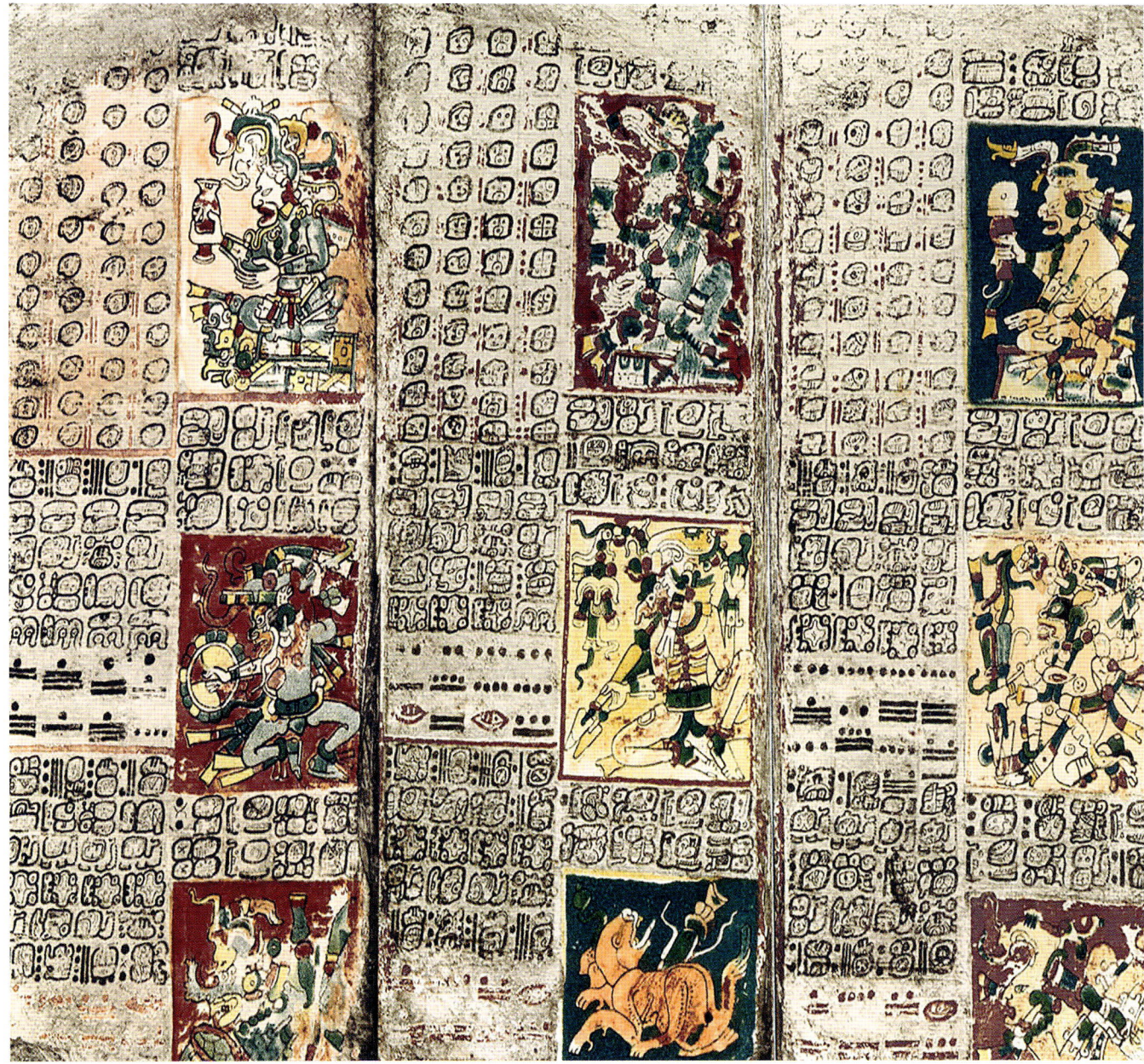

Guiding chart
This page of the *Dresden Codex*, a Maya manuscript from the 11th century CE, tracks the movements of Venus to advise on matters like the proper time to go to war or to perform rituals.

"The hunters, who had celebrated one festival in the month *Sip*, now celebrated another in the month *Sac*, on a day set by the priest."

SPANISH BISHOP DIEGO DE LANDA, *RELACIÓN DE LAS COSAS DE YUCATÁN*, 1566

260 days before all combinations were produced – approximately the length of time it took from human conception to childbirth, and also the time it took for maize (see pp. 104–05) to grow.

Astrological influence

Maya astrology was initially based on accurate astronomical observations. By noting the positions of the stars, planets, Sun, and Moon, astronomers were able to mark important dates for agriculture. Rituals designed to appease the gods, such as those to guarantee a good harvest, had to be performed at the correct time, so astrologers had to keep track of time. Certain temples and locations were tied to specific date combinations when they would be used to host rituals.

Religious and royal buildings of the Maya were often inscribed with astrological symbols, while the buildings themselves were designed with astronomical events in mind, so that their architecture aligned with the movement of bright stars or the Sun. The Maya pyramid at Chichén Itzá (in Yucatán, Mexico) is designed so that on the spring and autumn equinoxes, shadows create the shape of a great snake slithering down its steps, honouring the serpent god Kukulcán.

Sacred days

Those skilled in astronomy became advisers to rulers, and astronomy and astrology were pillars of Maya religion. The title often used for Maya priests was *ah k'in* (calendrical priest), due to their importance in timing rituals and celebrations.

Myths were linked to key dates as ascertained by the calendar cycles. For example, the Maya dated the creation of humans to 3114 BCE. Their Long Count calendar tracked the passing of time since creation, accounting for a "Great Cycle" of 5,125 years, or 13 *baktuns*, ending on 21 December 2012. (On this date, there was widespread fear of an apocalyse, due to the system being misunderstood.)

Bloodletting ritual
This Maya relief contains a specific date in the calendar round (5 *Imix* 4 *Mak*) and shows the goddess Lady Xook performing a blood sacrifice to summon the vision of a serpent.

Priests also read meaning into the dates generated by the two-calendar system. Surviving codices record detailed observations of Venus and horoscopes generated from studying the calendar and heavens. The name of each day in the *Tzolk'in* calendar was associated with a specific meaning – such as *Ben* and "maize" or *Eb* and "rain" – which could be interpreted by trained priests to give advice to petitioners. Each day was also ruled by

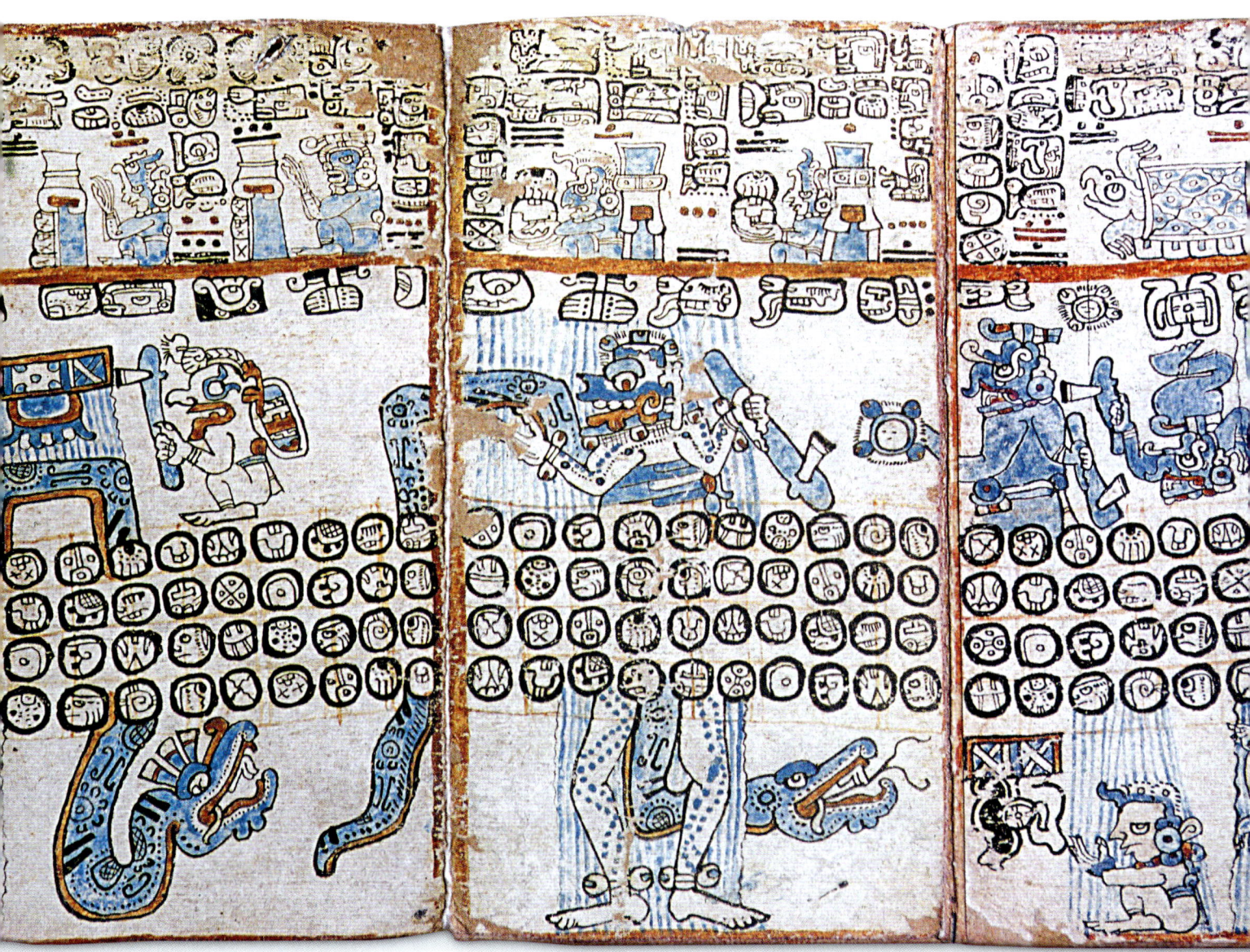

a different deity. The days were respresented in charts by a standardized set of pictoral glyphs. Codices from other Mesoamerican civilizations show similar beliefs: a surviving Mexica codex portrays a 13-day period on each page and the gods associated with each day.

These charts were consulted by priests to advise people on propitious days to perform certain acts. For instance, no ritual should be performed on a Tzi day, while Keej was the correct day to ask for favours and honour the dead. Whether the named day occurred with a low or high number also affected the advice given. The Mexica were often named after the day on which they were born and person's fate was tied to their birth date. In modern Maya communities, "day-keepers" still track the Tzolk'in calendar to perform rituals at the right time and answer questions posed to them.

Complex combinations
The *Madrid Codex* contains a Maya pictorial record of the *Tzolk'in* calendar showing each combination of days and numbers, along with the gods and practices associated with each day.

Fortunes in a dish
Greek lecanomancy

Long before polished bronze or mirrors were used in scrying (see p. 278), another reflective surface, water, was used for divination. In a method of divination known as hydromancy, the movement or appearance of water might be used to see a vision or receive an omen. This practice involved throwing pebbles into the water and interpreting the ripples, or visiting a shrine – such as the one dedicated to Apollo Thryxeus in Lycia – where the questioner would gaze into a sacred spring to receive a vision. Lecanomancy (from the Greek *lecanos*, or pot) was a form of hydromancy that used a clay or glass vessel filled with water for divination.

Oil and water

The practice of lecanomancy is mentioned in the Old Testament Book of Genesis and was recorded in ancient Babylon around 1600 BCE. Babylonian lecanomancy involved dropping oil into a vessel filled with water and then interpreting the oil's movement – if it rose to the surface, for example, it signified an unsuccessful military campaign; if the oil split in two, it meant a sick person would die.

The lecanomantic tradition was passed on by the Hittites and Assyrians, but by the time it reached the Greeks, the mode of divination had altered. Although the comic dramatist Aristophanes included a scene in *Acharnians* in which the general Lamachos sees a vision of an old man (his rival) reflected on a bronze shield, lecanomancy was mainly used for summoning spirits, rather than directly seeing into the future.

Omen in oil
Dating from around 1600 BCE, this Babylonian cuneiform tablet describes the interpretation of omens relating to the appearance of oil when it is poured into a vessel filled with water.

Power of reflection
This Roman fresco (c. 1 CE) from Pompeii depicts the story of Narcissus, who wasted away after falling in love with his own reflection in water – a mythic commentary on the power of reflective surfaces.

The *Paris Magical Codex*, one of the Greek Magical Papyri (see p. 45), dating from the 4th century CE, details several lecanomantic rituals. One involved pouring water into a bronze vessel to summon a deity – with rainwater used to invoke heavenly gods, saltwater to call up the gods of the Underworld, spring water for consulting the dead, and river water to bring forth the god Osiris. Green olive oil was then added to the water, whereupon the deity or spirit would appear. In another ritual, a white saucer was filled with water and olive oil, a magic formula inscribed on it with myrrh ink, and then the spirit of Aphrodite would reveal the future.

Greek diviners continued to use lecanomancy at least into Byzantine times (c. 4th century CE). The practice was adopted by the Romans, and survived as part of the repertoire of medieval and early modern European diviners, as well as in the Islamic world, where lecanomantic bowls inscribed with signs of the zodiac were used.

Awaiting a prophecy
The inside of a cup from c.430 BCE shows the goddess Themis as a priestess at Delphi. She gazes into a dish of water, awaiting a prophecy on the birth of Theseus, son of the watching King Aegeus.

Head of Èsù

Cowrie shells

Casting place
Used for summoning the gods and recording the outcome of a casting, the *opon Ifá* (divining tray) is the most important "wife of Ifa" (divination item). Trays often feature the messenger *òrìsà* Èsù on their rim.

The rim of the tray is decorated with animals important to Yoruba beliefs

Sacred signs in the dust
Ifá divination

The Yoruba people of Nigeria and Benin practise a type of divination known as Ifá. According to Yoruba oral traditions, Ifá was brought to humans by Orunmila, a seer born in the ancient Yoruba city state of Ile Ife around 500 BCE. It has since become a cornerstone of Yoruba cultural identity, and Orunmila – also sometimes known as Ifá – is deified as the òrìsà (god) of Wisdom.

Ifá diviners are called bàbáláwos (male diviners) or ìyánífás (female diviners). During divination, the diviner uses an iroke, or tapper – usually a long carved piece of wood or bone with a pointed end – to summon spirits by tapping an opon Ifá (divining tray). Diviners typically use 16 ikin (palm nuts) or cowrie shells and, with a question for the spirits in mind, cast lots by transferring the ikin from their left hand to their right. Alternatively, they may use an opele (a divining chain made from eight palm-nut shell-halves) or, for yes or no answers, ibo (single shells or stones). Depending on the outcomes of the lots cast, the diviner draws a series of short lines on the tray, which is covered in white or yellow divining powder called iyerosun. This pattern of lines can then be interpreted.

Corresponding verses
The lines drawn by the diviner correspond to the verses of the Odu Ifá – a collection of myths, incantations, proverbs, and songs that contain Yoruba ethics and morals, rituals, sacrifices,

Cowrie cup
This ivory agere Ifá (Yoruba divination vessel) depicts a kneeling female figure. These vessels are made to hold the palm nuts or cowries used in divination.

and other spiritual matters. There are 256 odu (verses), each divided into an ever-growing number of ese (sub-verses). A skilled Ifá diviner will read the patterns drawn on the tray by chanting the relevant verses and will then interpret them to advise their clients about offerings or sacrifices necessary to resolve the issue in question.

Modern divination
Ifá divination is still practised today in Nigeria and Benin. It is also practised in the vast African diaspora to which Yoruba people belong, either through voluntary migration or involuntarily, as a result of the transatlantic slave trade.

Traditionally, Ifá diviners learned the Odu Ifá through a process of memorization that could take up to 30 years. While the tools of Ifá divination have generally remained the same, the Odu Ifá is now published in books and some diviners even use modern technology, such as apps, to serve their clients. The importance of Ifá divination to the Yoruba remains unchanged. All beings in the Yoruba cosmos subscribe to Orunmila's wisdom, and even primordial deities such as the òrìsàs and Olodumare – the Supreme Being of Yoruba cosmology – practise Ifá.

Calling for spirits
A kneeling figure is commonly found carved on tappers, and indicates the diviner's humility, respect, or surrender to authority figures, the òrìsàs, or even to destiny itself.

> "Ifá says that we will bear a son who comes from heaven carrying his 'calabash of destiny'."
>
> VERSE FROM THE ODU IFÁ

The threads of fate

Old Norse *seiðr* and divination

The Norse Viking peoples of ancient Scandinavia believed that the *ørlog*, or destiny of a person – and that of the world – was predetermined, fixed immutably by the Norns, three sisters who wove each individual's fate into a tapestry at the foot of Yggdrasil, the great world tree. Knowledge of the future was available only to specialists, almost exclusively women, who engaged in magical rituals to access it. To help make their predictions, they employed various divinatory practices, such as casting wooden lots cut from birch bark, examining the bubbles of fermenting beer, and studying the shapes made by mottled lead when it was tossed into cold water; but the principal method was *seiðr* ("binding"). This was a form of shamanism practised by seeresses known as *völur* (singular, *völva*) who could contact spirits to help them predict the future.

Seeress at work

The methods and appearance of the *völur* are described in Norse sagas. In the *Saga of Erik the Red*, a *völva* named Thörbjorg visits a farm in Greenland where she spends days preparing to make her predictions. She sits on a cushion stuffed with chicken feathers, eating porridge made from kid's milk and consuming animal hearts, before secluding herself with female assistants and entering a trance-like state, brought on by chanting. She predicts marriages, deaths, and the general fate of the local community.

In the saga, the *völva* is a striking figure dressed in unusual clothing – a necklace of glass beads and a black lambskin hood lined with white catkin. She carries an iron staff with a bronze knob and a pouch containing amulets. Burials – such as one found at Fyrkat in Denmark that is thought to belong to a *völva* – confirm this picture. Items discovered at this grave site, for example, included a metal staff, wild animal bones, owl pellets, and the seeds of the hallucinogenic herb henbane – which may have helped induce the *völva*'s trance.

Fate of the gods

Although knowledge of *seiðr* was said to have been gifted to humanity by the goddess Freyja, even the gods were said to consult the *völur*, as they could not know the will of the Norns. In the *Völuspá*, part of the *Poetic Edda* myth cycle, the supreme god Odin consults a *völva* to discover the fate of the gods. He learns of Ragnarok, the final battle at the end of the world in which nearly all of them will perish. Knowing this fate, however, still leaves Odin – like all those to whom the *völva*'s *seiðr* revealed the future – powerless to avoid it.

Bringer of knowledge
This 10th-century CE pendant from Tissø in Denmark shows Freyja, Norse goddess of love. She was said to have brought knowledge of *seiðr* to humanity and the Aesir, the group of gods that included Odin.

Fateful sisters
The three Norns were said to look into the waters of Urðbrunnr – a magical well at the foot of the world tree – and see the future, which they then fixed by weaving it into a tapestry.

Visiting the *völva*
This engraving by Wilhelm Wagner (1901) shows Odin, with his eight-legged horse, Sleipnir, nearby, consulting the seeress. She tells him that he is destined to die, swallowed by the giant wolf Fenrir at Ragnarok.

Keepers of secret knowledge
Druidic seers

Druids were the religious elite of the Celts of northwest Europe, believed to possess secret knowledge of the natural world and the ability to predict the future. Their name derives from the Old Irish *drui* ("one who sees all") and, acting as counsellors to Celtic rulers, they were at the height of their powers prior to the Roman conquests of Gaul (in the 1st century BCE) and Britain (in the 1st century CE). After that, they survived only in Ireland, where druids practised until the island's conversion to Christianity in the 6th century. Historians must rely on fragmentary mentions by Roman and Greek authors, as well as far later Irish mythological cycles, for knowledge of druids and their beliefs and practices, as they left no written sources behind.

Classical observations

Roman statesman Julius Caesar, whose conquest of Gaul in c. 50 BCE brought him into direct contact with druids, wrote that they held power over all religious matters, taught young men, and acted as judges. He also observed that their education took 20 years, and that a single chief druid presided over their annual meetings convened to decide legal cases.

Greek historian Diodorus Siculus, also writing in c. 50 BCE, said that the Celtic Gauls had three classes of learned men: bards, *vates* (or prophets), and druids, who concerned themselves with the workings of nature. However, when the Roman orator Cicero met a druid, Diviaticus, who was visiting Rome from Gaul, the druid told Cicero that it was druids and not *vates* who had the power of predicting the future in Celtic societies. They did this through augury, studying the behaviour of birds as omens (see pp. 52–53), and their understanding of natural processes.

Classical authors such as Tacitus, writing in the 1st century CE, also gave accounts of druids examining omens "in the palpitating entrails of men", in the entrails of sacrificial animals, and in the flight of birds. Some possible evidence that druids performed human sacrifices comes from

Sharing wisdom
In keeping with their association with sacred groves of trees and their dedication to transmitting their knowledge, a group of druids is depicted listening to a teacher expounding druidic lore.

> "These men foretell the future by means of the flight or cries of birds and of the slaughter of sacred animals, and they have all the multitude subservient to them."
>
> **DIODORUS SICULUS,** *BIBLIOTHECA HISTORICA,* 36 BCE

Druidic seers

Spoons of fate Dating from 50 BCE–100 CE, these bronze spoons, found at Penbryn, in Wales, may have been used for divining, with water dropping from a hole in one onto the quadrants carved into the other.

Water flows out of the spoon through this hole

Spoon edges decorated with Celtic motifs

Carved lines divide spoon into quarters

Lindow Man – the c. 1st-century CE victim of a ritualistic killing, who had been garrotted and stabbed before being left in an English peat bog (in what is now Cheshire), which preserved the body.

Irish legends

Far more detailed information comes from medieval Irish sources, which assign druids specific magical powers. They describe divination using the sounds made by birds (such as the croaking of ravens) and the examination of sheep's shoulder blades (a form of scapulimancy; see pp. 18–19), as well as direct vision, or *imbas forosnai* ("knowledge that illuminates"), granted to a druid. In the *tabh fess*, or "bull feast", druids would eat the meat of a sacrificial bull, then wrap themselves in the dead animal's hide to receive a vision. Other druidic divination methods included casting lots made of sticks carved with *Ogham* (Celtic runic symbols), or incubation, sleeping in sacred places to receive messages in dreams (see pp. 44–45).

One druid, Cathbad, was described in the Ulster cycle of Irish myths, divining the auspicious days for activities, but also acting as an adviser to kings and as a teacher of traditional knowledge. Cathbad performed exactly the roles Julius Caesar had attributed to druids, suggesting that the Irish sources contain some real recollections of druids' original divinatory activities.

Clouds, myths, and magic

One special skill associated with the druids was that of the *néladoir* ("cloud-diviner"), who could discern patterns in the clouds to foretell the future. In the 12th-century *Acallam na Senórach* ("Tales of the Irish Elders"), mythical hero Fionn mac Cumhall asks the druid Cainnelesciath the meaning of some clouds. He is told that the red cloud is for the blood to be spilled in the coming battle, and the grey is the colour of clashing weapons. In later stories, even the priest-teacher of the Christian saint Columba was said to have consulted the clouds for advice.

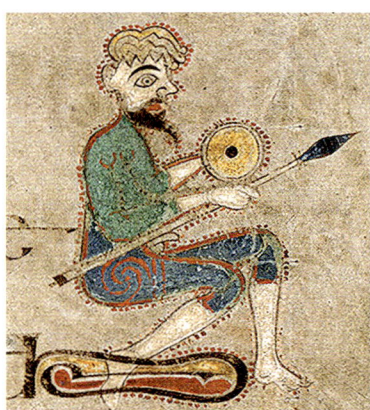

Celtic warriors, as depicted in the Book of Kells, a 9th-century gospel, are said to have consulted druids about their fate in battle.

A star is born
The origins of Hellenistic astrology

Empire-builder
Like the Greek-Egyptian hybrid god Zeus-Ammon, Alexander the Great wears ram's horns on this 4th- or 3rd-century BCE silver coin. Alexander was said to have been born at a favourable time, when the Moon was full in Taurus and the Sun was in Scorpio.

The precursor of modern Western astrology, Hellenistic astrology developed in Egypt during the reign of the Greek Ptolemaic dynasty, from the 4th century BCE. It evolved from a combination of science, myth, religion, and philosophy into a sophisticated system that spread across the Greco-Roman world and lasted until the 5th century CE.

Melting pot of ideas
Hellenistic astrology was a blend of three cultural and scientific astrological traditions: the astral omens, religious rituals involving the stars, invention of the zodiac, and birth charts of Mesopotamia and Babylonia (see pp. 24–27); the Egyptian tradition of keeping time in the form of decanal star charts (see pp. 28–29); and Greek cosmology based on the idea of universal sympathy and mathematics. It also drew on Egyptian temple culture, particularly the belief that the soul could ascend to the stars (see pp. 30–31). Alexander the Great's conquests in Southwest Asia and the Mediterranean region made it possible for these astrological ideas to spread, written in the Greek language and carried by scholars from east to west and back again. The city of Alexandria, founded in Egypt around 332 BCE, became a hub of intellectual pursuits. In the 2nd century CE, it was also home to Claudius Ptolemy, author of one of the key astrological manuals of the Hellenistic era, the *Tetrabiblos* (see pp. 86–89).

Egypt was not the only place where Hellenistic astrology flourished. Berossus, a Babylonian priest, is thought to have established a school of astrology and astronomy on the Greek island of Kos around 280 BCE. Kos was also the site of a Hippocratic medical school. Hippocrates' ideas that human personality, sex, and physical wellbeing were determined by an individual's proportion of hot, cold, wet, and dry qualities were later built upon in both astrology and medicine (see pp. 164–65).

Philosophy and the cosmos
Ancient Greek concepts of how and from which elements the cosmos was built contributed to the development of Hellenistic astrology. The universe was envisaged as a beautiful and harmonious living being, in which the heavens and Earth were interconnected and shared the same primary qualities. According to the 4th-century BCE philosopher Plato, each human soul is assigned to a star, and the cosmos itself has a soul, which he called the *anima mundi* ("world soul").

Starry skies
The ancient Egyptians believed that the sky was a great blue sea in which the gods – the stars – swam from dusk till dawn. The tomb of Pharaoh Seti I at Thebes depicts the major northern constellations.

Intellectual hub
The Great Library of Alexandria was one of the largest and most important of its kind in the ancient world, housing many astronomical and astrological treatises.

Planetary god
Depicted on this amulet, Kronos was the Greek god of agriculture, administration, and the elderly. He was associated with Saturn, the most malicious planet in Hellenistic thought, creating loneliness, anxiety, misery, and hard work – but possibly also great prospects.

The human soul is reincarnated after death, ascending from Earth to the sphere of the fixed stars. There, helped by the guardian spirit, the Agathos Daimon, the soul chooses its new life and descends through the planetary spheres to be reborn. Plato's pupil Aristotle's description of an Earth-centred cosmos made up of four elements (fire, air, water, and earth) influenced the astrological doctrine of the hot, cold, wet, and dry qualities of the planets and signs of the zodiac (see pp.86–89), while the Stoic Zeno of Citium's contribution to Hellenistic astrology was that *pneuma*, the active principle or soul, organizes both the individual and the cosmos through the law of *symphateia* (or cosmic sympathy; see pp.78–79).

Celestial bodies

The planets became the main elements of the Hellenistic astrological system. According to Aristotle's conception of the cosmos, which influenced the view of the heavens and provided the rationale for astrological practice, Earth is at the centre of the universe, surrounded by the eternally revolving spheres of the seven planets in the so-called Chaldean (Babylonian) order, from the most distant and slowest to the nearest and fastest: Saturn, Jupiter, Mars, the Sun, Venus, Mercury, and the Moon. Although the idea of associating mythical gods with the planets was invented in ancient Mesopotamia, the Greeks popularized the concept, successfully applying

> ### Sacred mathematics
>
> According to the enigmatic and influential 6th-century BCE Greek intellectual Pythagoras and his followers, numbers explain the true nature of the universe. The two main principles of the harmonious One and the disharmonious Two form the balance of opposites on which all living things and the cosmos itself are built. Pythagoras's thoughts on the interrelationships between harmony in the cosmos, harmony in society, and the power of numbers were influential in the development of Hellenistic astrological doctrine.
>
>
>
> **Philosopher and mathematician** Pythagoras taught that numbers had mystical qualities.

> "Perhaps there is a pattern set up in the heavens for one who desires to see it…"
>
> **PLATO**, *THE REPUBLIC*, C. 375 BCE

the mythical qualities of the gods and their names to the two luminaries, the Sun (Helios) and the Moon (Selene), and to the five planets: Mercury (Hermes), Venus (Aphrodite), Mars (Ares), Jupiter (Zeus), and Saturn (Kronos). In this new form of astrology, widespread across the Greco-Roman world, the planets, like capricious gods, could control and influence human destiny – a notion that had long existed in Babylonian astrology.

Lasting literature

To lend credibility to their work, many early Hellenistic astrologers claimed that the doctrine was established by the legendary Egyptian priests Nechepso and Petosiris, but that none of their treaties survived. Texts were also attributed to the legendary figure Hermes Trismegistus, believed to be the father of astrology and alchemy. These "Hermetic" works, the earliest of which were written in Greek and may date from the 2nd or 3rd century BCE, were a blend of ancient magical, astrological, alchemical, and scientific ideas. The most famous example, the *Corpus Hermeticum*, is a collection of religious and philosophical texts written in Greek and Latin, with strong links to Egyptian temple practices. In Hermetic literature, the celestial spheres and planets are presented as messengers of fate, and to look at and contemplate the sky is to know destiny. For the first Hellenistic astrologers, therefore, astrology was a tool for understanding and accepting fate.

Following Rome's conquest of Egypt in 30 BCE, Hellenistic astrology continued to flourish. Roman emperors such as Augustus, Tiberius, and Nero used the practice to bolster their authority and power (see pp. 106–07). Two astrological texts written in Latin have survived from the Hellenistic period: 1st-century CE Roman poet Marcus Manilius's *Astronomica* (see pp. 78–79) and Julius Firmicus Maternus's *Mathesis* (c. 337–40 CE). The *Astronomica*, written in hexameters, is the earliest complete Hellenistic manual in existence, and has influenced generations of astrologers.

Father of astrology
Hermes Trismegistus was thought to have invented astrology. He was a syncretic mix of the Greek god Hermes and Thoth, the Egyptian god of writing and magic.

Guided by stars
200 BCE–1100 CE

Introduction

By 200 BCE astrology had begun to take shape in its varying forms around the globe. It had long been a central part of Chinese imperial culture: the emperor was seen as an earthly representative of the heavens, and in the sky he was signified by the north celestial pole (the projection upwards of Earth's north pole). In the northern hemisphere, all the stars rotate around the north celestial pole, so it was said that in the Chinese Empire, all people rotated around, and obeyed, their emperor. A Chinese astrologer's task was to read the heavens and preserve stability across the emperor's realm, for the collective good. The concept of harmony was at the heart of early Chinese cosmology and it was thought that if the binary forces of yin and yang could be balanced, then harmony would be preserved both in heaven and on Earth.

To the west, the ancient Greeks also developed concepts of cosmic harmony, based on the work of the 6th-century BCE philosopher Pythagoras. He had argued that the universe was constructed according to the same geometrical patterns that produce musical tones, and deduced that if it were possible to hear the sounds the planets made as they circled Earth, they would add up to the "harmony of the spheres".

Meanwhile, in ancient Mesopotamia, the Babylonians had invented natal astrology – the use of planetary positions at birth to analyse personality and personal destiny. They had also devised the 12 signs of the zodiac, from Aries to Pisces, which remain a feature of modern astrology. The horoscope, a complex diagram that portrays the planets and zodiac signs for a precise time and place, was invented around 200 BCE as a result of interaction between Babylonian, Egyptian, and Greek scholars. Hellenistic astrologers formalized these concepts, establishing the fundamental structure of astrological method and meaning that has persisted to the present day and is now known as Western astrology.

Indian astrologers adopted horoscopic astrology from the Greeks around 100–200 CE, and married it to their religion, deities, and belief in reincarnation and karma – the law that

The tropical zodiac *see* p. 89

Protective power of runes *see* p. 99

Heavenly sign *see* p. 108

human lives can be influenced by their actions in a past life, and that present actions will influence future lives. The central tenet of Indian astrology is that by understanding the potential, both fortunate and unfortunate, that is revealed in planetary patterns, the future can be changed through appropriate actions, prayers, offerings, and *pujas* (devotional rituals).

While Indian astrology blossomed, astrological practice went into decline in the Roman Empire from around 300 CE. This was partly due to the adoption of Christianity as the state religion: early Christian theologians saw astrologers as rivals and quoted Old Testament texts condemning them. Yet astrology survived in Persia, which had been conquered by the Arabs by 654. In the late 700s, Arabic-speaking scholars rediscovered the practice, importing ancient Greek texts and Indian astrological works written in Sanskrit. From then until the year 1100, the tradition of horoscopic astrology that had begun in Mesopotamia flourished across the Arabic and Islamic world, from Spain in the west to Southeast Asia in the east, and simultaneously spread along the Silk Road trade route from India to China and Japan.

> "Bad government breeds bad qi; bad qi breeds disasters… When the Way of Order is lost below, the patterns of Heaven change above."
>
> **CHINESE PHILOSOPHER LU JIA**, c. 228–140 BCE

Destined for Mughal greatness see p. 115

Japanese divinatory ritual see p. 120

The right time to found a city see p. 128

Mapping the skies
The first star catalogue

Although Greek astronomers had observed the skies for centuries, devising complex theories of circular orbits to explain the motion of the planets and mapping patterns in the stars, they had not created a comprehensive catalogue of celestial bodies. The first was produced by Hipparchus of Nicaea (c. 190–120 BCE), one of the greatest astronomers of the Hellenistic period. Unfortunately, relatively little is known about his life, except that he made most of his observations from Rhodes and Alexandria. His only surviving work is a commentary on the *Phaenomena of Eudoxus and Aratus*, an astronomical poem, and most of what is known of his writings derives from their use by Ptolemy (see pp. 86–89) in the 2nd century CE.

A skilled mathematician, Hipparchus applied the newly developed techniques of trigonometry to his observations of the stars and planets to make a

Astronomer at work
This illustration from 1911 shows Hipparchus at work in his observatory with a globe version of his star map. In reality, ancient Greek astronomers did not have telescopes but made all their observations with the naked eye.

number of key advances. He made very accurate calculations of the lunar month, estimated the sizes of the Moon and the Sun, and devised a 345-month cycle for predicting lunar eclipses. He also estimated the length of the year – a calculation that varied only 6.5 minutes from that made by modern astronomers.

Groundbreaking observations

The star catalogue compiled by Hipparchus included descriptions of around 850 stars visible to the naked eye. Although this inventory has not survived, it was used by Ptolemy as the basis for his *Almagest*, which catalogued 1,048 stars and nebulas, organized into 48 constellations. Rather than simply noting the patterns he saw in the sky, Hipparchus's great advance was to use a system of celestial coordinates – notations of latitude and longitude based on a hypothetical projection outwards of Earth's equator – which Ptolemy partially adapted.

In examining observations made by his Greek predecessors, and by Babylonian astronomers since the 6th century BCE, Hipparchus noted a curious phenomenon. It was well known that as the seasons changed, the positions of the stars in the sky varied relative to the Sun – but it was thought that this series of location points was the same each year. Looking at observations recorded over periods of several centuries, Hipparchus realized that this was not true. He found that the position of Spica, a star in the constellation Virgo and one of the brightest in the night sky, had varied by two degrees since the astronomer Timocharis of Alexandria had observed it around 290 BCE. This meant that the Sun's location point relative to the stars at the equinoxes (the period in autumn and spring when days and nights are of equal length) was marginally different each year, shifting steadily westward at a rate he calculated to be one degree every 78 years (close to the true value of one degree every 72 years).

Celestial mechanism
Hipparchus's work may have inspired the Antikythera mechanism (shown here in a reconstruction), which was built shortly after his death. A type of mini computer, it was used to model planetary orbits and predict eclipses.

Precession of the equinoxes

Because Earth is not quite a sphere, but bulges at the equator, the gravitational pull of the Sun and Moon is greatest there – their closest point to Earth. This pull causes Earth to wobble on its axis and slow fractionally in its orbit. One result is that the Sun's position on the first day of spring (the vernal equinox) appears to recede westwards relative to the constellations, which in turn delays the time of the equinox by a few hours each year (until it is reset by the extra day in a leap year). Another effect is that the Pole Star changes over time. Each wobble traces a circle in the sky over a period of 25,722 years.

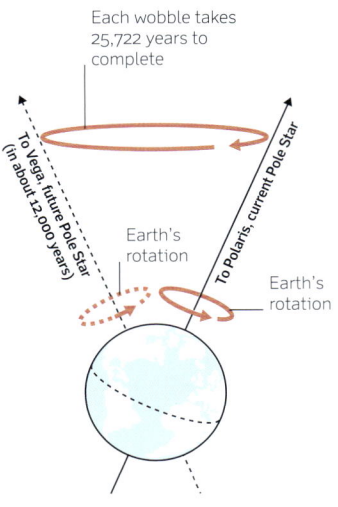

Each wobble takes 25,722 years to complete

To Vega, future Pole Star (in about 12,000 years)

To Polaris, current Pole Star

Earth's rotation

Earth's rotation

Hipparchus's discovery of the precession of the equinoxes (see above) meant that later astrologers had to choose between using a tropical zodiac, which is fixed relative to the seasons and the position of the Sun (so the spring equinox always signals the start of Aries), and a sidereal zodiac, which is tied to the observable position of fixed stars in the night sky (so the date of Aries changes).

Each planet (here, Mars) has its own ring marked with a small stone

Written in the stars
Stoic astrology

In ancient Greece, the concept of fate was part of everyday life, and was personified by the goddess Ananke and her offspring, the Fates. Homer wrote about fate in the *Iliad* (c. 850 BCE), sparking debate as to whether or not it was possible to control or influence destiny. Stoic philosophers, led by Zeno of Citium, entered the debate around 300 BCE, and their arguments about the interconnectedness of all elements of the visible and invisible world contributed to the growth of Hellenistic astrology.

Fate and free will
The Stoic view of fate could be reduced to the simple statement that whatever happened was meant to happen, and could not be otherwise. Free will was defined as a reasonable acceptance of fate. No one could escape fate, so the only way to live according to the will of the gods was to accept it. Stoics also believed that people could unite with the divine mind by contemplating the sky and learning about the structure and the mechanism of the cosmos. According to the doctrine of cosmic sympathy, all living beings are connected to the heavenly bodies through their essential natures, or "sympathies", and celestial bodies could therefore determine human destinies. For Stoics, astrology was a tool for understanding fate and predicting the future.

Early Hellenistic astrologers adapted Stoic ideas to explain the workings of the cosmos and human life. The word *moira*, used by Homer to signify a "lot" (portion) of fate assigned to each person, was taken up by astrologers to mean a degree of the zodiac. In Hellenistic astrology, the degree to which the ascendant (see p. 81) rises at the time of birth indicates the destiny the gods have assigned.

Determined at birth
The Roman poet Manilius, who wrote the *Astronomica*, an instructional poem on astrology, in the 1st century CE, believed that what happens in life, even the point of death, is predicted at birth and written in a person's horoscope. In his words, *nascentes morimur* ("at birth, we die"). He took the Stoic view of a living, interconnected cosmos and fate, arguing that the stars both influence human nature and write each person's inescapable destiny. According to Manilius, the only thing people can do to accept their fate and maintain balance in their lives is to be rational and aware of what lies ahead; in other words, to know and accept the future.

In the *Astronomica*, Manilius also presents the Stoic argument that the divine mind (*ratio*) and breath (*pneuma*) permeate and animate the entire cosmos, which operates according to predictable and recurring laws. Contemplating celestial phenomena and the planetary bodies, and knowing the cycles of the planets, fixed stars, and constellations, helps people to come closer to God, or to develop their own divine nature.

Interconnected cosmos
The Stoic idea of sympathy was based on the idea of a living cosmos in which all beings can influence one another, as depicted in this 1620 illustration of the macrocosm (the wider universe) and microcosm (life on Earth).

Message from the stars
The frontispiece to this 1675 English translation of Manilius's *Astronomica* shows Pan (the Greek god of nature, left) and Urania (the muse of astrology, above), with Mercury (right), as the messenger between earthly beings and the heavens.

Changing fortunes
Hellenistic horoscopes

By the 1st century BCE, Hellenistic astrology had become the dominant form of astrology in the Mediterranean region (see pp. 68–71). Its scheme of the heavens from which astrological predictions were made included four basic components: the zodiac, the planets, the 12 places (houses), and the planetary aspects. These components served as a map for understanding human character and fate, and became the system of astrological interpretation that could be learned by all budding astrologers. Vettius Valens outlined this practical approach in his *Anthologiae* ("Anthologies", 2nd century CE), the nine surviving volumes of which feature more than 130 horoscope examples, complete with commentary.

Signs and planets
In the Hellenistic system, the zodiac was made up of 12 signs, each 30 degrees in length. The signs shared their names and mythological symbolism with the constellation from which they evolved. Early Hellenistic astrologers used the Babylonian zodiac (sidereal, related to the fixed stars; see p. 27), but the tropical zodiac (related to the seasons) introduced by Claudius Ptolemy in the 2nd century CE (see p. 89) ultimately became the main system in Western astrology.

Like the signs of the zodiac, the seven planets of Hellenistic astrology (the Moon, the Sun, Mercury, Venus, Mars, Jupiter, and Saturn) symbolized different qualities, and were tied to the characters and functions of ancient Greek and Roman gods. The qualities of Mars, for example, were male, hot, and dry, so the planet was considered destructive, and it was associated with Ares (Mars in Roman mythology), god of war, brutality, and ambition. Planetary characteristics and strength were thought to vary according to the sign they were occupying, and the degrees (subsections) within that sign. Planets were happier in some signs than in others.

Places and aspects
Every day the Sun, Moon, and planets move along the ecliptic (see pp. 24–27) from east to west, regularly visiting the same places and parts of the sky above and below the horizon, due to Earth's 24-hour rotation on its axis. Inspired by the Egyptian system of decans and seasonal hours (see pp. 28–29), Hellenistic astrologers divided the sky into 12 places (later known as houses), and used this scheme to give additional meaning to planetary positions in a horoscope. As set out by Valens, each place signifies a different area of human activity: life, body, and mind (1st); possessions (2nd); siblings, other relatives, and authority (3rd); home, parents, and hidden matters (4th);

Astrologer's toolkit
Discovered at Grand in France, this wooden astrological board from the Roman period features the symbols of the zodiac, the Moon, the Sun, and the planetary gods assigned to the decans.

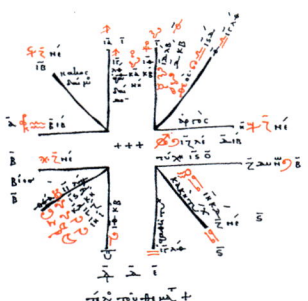

Sigils and symbols
Hellenistic astrologers used horoscopes for teaching astrology and in client consultations. This Greek example shows the planets, signs, and points of the sky (in red), and the places.

House division

Hellenistic astrologers used different place or house divisions, depending on their needs. The most popular, both used by Valens, were whole-sign houses and equal houses. The whole-sign system (right) was favoured in antiquity for its simplicity, as each sign of the zodiac encompasses a whole house. The ascendant (the sign rising on the eastern horizon at the time of birth) determines the first house. Like the whole-sign system, the equal-house system divides the horoscope into 12 houses of 30 degrees each, but the first house begins at the exact degree of the ascendant, rather than at the start of the zodiac sign.

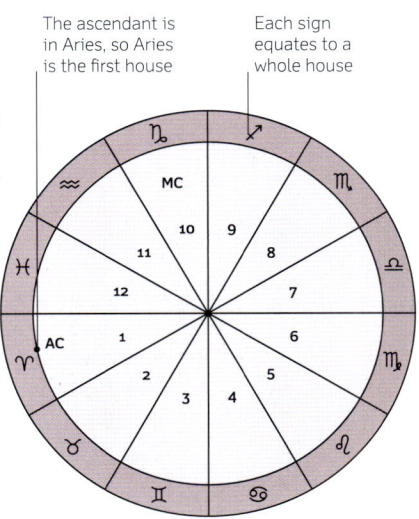

The ascendant is in Aries, so Aries is the first house

Each sign equates to a whole house

Crowning glory
This monumental relief of the Moon and stars in the royal constellation of Leo – possibly an early form of horoscope – was built on Mount Nemrut (in modern-day Türkiye) for the coronation of the Hellenistic king Antiochus I of Commagene (r. c. 69–34 BCE).

popular among the wider population, and was practised in Egyptian temples, Greek sanctuaries, and royal courts alike. From the 1st century BCE, anyone could order a birth chart and so apply astrological knowledge to everyday life.

As well as drawing up birth charts, astrologers gave advice on when to schedule an important event such as a journey or a wedding, or when to start a business. An astrologer needed to know what the purpose of the event was in order to choose a planetary god to protect it. The next step was then to find an auspicious moment for the event to take place, based on the relative positions of the stars, planets, and other celestial bodies. For example, the hour ruled by Mercury would be favourable for the start of a journey over which this god was the guardian.

Ordinary people carried astrological talismans in the hope that they would have the power to avert or solve problems, while rulers used astrological symbolism to try to associate the stars with their authority. Augustus, the first Roman emperor, had a coin stamped with the symbol of Capricorn, the zodiac sign containing the Moon in his birth chart.

children and happiness (5th); slaves, injuries, and illness (6th); marriage (7th); death and inheritance (8th), travel, divination, and deities (9th); fortune, reputation, profession, and career (10th); friends and gifts (11th); dangers, enemies, and suffering (12th).

Aspects, another key part of Hellenistic astrology, are mathematically measured distances between celestial bodies that show how the planets interact. Two good aspects – sextile (60 degrees) and trine (120 degrees) – were thought to make the planets friendly and cooperative, while two bad ones – square (90 degrees) and opposition (180 degrees) – forced the planets to fight and hate each other.

Everyday astrology

Schools and astrological manuals that outlined the Hellenistic approach helped to make astrology more accessible in an era when seeking answers from the gods was a common practice. Initially reserved for kings and aristocrats, Hellenistic astrology soon became

Practical approach

Valens' *Anthologiae* are widely considered the most important manual of practical astrology to survive to modern times. Unlike Ptolemy, who focused on the theoretical side of astrology, Valens taught its practice, describing, for example, how to use the 12 places (houses) to explain aspects of a person's life, such as work, money, relationships, or health – topics that remain popular among astrologers' clients today.

Hellenistic astrologers and their clients, regardless of wealth or power, were preoccupied with longevity and death. Valens responded to this by detailing which planetary rulers to expect over the coming years, and how they might affect people's lives. The benefic (good) planets Venus and Jupiter indicated happy and prosperous years, while the malefic (bad) planets Mars and Saturn heralded periods of sorrow, trouble, and risk of death.

Astrological aid
This silver medallion, probably a talisman, was found in the 2,100-year-old grave of a priestess in modern-day Türkiye. It features the goddess Aphrodite (Venus), surrounded by 10 zodiac signs.

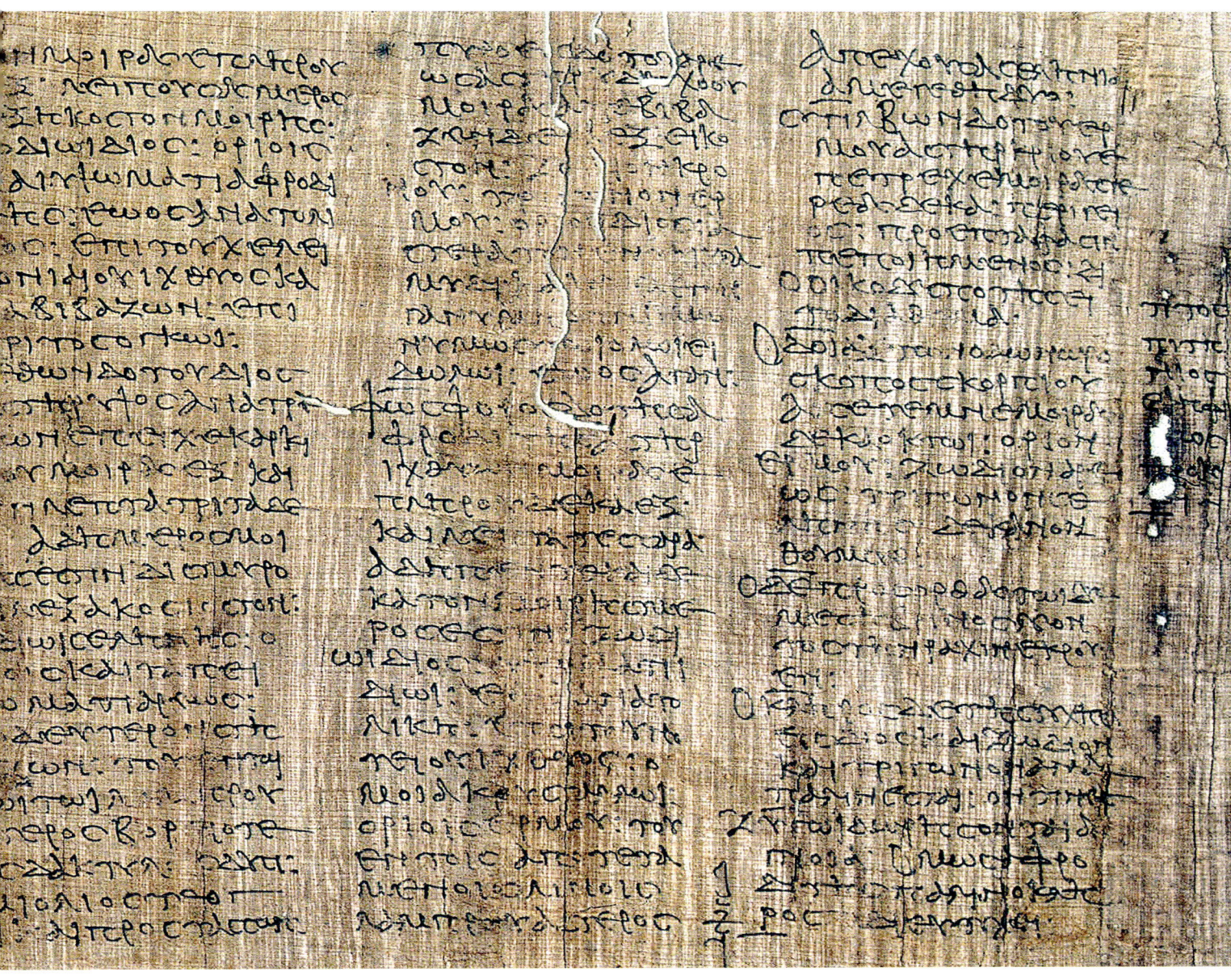

> "Fate has decreed for each person the immutable working out of events, reinforcing this decree with many opportunities for good or bad consequences."
>
> **VETTIUS VALENS**, ANTHOLOGIAE BOOK V, 2ND CENTURY CE

Birth record
Horoscopes were rarely delivered in writing, but some literary examples have survived. This papyrus details the horoscope of a child born in the evening of 31 March 81 CE, cast by the astrologer Titus Pitenius.

A geocentric universe

Important schools of thought in the classical world, chiefly those of Plato and the Stoics (see pp. 78–79), believed that the cosmos was a perfect creation of the divine mind, so it must be perfectly organized and ideally proportioned, and everything in it must have a purpose. The geocentric cosmos – a concept of the universe with Earth at its centre – was developed from the 4th century BCE by Greek thinkers, including Plato and Aristotle. But it was the 2nd-century CE astrologer-astronomer Claudius Ptolemy (see pp. 86–89) who transformed it into an enduring astronomical model, which he presented in his *Almagest* and *Planetary Hypotheses*, along with tables of planetary positions.

Ptolemy described the universe as a sphere, with the visible celestial bodies of the cosmos as successive spherical planes above the stationary Earth. This geocentric concept of the celestial sphere was presented as a sevenfold model, with seven planetary spheres of the heavens: first, the Moon (the body closest to Earth), followed by Mercury, Venus, the Sun, Mars, Jupiter, and Saturn (the planet furthest from Earth). The eighth and most distant sphere was the circle of fixed stars, which were grouped into 48 constellations.

> "…when I trace at my pleasure the windings to and fro of the heavenly bodies I no longer touch Earth with my feet…"
>
> **PTOLEMY**, THE *ALMAGEST*, C. 150 CE

The planetary spheres, depicted here by Andreas Cellarius in 1661, reflect the ancient concept of the cosmos as a beautiful and harmonious order.

Claudius Ptolemy
This 15th-century painting depicts the astronomer, mathematician, astrologer, and geographer Ptolemy, who lived in Alexandria in the 2nd century CE. His theoretical work enabled astrology to maintain the status of esteemed science until the early modern era.

A causal science
Formalizing Hellenistic astrology

A handful of astrological textbooks from the 1st and 2nd centuries CE shaped the art of astrology and influenced astrological practice for two millennia. These include Manilius's *Astronomica* (see pp. 78–79), Vettius Valens' *Anthologiae* (see pp. 80–83), Dorotheus of Sidon's *Carmen Astrologicum* (a poem largely focused on natal astrology), and the most important manual for the development of Western astrology, Claudius Ptolemy's *Tetrabiblos*.

Divine wisdom or natural science?
In the Greco-Roman world, astrology derived its authority from its status as both a *techne* (art, craft, technique, or skill) and an *episteme* (knowledge). Some astrologers, such as Valens, regarded it as divine wisdom. Others, like Ptolemy, saw astrology as a science interconnected with other scientific disciplines such as meteorology and medicine. According to Ptolemy, astrology should be based on natural, physical causes, with set rules and procedures. Like physicians, he argued, astrologers try to predict an outcome from data; they just do so by examining a birth chart rather than a body.

Ptolemy claimed that celestial bodies influence Earth in such a way that they determine, to some extent, the life and character of human beings. He gave the example of the power and heat of the Sun, which affects all bodies in the universe and the seasonal changes on Earth. However, he limited his discourse to scientific arguments, and did not address the question of the divinity of the planets (see p. 81). Ptolemy also made a distinction between natural astrology, which focused on the cycles of the planets and their influence on the weather and human health, and judicial astrology, which dealt with individual predictions.

In the *Tetrabiblos*, Ptolemy presented the foundations of Hellenistic astrological doctrine – based on centuries of astronomical observations from ancient Babylonia, Egypt, and Greece – in a methodical way. Its four books (from which the *Tetrabiblos* gets its name) are devoted to the basic principles of astrology and its various branches. Ptolemy also applied a scientific approach to the question of whether or not human life is determined by the stars, arguing that a birth chart does not explain everything that will happen in a person's life, since there are other equally important factors – such as the influence of upbringing, heredity, and the nature of a person's environment.

Qualities and oppositions
Ptolemy revised the astrological tradition in the *Tetrabiblos*, strengthening its mathematical and astronomical foundations and linking astrology to natural philosophy (see pp. 68–71). The planets were assigned Aristotle's qualities – wet or dry, hot

Birth data
This miniature from a 14th-century translation of the *Tetrabiblos* shows an astrologer studying the chart of a newborn. Ptolemy stressed the importance of calculating the exact degree of the ascendant at birth to obtain the most accurate data for predictions.

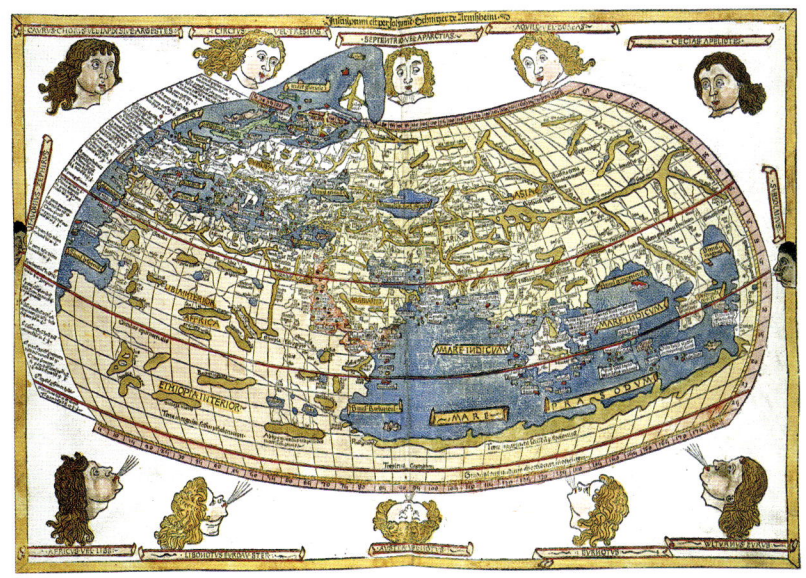

Ptolemaic map
Ptolemy assigned the zodiac signs and planets to different regions of the world and their inhabitants, claiming that the character of these places was influenced by astrological factors.

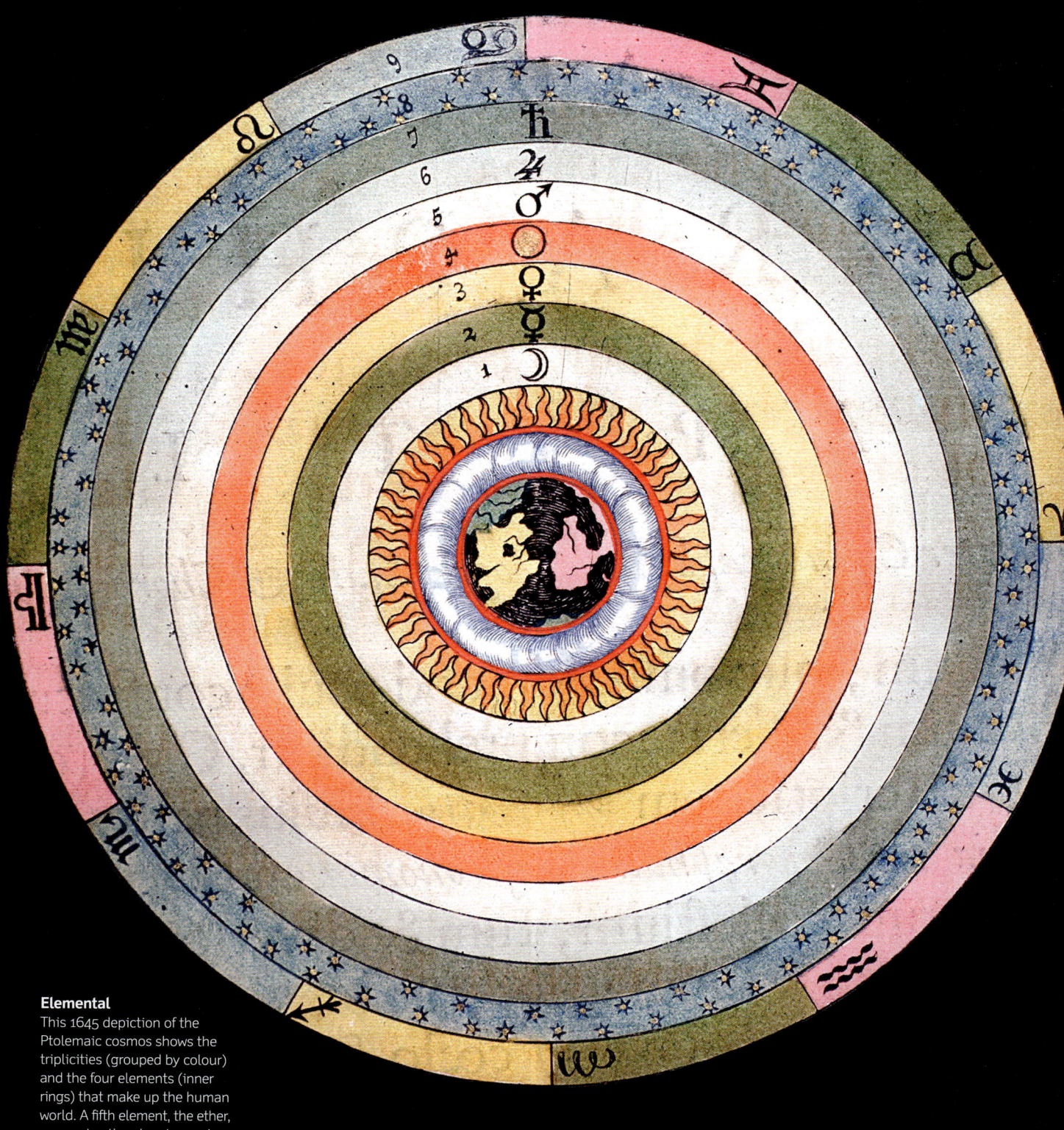

Elemental
This 1645 depiction of the Ptolemaic cosmos shows the triplicities (grouped by colour) and the four elements (inner rings) that make up the human world. A fifth element, the ether, permeates the planetary spheres.

or cold – so they could be described as physical entities with two basic properties. The classical planets furthest from the Sun's warmth, Saturn and the Moon, were cold, while those nearest the Sun, Mars and Venus, were hot. A planet's position also determined whether it was considered wet or dry.

Like the planets, the zodiac signs were categorized according to these four qualities, and put in groups of three called triplicities. Each triplicity connected signs that were 120 degrees apart. Valens was the first astrologer to associate the triplicities with the elements: fire signs (Aries, Leo, Sagittarius) are hot and dry; earth signs (Taurus, Virgo, Capricorn) are cold and dry; air signs (Gemini, Libra, Aquarius) are hot and wet; and water signs (Cancer, Scorpio, Pisces) are cold and wet.

Ptolemy further grouped the planets according to their opposing qualities: diurnal and nocturnal; masculine and feminine (with Mercury being both); benefic (good) and malefic (bad). The opposition of the benefic and malefic planets was crucial in interpreting the good and bad influences in a person's character. Venus, Jupiter, and the Moon were thought to be benefic, representing moderate heat and moisture – the fertile and active qualities in nature. On the other hand, Mars and Saturn were considered harmful because of their excessive dryness and heat (Mars) or cold (Saturn). The Sun and Mercury could change their nature depending on which planet they were in aspect with (see p. 82).

Lasting legacy

In the Hellenistic era, most astrologers used the Babylonian sidereal zodiac (see p. 27), which was based on the visible positions of the constellations and, at that time, was aligned with the seasons. However, Ptolemy realized that the precession of the equinoxes (see p. 77) would eventually cause the zodiacal constellations to move away from the seasons they were associated with. To maintain the seasonal qualities of the zodiac signs, he fixed the first degree of the so-called tropical zodiac (0° Aries) to the first day of astronomical spring (the vernal equinox). It is thanks to Ptolemy that Western astrologers today use the tropical zodiac.

With the decline of the Roman Empire and the rise of Christianity from the early 4th century CE, Hellenistic astrology gradually fell out of favour in its western heartlands. However, it was transmitted to the Islamic world, survived in Persia, and influenced the development of Indian astrology (see pp. 112–17). The survival of Hellenistic astrology is largely thanks to Arabic translations of the work of Ptolemy, considered by Arab thinkers to be one of the greatest scientists of antiquity. His *Procheiroi kanones* ("Handy Tables"), a set of astronomical tables with instructions for use (taken from the *Almagest*, Ptolemy's astronomy manual), became an essential practical tool for later astronomers and astrologers. The *Tetrabiblos*, which was rediscovered in Europe in the 12th century when it was translated into Latin, became the main source of knowledge for medieval astrologers. This seminal work remained in use until the 18th century.

Touch of malice
This 16th-century painting shows Saturn, the cold, dry, malefic planet, in human form. Saturn ruled the signs of Capricorn and Aquarius, which were opposite the signs of Leo (ruled by the Sun) and Cancer (Moon).

Tropical zodiac
Ptolemy linked the zodiac to the Sun's annual cycle. According to his tropical zodiac, shown in this image from a Byzantine edition of the *Tetrabiblos*, when the Sun enters Aries, spring begins.

♈ **Aries (roughly 21 Mar.–19 Apr.)** is a masculine, cardinal, fire sign that is ruled by Mars, the warrior planet. Valens described Ariens as "brilliant, distinguished… just, hard on offenders, free, governing".

♉ **Taurus (20 Apr.–20 May)** is a feminine, fixed, earth sign ruled by Venus, planet of beauty, love, and harmony. Valens called Taureans "toilsome, good at keeping things, pleasure-loving… generous".

Signs of the Western zodiac

Ancient astronomers divided the zodiac – the constellations the Sun appears to pass through – into 12 signs, each equivalent to 30 days of the year. These signs were grouped into elements, qualities, polarities (masculine or feminine), and modalities (cardinal, fixed, mutable) to guide astrological interpretation. Hellenistic astrologer Vettius Valens (see pp. 80–83) attributed characteristics to each sign.

The Gemini twins are associated with Castor and Pollux, twins from Greek mythology

♊ **Gemini (21 May–20 June)** is a masculine, mutable, air sign ruled by Mercury, the planet of communication, changeability, and intellect. Valens called Geminis "sensible people, practitioners of curious arts". He saw Gemini as bicorporeal (represented by two figures).

Signs of the Western zodiac

From the 12th-century "Hunterian Psalter"

♋ **Cancer (21 June–22 July)** is ruled by the Moon, indicating emotion and intuition. It is a feminine, cardinal, water sign. Valens called the crabs of Cancer "changeable, public, popular, civic".

♌ **Leo (23 July–22 Aug.)** is a masculine, fixed, fire sign ruled by the Sun – the luminary indicating identity and vitality. Valens described Leos as "distinguished, noble, steady, just, haters of evil".

♍ **Virgo (23 Aug.–22 Sept.)** is a feminine, mutable, earth sign ruled by Mercury, the planet of reason and keen analysis. Virgos, to Valens, are "noble, modest, religious, burdened with care".

♎ **Libra (23 Sept.–22 Oct.)** is a masculine, cardinal, air sign ruled by Venus, the planet governing beauty, love, and harmony. Valens described Librans as "noble and just" but "average in fortune".

♏ **Scorpio (23 Oct.–21 Nov.)** is ruled by Mars in classical astrology, and by Pluto in modern astrology. It is a feminine, fixed, water sign. Valens decried Scorpios as "traitors" and "connivers".

♐ **Sagittarius (22 Nov.–21 Dec.)** is a masculine, mutable, fire sign that is ruled by Jupiter, planet of wisdom, growth, and abundance. According to Valens, these heavenly archers "seek a noble reputation".

♑ **Capricorn (22 Dec.–19 Jan.)** is a feminine, cardinal, earth sign ruled by Saturn, planet of perseverance and discipline. Capricorns are "burdened with care" and "always criticizing" (Valens).

♒ **Aquarius (20 Jan.–18 Feb.)** is a masculine, fixed, air sign ruled classically by Saturn, and by Uranus in modern astrology. Valens called Aquarians "deceitful, tricky" but "occasionally generous".

♓ **Pisces (19 Feb.–20 Mar.)** is ruled classically by Jupiter, and by Neptune in modern astrology. It is a feminine, mutable, water sign that Valens associated with the unsteady and unreliable.

♄ **Saturn** is described by Vettius Valens in the *Anthologies* (see pp. 80–83) as indicative of "great ranks", yet if poorly placed, "imprisonment, chains, grief". Saturn rules Capricorn and Aquarius, symbolizing wisdom, stability, and persistence, and indicating life's inevitable challenges.

Sickle represents the god Saturn's association with agriculture

Renaissance depiction of Saturn from the *Spherae coelestis et planetarum descriptio*

Aquarius, the water-bearer

Capricorn, the sign of the goat

♃ **Jupiter** is known in classical astrology as the "Great Fortune" as it symbolizes prosperity and good luck. It rules Sagittarius and Pisces; those born under its influence are described as "jovial".

♂ **Mars**, the warrior, symbolizes strength, endurance, passion, and a "martial" temperament. It rules Aries and Scorpio and, when poorly placed, can indicate aggression, impulsiveness, and conflict.

The planets

Classical astrology is based on the movements, positions, and aspects of seven planets: Saturn, Jupiter, Mars, the Sun, Venus, Mercury, and the Moon. In the 2nd-century CE *Tetrabiblos* (see pp. 86–89), Ptolemy described the planets according to the cosmology and natural philosophy of his time, attributing their perceived powers over the terrestrial world to essential qualities (hot, cold, moist, and dry). As with the zodiac signs (see pp. 90–91), Valens recorded each planet's characteristics in his *Anthologies*.

The planets 93

☉ **The Sun** is the "greater luminary" and ruler of Leo, and represents good fortune, vitality, fame, and creativity. However, if poorly placed in a chart, it can indicate arrogance, egoism, and pride.

The outer planets

Invisible to the naked eye, the three "outer" planets (Uranus, Neptune, and Pluto) were discovered after the invention of the telescope. Astrologers assigned them meanings based on historical events of the time. Uranus, discovered in 1781 (just before the French Revolution), was associated with uprisings, progress, equality, and democracy. Neptune, spotted in 1846 at the peak of the Romantic movement, was linked with peace and idealism. Dwarf planet Pluto corresponded with nuclear weapons and psychoanalysis, developing fields in the 1930s.

The outer planet Neptune was depicted in *Le Tarot Astrologique* ("Astrological Tarot", 1927) by French occultist Georges Muchery.

♀ **Venus** denotes fortune, beauty, sexuality, love, and desire, but if poorly placed, it can indicate indulgence, excessive romanticism, jealousy, superficiality, and difficulties in relationships.

Valens wrote that Mercury is the "lord of brothers and of younger children"

Caduceus, symbol of medicine or commerce

Mercury is depicted with its signs, Virgo and Gemini (left)

☽ **The Moon** is the "lesser luminary" and ruler of Cancer. It symbolizes the physical body, emotions, and intuition. If poorly placed in a chart, it can indicate emotional instability and moodiness.

☿ **Mercury** can bestow "forethought and intelligence", according to Valens, or if poorly placed, can "make everything capricious in the outcome". Mercury rules Gemini and Virgo, and can indicate versatility and a "mercurial" temperament.

Reading Western birth charts

A Western birth chart is a map of the sky, as viewed from Earth, at the moment of a person's birth. Reading the chart involves interpreting the positions of the planets, including the Moon and Sun (the "luminaries"), and the cardinal points or angles (the ascendant, midheaven, descendant, and imum coeli) in relation to 12 houses and the zodiac signs. The planetary aspects, angular distances between celestial bodies, dictate the strength and nature of their interaction.

The aspects
On a birth chart, the angular distances between elements are called "aspects". These govern the dynamics between planets and luminaries, which might be harmonious or discordant.

Conjunction ☌	A conjunction occurs when two or more planets are in the same zodiac sign or close to the same degree; their energies are combined and strengthened.
Semisextile ⚺	In this aspect, two planets are 30° (one zodiac sign) apart. Because of their positions in opposing zodiac signs, the planets have no traits in common.
Semisquare ∠	Planets are 45° apart in this aspect, creating a stressful but dynamic relationship between the two planets involved.
Sextile ✶	This beneficial aspect occurs when two planets are 60° (two zodiac signs) apart. They cooperate and positively motivate each other to produce harmony.
Square □	This negative aspect occurs when planets are 90° apart. It creates clashing energies and tension because the planets are in incompatible zodiac signs.
Trine △	Considered an auspicious aspect, bringing luck and harmony, a trine forms when there is a 120° angle between planets in zodiac signs of the same element.
Quincunx ⚻	Sometimes called an "inconjuct", planets are 150° (five zodiac signs) apart in this aspect. They cannot properly cooperate in this position, causing tension.
Opposition ☍	Planets in opposition are 180° apart – on opposite sides of the sky. This may cause tension and conflict or a cooperative and harmonious partnership.

The houses
A birth chart is divided into 12 sections or "houses", each representing a different area of life. When planets enter a house, they influence the corresponding life area.

First house	The sign of the "self", the first house represents physical appearance, personality, self-identity, and approach to life.
Second house	This house represents money, and how this is earned and spent. It also relates to the value system followed.
Third house	Communication (including relationships with siblings and neighbours) and education are covered by the third house.
Fourth house	Representing home, family, and tradition, the fourth house symbolizes personal space and security.
Fifth house	The fifth house stands for self-expression, creativity, and ingenuity. It is also associated with passion and romance.
Sixth house	Work, daily schedules, lifestyle, health and illness, cleaning, tidying, and pets are represented by the sixth house.
Seventh house	This house represents all types of relationships and collaborations, including marriages and work partnerships.
Eighth house	The eighth house covers shared assets and interactions, processes of transformation, and life-threatening experiences.
Ninth house	Symbolizing broadening horizons, the ninth house is linked to travel, higher education, cultural experiences, and spirituality.
Tenth house	This house stands for ambitions and aspirations. It represents career, reputation, leadership, and also personal legacy.
Eleventh house	Friendships, hobbies, community groups, and other social organizations are covered by the eleventh house.
Twelfth house	Representing the subconscious mind, this house covers art, spirituality, and intuition, plus hidden enemies and isolation.

Planets, luminaries, and nodes
The positions of these celestial elements in the 12 houses and zodiac signs influence behaviour, purpose, and destiny.

Moon ☾	Sun ☉	Mercury ☿	Venus ♀
Mars ♂	Jupiter ♃	Saturn ♄	Uranus ♅
Neptune ♆	Pluto ♇	North node ☊	South node ☋

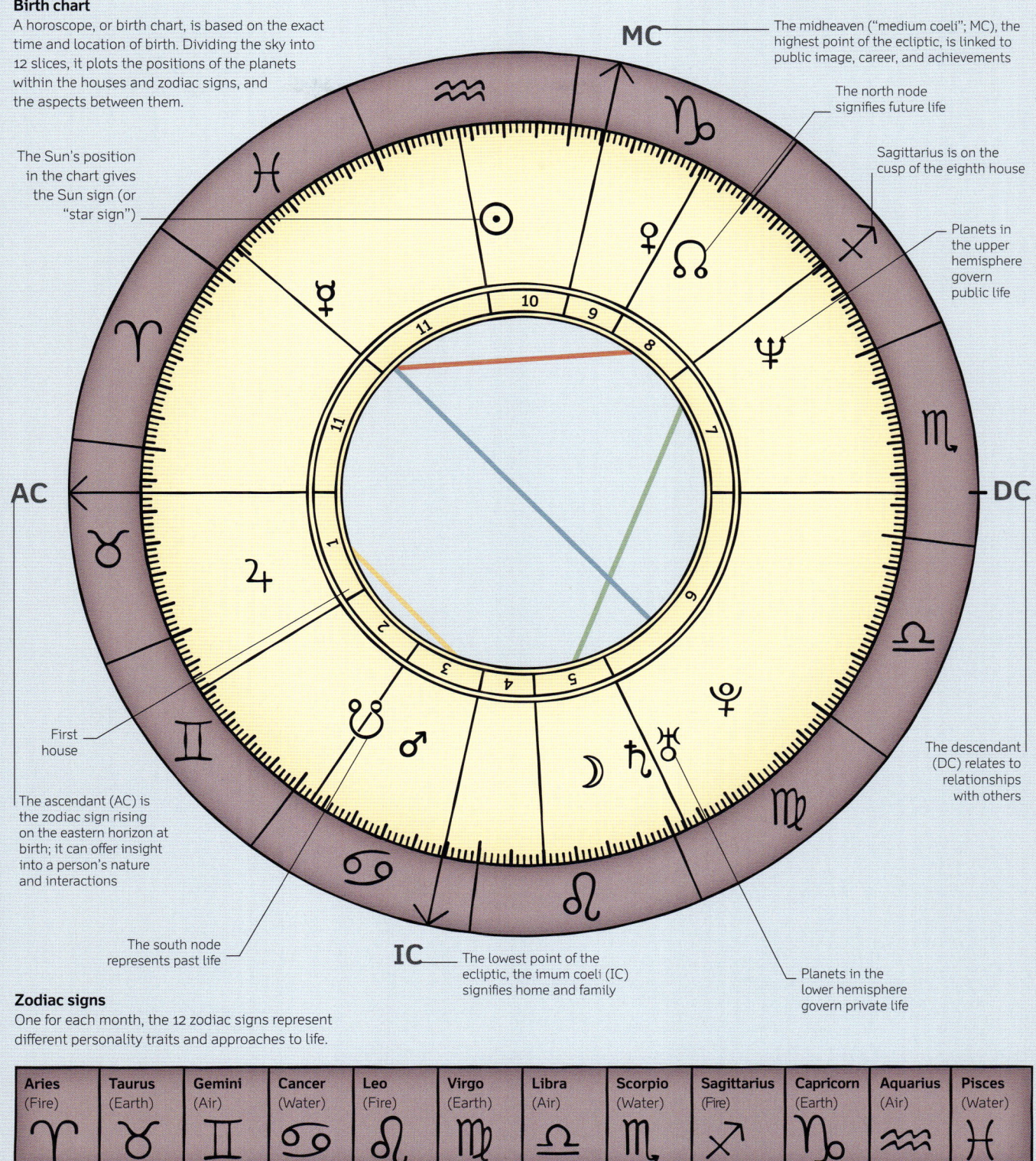

The Magi and the Star of Bethlehem

The Gospel of Matthew, in its description of Jesus' birth, describes how *magoi* travelling from the East followed a star to find the new King of the Jews. When the star stopped over the place where a child had been born, they bowed down to Jesus and delivered costly gifts. The word *magoi* is usually translated as "wise men" from the East, but actually refers to Magi – priests of Zoroastrianism. In ancient sources, the Magi were considered to be skilled in sorcery, prophecy, and astrology.

Only one gospel mentions the star and the Magi, leading some scholars to read it as a literary device – underlining the cosmic significance of Jesus' birth in Christianity – and not a real cosmological event. Others suggest that it was a natural astronomical phenomenon such as a comet, a supernova, or the conjunction of planets, and that, rather than literally following a guiding star, the Magi could have divined Jesus' birth from astrological observations, then embarked on their journey to find him.

> "…and, lo, the star, which they saw in the East, went before them, till it came and stood over where the young child was."
>
> THE BIBLE, MATTHEW 2:9, KING JAMES VERSION

The star, shown in radiant gold, is a common motif in Christian nativity paintings, such as this 15th-century example by Giovanni di Paolo.

The magic of letters
Runes

Used as letters, runes formed the writing system of Germanic tribes in Europe before they adopted the Latin alphabet, along with Christianity, from the 5th century CE onwards. However, even after this date, and despite a 16th-century ban on their use by the Church, runes continued to be employed for specialist tasks. These included divinatory practices and magic, based on runes' strong associations with secret knowledge and the supernatural powers of the Norse gods.

Ancient alphabet

The earliest generally accepted runic inscriptions date from around 150 CE, although some pre-runic symbols have been identified on Bronze Age rock carvings, mainly in Sweden. Like other alphabets from the same period, runes were formed using angular shapes (but no horizontal strokes), so that they could be easily carved into hard surfaces such as wood, metal, bone, or stone. Runic inscriptions were written from left to right or right to left, the direction sometimes alternating sentence by sentence. There were no capital letters and runes were written without spaces between words, although sometimes points were used to separate words and sentences.

Scandinavian runes are known as futhark, named after the first six letters of the runic alphabet (f, u, þ, a, r, and k). The oldest version of this alphabet, Elder Futhark, had 24 letters, each corresponding to a single sound. Letters were further grouped into three aettir (families) of eight; the original names of the aettir are not known, but in modern times they have been linked to the deities Freyja, Hagall, and Tyr (see pp. 102–03). The division into aettir allowed for ciphers and a type of runic "shorthand". Ciphers sometimes used the number of the aett (one, two, or three) as well as the number of the rune within the aett (between one and eight) to create a secret code.

By around 750 CE, a condensed alphabet of just 16 letters – the Younger Futhark – had diverged from the Elder Futhark. Other variants included the Anglo-Saxon Futhorc, which was used from the 5th century onwards in Britain and Frisia (a region along the North Sea coast of present-day Germany and the Netherlands). This alphabet had two additional runes to the Elder Futhark, and later expanded to include 33 runes.

Signs of destiny

According to Norse mythology, runes have existed since the beginning of time and have divine origins. This contributed to beliefs that the letters were a direct means of communication between the human and supernatural realms and could convey powerful, even hidden, messages – the word "rune" means "secret" or "mystery".

The Old Norse poem Hávamál ("Sayings of the High One"), composed between the 9th and 10th centuries CE, describes how three Norns (supernatural female beings) shape fate by carving runes into the trunk of the world tree, Yggdrasil. Desperate to acquire some of their power and wisdom, the god Odin hangs himself from Yggdrasil, in a self-imposed ordeal, to win mastery of the runes (see p. 100). In some legends, Odin then bestows knowledge of the runes on humanity so they can learn their destiny. Another poem from the same period, the Rígsmál, describes how the god Ríg (also known as Heimdall) has three sons, Thrall (slave), Churl (freeman), and Jarl (noble), by human women – the ancestors of the three classes of humans. Ríg teaches the runes to Jarl, and so they enter human knowledge.

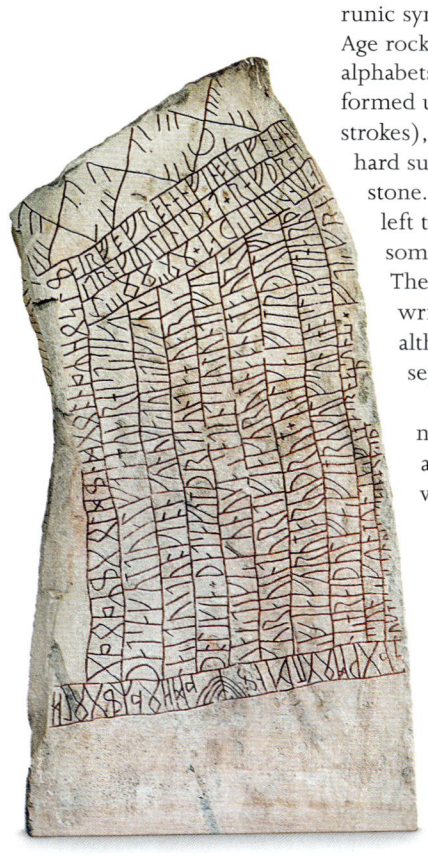

Secret code
The 9th-century Rök Stone in Sweden has the longest known runic inscription in stone. Its message is partially encrypted, using both displacement and cipher runes, possibly to obscure a magical purpose.

Runes 99

The runes are arranged in groups of eight

Power of Odin
This Swedish bracteate (decorative medal) from 400–550 CE is thought to depict the god Odin and his symbol, a raven, surrounded by the 24 runes of the Elder Futhark alphabet. It was probably an amulet designed to protect the wearer.

Dots divide the runes into three *aettir* (families)

> "All will prove true that thou askest of runes —
> those that are come from the gods."
>
> HÁVAMÁL, STANZA 79

The 1st-century Roman writer Tacitus is the main source for how humans used this rune knowledge in relation to destiny. In his *Germania* (98 CE), a study of the German tribes north of Rome, Tacitus describes how specialist rune casters threw lots by marking strips of wood with signs before casting them onto a white cloth. After offering a prayer to the gods, the rune caster picked up three strips and read their meaning from the signs scored on them. The result might imply the gods' blesssing for an enterprise or, conversely, their disapproval.

Runic magic

Knowledge of runes meant more than simply understanding their role as letters. Runes were regarded as potent symbols that could channel the power of the gods, directly influencing fate. The rune Tiwaz, for example, resembles an arrow or spear and was associated with Tyr, the god of the skies and of war. Its use on a sword or shield might bring its owner strength and victory in battle. The rune Hagalaz, on the other hand, symbolizes hail, and is associated with the destructive power of nature. This might signify a hard fate in a divinatory reading, or provide a useful force when inscribed in a curse or spell.

Carved on objects such as pendants, combs, or bones, runes were often used to create amulets for protection against bad luck or sickness. A common runic charm word was *alu* (Ansuz, Laguz, Uruz), which appears in many inscriptions between the 3rd and 8th centuries. Its literal meaning is "ale", but its magical meaning is unclear. The word *auja* (Ansuz, Uruz, Jera, Ansuz), used on buckles and jewellery, appears to mean "good luck" or "protection". It sometimes appears as *gebu auja* — "I give luck" or "I give protection".

Magical formulas were also created using multiples of runes. Sometimes these are listed in succession, as on the Lindholm amulet (c. 2nd–4th century CE), which features eight Ansuz runes in a row, possibly invoking eight gods. Stacking or combining runes to form a single glyph, known as a bindrune, could intensify their power. The Swedish Kylver Stone (400 CE) features a common bindrune — stacked Tiwaz runes that form a tree-like shape — that probably represents a call to channel the full force of the god Tyr.

The Old Norse *Saga of Egill*, recorded in the 13th century, provides a sense of the power and status of rune masters, credited with accessing the power of the gods and influencing human destiny through reading, carving, and casting runes. In the story, Egill is asked to visit a farmer's daughter who is seriously ill, and notices malicious runes carved on a whalebone above her bedpost. He destroys the runes, and carves new ones, placing them under her pillow, which saves her life. Egill leaves with a significant warning: "Runes none should grave ever who knows not to read them."

Protective magic
This Anglo-Saxon ring from the 9th century is inscribed with runes thought to spell out a magical charm, probably to stop bleeding.

The significance of nine

The power of runes is tied to the legendary and magical associations of the number nine in Norse mythology. According to Norse belief, the universe was divided into nine realms that were connected by the world tree, Yggdrasil. The number nine was also associated with the god Odin, who hung himself from Yggdrasil for nine days and nights to prove that he was worthy of mastering the runes. Nine therefore came to symbolize wisdom, completeness, and a connection between the divine and earthly realms. This is reflected in the common practice of casting nine runes for a divinatory reading that gives a comprehensive view of a situation.

Odin's sacrifice involved piercing himself with his own spear and refusing food and drink while he hung from the world tree.

Deciders of destiny
Johan Ludwig Lund's 1844 painting shows the three Norns – Uld, Verdandi, and Skuld – ready to judge actions in the past (left), present (centre), and future (right).

Freyja's *aett* is associated with creation and practical matters linked to love, life, and happiness.

Fehu *Cattle*
The rune of fulfilment and abundance, Fehu signifies success and material reward, as well as achievement and good health.

Uruz *Auroch*
Linked to strength, tenacity, and courage, Uruz implies that success is near, but will require hard work and resourcefulness.

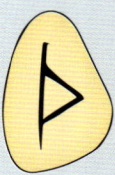
Thurisaz *Giant*
This rune suggests danger, hardship, and conflict are imminent and should be faced, but help and support may be close at hand.

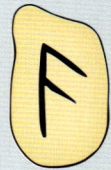
Ansuz *Mouth*
The rune of wisdom and communication, Ansuz suggests that inspiration and good advice is on hand to help with decisions.

Raidho *Wheel*
Travel or an inner personal journey is indicated by Raidho. This might involve making a decision to enact a change.

Kenaz *Torch*
The rune of creativity, enlightenment, and inspiration, Kenaz suggests a revelation that offers a solution to a problem.

Gebo *Gift*
To do with exchange and joining forces for mutual benefit, Gebo also relates to good relationships, balance, and generosity.

Wunjo *Joy*
The rune of fulfilment and accomplishment, Wunjo signals long-lasting wellbeing, as well as social and domestic harmony.

Hagall's *aett* is concerned with psychological matters, achievement, money, power, and success.

Hagalaz *Hail*
This rune signals a short but hard setback and the need for willpower and concentration to weather the storm.

Nauthiz *Need*
Highlighting discontent and hardship, Nauthiz suggests the need to face fears and address changes.

Isa *Ice*
Signifying a period of inactivity and withdrawal, Isa suggests the need for quiet reflection and appraisal.

Jera *Harvest*
This rune indicates it is time to reap the benefits of hard work and to take stock of achievements, even if they have taken time.

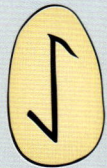
Eihwaz *Yew*
A symbol of balance and stability, this suggests difficulties can be overcome through perseverance and self-discipline.

Perthro *Dice cup*
A reminder that much of life is down to chance, this rune implies that hidden information may soon be revealed.

Algiz *Elk*
Standing for defence and protection, Algiz implies that help is there. While warning of danger, it suggests a positive outcome.

Sowelo *Sun*
This rune symbolizes success, healing, and victory. It heralds a time of good fortune and the celebration of achieved goals.

Tyr's *aett* is linked to relationships, justice, understanding, and establishing order.

Tiwaz *The god Tyr*
Signifying strength, responsibility, and courage, Tiwaz suggests victory, although this might require a sacrifice.

Berkano *Birch*
The rune of fertility, birth, and growth, this brings healing and renewal, and also suggests taking a new direction.

Ehwaz *Horse*
This is about making steady progress through teamwork. It suggests trust and loyalty will combine to bring harmony.

Mannaz *Man*
Signifying all of humanity, Mannaz is a reminder to focus on community and cooperation to ensure future harmony.

Laguz *Water*
Representing the flow of emotions, intuition, and the unconscious, Laguz stands for all that is hidden. It can also signify renewal.

Inguz *The god Ing*
Signalling potential and new beginnings, the fertility rune Inguz suggests that it is time to embrace change positively.

Dagaz *Day*
Suggesting hope and happiness, this rune of awakening symbolizes the end of a cycle and the start of a new enterprise.

Othala *Heritage*
This symbol of lasting legacy represents inheritance and suggests aligning values with what is truly important.

Reading runes

Traditionally, runes are cast randomly onto a cloth and their positions in relation to one another are interpreted to answer a question. However, modern rune readers often lay them out in spreads (the numbered examples below give the order in which each spread is constructed). In terms of timing, the past usually refers to the past three months, and the future refers to the next three months.

Single rune draw
One rune is picked at random to suggest the strengths and qualities needed to tackle a current problem. A rune can also be selected each morning to see how the day will go.

Three-rune spread
This selection offers a short and focused answer to a problem. It can also be used to place issues in context, looking at how the past influences the present.

Problem and solution variation

1 The current situation
2 Challenges and obstacles
3 Possible solution or action required

Past, present, future variation

1 Past influences
2 What is happening now
3 Likely outcome of the situation

Five-rune spread
This spread can provide a deeper understanding of the components of a problem that needs solving, or can be used to analyse and provide guidance on a more complex issue.

1 Current problem and attitude towards it
2 Obstacles that must be overcome
3 The best action to take
4 What must be accepted, as it cannot be changed
5 The likely outcome if action is taken

Seven-rune spread
In this runic "V" shape, the placement of the fourth rune at the base literally points to the best possible course of action in relation to the problem.

1 The influences of the past
2 Present circumstances
3 General prospects and hopes for the future
4 The best possible course of action
5 Attitude or feelings about the situation
6 Potential problems that may delay or frustrate plans
7 The likely outcome

Nine-rune spread
The number nine is significant in Norse tradition (see p. 100). This spread gives the greatest insight, taking into account other relevant people and outside circumstances.

1 The past and its bearing on the situation
2 Attitude towards the outcome
3 Hidden influences acting now
4 How current influences might affect the outcome
5 The present situation
6 Feelings about past events
7 Current attitude to present events
8 Hidden influences that acted in the past
9 The best possible outcome
(The runes are read from left to right, bottom row, middle row, top row.)

First casters
This panel from the *Codex Borbonicus*, a Mexica manuscript from the 1520s, shows the ancestors of all humans, Oxomoco and Cipactonal, throwing maize kernels for divination.

"…if the maize kernels fall face up, the fortune is good… and the contrary if the maize falls face down."

HERNANDO RUIZ DE ALARCÓN, 1629

Seeds of fate

Mesoamerican maize reading

Maize was first domesticated around 9,000 years ago in southern Mexico and became one of the most important crops for numerous cultures in Mesoamerica (see pp. 56–59). Many Mesoamerican cultures regarded maize as divine. A number of their gods were depicted as either carrying maize cobs or surrounded by the leaves of a maize plant. The Mexica (Aztec) maize god Centeotl is one example of this – he was usually depicted as a warrior with maize sprouting from his head and carrying a maize sceptre, while his consort, Chicomecóatl, carried ears of corn in each hand.

Reading the grains

Several Mesoamerican codices – books made from squares of animal skin – have survived the region's colonization by Europeans, and the images preserved on them show people casting handfuls of maize kernels in a ritual setting. This practice was a form of divination used to gain knowledge of the present and future.

Spanish sources also described the process. In 1629, Hernado Ruiz de Alarcón, a Spanish priest working in New Spain (Mexico), wrote the *Treatise on the superstitions and customs among the native Indians of New Spain*, which details the process of Nahua maize divination. To read the maize "dry", the diviner first selected a number of flawless kernels and threw them in the air, and then caught them while invoking various gods. They then tossed the kernels onto a cloth and observed how the maize fell. If the kernels fell face up, it meant good fortune, while face down meant the opposite. How the kernels fell in relation to each other was also significant. This method was used for finding lost people and items, identifying diseases, and prescribing cures. It is still used today by a number of peoples, including the Maya, Mixe, and Nahua, whose practitioners keep the sacred calendar and interpret divine signs.

In "wet" maize divination, the maize was tossed into water. If the maize sank, the prediction was positive, and if it floated (or how it floated) could be interpreted negatively. This form of divination was particularly used for medical matters, to reveal whether an illness had natural or supernatural causes, and to suggest a cure.

> ### Maize and mythology
>
> Maize was a staple crop for the Maya, one of the most prominent Mesoamerican civilizations, and played a central role in their religious beliefs, with several gods personifiying maize.
>
> Maize also featured in Maya beliefs about human origins. When the gods discovered a mountain overgrown with white and yellow maize, they ground it into paste to make dough, which they shaped into the first humans. Maize fed the Maya, and the Maya were maize.

Hun Hunahpu (the Maya maize god) is depicted in this 8th-century CE statue, found in a Maya pyramid.

Questions and cures
A Mexica *ticitl* (physician) casts maize kernels to divine an illness in the presence of the wind god Ehecatl-Quetzalcoatl in this image from the 16th-century *Codex Magliabechiano*.

Destined for greatness
Astrology and politics in imperial Rome

Imperial sign
The reverse side of a coin of Augustus issued in 27 BCE bears the astrological sign of Capricorn – the emperor's Moon sign – carrying a cornucopia (representing prosperity) and a globe (symbolizing power).

Knowledge of Babylonian astrological techniques reached Rome via the Hellenistic world and became popular in aristocratic circles by the 1st century BCE. Some, such as the politician Cicero, lampooned the practice, citing the astrologers' wholly false predictions that the three leaders Crassus, Pompey, and Julius Caesar would all die of old age – they were assassinated or died in battle – but most took to it as a way the gods could make their will known through celestial signs.

Although it was not state-controlled, as it was in ancient Mesopotamia, Roman emperors exploited the propaganda possibilities of astrology in confirming their right to rule. The historian Suetonius recorded that the astrologer Publius Nigidius Figulus had prophesied Augustus's greatness at his birth. The emperor himself used the appearance of the *Sidus Iulium*, or Julian star – most likely a comet – that appeared during the funeral games of Julius Caesar in 44 BCE as a sign that he was Caesar's political heir. Nero, in turn, was proclaimed Roman emperor at noon on 13 October 54 CE, the precise time his mother's astrologers had deemed auspicious.

A risky business

Astrology held dangers, too. Tiberius took to hurling astrologers into the sea if he disliked their predictions, and the art was banned 13 times between the death of Caesar and that of Marcus Aurelius in 180 CE. Largely, though, the victims were those who consulted astrologers, either concerning the health of the emperors – which could be construed as treason – or, even worse, who had horoscopes cast that predicted their own rise to power. In 16 CE, Drusus Libo, Pompey's great-grandson, was found to have consulted an astrologer about his prospects of becoming emperor. He died by suicide before his trial had ended.

Astrology destabilized the Roman state in other ways. Nero murdered his mother, Agrippina – it was said, to fulfil an astrological prediction – who years earlier had used the accusation of consulting astrologers to dispose of Lollia Paulina, her rival for the hand in marriage of Emperor Claudius. The revolt in 96 CE of Nerva against Domitian – a tyrant who had executed several aristocrats whose horoscopes predicted imperial office – was led by high-ranking Romans wishing to avoid the same fate. Even Septimius Severus, emperor from 193 CE, may not have taken up office if he had not escaped an accusation of using astrology four years earlier.

By the 4th century CE, the role of the astrologer had become so politically charged and its practice so fraught with danger for both practitioners and clients that the astrologer Julius Firmicus Maternus counselled avoiding political matters at all costs. His advice, though, was largely rendered redundant, since nearly all emperors were Christian after Constantine's legalization of the religion in 313 CE (see pp. 108–09). With God, not the stars, now determining imperial destinies, there was no longer a need for astrology to be considered treasonous.

Sol Invictus

Sol, the Sun, long recognized as an important deity, became increasingly identified with the emperor from the time of Nero (r. 54–68 CE), who had been depicted on coins with sunbeams radiating from his crown. It was under Aurelian in 274 CE that the cult of Sol Invictus ("the unconquered Sun") really became established and he came to be regarded as the supreme deity. Elements of the cult influenced early Christianity, as Sol Invictus's birthday was said to be 25 December, the same as that of Jesus Christ.

This limestone relief from Roman Lugdunum (modern-day Lyon, France) depicts Sol and dates from the 2nd–3rd century CE.

"Beware of replying to anyone about the condition of the State or the life of the Roman emperor. For it is not right, nor is it permitted…"

JULIUS FIRMICUS MATERNUS, *MATHESIS* 2.30.4, 4TH CENTURY CE

Christian emperors
This 10th-century mosaic shows Justinian (left) and Constantine (right) offering Constantinople (modern Istanbul) to Mary and baby Jesus. After Constantine's conversion, emperors looked to God, not astrologers, for guidance in Roman affairs.

108

Constantine's vision

In 312 CE, Emperor Constantine won a battle against his arch-rival Maxentius at the Milvian Bridge outside Rome – a victory that made him master of the western half of the Roman Empire. Before the battle, Constantine was said to have witnessed a heavenly sign, a cross of light in the sky, with the words *In hoc signo vince* ("In this sign, conquer"). He instructed his troops to paint the cross on their shields, and attributed his subsequent victory to God.

This account of the event was written decades later by a Christian author, Eusebius. Another version, by Lactantius, does not mention the cross – only a dream instructing the emperor and his soldiers to inscribe the Christian Chi-Rho symbol on their shields. A third variation tells how some years earlier, Constantine had a vision in the sky of the pagan god Apollo offering him a laurel wreath. Whichever version is true, the stories show the importance vested by the Romans in heavenly signs, and Constantine certainly favoured Christianity thereafter – he made it legal by the Edict of Milan in 313 CE, confirmed that the Christian seven-day week would replace the traditional Roman eight-day one from 321 CE, and converted to Christianity on his deathbed.

> "About the time of the midday Sun… he saw with his own eyes, up in the sky… a cross-shaped trophy formed from light…"

EUSEBIUS OF CAESAREA, *LIFE OF CONSTANTINE*, 4TH CENTURY

Constantine sees the fiery cross in the sky above the Milvian Bridge in this image from a 9th-century manuscript.

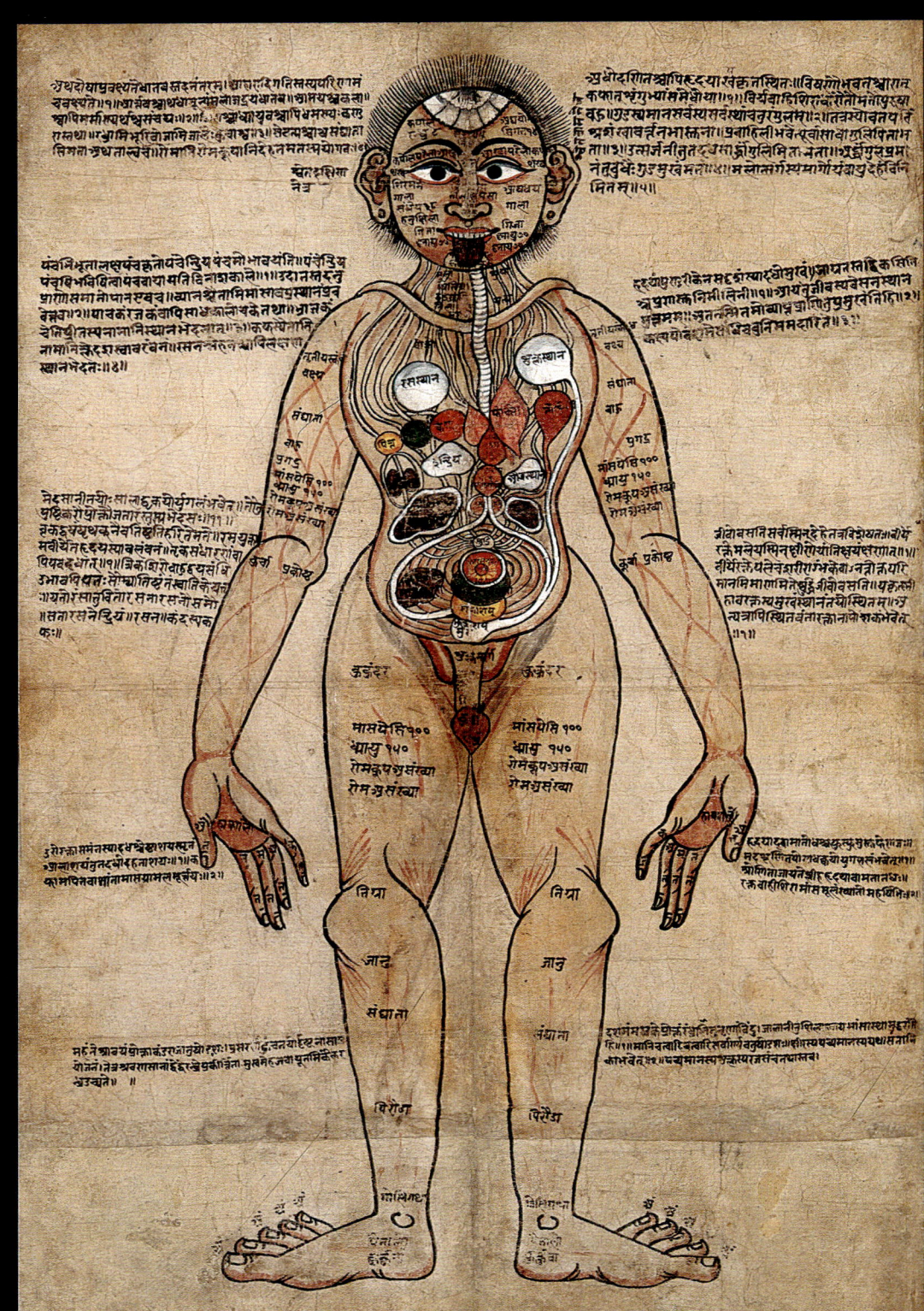

Ayurvedic anatomy
In this 18th-century illustration, the male body is interpreted according to Ayurvedic principles. Each organ is linked to its governing *dosha* – those coloured white, for example, are associated with the *kapha dosha*.

A long and healthy life
The birth of Ayurvedic medicine

The "science of life", Ayurveda is a system of healing developed in India over 3,000 years ago and still used widely today. The practice was first described in ancient Hindu scriptures, the *Vedas* (1500–500 BCE), but was refined between 800 BCE and 1000 CE. During this period, foundational texts such as the *Suśruta Saṃhitā* ("Sushruta's Compendium"), a Sanskrit treatise on medicine written by ancient Indian surgeon Sushruta in the 6th century BCE, and the *Charaka Saṃhitā* ("Charaka's Compendium"), composed in the 2nd century BCE, set out Ayurveda's key tenets.

Ayurveda is based on the principle that good health results from balancing three *doshas*, or energies, within the body; ill health and disease occur when these energies are imbalanced. The *doshas* are *pitta*, which is linked to fire and a fiery temperament; *vata*, associated with water and creativity; and *kapha*, which is tied to earth and a solid, strong disposition. An imbalance in one of the *doshas* is believed to affect particular organs or tissues. Excessive *pitta*, for example, may cause ulcers, digestive problems, and arthritis; too much *vata* may result in joint pain or constipation; a surplus of *kapha* is thought to lead to obesity and diabetes. Ayurvedic doctors treat these imbalances using meditation, dietary changes, and herbal medicines. Since the earliest days of Ayurvedic practice, they have also made use of the ancient Vedic system of astrology known as *jyotiḥśāstra* (see pp. 112–15). This form of astrology is used to guide diagnoses and prescriptions, and also to determine the best time for treatment.

Planet-driven health

Ayurvedic astrology is based on the notion that the positions of nine celestial bodies (the *navagrahas*) within the 12 zodiac signs at the time of a person's birth predispose them to certain ailments. This makes a natal chart an important predictive and diagnostic tool, as it shows the relative influence of the Sun, Moon, and planets on health at birth. The planet Mars, for example, is associated with the *pitta dosha*, and is believed to govern blood and muscles. Given a significant position on a birth chart (see pp. 116–17), it may predispose an individual to blood disorders and inflammation. The location of these celestial bodies within the astrological houses on a birth chart is also significant, because each house is associated with specific organs and afflictions. Planetary action in the first house, which rules the head, for example, may lead to issues such as headaches, while the third house governs the lungs and is linked to respiratory diseases.

By referencing astrology, Ayurvedic treatments can be timed to coincide with periods when the influence of a planet linked to a particular disorder is especially strong. The movement of planets can also be studied to predict future health issues – a transit of Saturn, for example, may signify that there will be a protracted recovery. Once planetary influences are identified as a cause or contributing factor to a health problem, the standard range of Ayurvedic cures to balance the *doshas* can be deployed. Sometimes, these include the additional use of amulets linked by their colour, or other properties, to the planet responsible for the issue.

Making a diagnosis
Ayurvedic practice is a holistic approach, melding physical examination and consideration of the *doshas* with astrological information. In this 19th-century painting, an Ayurvedic doctor begins his consultation by checking the pulse of a patient.

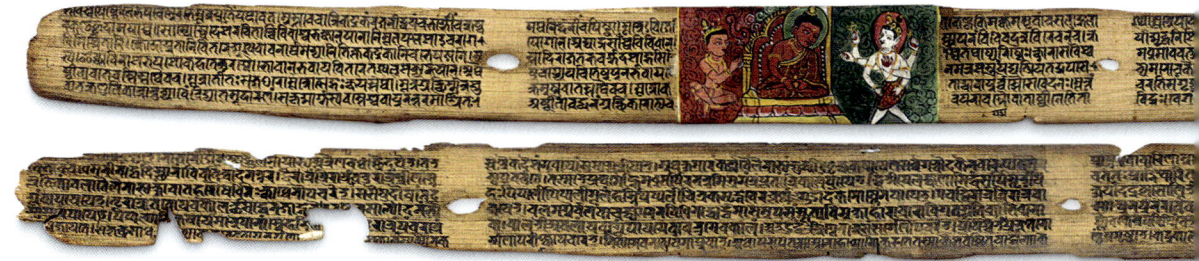

Ancient medical text
This 12th-century copy of the *Suśruta Saṃhitā* is inscribed on palm leaves. As well as astrological content, the work contains one of the earliest accounts of plastic surgery.

> "This science reveals the ripening of all such karman (deed) that was accumulated in the other life, good or bad, just as a lamp reveals objects in the darkness."

VARĀHAMIHIRA DESCRIBING HOROSCOPIC ASTROLOGY, *LAGHUJĀTAKA* 1.3 (TR. ANUPAM KUMAR SUMAN)

Zodiac wheel
The signs of the zodiac encircle a lotus flower on this 12th-century stone carving, illustrating the fusion of Hellenistic and Vedic concepts in Indian astrology.

Charting one's fortunes
Indian astrology

Jyotiḥśāstra, meaning "science of light", was first described in Hindu sacred texts, the *Vedas*, in the 2nd millennium BCE (see pp. 32–33). These texts refer to a practice based on observational astronomy (*gaṇita*), with no mention of predictive astrology aside from an occasional reference to omens. However, early Buddhist texts such as the *Brahmajālasutta* ("The Divine or Supreme Net of Views") suggest that new forms of astrology were in use by the 5th century BCE. These works describe divination based on the interpretation of omens (*saṁhitā*) as well as the use of mundane astrology, which deals with the fate of nations, states, or cities. This type of prognostication is detailed more systematically in the *Gargasaṁhitā* ("Astrology of Garga"), written around 100 BCE.

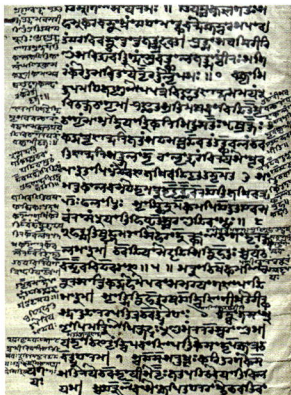

Discussions of destiny
In this page from a copy of his 6th-century work the *Yogāyātra*, Indian astrologer Varāhamihira discusses how human effort and fate can both influence destiny for better or worse.

Hellenistic horoscopic influences
Although natal astrology (*phalita jyotiṣa*) appears in the Buddhist text *Śārdūlakarṇāvadāna* (100 CE), which describes a person's characteristics based on the Moon's position in a particular *nakṣatra* at birth, the clearest evidence of early horoscopy (*horā*) in India is found in 2nd-century CE texts. These show the gradual assimilation of Hellenistic astrological ideas into Indian practice – the result of cultural and economic exchange with ancient Greece. The *Yavanajātaka* ("Greek Horoscopy"), composed around 150 CE, is one of the first works to describe horoscopic methods that combine zodiac-sign-based Hellenistic astrology with Vedic approaches based on the Moon's position in the 27 *nakṣatras*.

The process of synthesis was completed in the 6th century by the Indian astrologer Varāhamihira. In two seminal texts, the *Bṛhajjātaka* ("Big Volume on Horoscopy") and *Bṛhatsaṁhitā* ("Big Volume on Omenology"), he mathematically amalgamated the ecliptic positions of the 12 zodiac signs with the *nakṣatras* to give one predictive measurement: each sign (*rāśis*) encompassed two-and-a-quarter *nakṣatras*. He also substituted Vedic gods for the Greek gods traditionally associated with the planets: Indra, for example, replaced Zeus as ruler of Jupiter. Varāhamihira's systematization and modification of ancient Vedic traditions to include Hellenistic elements still forms the basis for the practice of Indian astrology today.

The power of karma
Varāhamihira's new form of astrology included one core philosophical concept absent from Hellenistic interpretations of the heavens – the metaphysics of karma (*karman*). According to ancient Vedic thought, karma – a universal law of cause and effect in which every action, word, or thought sets in motion a chain of events that will eventually return to the individual – shapes human destiny across lifetimes. For Varāhamihira, karma provided a philosophical basis for horoscopy.

Planetary shrine
Many Indian temples include shrines to the nine planetary bodies (*navagrahas*) that shape destiny. In this example from Tamil Nadu, southern India, the celestial bodies are represented by their ruling deities.

This meant that a horoscope functioned as an expression of the deeds enacted by an individual in past lives, with the position of each celestial body representing the resultant karma. These planetary bodies were the *navagrahas*, or "nine planets", made up of the Sun, the Moon, Mars, Mercury, Jupiter, Venus, Saturn, and the "shadow planets" Rahu and Ketu (the north and south nodes of the Moon). The position of each *graha* (planet) in a horoscope indicates which type of karma may dominate at a particular time, and can therefore guide positive choices or actions to influence destiny. Each *graha* is ruled by a different deity, who may be petitioned or worshipped in the hope of mitigating bad karma inherited from previous deeds or of fostering good karma, with the aim of improving future outcomes.

Complex calculations

In the centuries following Varāhamihira, methods for preparing and interpreting horoscopes became increasingly sophisticated. Unlike Western charts, Indian horoscopes began to include analysis of planetary periods, or *daśā* (literally "states"), to give more detailed information on the circumstances influencing a person at a particular point in time. Each *daśā* is controlled by one of the *navagrahas*, so analysing these periods provided a system for assessing the effects of planetary forces over a lifetime. Several *daśā* systems developed, each assessing different lengths of time. The *Vimśottarī daśā* became the most popular and is still in use. This system analyses periods of 120 years and allocates each *graha*, or planetary force, a *daśā* of different duration: the Sun's period of influence is 6 years, the Moon's 10 years, Venus is 20 years, Mars 7 years, Jupiter 16 years, Saturn 19 years, Mercury 17 years, Rahu 18 years, and Ketu 7 years. Whether a *daśā* brings good times or bad depends on the nature of its associated *graha* (Venus, for example, is regarded as benevolent, Saturn malign) as well as the *graha*'s movement through the signs and houses of the zodiac during this period.

Celestial calculations known as *aṣṭakavarga* ("eight-fold division") added another tool to horoscopic practice. Using this method, astrologers determined the strength of each house in a horoscope by evaluating planetary transits. Each planetary body was assigned points between one and eight based on its position in a house. The points were then added together to determine the overall strength and influence of the planet at a given time. Powerful combinations of planets, known as *yogas*, or "unions", were also believed to significantly influence the course of a person's life by determining the level of success or failure. Certain unions, such as the *Raj yoga*, were considered auspicious; others less favourable. The thousands of different *yogas* indicate the complexity and comprehensive nature of the horoscopic system that developed over time. Recorded in manuals for prediction, these methods still guide the practice of Indian astrology today.

Following tradition
This modern chart reflects astrological methods that have been refined over the past 2,000 years. It includes complex mathematical calculations relating to planetary phases (*daśā*), transits, and significant conjunctions (*yogas*), which the astrologer must interpret before making a prediction.

Predicting success
A retrospective tribute to the start of a successful dynasty, this 17th-century miniature from a chronicle of the reign of third Mughal emperor Akbar (r. 1556–1605) shows astrologers casting horoscopes at the birth of his great ancestor, the conqueror Timur, in 1336.

Reading Indian birth charts

An Indian birth chart (*kuṇḍalī*) is a two-dimensional representation of the sky at the moment of birth. There are several different ways of drawing up a chart, but the most common is the diamond pattern, or North Indian style. The positions of the zodiac constellations and planetary bodies (*navagrahas*) in 12 houses and 27 lunar mansions (*nakṣatras*) dictate their positive or negative effects. These influences are analysed to gain insight into the individual's personality, to guide important decisions, and to make predictions about the future.

The 12 zodiac signs, shown as numbers on an Indian birth chart, are each governed by a ruling planet.

Aries (1) (*Meṣa*) Planet: Mars	Taurus (2) (*Vṛṣabha*) Planet: Venus	Gemini (3) (*Mithuna*) Planet: Mercury	Cancer (4) (*Karka*) Planet: Moon
Leo (5) (*Siṁha*) Planet: Sun	Virgo (6) (*Kanyā*) Planet: Mercury	Libra (7) (*Tulā*) Planet: Venus	Scorpio (8) (*Vṛścika*) Planet: Mars
Sagittarius (9) (*Dhanu*) Planet: Jupiter	Capricorn (10) (*Makara*) Planet: Saturn	Aquarius (11) (*Kumbha*) Planet: Saturn	Pisces (12) (*Mīna*) Planet: Jupiter

The nine planetary bodies (*navagrahas*) – two luminaries, five planets, and two nodes or "shadow planets" – govern different aspects of life.

Sun (*Sūrya*)	Mercury (*Budha*)	Saturn (*Śani*)
Moon (*Candra*)	Jupiter (*Guru*)	Ketu (South node of the Moon)
Mars (*Maṅgala*)	Venus (*Śukra*)	Rāhu (North node of the Moon)

The lunar mansions (*nakṣatras*) represent 27 divisions of the Moon's path around Earth, each spanning 13 degrees (°) and 20 minutes (').

1 Aśvinī Aries 0°00'–13°20'	10 Maghā Leo 0°00–13°20'	19 Mūla Sagittarius 0°00–13°20'
2 Bharaṇī Aries 13°20'–26°40'	11 Pūrva-Phālgunī Leo 13°20'–26°40'	20 Pūrva-Āṣāḍha Sagittarius 13°20'–26°40'
3 Kṛttikā Aries 26°40'–10°00'	12 Uttara-Phālgunī Leo 26°40'–10°00'	21 Uttara-Āṣāḍha Sagittarius 26°40'–10°00'
4 Rohiṇī Taurus 10°00'–23°20'	13 Hasta Virgo 10°00'–23°20'	22 Śrāvaṇa Capricorn 10°00'–23°20'
5 Mṛgaśirā Taurus 23°20'–6°40'	14 Citrā Virgo 23°20'–6°40'	23 Dhaniṣṭha Capricorn 23°20'–6°40'
6 Ārdrā Gemini 6°40'–20°00'	15 Svātī Libra 6°40'–20°00'	24 Śatabhiṣā Aquarius 6°40'–20°00'
7 Punarvasu Gemini 20°00'–3°20'	16 Viśākhā Libra 20°00'–3°20'	25 Pūrva-Bhādrapada Aquarius 20°00'–3°20'
8 Puṣya Cancer 3°20'–16°40	17 Anurādhā Scorpio 3°20'–16°40	26 Uttara-Bhādrapa Pisces 3°20'–16°40
9 Āśleṣā Cancer 16°40'–30°00	18 Jyeṣṭhā Scorpio 16°40'–30°00	27 Revatī Pisces 16°40'–30°00

The 12 houses (*bhavas*) are grouped in different ways, and each house occupies a whole zodiac sign.

Kendra, Paṇaphara, Āpoklima (Angular, succedent, and cadent houses)	Varāhamihira's original classification was probably influenced by the Greek tradition. He grouped the houses as "angular" (1st, 4th, 7th, 10th), "succedent" (2nd, 5th, 8th, 11th), or "cadent" (3rd, 6th, 9th, 12th).
Puruṣārtha (The four goals of life)	According to Hindu philosophy these are: *Dharma* (purpose) – 1st, 5th, and 9th houses; *Artha* (wealth) – 2nd, 6th, and 10th houses; *Kāma* (desires) – 3rd, 7th, and 11th houses; *Mokṣa* (liberation) – 4th, 8th, and 12th houses.
Kendra (Cardinal or angular houses)	The 1st, 4th, 7th, and 10th houses. These houses form the centre of the birth chart and are the most powerful. Planets that are stationed in these houses can exert either positive or negative influences.
Trikoṇa (Trine houses)	The 1st, 5th, and 9th houses. These benefic (good) houses form a triangle in the North Indian birth chart. When their planetary rulers are in conjunction with those of the *kendra* houses, they confer luck and prosperity.
Duṣṭa (Bad houses)	The 6th, 8th, and 12th houses. These houses, their rulers, and the planets within them tend to create obstacles and suffering – unless a planetary ruler, or "house lord", is occupying its own house.

Reading Indian birth charts

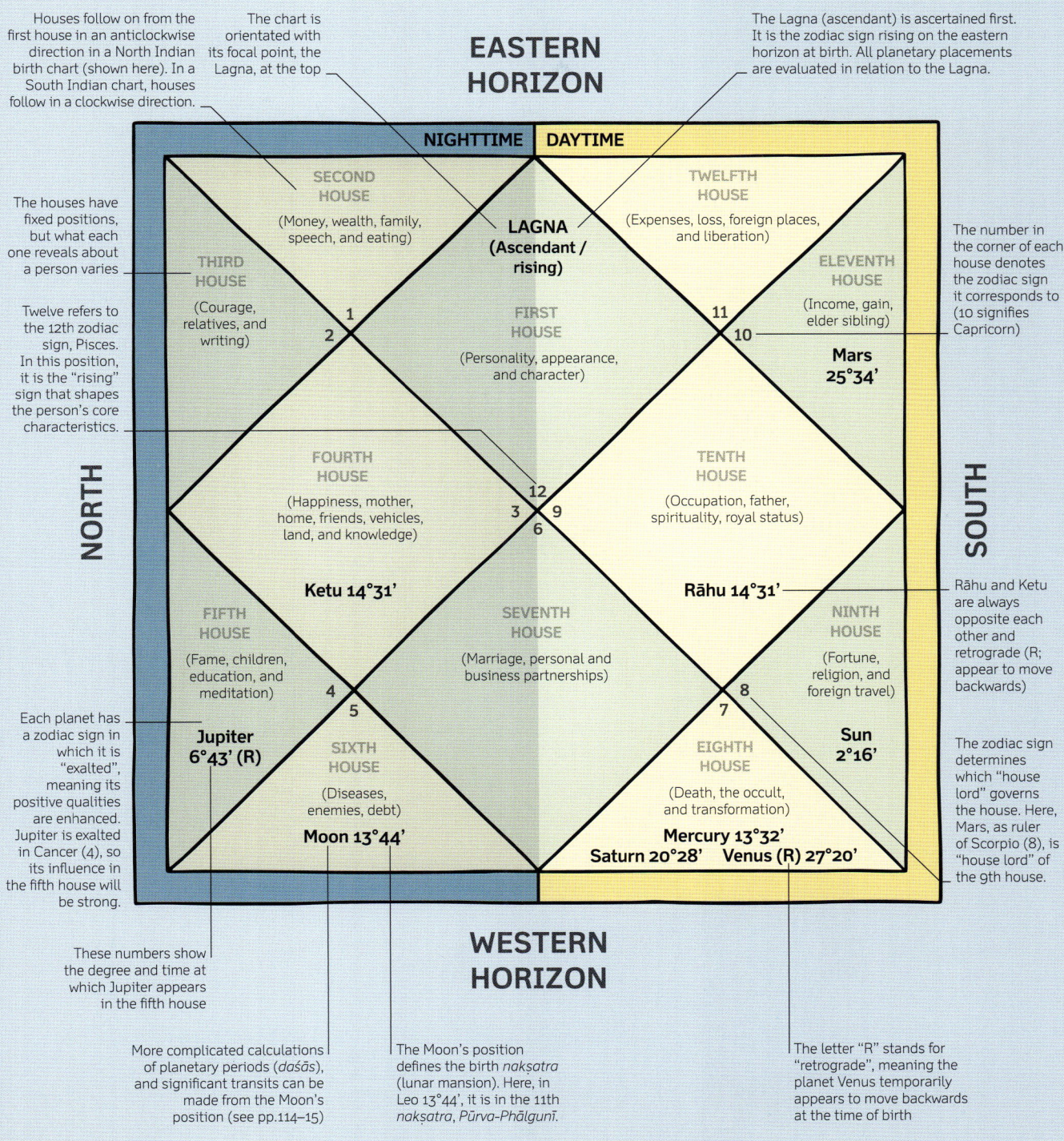

Notes from above
Chinese spirit-writing

Immortal sage
Lü Dongbin, one of the Baxian – the Eight Immortal Sages of Daoism – is shown on this 16th-century scroll. He was highly revered and had many *fuji* spirit-writing altars dedicated to him.

Spirit-writing, or *fuji*, emerged in China from a long tradition of communication with the gods that dates back to at least the 2nd millennium BCE, when Shang dynasty rulers used the bone of turtle shells for divination (see pp. 18–19). The Chinese belief that writing was the most effective way of communicating with the spirits led priests of the Tianshidao (Heavenly Master) school of Daoism, which developed under the Eastern Han (25–220 CE), to leave written petitions to the gods. In turn, the gods would transmit their divine revelations in written form back to the priests.

Fuji first appeared in the 5th century CE among female silk workers devoted to the goddess Zigu, the Purple Maiden, whose advice they sought regarding textile production. The ritual involved one or two spirit mediums, each holding one end of a bifurcated wooden stick made from peach or willow – woods believed to repel evil forces – over a wooden planchette, or tablet, sprinkled with sand or ashes. Moved by the spirit of the deity, they would trace out an answer to their question onto the planchette, character by character. The two mediums were considered to represent the complementary cosmic forces of yin and yang, with the yang medium standing on the left of the altar said to represent "heaven's hand" – the main mover of the stick that created the message. A reader was present to announce what had been written and a scribe would record the divine communication onto paper.

Spirit-writing cults

From its humble beginnings, *fuji* gained popularity among the elite literati class during the Song dynasty (960–1279 CE). Clubs devoted to its practice were formed – to communicate with dead ancestors, for divination on matters concerning career and family, and as a form of entertainment. Altars were set up dedicated to *fuji* and during the subsequent Ming dynasty (1368–1644), spirit-writing was taken up by Daoist priests as an element in their ritual repertoire – to seek blessings, counsel, or cures from the gods.

From 1644, under the Qing dynasty, spirit-writing was practised by groups of lay people, as well as priests and the elite. These groups established spirit-writing cults dedicated to Daoist sages, such as Patriarch Lü (Lü Dongbin), and some claimed to receive wider revelations from the gods. For example, the *Lüzu quanshu*, a Daoist text, was apparently spirit-written through *fuji*.

Although intermittently suppressed by the central authorities during the 19th century, *fuji* survived, and new spirit-writing cults emerged at times of social instability, such as after the fall of the imperial regime in 1911. Today, it continues to be practised in Daoist temples. Fuji inspired the development of planchette seances in the mid-19th century in Europe and the US, in which similar spirit-writing was produced – ultimately leading to the creation of the first Ouija boards in the 1890s.

***Fuji* ceremony**
This 19th-century plaster model shows a *fuji* ritual in which two mediums are requesting a prescription from Yao Wang, god of medicine. A reader (far left) and a scribe (far right) are poised to record the message.

Chinese spirit-writing 119

"If something is in your fate, you will always receive it, [but] if something is not in your fate, do not force it."

CHINESE PROVERB

Writing practice
This painting, from an illustrated edition of the 18th-century novel *The Dream of the Red Chamber* by Cao Xuequin, shows women who are thought to be practising spirit-writing.

The way of yin and yang

Onmyōdō in Japan

The main Japanese divinatory practice for over a thousand years, onmyōdō has its roots in the Chinese philosophy of the cosmic balance of yin and yang, and the interaction between fire, wood, earth, metal, and water: the five elements making up the universe.

The basis of the system was introduced to Japan from China in the 6th century CE by, among others, a visiting Korean monk, Gwalleuk, who brought divinatory manuscripts with him. Offering a formal framework for making decisions and avoiding inauspicious dates, times, or directions, the new techniques were taken up by the imperial court, and in 701 CE Emperor Monmu (683–707) established the Onmyōryō (Divination Bureau). Its officials included six onmyōji responsible for yin-yang divination, as well as specialists in tenmōn

Casting lots
An onmyōji performs divination using counting rods in this illustration from the Tamamo-no-Mae, a 17th-century text about the life of Tamamo, a fox–spirit.

(astrology), koyomi (calendar studies), and rōkōki (timekeeping). At first, the onmyōji were almost exclusively devoted to advising members of the imperial court, interpreting omens, or judging the correct time or manner in which to carry out official activities such as military campaigns or the movements of the emperor within the imperial capital, Kyoto.

Gradually, the roles of the officials within the Onmyōryō blurred until the onmyōji performed them all, becoming generalist magical practitioners. By the latter part of the Heian period (794–1185), their ranks were dominated by the Abe and Kamo families, while Buddhist monks, who previously practised divination, were forbidden to do so. No longer exclusively serving the imperial household, the onmyōji now also offered their services to noble clans who sought their advice.

Grand rituals such as the Shikaku-shikyōosai in Kyoto, performed to secure the four main exit roads from the imperial city and seal them against evil spirits, continued to take place. However, onmyōdō was increasingly used by influential families to appease the kami (Shinto deities), or to ward off illness and other misfortune. The means the onmyōji used were varied – sometimes through spells, or the use of ofuda (protective talismans), or by astrological divination to determine auspicious days and hours, and offerings to the five planets, 12 zodiac deities, and 28 lunar mansions (see pp. 124–27).

The onmyōji absorbed beliefs from esoteric Buddhism concerning astral deities and gods such as Daishōgun, and adopted the practice of feng shui – the layout of buildings and cities according to the most harmonious flow of energy within them (see pp. 36–37). They also performed exorcisms, and summoned up shikigami, conjured spirits who were bound to do their bidding by being trapped in folded paper shapes.

Eventual decline

Onmyōdō received further official recognition in 1683 when the Tsuchimikado family were appointed official overseers, charged with licensing all forms of divination and ensuring the adequate training of practising onmyōji. However, following the Meiji restoration in 1868, when the emperors were restored to real power after centuries of subjugation to the authority of the Tokugawa shoguns, the new regime forbade hybrid Buddhist–Shinto practices. Onmyōdō, which had absorbed so much from Japan's various religious traditions, lost imperial favour and was banned. Although some onmyōji carried on, attached to shrines as priests, their central role in Japan's landscape of magic and divination was over.

Directional deity
This 11th–12th-century wooden sculpture shows Daishōgun, god of the four cardinal directions. Deciding on a safe direction of travel was an important element in onmyōdō, so enlisting Daishōgun's aid was vital.

Master diviner

Japan's most renowned onmyōji, Abe no Seimei (921–1005), was a diviner, astrologer, and exorcist who, at the age of 80, was appointed "Master of onmyōdō". Legend stated that he was only part-human, his mother being a kitsune, or fox spirit, whom his mortal father married. Abe was said to have correctly predicted the date of the abdication of Emperor Kazan in 986. He also apparently had an ability to find lost objects simply by thinking about them. The five-pointed star that became a symbol of onmyōdō and Japanese mysticism in general was derived from Abe's personal seal and was called the Seimei Kikyō, or Seal of Seimei.

Abe no Seimei contemplates a manuscript in this mid-19th-century ink drawing.

Chinese constellations

Chinese astronomers developed their own system of constellations entirely separate from those of ancient Mesopotamia and Greece, as demonstrated by a star map rediscovered at Dunhuang, China, in the early 20th century. Probably dating from the 7th or early 8th century CE, this scroll shows 1,345 separate stars, arranged in 257 small groups or "asterisms", and it offers a valuable insight into how the Chinese viewed the heavens.

Twelve panels provide coverage of the sky, centred on the celestial equator, which Chinese astronomers divided into 12 sections. These, in turn, were associated with Jupiter's revolution period of approximately 12 years. As well as asterisms, the panels show the 28 lunar mansions (see pp. 124–27) with their leading stars. A final 13th panel depicts the celestial north pole, including the North Star and its surrounding asterisms. This region of the sky was significant in Chinese political ideology as it represented the emperor (the North Star) as the supreme ruler around which all activity occurred. The asterisms were believed to correspond to other members of the royal family, court officials, and various rooms in the royal palace.

> "At the 11th month, the spirit yang contracts, the spirit yin expands, the 10,000 beings disappear into the darkness."

TEXT FROM THE FIRST CHART OF THE *DUNHUANG STAR ATLAS*

The 13th chart from the *Dunhuang Star Atlas* shows the stars of the celestial north pole (right) alongside the god of lightning (left).

電神

自尖二度於胃九度七度於辰狂田為星紀者言統己万物之終故曰星紀吳越之分也

Ideas from afar
East Asian horoscopy

Long before regular contact with other civilizations, Chinese astronomers developed their own system of observational astronomy based on the passage of the Moon through 28 stations or "lunar mansions". They also independently discovered and noted the motions of the five planets, which they linked to the five elements: water to Mercury, fire to Mars, wood to Jupiter, metal to Venus, and earth to Saturn. They associated the Moon with the universal force of yin, and the Sun with yang, and speculated on how celestial influences might affect the flow of energy (qi) on Earth (see pp. 34–35). Chinese rulers considered all these factors when taking decisions, from planning the design of a city to initiating a war. They also carefully monitored the heavens for any anomalies that might be interpreted as omens, such as comets or eclipses, believing that these signs might signify a looming disaster or, conversely, an imminent success (see pp. 38–39). The sensitive implications of this celestial knowledge meant that astronomy was a restricted profession, closely controlled by the imperial court: only authorized people could study the subject in detail. The court also retained the executive right to draft and issue an annual calendar – anyone drafting alternative versions was challenging the authority of the emperor.

Travelling traditions
The prognostic potential of linking a calendar to observed celestial movements had already been realized in astrological traditions outside China. The Babylonians devised the system of 12 zodiac signs and recorded the motions of the planets on clay tablets in the 5th century BCE (see pp. 24–27), while the first horoscopes were cast in Alexandria, Egypt, in the 2nd century BCE (see pp. 80–83) – bringing together Babylonian, Egyptian, and Greek astrological ideas and practices. A horoscope (literally the "marker of the hour") is a chart that displays the 12 zodiac signs and the positions of the planets in those signs at a given moment in time, especially the time of a person's birth. Astrologers would calculate and create these charts for clients and then interpret the fortunes and disasters that they might expect in life.

Horoscopy spread to Europe, Persia, and then to India between the 3rd and 4th centuries CE. Here, Hindu astrologers incorporated the practice into their own system of 27 lunar mansions, the *nakṣatras* (see pp. 32–33). Indian Buddhists initially rejected astrology, with monks and nuns prohibited from its practice. However, the rules were not strictly enforced and, over time, some Buddhists – particularly those following Mahayana teachings – began to incorporate astrology into their doctrines and rituals. By the 7th century, calculations based on astrological beliefs had become an essential tool for timing rituals in the new esoteric or Tantric form of Buddhism that was gaining popularity in India. Tantric texts, carried along the Silk Road trade route by Buddhist monks, would ultimately bring the practice of horoscopy from India to China.

Lunar mansion god
This painting by Chinese astronomer and artist Liang Lingzan (c. 690–757 CE) illustrates one of the deities associated with the 28 lunar mansions of traditional Chinese astronomy.

Astrological mandala
Known as the "Garbhadhātu-mandala", this representation of the universe from a 7th-century Buddhist text shows the early influence of astrology on Indian Buddhism. The 12 zodiac signs are depicted as deities.

Key

1 The Buddha is seated on an ox cart, surrounded by the five planets, depicted in human form.
2 Mars appears as a four-armed red warrior.
3 Venus is shown as a beautiful woman playing the Chinese lute.
4 Saturn appears as a Brahmin (a Hindu priest) leading a bull.
5 Jupiter is illustrated as an official, holding flowers.
6 Mercury is represented as a woman and a scribe, holding brush and paper.

Astral influencer
This Chinese painting from 897 CE fuses Buddhist ideas and astrological concepts. It reflects the belief that the Buddha (centre) can placate the planets, thereby preventing misfortunes.

> "He examined the pearl-adorned turning sphere, with its transverse tube of jade, and reduced to a harmonious system (the movements of) the Seven Directors."

CHINESE LEGEND FROM THE *SHANGSHU* ("BOOK OF DOCUMENTS")

Astrology and Chinese Buddhism

Buddhism gained popularity in China during the Tang dynasty (618–907 CE) with the arrival and translation of Indian Buddhist scriptures. In 724 CE, astronomer and Chinese Buddhist monk Yixing and the Indian monk Śubhakarasimha, both employed by the Chinese court, translated the *Mahāvairocana-sūtra*. Containing a mandala (diagram symbolizing the universe) featuring the signs of the zodiac, the planets, and the 28 *nakṣatras*, this Buddhist text shows how astrology was becoming integrated with religious concepts. Such texts promoted the notions that knowledge of astrology was necessary for the proper timing of religious rituals and that the planets embodied more than elemental forces – they represented deities or divine powers worthy of worship.

In 759 CE, the Buddhist monk Amoghavajra drafted the *Xiuyao jing* ("Treatise on Lunar Mansions and Planets"). This authoritative manual was the first to give detailed instructions on using astrology to time rituals. It equated the lunar mansions of Chinese astronomy with the Indian *nakṣatras* system and introduced ideas related to horsocopy – specifically that predictions could be made about a person based on the time of their birth. All the astrological calculations in Amoghavajra's text were based on Buddhist cosmology, which envisioned the world as a flat disc (rather than as a globe). According to this model, the Sun and Moon revolve around Mount Sumeru, which forms the centre of the spiritual and physical universe.

Personal destiny

By 800 CE, Persian as well as Indian astronomers were being employed at the Chinese court. They introduced and translated texts that dealt specifically with horoscopy, sparking a wave of interest in the practice. Unlike earlier forms of Chinese astral divination, which focused on omens relating to rulers or the country in general, horoscopes revealed the fate of the individual, giving them widespread appeal. Horoscopy was soon taken up by Daoist priests, as well as famous poets such as Han Yu and Du Mu. Followers of Buddhism also popularized the practice, embracing birth charts and a new pantheon of astral deities as a means to explain – and influence – fate.

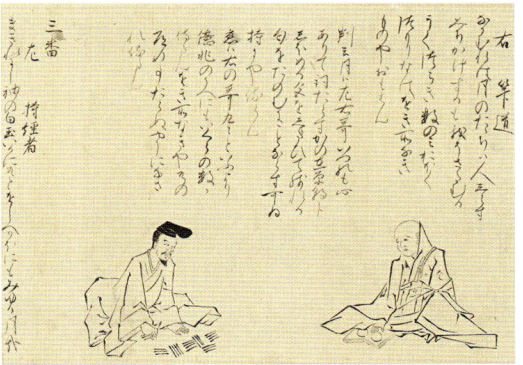

Casting a horoscope
This 13th-century Japanese illustration shows the Chinese method for casting horoscopes, introduced into Japan in the 9th century. While a mathematician (left) casts and counts rods, the astrologer-monk (right) examines the horoscope.

In the early 9th century, the Buddhist monk Kūkai took Amoghavajra's *Xiuyao jing* to Japan. Subsequent generations of monks introduced more texts, establishing the Chinese system of horoscopy in a new Japanese context. By the late 10th century, a lineage of astrologer-monks unique to Japan had emerged. Called the *sukuyōdō*, they incorporated astrology and the worship of planets into their belief system and rituals. Influential in Japanese aristocratic circles, they read clients' horoscopes and offered advice on which planets to pray to in order to avert predicted disasters. While this caste of astrologers had vanished by the late 14th century, much of what is known of early Chinese horoscopy was preserved in this Japanese tradition.

Deities and the seven-day week

Along with horoscopy, Indian and Persian texts introduced the concept of the seven-day week to China, where it was first adopted by Daoists around the 9th century. According to this system, each day, and each hour of the day, is ruled by one of the seven planets in the form of an astral deity. The sequence begins with Saturn, followed by Jupiter, Mars, the Sun, Venus, Mercury, then the Moon. The characteristics of each planet determine whether a day or time is opportune or inauspicious for an activity: Saturn's link with loneliness, for example, warns against marriage under its influence.

Venus, associated with merrymaking, is usually shown playing a lute, as in this 9th-century illustration.

Heaven on Earth
The founding of Baghdad

Designed as a perfectly round city, fashioned after a geocentric model of the cosmos, Baghdad was intended to represent the order of the heavens on Earth and provide its Abbasid rulers (750–1258) with a gloss of divine authority. The details of its construction, however, involved celestial foundations that ran deeper than the shape of its walls.

Astrology shaped the Abbasid dynasty's perception of time, history, and the unfolding of events. The Abbasids believed terrestrial affairs were directly connected to celestial movements, and equated knowledge of astrology to understanding the mechanisms of fate and causality. Therefore, when they decided to build a new capital for their nascent empire, the Abbasids used electional astrology – examining the heavens to elect a moment when celestial configurations promised their caliphate enduring glory, prosperity, and power. Unlike other forms of astrology, which usually interpret an existing or past situation, electional astrology seeks to influence future events by choosing the most auspicious time for their inception. The 9th- to 12th-century accounts of al-Ya'qubi, ibn al-Faqih, al-Biruni, and al-Hamawi confirm that Abbasid caliph al-Mansur (714–775 CE) laid the first brick of Baghdad at a time specified by astrologers.

Astrology in the service of power
The Abbasids needed to create a new capital to assert the legitimacy and superiority of their reign after overthrowing the Umayyad dynasty in 750 CE. According to al-Ya'qubi, al-Mansur appointed two astrologers, Masha'allah ibn Athari and Naubakht, to elect an auspicious moment for the task. Historical sources indicate that the date chosen was 30 July

Esteemed astrologer
This engraving of Persian-Jewish astrologer Masha'allah ibn Athari (c. 740–815 CE) is from the Latin translation of his astronomy treatise *De scientia motus orbis* ("On Science of the Movement of Spheres"), printed in 1504.

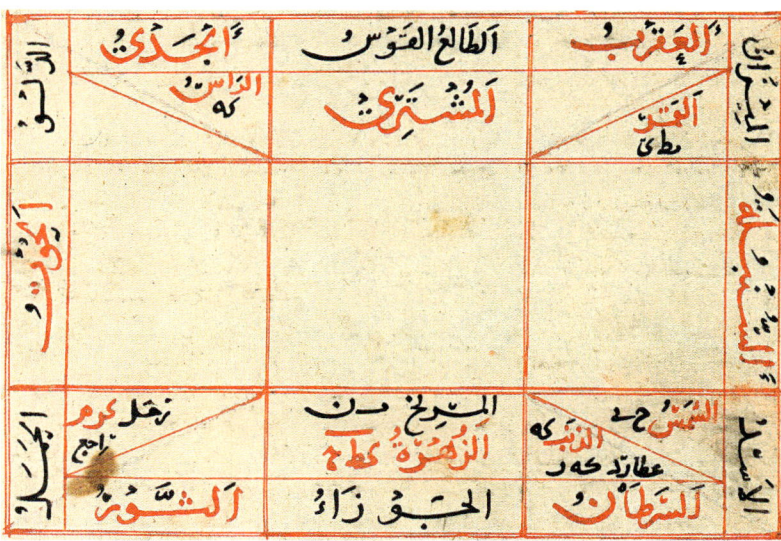

762. Al-Hamawi wrote that Naubakht assured al-Mansur that the horoscope for this date predicted Baghdad's "long-lasting presence, the abundance of its buildings, and the people's dependence on what it contained." Founded as al-Mansur's *Madinat al-Salam* ("City of Peace"), Baghdad was intended to become the cosmic centre of the Islamic empire.

The horoscope given for Baghdad in al-Biruni's *Al-athar al-baqiya* ("The Chronology of Ancient Nations") places Sagittarius and its ruler Jupiter in the ascendant. This placement renders Jupiter, the planet of great fortune and wisdom, exceptionally potent and capable of fulfilling its promises. Jupiter bestows its blessings upon the planet of kings and rulers, the Sun, through a harmonious aspect, suggesting a favourable influence on the Abbasid caliphs. Situated above the horizon in the royal sign of Leo, the Sun appears to consolidate the rulers' power and status. An ominous sign, however, is Mars's presence in the descendant, which may explain Naubakht's remark to al-Mansur, "No caliph will ever die there of natural causes."

Foundation chart
Persian scholar al-Biruni included this horoscope for Baghdad – thought to be a copy of Naubakht's original – in his *Al-athar al-baqiya* (1000 CE).

Bridging theory and science
Astrology in Abu Ma'shar's treatises

Born in Balkh, Khorasan (modern Afghanistan), Abu Ma'shar al-Balkhi (787–886 CE) was attracted to the thriving intellectual centre of Baghdad some time during the reign of caliph al-Ma'mun (r. 813–833 CE). Initially a scholar of *hadith* (the traditions of the Prophet Muhammad), at the age of 47 he was motivated to study astrology – an art he had vehemently attacked – after a heated debate with a fellow scholar, Arabic philosopher al-Kindi. Abu Ma'shar would go on to become one of the most prolific and influential medieval astrologers in the Islamic world, advising princes, teaching students, and writing more than 30 books. These authoritative works synthesized ancient knowledge, presented a new philosophy of astrology underpinned by advances in astronomy, and standardized astrological practice. Translated into Latin during the 12th century, they also became core texts for Western astrologers.

Celestial influencers
This miniature from *Kitab al-mawalid* ("Book on Nativities"), attributed to Abu Ma'shar, depicts the planets in human form, including Venus (top left) and the Moon atop the Bull (right).

The fruit of astronomy
In *Kitab al-madkhal al-kabir 'ala 'ilm ahkam al-nujum* ("Great Introduction to the Science of Astrology"), Abu Ma'shar continues a centuries-long debate on the validity and aims of astrology begun by Greek astrologer Claudius Ptolemy in his *Tetrabiblos* (see pp. 86–89). Abu Ma'shar presents a theory of astrology grounded in Aristotelian philosophy, while admitting that the practice lacks the certainty of astronomy. He argues that this weakness can be rectified by refining mathematical astronomy and observational methods because, in his view, astrology is the "fruit" of astronomy.

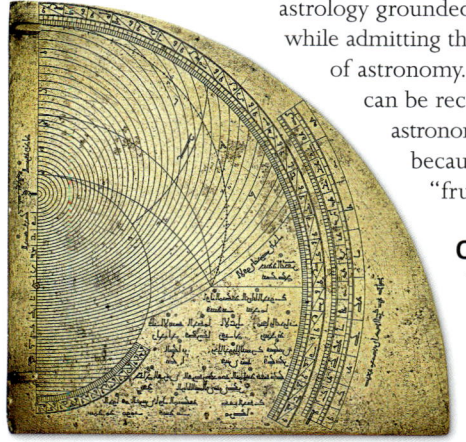

Astrolabic quadrant
Ninth-century Baghdad was a centre for the production of quadrants. These tools, used to measure celestial positions, were crucial for the accurate predictions advocated by Abu Ma'shar.

Conjunctions and cycles
Widely consulted as a guide to history, Abu Ma'shar's *Kitab al-milal wal-'l-duwal* ("Book on Religions and Dynasties") explains the function of mundane astrology – how the planets influence world events. Focusing on Saturn and Jupiter, which are regarded as "superior planets" with long-lasting effects on history, Abu Ma'shar links their conjunctions to the rise and fall of nations, dynasties, civilizations, and religions. A "Lesser Conjunction" occurs when the planets conjoin once every 20 years, effecting short-term changes. In contrast, a "Greater Conjunction" occurs when the planets conjoin in a new triplicity (portion of the zodiac that shares the same governing element – earth, air, fire, or water), indicating more dramatic historical transformations, such as the collapse of an entire civilization.

Astrology in Abu Ma'shar's treatises 131

Progressing science
This 15th-century Persian miniature shows astronomy students learning to use astrolabes (one overhead; one held by a student). These instruments were used to calculate time, determine direction, and read horoscopes.

A star-studded era
Astrology in the Islamic Golden Age

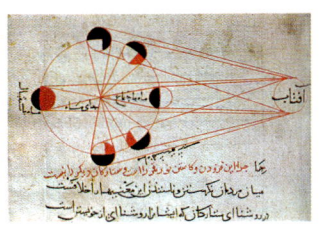

Lunar phases
This illustration of the phases of the Moon (with the Sun, far right) is from *Kitab al-tafhim li-awa'il sina'at al-tanjim* ("Book of Instruction on the Principles of Astrology") by Iranian scholar al-Biruni.

The founding of the new Abbasid empire in the 8th century, centred on Baghdad (see pp. 128–29), marked the beginning of an extraordinary era of scientific, cultural, and economic achievements. Known as the Islamic Golden Age, this period is traditionally viewed as extending from the reign of Abbasid caliph Harun al-Rashid (r. 786–809 CE) until the sack of Baghdad by the Mongols in 1258. Today, however, historians of science argue that this age of advancement did not end with the collapse of Abbasid rule, but continued until the 17th century in different Islamic cultural centres, such as Cairo, Córdoba, Samarkand, and Istanbul.

Intellectual and cultural growth during this era was invigorated by an environment that fostered inquiry and innovation. The founding of *Bayt al-hikma* (the "House of Wisdom") – a major centre of learning – triggered an unprecedented translation movement that preserved ancient knowledge from Greek, Persian, and Indian texts and integrated it with Islamic thought. Generous state patronage motivated scholars to contribute to the growing body of knowledge.

Scientific output, and the circulation of ideas, was also greatly enhanced by the introduction of papermaking from China. Paper was more durable and easier to manufacture than papyrus and easily bound into books. Notable works from this period include al-Battani's *al-Zij al-Sabi* ("Sabian Astronomical Tables"), ibn al-Haytham's *Kitab al-manazir* ("Book of Optics"), and Ibn Sina's *al-Qanun fi al-tibb* ("The Canon of Medicine").

From observations to predictions

One of the most dynamic fields of scientific research during the Islamic Golden Age concerned the position and movement of celestial bodies. The religious rituals of Islam require knowledge of astronomical cycles, especially those of the Sun and the Moon. The Sun's movement helps to determine the timing of daily prayers. Sighting the new Moon marks the start of a month and guides religious observances in accordance with the Islamic lunar calendar. This religious necessity heightened interest in observational and theoretical astronomy, with the output recorded in a vast number of manuscripts. Many students of astronomy, such as 9th-century Persian scholar Abu Ma'shar al-Balkhi, also wrote influential astrological treatises, considering the relationship of these heavenly movements to events on Earth (see pp. 130–31).

While observations of the stars and planets provided a necessary empirical method for calculations, theoretical astronomy supplemented these observations with mathematical models that enhanced their accuracy and enabled astronomers to predict astronomical events, such as eclipses.

Astronomical instruments

Progress in observational and theoretical astronomy was driven by new observatories, which became centres of learning and research, and advances in the design of astronomical instruments, such as celestial globes. These three-dimensional models helped students to visualize the positions and movement of stars and constellations in relation to Earth (positioned at the sphere's imaginary centre).

This 13th-century celestial globe is a spherical map of the sky surrounding Earth.

Fixed stars
The constellation of Perseus as it appears on the celestial globe is depicted in Persian astronomer al-Sufi's *Kitab suwar al-kawakib al-thabita* ("Book of Fixed Stars", c. 964).

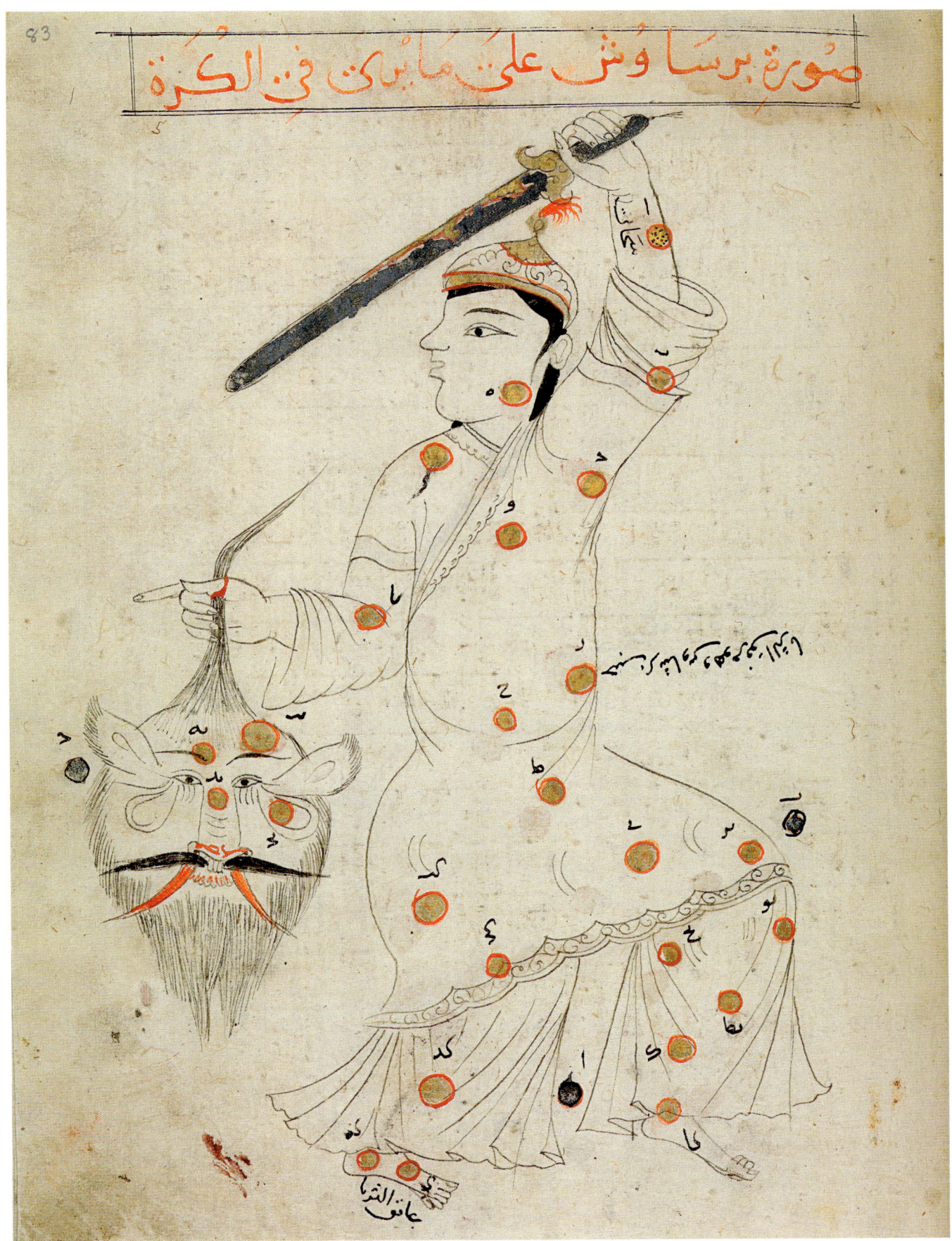

Classical cosmology

This miniature from Iranian cosmographer al-Qazwini's (1203-83) influential work *Aja'ib al-makhluqat* ("The Wonders of Creation") shows the seven classical planets anthropomorphized, with the Sun in the centre.

Theoretical astronomy also provided astrologers with a cosmological framework that helped them interpret celestial configurations. Prevailing views on cosmology – the structure of the universe and humans' place within this scheme – were Ptolemaic, or geocentric. Formulated by Greek astronomer Claudius Ptolemy in his astronomical treatise the *Almagest*, geocentric cosmology places Earth at the centre of the cosmos (see pp. 84–85). Earth is surrounded by layers of concentric circles representing the paths or spheres of the planets, starting in ascending order with the Moon, then Mercury, Venus, the Sun, Mars, Jupiter, and Saturn. In this scheme, the luminaries – the Moon and the Sun – determine rankings in the hierarchy of the geocentric model. Elements, objects, and living things on Earth are called "sublunar" because they are categorized below the Moon. Planets placed below the Sun, including the Moon, are termed "inferior" planets, whereas planets placed above it are "superior". The conjunction of superior planets was perceived by Abbasid astrologers to indicate major shifts in world history (see p. 130).

> "I have begun with geometry and proceeded to arithmetic and the science of numbers, then to the structure of the universe, and finally to judicial astrology."

AL-BIRUNI, *KITAB AL-TAFHIM LI-AWA'IL SINA'AT AL-TANJIM* ("BOOK OF INSTRUCTION ON THE PRINCIPLES OF ASTROLOGY"), 1029

Stars, planets, and enchanted realms

Above the seven spheres of the planets lies the belt of the "fixed stars", which is considered to contain 48 constellations, including the 12 zodiacal groupings. In his seminal treatise *Kitab suwar al-kawakib al-thabita* ("Book of Fixed Stars"), 10th-century Persian astronomer al-Sufi catalogued these constellations in astronomical tables, illustrated them from multiple perspectives, corrected the coordinates given in Ptolemy's *Almagest*, and revitalized descriptions of the constellations by linking them to pre-Islamic Arabic lore. The enchanted stories in al-Sufi's book were enhanced by anthropomorphizing the constellations – describing them as having human characteristics.

Following Indian traditions, Islamic texts also anthropomorphized the planets using a system of astrological correspondences – where planets "correspond" to specific human attributes and qualities. For instance, Venus, the planet of beauty and art, is portrayed as a female musician, while Mars, the planet of war and destruction, is depicted as a warrior with a sword and severed head. Images of the zodiacal constellations and planets were also believed to imbue objects with talismanic powers related to the planet or the zodiac sign depicted.

Popularity in the face of polemic

The belief by adherents of astrology that celestial configurations cause events in the sublunar world contradicted several fundamental Islamic principles, especially *tawhid* (absolute monotheism), which asserts that no entity shares God's authority and influence. Muslim theologians wrote polemics to challenge and critique astrology on this basis, but these seem to have done little to lessen its popularity. The multiple astrological manuals listed by 10th-century bibliographer and bookseller ibn al-Nadim attest to a public eager for accessible astrological instruction on subjects ranging from birth-chart analysis to choosing auspicious times for events and tasks. At the other end of the social spectrum, astrologers continued to be employed at the Abbasid court, advising rulers on matters of state.

Powerful talismans
The signs of the zodiac and their ruling planets that decorate this late 12th- to early 13th-century ewer from Iran or Afghanistan were believed to enhance the object's auspicious powers.

Lunar effect
The Moon's influence on the zodiac signs of Gemini, Cancer, and Leo is depicted in this 14th-century manuscript of *Mu'nis al-ahrar* ("The Free Man's Companion"), by Persian poet al-Jajarmi.

Iskandar's nativity chart

On 18 April 1411, court astrologer Mahmud ibn Yahya ibn al-Hasan al-Kashi cast a horoscope for the Timurid prince Jalal al-Din Iskandar (1384–1415), recently appointed ruler of Shiraz and Isfahan, and grandson of the founder of the Timurid Empire, Timur Lenk. The details of this prediction, along with an exquisitely decorated birth chart recording planetary positions at the time of Iskandar's birth, form the manuscript of the 15th-century *Kitab-i viladat-i Iskandar* ("Book of birth of Iskandar").

The horoscope appears as a wheel (heaven) divided into 12 sectors, each representing a zodiac sign and corresponding to an astrological house. Anthropomorphized planets occupy four of the houses (see p. 134), while four angels are placed in the outside corners of the wheel. As is customary in Islamic horoscopes, the ascendant, or rising sign, is located at the top of the wheel in the 12 o'clock position, in Capricorn. The text of the horoscope says that the placement of the third house's lord, Jupiter, in the sixth house indicates "harm from friends, relatives, and loved ones". Indeed, Iskandar was executed by his uncle Shahrukh only five years into his reign.

> "May God perpetuate the rule and authority of the son of princes, Iskandar, and make his abode above the two celestial poles."
>
> **MAHMUD IBN YAHYA IBN AL-HASAN**, *KITAB-I VILADAT-I ISKANDAR*, 15TH CENTURY

Iskandar's horoscope in the *Kitab-i viladat-i Iskandar* reflects Islamic cosmology and the prince's political and religious convictions.

Lines traced in the sand
Arabic geomancy

Known in Arabic as *'ilm al-raml* ("the science of sand") or *khatt al-raml* ("tracing lines in the sand"), the divinatory practice of geomancy has mysterious roots. The *hadith* ("prophetic tradition") of Prophet Muhammad tells of a prophet who "drew lines, so if anyone does this in the same way, it is permissible." Arab historian Abd al-Rahman ibn Khaldun wrote in his *Muqaddima* ("Introduction", 1377) that Muslim diviners who traced lines in the sand frequently referred to this *hadith* to lend legitimacy to their practice. When it was introduced into the medieval West, probably through 12th-century translations of Arabic texts by Spanish priest Hugo of Santalla, it acquired the Latin name *geomantia*, from the Greek words *gaia* ("earth") and *manteia* ("divination") – "divination by the earth".

Mechanical predictions
This sophisticated device, made in 1241, functions like a divinatory chart or tableau. Turning the dials generates geomantic figures that are interpreted in relation to the astrological inscriptions under each window.

Shrouded in myth, some accounts of the origins of geomancy attribute it to legendary figures such as the Angel Gabriel, who is said to have taught the practice to the prophet Idris (often equated with Enoch from the Bible or with the mystical figure Hermes Trismegistus). Idris is thought to have transmitted this knowledge to an enigmatic Indian figure, Tumtum al-Hindi, who, in turn, is credited with introducing geomancy to the Arabic-speaking Islamic world by teaching it to Khalaf al-Barbari, a historical figure and contemporary of Prophet Muhammad. From al-Barbari, a lineage of masters and pupils commenced, culminating in the teachings of one of the greatest authorities on geomancy, Abu 'Abdullah Muhammad ibn 'Uthman al-Zanati, who is known to have been active in the late 12th or early 13th century. The toponymic (geographic) surnames of the geomancy masters suggest that the practice may have originated in India and North Africa (the surnames al-Barbari and al-Zanati indicate Berber origins).

From sand to stars

In the 13th century, astrologers began producing numerous treatises on geomancy. Among these was Abdulla ibn Mahfuf's extensive tract the *Kitab fi 'ilm al-raml* ("Book on Geomancy"), which codified geomantic practices. The renowned astronomer, mathematician, and philosopher Nasir al-Din al-Tusi also contributed several divinatory texts, including *al-Risala al-sultaniyya fi 'ilm al-raml* ("The Royal Epistle on Geomancy").

The works by ibn Mahfuf and al-Tusi reflect the development of a complex method of geomancy – often attributed to al-Zanati – that integrated astrology and geomantic practices. In this system, the 16 geomantic figures were associated with planets, zodiac signs, astrological houses, and the four cardinal directions; they were then arranged in diagrams or astrological charts for analysis (see pp. 140–41). This new form of practice led to a diversification of geomantic applications.

Relating the geomantic figures to astrological signs established connections to the four elements (fire, water, earth, and air) and, subsequently, to the four classical humours (blood, phlegm, yellow bile, and black bile). Geomancers developed a diagnostic method similar to medical astrology (see pp. 164–67) that correlated human body parts with the 16 geomantic figures. The figure "Laetitia", for example, was associated with the head, "Rubeus" with the throat, and "Puella" with the right shoulder. This practice ultimately led to the creation of geomantic talismans designed to target illnesses affecting specific body parts.

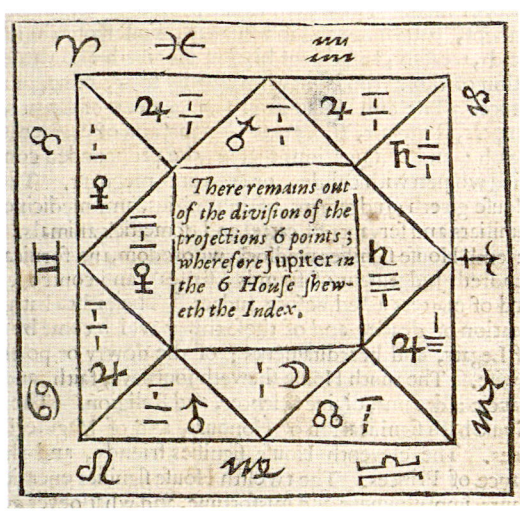

Astrology meets geomancy
Geomantic figures are arranged in astrological houses in this 16th-century chart. Taken from an occult text by Cornelius Agrippa, it shows how Arabic methods influenced Western practice.

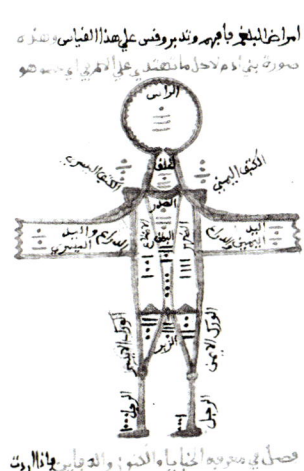

Geomantic diagnosis
This illustration from an 18th-century geomantic manuscript, attributed to the Prophet Idris, shows how the 16 geomantic figures were correlated with human body parts for the purposes of diagnosing disease.

> "…to discover the supernatural and know the future, [they] invented a craft they called 'sand writing' [geomancy], after the material one uses for it."
>
> **ABD AL-RAHMAN IBN KHALDUN**, THE *MUQADDIMA* ("INTRODUCTION"), 1377

House	Name	Meaning
1	*Vita* ("Life")	House of life and the questioner
2	*Lucrum* ("Profit")	House of substance and riches
3	*Fratres* ("Brothers")	House of siblings and short journeys
4	*Genitor* ("Parent")	House of fathers and things hidden
5	*Nati* ("Children")	House of messengers and rumours
6	*Valetudo* ("Health")	House of diseases and servants
7	*Uxor* ("Spouse")	House of spouses and controversies
8	*Mors* ("Death")	House of death and inheritance
9	*Itineris* ("Journey")	House of sciences and long journeys
10	*Regnum* ("Kingdom")	House of honours and authorities
11	*Benefacta* ("Benefit")	House of friends and wishes
12	*Carcer* ("Prison")	House of enemies and imprisonment

The astrological houses govern different areas of life and can provide answers for targeted questions: answers about financial success, for example, might be sought in the second house.

Practising geomancy

Geomancy relies on randomly generated figures, each with their own astrological associations, which are arranged in a tableau for analysis. Considering a question, the geomancer draws series of marks, which are added and stacked in a prescribed fashion to form a geomantic figure. The first four figures created are called the "mothers"; from these four "daughters" are derived, then four "nieces", two "witnesses", and a "judge". The figures are then arranged in a tableau (see the geomantic shield chart, opposite) where their positions and associations are interpreted in conjunction with astrological tables and texts.

The astrological associations of the geomantic figures in this table are derived from German occultist Agrippa's *Fourth Book of Occult Philosophy* from 1559.

Figure	Name	Associations	Figure	Name	Associations
	Via ("Way")	Water Moon Cancer		*Laetitia* ("Joy")	Fire Jupiter Sagittarius
	Populus ("People")	Water Moon Cancer		*Tristitia* ("Sorrow")	Air Saturn Aquarius
	Conjunctio ("Conjunction")	Earth Mercury Virgo		*Puella* ("Maid")	Earth Venus Taurus
	Carcer ("Prison")	Earth Saturn Capricorn		*Puer* ("Child")	Fire Mars Aries
	Fortuna Major "Greater Fortune"	Fire Sun Leo		*Albus* ("White")	Air Mercury Gemini
	Fortuna Minor "Lesser Fortune"	Fire Sun Leo		*Rubeus* ("Red")	Water Mars Scorpio
	Aquisitio ("Acquisition")	Water Jupiter Pisces		*Caput Dragonis* ("Dragon's Head")	Earth North node Capricorn
	Amissio ("Loss")	Air Venus Libra		*Cauda Dragonis* ("Dragon's Tail")	Water South node Scorpio

Practising geomancy

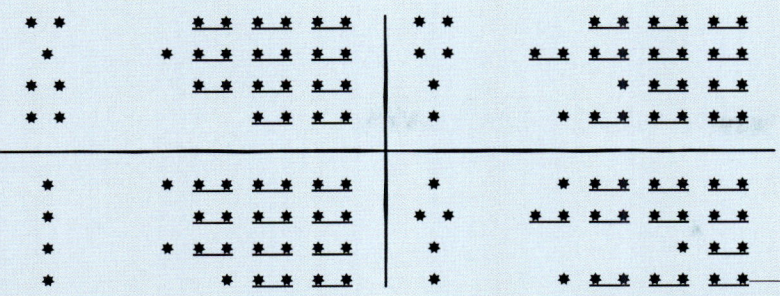

Count off the marks in pairs

The four "mothers" are the foundational figures of any tableau. To create the "mothers", quickly draw 16 lines of marks (shown here as stars). Group the lines into four sets of four lines. Count off the marks in each line: for an odd number, make a single mark; for an even number, make two marks. These marks create a new figure – a "mother".

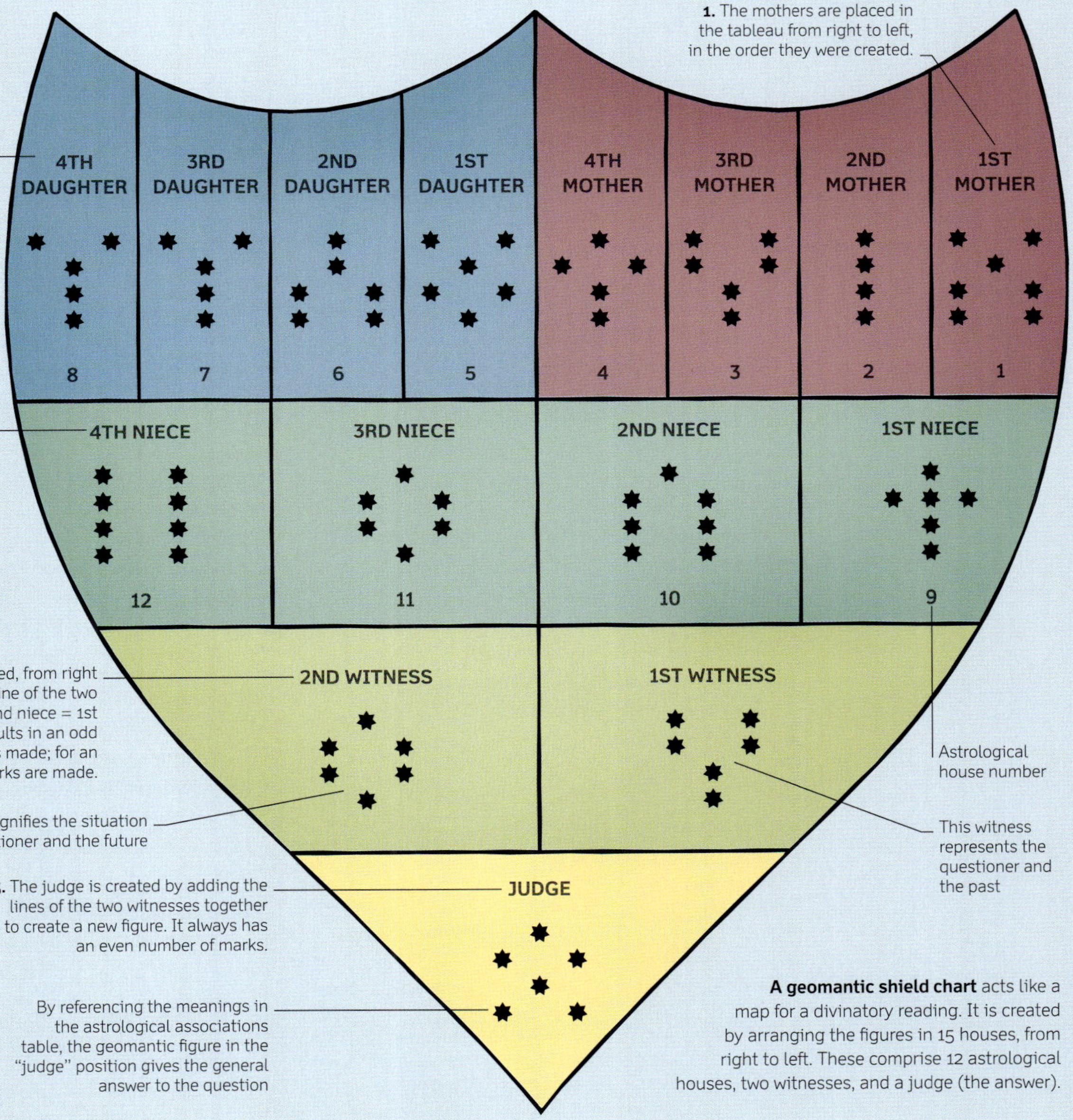

1. The mothers are placed in the tableau from right to left, in the order they were created.

2. Marks from the first line of the mothers are stacked (from right to left) to create the 1st daughter. The second line of the mothers is stacked to create the 2nd daughter, and so on.

| 4TH DAUGHTER | 3RD DAUGHTER | 2ND DAUGHTER | 1ST DAUGHTER | 4TH MOTHER | 3RD MOTHER | 2ND MOTHER | 1ST MOTHER |
| 8 | 7 | 6 | 5 | 4 | 3 | 2 | 1 |

3. The nieces are created, from right to left, by adding each line of the two figures above (1st mother + 2nd mother = 1st niece). Where the line addition produces an odd number, one new mark is made; for an even number, two marks are made.

| 4TH NIECE | 3RD NIECE | 2ND NIECE | 1ST NIECE |
| 12 | 11 | 10 | 9 |

4. The witnesses are created, from right to left, by adding each line of the two figures above (1st and 2nd niece = 1st witness). Where a line results in an odd number, one new mark is made; for an even number, two marks are made.

| 2ND WITNESS | 1ST WITNESS |

This witness signifies the situation affecting the questioner and the future

Astrological house number

This witness represents the questioner and the past

5. The judge is created by adding the lines of the two witnesses together to create a new figure. It always has an even number of marks.

JUDGE

By referencing the meanings in the astrological associations table, the geomantic figure in the "judge" position gives the general answer to the question

A geomantic shield chart acts like a map for a divinatory reading. It is created by arranging the figures in 15 houses, from right to left. These comprise 12 astrological houses, two witnesses, and a judge (the answer).

The power of names
Islamic onomancy

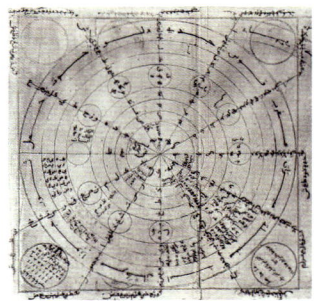

Deeper truth
The *za'irja*, an onomantic tool, was thought to be able to generate ideas from numbers and celestial data. It may have influenced the 13th-century Spanish mystic Ramon Llull in his creation of a logic machine, the *Ars Magna*.

Onomancy, derived from the Greek words *ónoma* ("name") and *manteia* ("divination"), is a divinatory practice based on the belief that names, phrases, and letters encode esoteric (inner) meanings and powers that are represented by numerical values. Onomancers assign a number to each letter or groups of letters, then perform mathematical calculations in order to reveal hidden meanings relating to the future or the outcome of events. Textual evidence suggests the practice dates back to antiquity, with onomancy first referenced in ancient Greek, then found in Semitic languages, such as Ethiopic, Syriac, Hebrew, and eventually Arabic.

Arab historian and sociologist Abd al-Rahman ibn Khaldun gives a detailed account of onomancy in his 14th-century magnum opus, the *Muqaddima* ("Introduction"). He describes how the practice (which he calls *simiya*) gained popularity in the Muslim world in tandem with new mystical beliefs that the esoteric qualities of names and letters permeated all aspects of existence, from the planetary spheres to the world of elements. Onomancers claimed that they could manipulate (*tassaruf*) the natural world and disrupt its natural order (*khawariq al-'ada*) through their knowledge of the hidden powers of words. In Islam, onomancy also draws upon the knowledge of, and potency attributed to, the names of Allah (*asma' Allah al-husna*), the angelic entities (*mala'ika*), and the spiritual souls (*nufus rabbaniyya*).

According to ibn Khaldun, notable 13th-century figures who wrote on the topic were Muhammad ibn 'Arabi from Andalusia and Ahmad al-Buni from the Algerian city Buna. Al-Buni's *Shams al-ma'arif wa lata'if al-awarif* ("The Sun of Gnosis and Subtleties of Gnostics") is regarded as one of the key works on onomancy.

Deciphering letters and numbers

Ibn Khaldun notes a lack of consensus among onomancers regarding the method for extracting the esoteric values of names. Some began by categorizing letters into four groups corresponding to the four elements: earth, water, air, and fire. Others linked the 28 letters of the Arabic alphabet to the 28 lunar mansions (divisions of the sky the Moon passes through on its orbit around Earth). A third group used a letter-number system known as *abjad*, where letters are grouped into three sets and given a numerical value. The first set of letters represented units, the second tens, and the third hundreds, with the final letter representing 1,000. Magical squares (*awfaq*) were then derived from the *abjad* and used to harness the power of names.

Tables for calculating answers to simple "yes/no" questions were also used (see pp. 154–55), as were mechanical devices such as the *za'irja*. Attributed to 12th-century Moroccan mystic Ahmad al-Sabti, this tool comprises a circular chart enclosing concentric circles that represent the planetary spheres and elements, and a complex numerical table.

Prophetic calculations
This "Table of Life and Death", in the form of two tables from a 19th-century copy of the *Kitab Sirr al-asrar* ("Secret of Secrets"), was used to answer "yes/no" questions.

Islamic onomancy **143**

Designs are created in engraved brass inlaid with silver

Magical words
The word *baduh* inscribed on the clasp of this 15th-century Mamluk casket was believed to possess powers derived from the esoteric qualities of its letters "b", "d", "w" ("u"), and "h".

Inscriptions add to the box's amuletic potency

Geometrical patterns are a common Mamluk design

"The person who works with words may mingle the powers of expressions and words with the powers of the stars."

ABD AL-RAHMAN IBN KHALDUN, *THE MUQADDIMA* ("INTRODUCTION"), 1377

Distant and divine
1100–1600

Introduction

The early 12th century saw a momentous shift in the culture of Western Europe, especially in England, Germany, and France. For more than 500 years in the West, the main guide to knowledge about the world had been the Christian scriptures, which asserted that God had created the world in six days (and rested on the seventh) and that the whole universe, including the stars, obeyed his commands. But then European scholars began to visit centres of learning in the Islamic world, the nearest of which were in Spain. There, they discovered texts in Arabic, including translations of earlier works from India, Persia, Greece, and Rome, which described the world in terms of the reasons why things happened. These texts did not deny God's power; they added to it. Among the first works to be translated from Arabic to Latin were those written by, or influenced by, the Greek philosopher Aristotle, who talked about the natural influences exerted by the planets. The burgeoning 12th-century vogue for astrology therefore tended to focus on physical conditions and medical matters.

By 1450, Western Europe was entering the Renaissance, and a fresh wave of cosmological and astrological texts were translated, emphasizing the planets' role in psychological and spiritual areas. The printing press made texts available to everyone who could read, and a new spirit of inquiry developed that would eventually lead, in the 17th century, to the emergence of modern science. Printing had a huge impact on astrology, through the production of annual – and sometimes monthly – almanacs. These carried all sorts of information about the coming period, including astronomical details such as the dates of new and full Moons, and advice on when best to perform particular activities, from planting crops to travelling, getting married, or even having a haircut.

The publication of Polish astronomer Nicolaus Copernicus's *De revolutionibus orbium coelestium* ("On the Revolutions of the Heavenly Spheres") in 1543 marked one of the greatest changes in the human understanding of the universe. Copernicus argued that the Sun, not Earth, was at the centre

Jewish astrologers at work *see* p. 158

Messages in Mexica mirrors *see* p. 163

Renaissance cosmos *see* p. 179

of the universe. Although his ideas were not fully accepted until the next century, as he was unable to offer the proof of actual observation, they ultimately caused scholars to question the credibility of astrology, with its geocentric approach.

Around the same time, Europeans encountered another astrological tradition, one that dated back perhaps a millennium or more and had flourished among the Maya and Mexica (Aztec) people of what are now Mexico and Central America. In 1521, the Spanish conquered the Mexica Empire, and later Spanish scholars documented their observations of Mexica omens and astrological practices. Mexica astrology attributed great importance to the planet Venus (which was associated with the god Quetzalcoatl and whose cycle could be used to time military activity), and to the 260-day *Tzolk'in* calendar, inherited from earlier traditions, which consisted of sequences of 20 days – each with a different meaning – and the Long Count, which timed long-term periods. According to some calculations, the latter was due to end in 2012, causing much excitement: back in the 1980s, New Age teachers had forecast the event would inaugurate a spiritual transformation.

> "The Sun is a benefic… It brings good fortune, it brings bad fortune, at one time it raises, at another time it brings down."
>
> **ABU MA'SHAR**, *KITAB MUKHTASAR AL-MADKHAL* (ABRIDGED VERSION OF THE "GREAT INTRODUCTION"), 9TH CENTURY

Sun-centred universe *see* p. 180

Birth chart of a future king *see* p. 188

Zodiac signs in miniature *see* p. 190

East meets West

Translating Arabic astrological texts

The centuries after the collapse of the Western Roman Empire in 476 CE left European scholars deprived of much classical knowledge, as key works such as Claudius Ptolemy's astronomy manual, the *Almagest*, had been lost. Though there was continued interest in astrology – then a branch of astronomy and part of the *quadrivium*, or programme of higher study (along with arithmetic, geometry, and music) – the lack of texts meant astronomical calculations beyond simple matters such as the date of Easter were not possible in Western Europe.

However, in the Islamic world, an astronomical tradition building on classical works was thriving. Scholars such as the 9th-century philosopher al-Kindi integrated Aristotelian philosophy with astrology and argued for a rational approach to the influence of celestial bodies on human affairs.

Disseminating ideas

Knowledge only travelled from the Islamic to the Christian world in areas where they bordered each other, such as in Sicily and Spain. Gerbert of Aurillac,

Astrologer-king
Thirteenth-century ruler Alfonso X of Castile is depicted here with scribes. Nicknamed "the Astrologer", he sponsored the translation of many works into Spanish, including the *Picatrix*, an Arabic manual of astrology and magic.

Translating Arabic astrological texts 149

> "I translated that author [al-Kindi] whom your diligence has often noted to be the most suitable and true judge amongst astrologers."

ROBERT OF KETTON, PREFACE TO HIS TRANSLATION OF AL-KINDI'S *FORTY CHAPTERS*, c.1138–43

Great translator

One of the pioneers of the 12th-century scientific renaissance in Europe, Adelard of Bath (c.1090–1160) spent seven years travelling in the Islamic world – including in Türkiye and Syria – learned Arabic, and translated many ancient Greek works from Arabic into Latin. These included Euclid's *Elements* and astronomical texts such as al-Khwarizmi's star tables, the *Kitab al-madkhal al-sagir* ("Smaller Introduction") of Abu Ma'shar, and a treatise on horoscopes by Thabit ibn Qurra. He drew on many Arabic texts to produce his greatest work, the *Quaestiones Naturales* ("Questions on Natural Science").

Adelard is on the left in this miniature from a 15th-century manuscript of the *Regulae Abaci*, his work on the abacus.

who became Pope Sylvester II in 999, spent several years in northern Spain, learning how to use the astrolabe and the abacus from Arabic sources in the neighbouring Islamic province of al-Andalus, which covered most of the Iberian Peninsula to the south. As Spain's Christian kingdoms expanded southwards into Islamic territory, the exchange of knowledge accelerated – particularly after the capture of Toledo in 1085. The city became a hub for the translation of works from Arabic into Latin, including Hermann of Carinthia's translation of Abu Ma'shar's *Kitab al-madkhal al-kabir 'ala 'ilm ahkam al-nujum* (see p.130), which became the most widely disseminated astrological text in medieval Europe.

The next 50 years saw even more translations – many the work of Mozarabs (Arabic-speaking Christians), such as Dominicus Gundissalinus, or Jewish scholars, such as Abraham bin Ezra, whose *Reshit Hokhmah* ("Beginning of Wisdom") brought Jewish astrological knowledge to Christian Spain. By 1176, Gerard of Cremona had translated 80 texts, the *Almagest* among them, allowing European astrologers to make their own calculations for the first time, including for birth horoscopes. Perhaps most influential of all was the *Picatrix*, a translation of the Arabic *Ghayat al-Hakim*, rendered in Spanish around 1250, and in Latin soon after.

Increased acceptance

Latin translations of texts, and some works in the vernacular, acted as a bridge between the ancient, Arabic, and Renaissance worlds. Astrology was now recognized as an academic discipline, with professorships at prestigious universities such as Bologna and works such as Ptolemy's *Tetrabiblos* (see pp.86–89) used as teaching materials.

Venus figure
The *Picatrix* contained instructions for the creation of astrological talismans, such as how to depict Venus. Wearing them was believed to ward off misfortunes predicted by astrology.

Crucifixion casting
This 15th-century stained-glass window from a church in Norfolk, England, depicts a New Testament scene, in which Roman soldiers cast lots at Christ's crucifixion.

Divining right from wrong
Reviving ancient practices

It is no coincidence that at the same time as the translation movement of Arabic texts into Latin began in the 11th century, the first European universities were founded (led by Bologna, which was established in 1088). This wave of scholarship led to a renewed interest in astrology, as many works were translated into Latin for the first time. Texts describing divinatory practices such as chiromancy (palm-reading), scapulimancy (reading the lines on the shoulder blades of sheep and other ruminant animals), and geomancy (see p. 153) were also translated in the medieval period, and ancient methods of interpreting signs and omens, among them scrying (gazing into reflective surfaces such as water or a mirror for signs; see pp. 278–79) and augury (see pp. 52–53), became popular once more.

Controversial practices
Divination was condemned by the Christian Church, notably in *Gratian's Decretum*, a canon law collection from the University of Bologna in the 1140s, and by Italian theologian Thomas Aquinas in the later 13th century. It nevertheless occupied a dubious space between acceptable and forbidden practice. Many Christian stories touched on what might be interpreted as forms of divination, such as casting lots, while the existence of Christian prophets in the Bible and in hagiography (writings about the lives of saints) raised questions about legitimate ways to predict the future. Yet the notion that Christian writings gave an acceptable veneer to divinatory practices was disputed, and it could equally be argued that divination was unacceptable in Christian society. Divination and magic had been linked since at least the late Roman Republic period (c. 133–44 BCE), and as Augustine argued in the 5th century CE, divination went against the doctrines of free will and divine providence, and operated by means of demonic power.

Some of the new medieval translations of divinatory texts into Latin provided rationales for using certain forms of divination, such as astrology. As long as astrologers predicted what was likely to happen (for example, the course of illness or what weather could be expected), rather than what would definitely happen, they were able to stay within the bounds of legitimate Christian practice.

Divine rays
Arab scholar al-Kindi's 9th-century *Kitab al-Shu'a'at* ("Book of the Rays") was translated into Latin as *De Radiis*. This work posited that stars emit celestial rays that allow them to influence events on Earth – hence the need for astrology. This theory fed into astral magical practices; people believed the rays' power could be captured in talismans for protection or to influence the future. The materials used to construct a talisman often corresponded to the planet of which power was invoked.

This gold ring from the 16th century depicts the Roman god Mars, and was possibly used for talismanic magic.

> "...open a Psalter and consider the first letter that will appear to you and you will see what you seek."
>
> NORTHERN ITALIAN MANTIC ALPHABET, 13TH CENTURY

After all, God controlled the natural world, including the stars, Moon, and planets. This argument could also be applied to other forms of divination, such as bibliomancy, or *sortes bibliae* (divination by opening books at random), and geomancy (drawing lines and dots in sand or on paper), as long as they were seen as ways of deciphering God's will.

Sand divination

Geomancy is a term Europeans originally applied to ancient Greek divination via the earth, and appears in the earliest condemnations of divination, such as that of Roman scholar Varro in the 1st century BCE. But during the medieval translation movement, the term was repurposed as texts about an Arabic practice called *ilm al-raml* ("science of the sand"; see pp. 138–39) began to circulate in Latin. Arab diviners originally drew lines and dots in the sand, but for practical reasons, their late medieval European counterparts tended to use ink and paper or parchment. How much this Arabic practice related to ancient Greek geomancy is unknown, since no original texts describing the latter have survived – references such as Varro's give no details about its methods.

The earliest translators of Arabic geomantic texts were Gerard of Cremona and Hugo of Santalla, working in 12th-century Castile and Aragon (in modern-day Spain) respectively. These authors recommended geomancy for medical prognosis (predicting the course of illness) as well as the prediction of other matters in a person's life.

Despite the practice being condemned by canon law, geomantic texts were owned by those at the highest levels of society. Richard II of England (r. 1377–99) was given a book on geomancy in 1391; the author wrote in the dedication that geomancy was much easier to understand than astrology. Other elite individuals who possessed

Fit for a king
Taken from an instruction book produced for Richard II, this section of geomantic text depicts two philosophers – a crowned king and a youth – with geomantic tables.

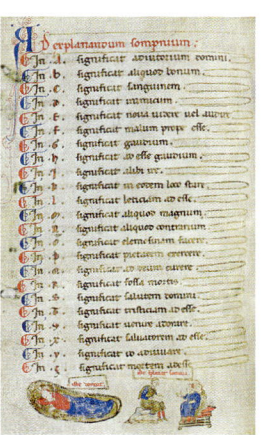

Listed letters
This 13th-century Italian manuscript shows a mantic alphabet, used for bibliomancy. Practitioners opened a Bible or Psalter at random and the first letter of the page was cross-referenced with the list here.

geomancies were the 14th-century rulers Wenceslaus IV of Bohemia and Charles V of France. Geomancies were translated into the vernacular in the later medieval period, indicating widespread enthusiasm for the art across literate society.

Searching the pages

Another popular form of divination, especially in clerical circles, bibliomancy worked by consulting a Bible or Psalter, selecting a page at random, and cross-referencing the first letter with a mantic (divinatory) alphabet to give an answer. Whether the use of a Christian book – and the purification rituals such as fasting and reciting prayers that were required beforehand – made the practice more or less acceptable is questionable: this context could give an impression of legitimacy, but could also be seen as a perversion of Christian rituals and texts. Interest in bibliomancy soon spread, as mantic alphabets became available in vernacular languages such as German, French, and English.

Dice divination

While the term *sortes sanctorum* ("lots of the saints") has sometimes been used to describe bibliomancy, the *Sortes Sanctorum* is also the name of a medieval text used for dice divination. The user rolls the dice, then consults the text. The right-hand column lists the arrangement of numbers that can be rolled by the dice, from C, C, C (3 x 6) down to I, I, I (3 x 1), with their corresponding interpretations.

This page is from a 12th-century manuscript of the *Sortes Sanctorum*, a guide to dice divination.

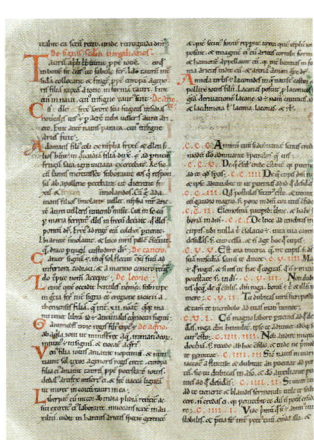

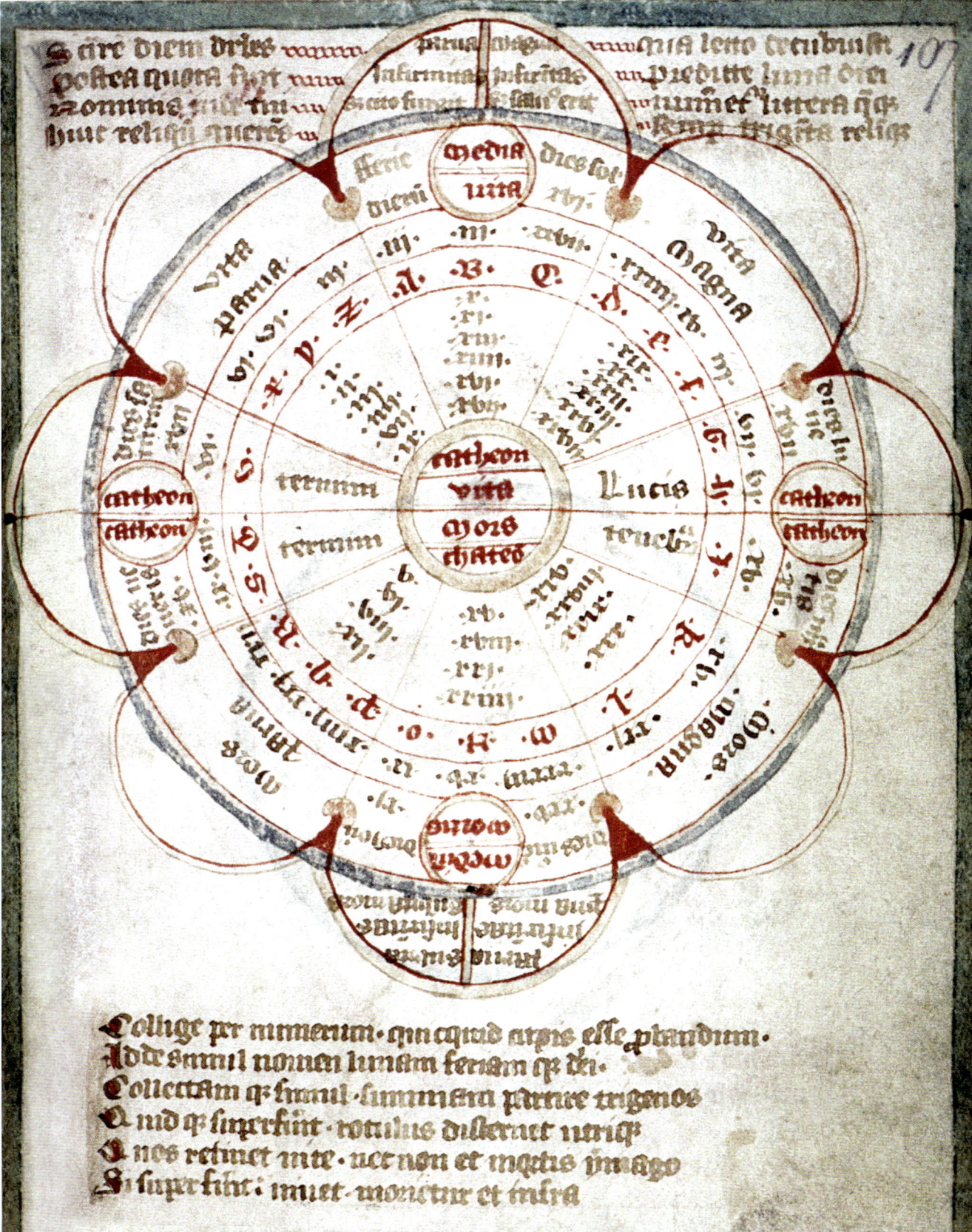

Life or death?
Divination in medieval Europe

The translation movement that began in the 11th century (see pp. 150–53) flourished at European centres of learning such as Toledo and Sicily. Arabic texts were translated into Latin, as were Arabic translations of ancient Greek works. The plethora of newly available texts led to a renewed interest in ancient divinatory practices among European scholars. Onomancy (divination based on words and numbers; see pp. 142–43) and chiromancy (palm-reading) are two of the most common divinatory methods mentioned in late medieval manuscripts.

Adding up answers
A figure known as the "Sphere of Life and Death" (or the "Sphere of Pythagoras", with whom onomancy is often associated) circulated in early medieval manuscripts, but in the 12th century, a different form of onomancy, the "Victorious and Vanquished", was also translated into Latin. The "Sphere" was used to answer "yes/no" questions, such as whether a sick person would live or die. The practitioner would add the numbers correlating to the letters of the ailing person's name, then add the numbers of the day of the Moon and of the planetary weekday when they fell ill. The total was divided by 30: if the remainder was a number in the top hemisphere of the diagram, the person would live; if it was in the bottom, they would die.

The "Victorious and Vanquished" answered questions with two possible answers, such as who would win a duel. Also based on addition and division, this approach listed all the combinations of remainders to show which "beat" the other.

Prognostic tool
This version of the "Sphere of Life and Death" was copied in England in c. 1375 into a book of prognostics, based on a manuscript of the English monk Matthew Paris, who died in 1259.

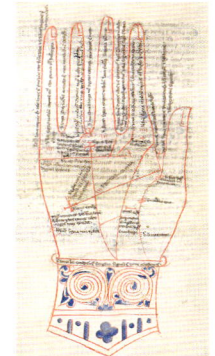

Handy diagram
This is one of a pair of annotated hands present in *Liber de chiromantia* ("The Book of Chiromancy"), produced in the 13th century, probably in England.

Unlike Greek or Arabic, Latin does not have a system where every letter in its alphabet has a matching number, so translators and copyists of onomancies used varying values as scribes tried to find the "right" matches.

Reading the lines
Medieval texts on chiromancy — which, like onomancy, was practised in ancient Greece — gave advice on reading the lines and bumps on a person's hand, in order to learn various things about that person's future, from longevity to luck in love. Some examples did not have diagrams, but versions that fused text with diagrams became common in the later medieval period.

The Eadwine Psalter
Made in c. 1160 at Canterbury Cathedral, England, and named after the monk who perhaps oversaw its creation, the Eadwine Psalter is a beautifully illustrated book of psalms and other religious material. It includes a dedication to Eadwine and the psalms in Latin, Old English, and Anglo-Norman, and notably ends with a section on chiromancy, followed by "Victorious and Vanquished" onomantic text. It might seem odd that material opposed to Christian doctrine appears in a book for monks, but divination fell somewhere between acceptable and unacceptable in a Christian context, depending on interpretation (see pp. 150–53).

The monk Eadwine, the Psalter's chief scribe, is depicted in its pages.

ligna anno.

Quarta subit mortem prostituit tertia sortem
Nor habet horas xiiij. dies x.
februarius habet dies xxviij. luna xxix.

			februarius	Ignacij epi et mris. iij. lc. Brigide virginis. sm vig.
ij	c	iiij	N	purificatio beate marie. duplum.
xi	f	iij	N	Blasij epi et martiris. duplum.
viij	g	ij	N	Dies eg.
	A	Nonas	N	Agathe virginis et mris. ix. lc.
xvi		viij	Id	Vedasti et amandi epōrum. iij. lc.
v		vij	Id	
xiij		vj	Id	Apolonie virginis et martiris.
ij	f	v	Id	Scolastice virginis. iij. lc.
		iiij	Id	
x	A	iij	Id	Eulalie virginis. sm.
		Idus	Id	
xviij		xvj	kl	Martij Valentini martiris. iij. lc.
vij	d	xv	kl	Sol in pisabus.
	f	xiiij	kl	
xv		xiij	kl	
iiij	g	xij	kl	Adam hic peccauit.
	A	xj	kl	
xij	b	x	kl	
j	c	ix	kl	
	d	viij	kl	Cathedra sancti petri. ix. lc. Iuuantuū vris.
ix	e	vij	kl	
	f	vj	kl	Mathie apli. duplum. locus byssent.
xvij	g	v	kl	
vj	A	iiij	kl	Dies eger.
	b	iij	kl	
xiiij	c	ij	kl	

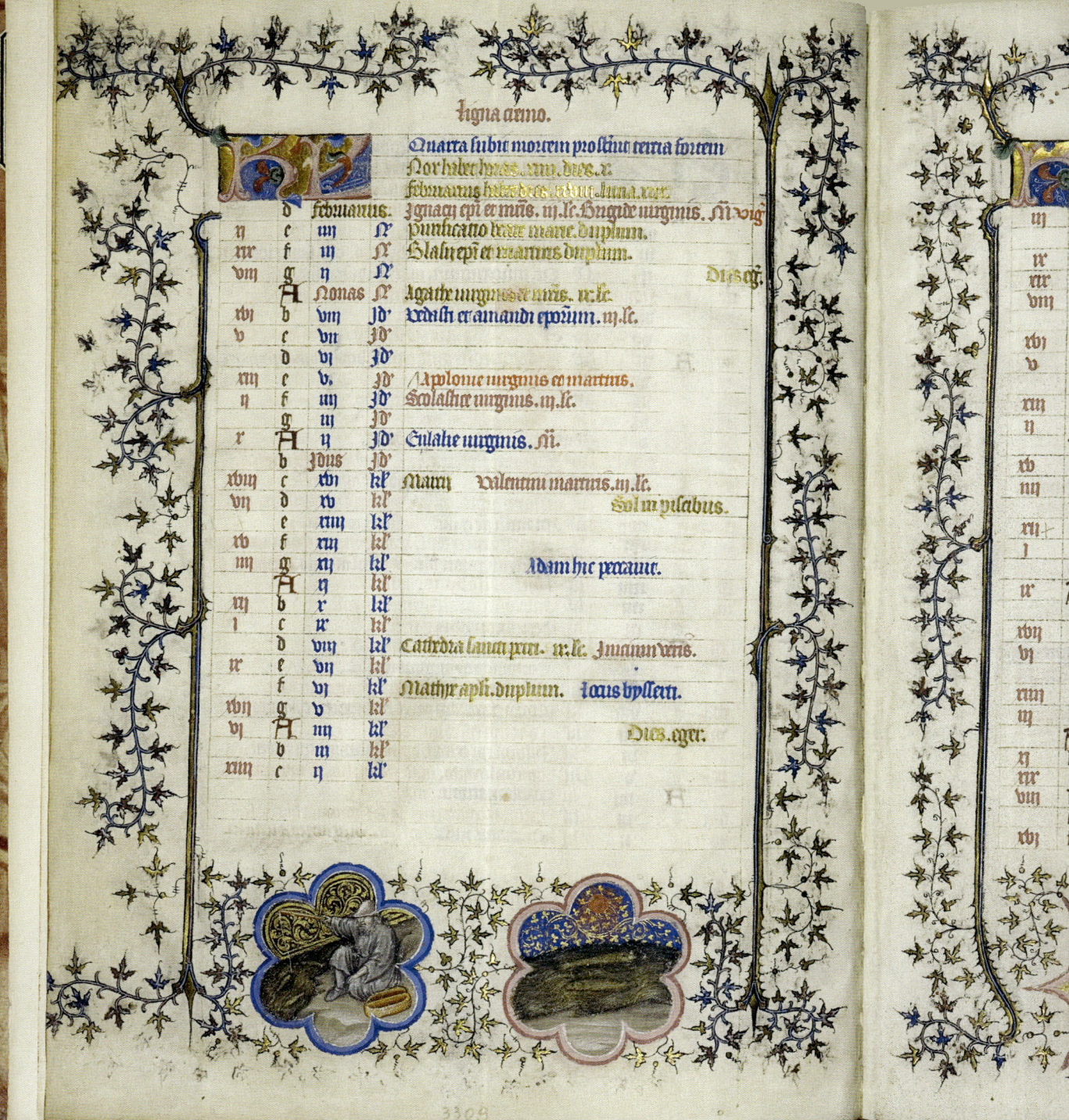

A dismal date in the diary

Many ancient cultures regarded certain days as unlucky, and the Romans considered three days a month as *dies atri*, on which beginning ventures such as journeys would bring misfortune. The concept of unlucky days was incorporated into Christian liturgical calendars, the earliest of which, dating from 354 CE, features 25 ill-omened days.

By the 9th century, unlucky days had become known as *dies aegyptiaci*, or "Egyptian days", arising from the belief that Egypt was particularly associated with the magical and astrological arts. Egyptian days were indicated on manuscript calendars by "D", standing for *dies mali*, whose meaning became corrupted from "bad days" to "dismal days". In medieval Europe there were generally 24 Egyptian days (two per month), explained as the 10 days on which God struck the Egyptians with blights such as plagues in the Book of Exodus, along with 14 other, minor plagues. On these days, activities such as surgery or business were best avoided, while those born on a dismal day would suffer a life of misfortune. As a way of remembering unlucky days, medieval authors wrote mnemonics, such as 13th-century Scottish cleric John of Sacrobosco's *Armis gunfe*, which condensed the 24 dismal days into 150 catchy syllables.

> "I believe it was in the unlucky days, that were the ten wounds of Egypt…"
>
> **GEOFFREY CHAUCER**, *THE BOOK OF THE DUCHESS*, c. 1369

Sick days (*dies eger*) in February and March are marked in gold on these illuminated pages from the late 14th-century "Parisian calendar".

Surveying the stars
Astrologer Abraham ibn Ezra (seated, centre) is shown at work, scrutinizing an astrolabe. A commonly used device for determining the positions of the stars and planets, it could be used for navigation, but was also an essential tool in making astrological predictions.

Spheres of influence
Jewish and Kabbalistic astrology

There are few direct references to astrology in the Hebrew Bible. Ancient high priests carried the Urim and Thumim, mysterious objects concealed in a pouch that enabled them to obtain oracles at times of need, but generally divination (in the sense of communicating with powers other than God) was not condoned. Knowledge of astrology became more widespread during the Jewish people's exile in Babylon in the 6th century BCE. While astrology was explicitly condemned by the Old Testament prophets, later Jewish scholars argued that it was acceptable as long as it did not imply a fate for the Jewish people, who were responsible only to God.

A Jewish tradition
In the medieval period, Jewish scholars gained access to translations of Arabic astrological treatises and produced their own works, such as *Sefer ha-yaqar* ("Precious Book", c. 970 CE), by Shabbetai Donnolo, which featured detailed charts of planetary positions, and the *Keter malkut* ("Royal Crown", c. 1050), by Solomon ibn Gabirol, which described the specific areas of influence each planet had on earthly affairs. The most influential scholar was Abraham ibn Ezra, from northern Spain, whose *Sefer re'sit hokhma* ("Beginning of Wisdom", 1148) included explanations of the signs of the zodiac and astrological terms.

The 13th and 14th centuries saw an increasing divergence between astronomy and astrology, usually treated as a single area of study. Jewish astronomers helped to compile the *Alfonsine Tables*, used to calculate planetary positions and celestial events such as eclipses, around 1270, and Jacob ben Makir's creation of an improved quadrant, the "quadrant of Israel", made it possible to measure the altitudes and relative positions of celestial bodies more accurately. Meanwhile, the *Sefer Milhamot ha-Shem* ("War of the Lord", 1329), by Levi ben Gershon (Gersonides), included a form of astrological determinism, accepting astral influences, but seeking a rational explanation.

In contrast, more esoteric forms of study also flourished – such as astral magic, based on the works of Judah Halevi, which taught that emanations from specific celestial bodies could be channelled into *segullot* (talismans) to affect earthly events.

Wise paths
Kabbalah, a form of mysticism, emerged in the 12th and 13th centuries among Jewish communities in Spain and southern France and was embodied in texts such as the *Sefer Raziel ha-Malakh* ("Book of the Angel Raziel"). It considered that the infinite energy of God was channelled to Earth through 10 manifestations, or *sefirot*. Understanding these was key to attaining wisdom. Each was linked to a specific celestial body – such as Hed ("divine mercy") to Jupiter or Tipharet ("beauty") to the Sun – with the pathways between them aligned with signs of the zodiac. Elements of Kabbalistic astrology were taken up by Christian occultists during the Renaissance, then transmitted to the Rosicrucians in the 17th century and occult revivalist movements such as the Hermetic Order of the Golden Dawn in the 19th century (see pp. 226–27).

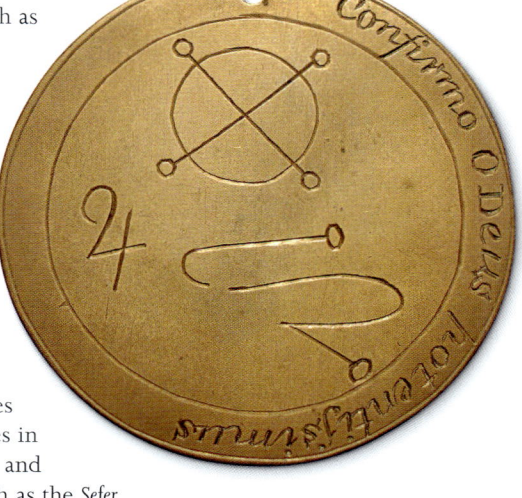

Protective disc
This amulet is inscribed with Kabbalistic symbols relating to Jupiter: the seal (top) and intelligence (bottom) of the planet, and its symbol (left). On the other side, there is a magic square and the number 136, which signifies one of the names of God.

> "Everything depends on the stars (*mazzal*), even the scroll of the Torah in the Sanctuary."
>
> *ZOHAR*, IDRA RABA SECTION, VERSE 149, c. 13TH CENTURY

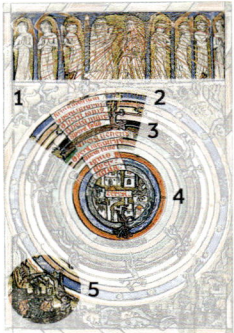

Key

1 God sits at the centre of the kingdom of Heaven.

2 The stars occupy the outermost sphere.

3 Each of the known planets has its own sphere, as do the Sun and Moon.

4 Earth is at the centre, encircled by the spheres of the elements.

5 Having fallen through the celestial spheres, demons land in Hell.

Cosmic order

This mid-14th-century illustration from the "Neville of Hornby Hours" shows Earth in the centre, surrounded by the celestial spheres. Demons fall from Heaven, through the cosmic spheres, into Hell.

Evil influence
Planetary demons

The Greek philosopher Aristotle's theory that the Sun, Moon, and planets orbited Earth in a series of concentric spheres had a profound influence on the medieval European view of the cosmos. Adapted to conform to Christian theology, with the outer spheres forming the realm of angels, and Earth in a corruptible region beneath the sphere of the Moon, this model became a way of understanding how evil forces might shape human affairs.

By the 13th century, there was growing interest in astrological magic, sparked by new translations of Arabic texts such as the *Ghayat al-Hakim* (known in Latin as the *Picatrix*; see pp. 148–49). These works described how the planets could sway human behaviour towards good or evil, leading scholars to consider how demons might harness these celestial influences to corrupt mankind.

Debating malign forces
William of Auvergne, bishop of Paris from 1228 to 1249, was one of the first medieval philosophers to study the relationship between planets and demons in manifesting evil. He rejected the notion that the planets could exert malign influence, given they were in God's domain, but suggested that demons gave the impression of having power over celestial bodies. The Italian theologian Thomas Aquinas, his contemporary, believed that the planets could influence human behaviour. He argued that while demons lacked the power to move the planets, they could manipulate celestial influences as they flowed to Earth. Aquinas also believed that demons could study lunar phases to ascertain when humans were at their most vulnerable to corruption.

The precise nature and location of demons were other aspects of the cosmological debate that continued to preoccupy theologians and astrologers. Aristotle had argued that evil demons fell through the celestial spheres, ending up deep in the Earth's core. Medieval scholars modified this concept, with some positing that demons were fallen angels that resided in the lower spheres of the cosmos.

According to Giorgio Anselmi, a teacher at the universities of Parma and Bologna in the 1440s, the four spheres affiliated to the elements (earth, air, fire, and water) each had their own demon, as did the cardinal directions (north, east, south, and west). Each planet also had a demon that could influence affairs associated with it, such as matters of the heart for Venus. Growing interest in discussions of this type was problematic for the Church, which worried that planetary demons were being ascribed powers reserved for God and the angels, and that these forces might be manipulated via astrological magic. The dangerous nature of this debate was proven in 1327 when Francesco Stabili (better known as Cecco d'Ascoli), a professor of astrology at Bologna, was burned at the stake for his teachings.

Magical seal Used for astrological magic, this "seal of God" (*sigillum Dei*), featuring the names of God and the angels, was believed to conjure and control planetary spirits.

Celestial Intelligences
Medieval theologians distinguished between various categories or orders of angels with differing levels of influence. Archangels and Angels were ranked lowest, while the most powerful had dominion over individual planets. The order of the Cherubim, for example, were responsible for Saturn, the Thrones for Jupiter and the Dominations for Mars. Another order of angels, the Intelligences, were thought to govern the physical movement of the planets and, via this, exert influence on humans and the physical world in a way denied to demons. Practitioners of astrological magic often created talismans to summon the angelic Intelligences to do their bidding.

A 14th-century illustration shows the nine orders of angels circling God, Christ, and the Virgin Mary.

Ways of seeing
Mexica obsidian mirrors

Gazing into reflective surfaces such as water and mirrors to receive signs, known as scrying, is an ancient divinatory practice (see pp. 278–79). In the Americas, the Olmec people (1200–400 BCE) viewed their reflection in polished minerals such as pyrite, believing such mirrors to act as portals to other worlds where priests could communicate with deities and spirits.

Gods and kings
The Mexica (Aztecs), who flourished in Mexico from 1100 to 1521 CE, inherited this practice. In the 13th century, they began to use obsidian, a shiny, black volcanic glass, to craft their mirrors. These objects were important to the Mexica, who, according to legend, were guided by a smoking mirror from their sacred homeland of Aztlan to the site where they later founded Tenochtitlán. Mirrors were associated with water, and the new city was built on an island in 1325, surrounded by what one writer called "the great water mirror".

Obsidian mirrors were crafted by polishing lumps of glass until they were flawlessly smooth. The work and patience required to make these mirrors made them elite objects, and they became associated with rulers, priests, and gods, leading to magical connotations. The concept of an obsidian mirror as magical even entered the Mexica language, Nahuatl, with the word for divination, *itzpopolhuia*, being derived from *itztli* ("obsidian"), and diviners calling their books of signs *tēzcatl*, meaning "mirror".

Mexica art and religion often feature obsidian mirrors. The god Tezcatlipoca, whose name means "Smoking Mirror", was closely associated with

Directions for wear
The images of obsidian mirrors in the *Codex Tepetlaoztoc*, a 16th-century Mexica manuscript, show how the mirrors were framed in wood or precious metals to be displayed or worn by priests and rulers.

both obsidian and divination. Images of the god usually show him wearing an obsidian mirror on his head or as a breastplate. Surviving examples of Mexica mirrors suggest that they were worn in this way by both priests and rulers. Known as the "mirror pierced on both sides", rulers of the Mexica would wear a mirror to allow them to communicate with the gods. As well as mirrors, the word *tēzcatl* could also refer to eyes — Mexica carvings of several gods had obsidian eyes — making mirrors objects with the power of sight.

Cultural theft
Little is known about the precise ways in which mirrors were used for divination by the Mexica, but evidence suggests that they were held in high

> "They carve these mirrors in many shapes: some round, others triangular, and others in other shapes…"
>
> **BERNARDINO DE SAHAGÚN**, THE *FLORENTINE CODEX*, BOOK 11

regard for their ability to reveal the past, present, and future. When the Mexica were conquered by the Spanish in 1521, valuable treasures were stolen and obsidian mirrors became prized possessions for European magicians. John Dee (see p. 189), who served as court astrologer to English queen Elizabeth I, famously used one in his attempts to communicate with angels, and later occultists used Mexica artefacts in their own divinatory rituals.

Glorious Tezcatlipoca
In this depiction from the 16th-century *Codex Borgia*, the Mexica god known as Smoking Mirror has obsidian mirrors attached to his head, chest, and foot.

Moctezuma's omen

The *Florentine Codex*, Spanish friar Bernardino de Sahagún's 17th-century study of the Mexica, records many omens noted by the Mexica in the final decades of their rule. One omen was interpreted by ruler Moctezuma II when a bird with a mirror on its head was captured. Moctezuma peered into the mirror and saw many warriors riding large, deer-like animals. Sure enough, Spanish *conquistadors* arrived on horseback soon after, signalling the downfall of the Mexica.

The mysterious bird with the mirror on its head was depicted in the *Florentine Codex* by Mexica artists working with de Sahagún.

The right remedy
Astro-medicine

Astrology has been used since the earliest times to gain information about illness, with evidence of this practice surviving from Babylon in ancient Mesopotamia (see p. 25). Astrologers and physicians alike consulted the heavens to work out diagnoses, the most suitable course of treatment, and when to administer it.

Body in balance
In ancient Greece, the Hippocratic writings of the 5th century BCE stated that health depended on the balance of the four humours — blood, yellow bile, black bile, and phlegm — existing in a unique formation for each person. The 2nd-century CE Greek physician Galen introduced the idea of the six "non naturals": air; food and drink; sleep and waking; exercise and rest; emissions and retentions; and the passions (emotions). These provoked the four states (hot, cold, wet, and dry) that affected the humours, causing illness.

Galen's theory of humours dominated medical thought up to the Renaissance and beyond. It conceptualized the body as a microcosm of the universe, whose four elements — earth, air, fire and water — mapped onto the four states, the four seasons, and four stages of human life. As well as affecting their health, a person's humoral make-up was thought to account for their emotions and character. For example, "melancholics" (those dominated by black bile) were considered fearful, despondent, and agitated. Any humoral imbalances could be mitigated by looking at the stars to work out the best times for treatment.

Dominant theory
This woodcut from Leonhard Thurneysser's *Quinta Essentia* (1574) shows the the four humours in relation to their corresponding elements and zodiac signs.

Time to take blood
Astrological diagrams of the body were common in late medieval and Renaissance manuscripts. The "Zodiac Man", for example, linked body parts to astrological signs (see pp. 178–79). Such diagrams helped medical practitioners work out the best times for treating particular body parts.

Astrological charts were useful for diagnosis as well as treatment. Having established which constellation the Moon was in when the patient fell ill, a physician would consult these charts to determine the best course of action. For example, bloodletting, which was believed to correct humoral imbalance, was most effective when the Moon was in a particular constellation. To give them an air of authority, physicians used volvelles, often worn on a belt for ease of consultation (and as visible indicators of knowledge), to calculate the position of the heavens. These were circular calendars with moveable parts for determining time, accuracy, and amount to bleed.

Lunar device
This volvelle from 1488–98 would have been used for working out the positions of the Sun and Moon in the zodiac, and the lunar phases.

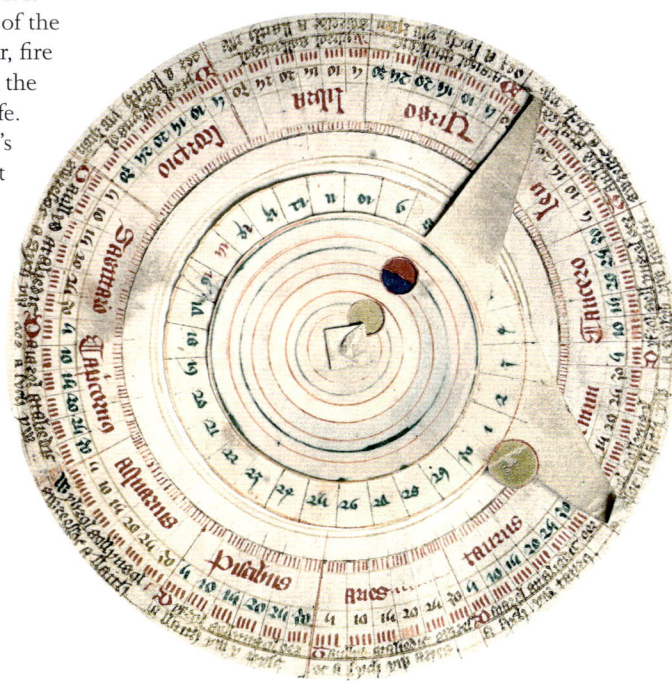

Astro-medicine

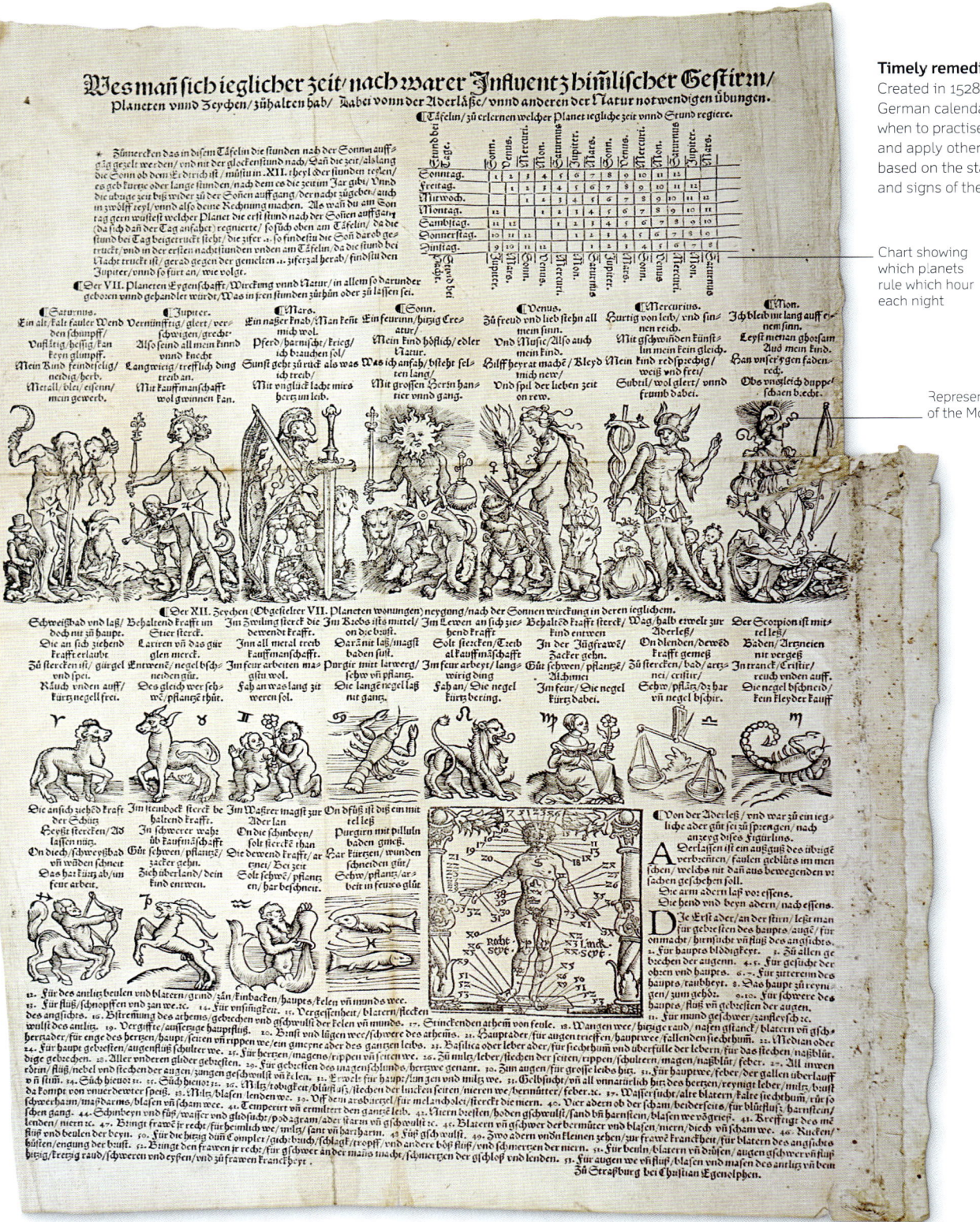

Timely remedies
Created in 1528–30, this German calendar explains when to practise bloodletting and apply other remedies, based on the stars, planets, and signs of the zodiac.

Chart showing which planets rule which hour each night

Representation of the Moon

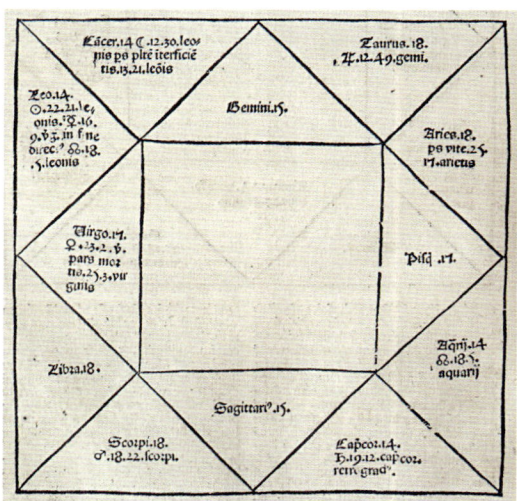

Predicting the end
This ominous horoscope was calculated by Jean Ganivet for the dean of Vienne on 7 August 1431, predicting he would die from his illness. It was published alongside other horoscopes in his 1496 *Amicus medicorum* ("Friend of the Physicians").

In the 15th century, *Aderlasskalendar* (bloodletting charts) of anatomical figures with zodiac signs became especially popular in Germany, and were often displayed in physicians' shops as professional emblems. The first printed versions were available from the 1450s.

Diagnosis and cure

Astrologer-physicians drew up predictions, such as horoscopes (based on the time of consultation), decumbitures (based on when a patient became ill), or nativities (based on birth date), to determine the course of a patient's illness and other pertinent information. French astrologer-physician Jean Ganivet cast multiple horoscopes, including a well-known prediction in 1431 that the sickly dean of Vienne would die. Two days later, he did.

Astrology was even applied to the health of entire populations; for example, the outbreak of bubonic plague in 1348 (known as the Black Death) was investigated by the medical faculty of the University of Paris later that year and ascribed to a malevolent conjunction of Mars, Jupiter, and Saturn that had taken place three years earlier.

The planets and stars were thought to control both ailments and the efficacy of remedies — especially plants and herbs. Medical authorities advised collecting plants when their associated planets were visible, worked out by consulting an almanac. It was believed that gathering plants at other times could make them less powerful or even render them completely ineffective.

Culpeper's compendium

The 17th-century English medical writer Nicholas Culpeper recommended astrology for treating the sick. His *English Physician*, first printed in 1652, became a bestseller. Later called the *Complete Herbal*, this illustrated compendium was intended to be bought and kept in the home, and was written to give ordinary people the skills to identify and pick plant remedies, as well as listing the conditions each remedy could treat. It also showed how these plants correlated with the seven classical planets.

Critical days

The Hippocratic writings of the 5th century BCE and, centuries later, those of Galen of Pergamon both described the "critical days" of illness. These were days on which a patient's ailment would get better or worse, in accordance with the phases of the Moon.

Galen's *On Critical Days* was translated into Arabic, and Arabic physicians included the influence of the stars in their calculations. This Galen-inspired astro-medicine spread from the Islamic world into Western Europe from 1200 CE during the translation movement (see pp. 150–53), remaining dominant in medical thought and practice throughout the later medieval period and into the Renaissance.

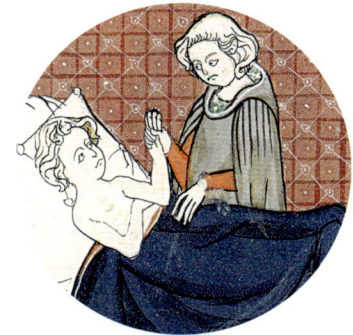

A doctor examines a patient in this illustration from *Oeuvres de Galien*, a 14th-century French translation of Galen's work.

Astro-medicine

The book was revised and enlarged in 1653, to create an edition including 328 separate plant descriptions: 322 of these were assigned a planet; 38 correlated to both a planet and a zodiac sign.

Culpeper linked both plants and stars to the work of God. He wrote in the introduction to his 1653 edition of the *Physical Directory* (a translation of the Royal College of Physicians' *Pharmacopoeia Londinensis* of 1618) that the universe created by God was linked to the body of man as macrocosm-microcosm. He deduced that the three realms of the macrocosm – physical (elemental), the stars (celestial), and God (intellectual) – must have their counterparts in the human body, the microcosm, and asserted that the stars (with God as the ultimate cause) must therefore be able to influence or cause the natural ailments of the human body, through nature (the direct cause).

Cooling remedy

These illustrations from an 18th-century edition of Culpeper's work show two types of hawkweed: mouse-ear (*Hieracium pilosella*, left) and mountain (*H. alpinum*, right). Associated with Saturn and said to be cooling, drying, and binding, the plant's "bitter milk" was thought to treat many ailments, including stomach issues, while its leaves could treat issues caused by "hot and salt phlegm", burns, and convulsions.

"Bitter milk" can be harvested from any part of the plant

Leaves applied with "meal and fair water" act as a poultice

Dried root is given in wine and vinegar to reduce swelling

> "…he that would know the reason of the operations of herbs must look up as high as the stars."
>
> **NICHOLAS CULPEPER**, *THE ENGLISH PHYSICIAN ENLARGED*, 1653

Divine inspiration
Ecstatic visions

From the earliest days of Christianity, certain worshippers were known to have intense visions in moments of deep contemplation that revealed the nature of God. Many visions were multisensory experiences, which felt real to the visionary; these were known as "ecstasie". Those who had ecstatic visions were called mystics. The ecstatic experience was both intensely painful and yet joyous. Saint Teresa of Avila described one vision as like being pierced with a flaming spear, causing her to cry out loud.

A mystical awakening
When a servant called Elizabeth Barton – later known as "The Holy Maid of Kent" – began having visions in 1525 her fame soon spread throughout England. Physical hardship, such as illness or fasting, might provoke ecstasies. Barton's began as a result of an illness, during which she was unable to eat or drink and experienced seizures. Barton claimed that her vision told her that a child in the house of Thomas Cobb – where Barton worked – would die, and that her own illness would be cured by God if she visited a local 12th-century chapel. Both predictions came true.

Over the next eight years, Barton continued to have prophetic visions, despite having recovered from her illness. These visions prompted her to encourage others to support the beliefs of the Catholic Church and to promote orthodoxy, and so she became a nun at St Sepulcre's convent in Canterbury, Kent. Many important Catholic authorities endorsed Barton, and she met King Henry VIII at least twice to discuss revelations from her visions. News of her prophecies even reached the Pope.

Unpopular prophecies
A letter from Sir Thomas More describes Elizabeth Barton as "the wykked woman of Canterbury" after she began to speak out in opposition to the actions of King Henry VIII.

Treasonous prophecy
When the English king sought a divorce from his wife, Catherine of Aragon, and moved to break with the Church in Rome, Barton's visions became dangerous for her. She warned that Henry would die if he divorced his Catholic queen and that he would be doomed to hell if he broke with the Catholic Church. With this prediction, Barton lost the king's favour and in 1533, she was arrested, along with several of her supporters, and condemned for treason. Barton was hanged in 1534.

Reform and counter-reform
In 1517, Martin Luther challenged key doctrines of the Catholic Church and initiated the Protestant Reformation, which divided communities across Europe. A Counter-Reformation was launched by Catholics to combat Protestantism, and mysticism played a key role. The upheaval in Christianity left people uncertain as to what the correct response by worshippers should be, but direct, personal revelation allowed individuals to navigate theological debates. Catholic mystics bolstered the Counter-Reformation by declaring that the renewal of the Catholic Church had to come from within each of the faithful.

Martin Luther published a list of 95 questions about corruption in the Catholic Church.

Ecstatic visions 169

In the throes of ecstasy
This 19th-century engraving shows Barton falling into an ecstatic vision in front of a statue of the Virgin Mary.
Modern scholars have suggested a potential link between ecstatic visions and epileptic seizures.

Key
1 God and the angels occupy the outermost sphere, with God shown as a cloud.
2 *Anima mundi*, the soul of the world, is depicted as a woman chained to God, who spans the heavens and Earth.
3 The planets and luminaries, with the stars in a ring beyond, appear in order of their distance from Earth.
4 The minerals lead and antimony are governed by Saturn, as indicated by the symbol (♄) and dotted line.

Cosmic harmony
Robert Fludd's illustration from *Utriusque Cosmi* ("History of the Two Worlds", 1617) depicts the correspondences within the cosmos, with its soul shown as a woman. Fludd's vision is of cosmic harmony, where everything is connected and in balance.

> "By this Spirit, therefore, every occult property is conveyed into herbs, stones, metals, and animals, through the Sun, Moon, planets, and through stars higher than the planets."
>
> **CORNELIUS AGRIPPA**, *THREE BOOKS OF OCCULT PHILOSOPHY*, 1531

As above, so below
Astrology in Renaissance Europe

From science and high politics to art and everyday life, astrology was a powerful force in Renaissance culture. Following its revival during the medieval period, its status continued to rise as astrologers held increasingly prominent positions in European society, fulfilling the role of today's meteorologists, epidemiologists, economists, and political pundits. Astrology was taught to university students while researchers sought to make it an empirical science. Although its practice was sometimes controversial, astrology remained a respected academic subject.

Cosmic connections

Renaissance astrology was based on theories about the structure of the cosmos. According to Aristotle, Earth (made of earth, air, fire, and water) is surrounded by concentric spheres that house the Moon, Sun, planets, and stars (see p. 70). On Earth things are constantly changing, but the motion of the heavenly spheres is perfect and predictable. Working from Aristotle's vision, astrologers explained that the movement of these spheres was responsible for all change — which Aristotle called "generation and corruption" — on Earth.

The idea of a link between the macrocosm (the wider universe) and the microcosm (the human being) provided Renaissance astrologers with a key for understanding just about all aspects of life. According to theories of a Great Chain of Being, the cosmos is a ladder running from God down to the smallest bits of matter. Many believed that different parts of this ladder "corresponded" with or reflected each other. For example, as a cold and dry planet, Saturn was associated with melancholy, a disease that took over human bodies when they were too cold and dry. This meant that herbs and medicines that were hot and wet could be used to counteract such a humoral imbalance and heal the body and mind (see pp. 164–67). Understanding the correspondences between different parts of the macrocosm and microcosm was therefore crucial for living life to the fullest.

Ancient science and philosophy were widely studied in the Renaissance. Scholars wanted to understand them better and update them based on what they knew to be true about the world. Astrological works were no exception. Hellenistic astrologer Claudius Ptolemy's writings (see pp. 86–89) fascinated many, and some came to view them as a more reliable guide to astrology than the Arabic writers who had dominated late medieval thought. Others turned to Platonic philosophy. Italian scholar Marsilio Ficino studied neo-Platonic ideas about the "soul" of the cosmos and connected them to astrology. By envisaging the planets as alive and ensouled themselves, he theorized that it might be possible for them to influence the human soul directly — a notion that medieval astrologers, concerned about free will, had rejected. Ficino experimented with ways to harness the influences of the stars using images and talismans. These devices could supposedly channel a planet's positive effects or ward against negative ones, like a shield.

Channelling Venus
This reconstruction of a silver talisman based on Renaissance descriptions is said to attract the powers of Venus, including fertility and peace. Each row and column add up to 175, the number of Kedemel, the spirit of Venus.

Astrology in art

From grand architecture and lavish frescoes to bowls, vases, and pen boxes, astrological imagery was ubiquitous in the Renaissance. Astrology's rich visual language, with its established motifs and symbols, made it accessible to those with low literacy and so useful for sending powerful messages. Rich families like the Medici of Florence exploited this, using the associations of the planets and zodiac to promote their dynasty. On the advice of Marsilio Ficino, some of the Medici's frescoes were purposely designed to capture and exploit celestial influences.

Easy to recognize, the zodiac signs adorn the face of St Mark's clock tower in Venice's Piazza San Marco.

Renaissance astrologers sought to give astrology a secure scientific footing, a project that involved collecting masses of astronomical data and comparing it to earthly events. Italian Girolamo Cardano analysed hundreds of birth charts alongside biographies of their owners, while monks at the Santa Prassede monastery in Rome used curated questionnaires. They aimed to identify patterns that would refine and strengthen existing theories.

Birth of a reformer
In this version of Martin Luther's natal chart, Luca Gaurico set Luther's birthday (a contested date) to 22 October 1484.

Astrological agony aunts

In the 15th and 16th centuries, astrology reached new heights of popularity. As printing grew in scale and sophistication, what was previously an academic subject became accessible to the public (see pp. 176–79). Astrologers' predictions could now incite a whole city to action and even cause collective panic, as in the case of an apocalyptic flood forecast in 1524 (which never arrived). Collections of natal charts became a bestselling genre: astrologers commented on the lives of celebrities, revealing compromising details. Luca Gaurico explained the sexual vices of Francesco Filelfo by the features of his natal chart, even claiming that the unpopular dead courtier had had "three enormous testicles". Other birth charts, such as that of Martin Luther, were used for religious and political ends.

People often turned to astrology to help them navigate the twists and turns of life. Renaissance astrologers saw patients who needed advice not just about their health, but their personal and professional lives, too. Some astrologers set up shop in busy marketplaces, while others had permanent clinics. Their clients hailed from all walks of life: men and women, old and young, rich and poor. Astrologers offered anything from prenatal guidance to detective work. They were also professional matchmakers, advising on suitable partnerships or using the stars to determine the virginity, fertility, and faithfulness of a potential spouse. In this sense, astrology focused less on the future, and more on decision-making in the present.

Censorship

The popularity of astrology troubled the Church, especially in the wake of the Reformation in the 16th century. While Lutherans tried to interpret heavenly signs, Calvinists thought astrology was too deterministic. The Roman Catholic Church cracked down on astrology in a bid to rid itself of "superstitions". Concerned about astrology's apparent threat to free will, it used the *Index of Prohibited Books* to ban texts that taught how to predict future events that depended on human decisions. (Books that taught astrology for the purposes of navigation, agriculture, or medicine were still allowed.) When astrologers forecast the death of Pope Urban VIII, he issued an official decree banning predictions of the death of popes, princes, or their families, on penalty of death. However, this legislation was difficult to enforce, and inquisitors, busy with their other censorship responsibilities, often turned a blind eye.

Advice for life
The third book of Ficino's *De triplici vita* ("Three Books on Life"), shown here in a codex made for King Matthias Corvinus of Hungary, is called *De vita coelitus comparanda* ("On obtaining life from the heavens").

> "Most important, the cosmos is itself an animal more unified than any other animal, the most perfect animal…"
>
> **MARSILIO FICINO**, *DE TRIPLICI VITA*, 1489

Astrology in Renaissance Europe 173

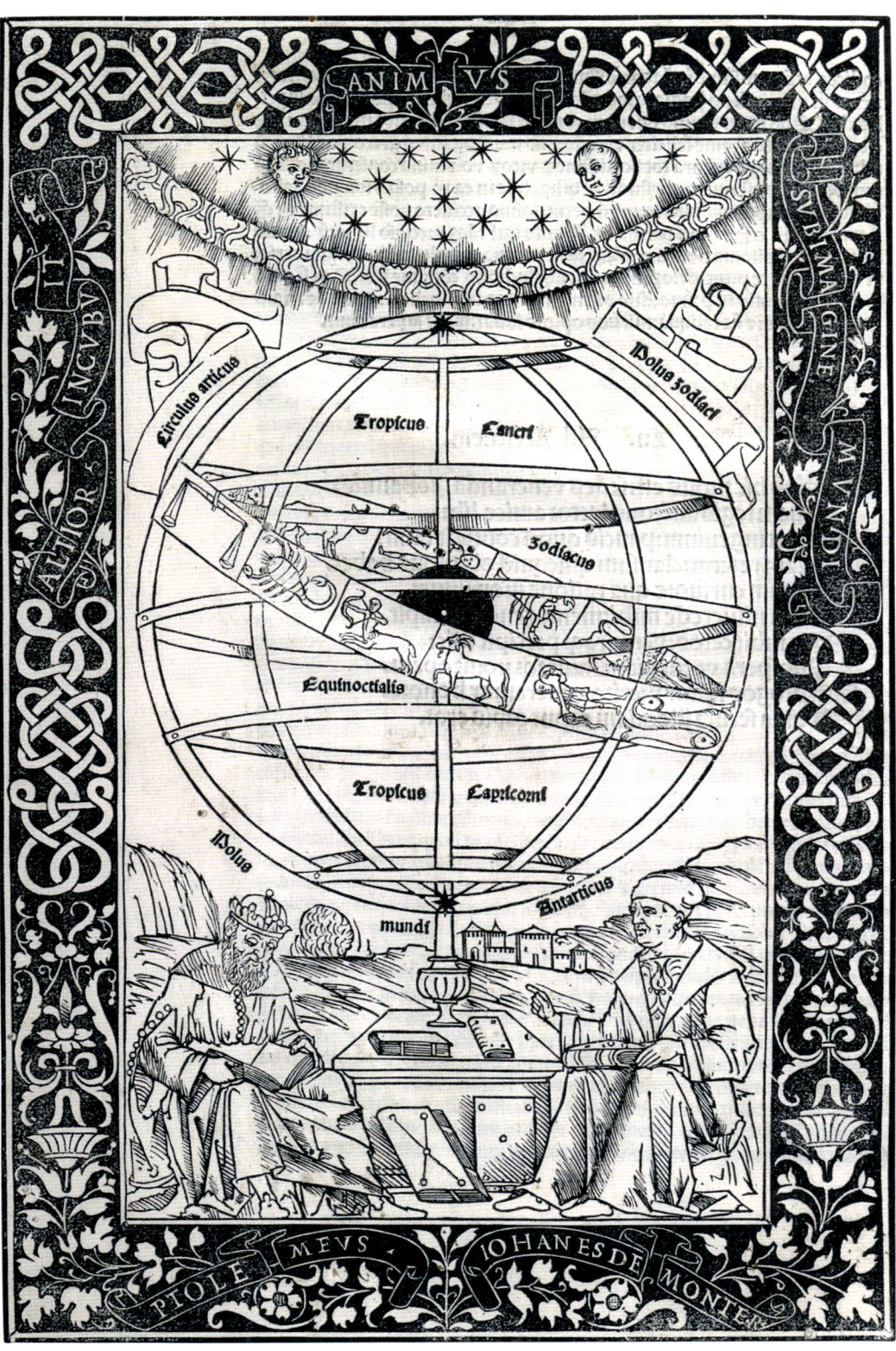

Astrologers at work
The frontispiece of Johannes Regiomontanus's *Epytoma in Almagestum Ptolemaei* ("Epitome of Ptolemy's Almagest", 1496) depicts the Renaissance astrologer working opposite Claudius Ptolemy, with an armillary sphere featuring the 12 zodiac signs between them.

Fateful prophecy

Michel de Nostredame, better known as Nostradamus, was the most famous astrologer-prophet of the Renaissance. A successful physician in Montpellier, France, he turned to astrology in the mid-16th century, at around the age of 50, and was soon running a prominent astrological boutique, casting horoscopes for the rich and famous. His skills as an astrologer were poor, but his prophetic poems became bestsellers. Nostradamus wrote in quatrains (four-line verses), which were notoriously cryptic. Despite this, admirers claim that many of his predictions have come true.

One quatrain seemingly predicted the death of Henri II in 1559. To celebrate his daughter's marriage, the French king organized a jousting tournament. The day was long and hot, but Henri displayed valiant strength against many combatants. As evening fell, he took on one last jouster: Gabriel de Lorges, Count of Montgomery. The young count's lance dealt a powerful blow, opening the visor of the king's helmet and piercing his eye. Henri fell, face bloody. An infection spread to his brain, and he suffered convulsions before dying 10 days later. Thus the "young lion" defeated the "older one", just as Nostradamus had predicted.

> "The young lion will overcome the older one,
> On the battlefield in a single combat; He will pierce his eyes…
> and he dies a cruel death."
>
> **NOSTRADAMUS,** *CENTURY I,* QUATRAIN 35

Henri II's tournament was held in the Place des Vosges in Paris. This engraving by Jean Perrissin was produced a decade after the event.

Pocket predictions
Astrological almanacs

Renaissance readers demanded on-the-go access to astrology. Many believed that almost every decision they made could benefit from the guidance of the stars. This was especially true when it came to making plans for the year ahead. Would the summer be fine? Was it a good year for a new business deal? When is the best time to have a bath? Such questions could be answered by consulting an almanac. These were similar to modern pocket diaries in that they contained a calendar as well as reference material like dates of holidays and tables of weights and measures. But, unlike a modern pocket diary, almanacs also included grand forecasts for the year to come.

What lies ahead

Astrology is often associated with predictions about individual people. Yet a large part of astrological practice was focused on the fortunes of entire villages, cities, and even countries. Renaissance astrologers made prognostications on a grand scale by using a chart called the horoscope for the revolution of the year, which was timed to the spring equinox. They also considered upcoming eclipses, comets, and planetary conjunctions. This astronomical data helped astrologers to make forecasts about the religion, politics, weather, and health of a community.

Gaspard Laet's predictions for the year 1496 are a good example of a general forecast. Based on the positions of Jupiter and the Sun, the Flemish astrologer predicted dangerous thunderstorms that would damage ships and destroy crops, and have knock-on effects on commerce and trade. The stars also indicated the possibility of pestilence in some regions. According to Laet, a breakdown in peace between princes and the clergy was to be expected as well, with a conjunction of Saturn and Mars exacerbating divisions. He warned that the

List of eclipses
Folding almanacs helped medical astrologers treat their patients by outlining auspicious (good) and inauspicious (bad) times to perform procedures. This lavish example, listing eclipses, was produced in England in c. 1415–20.

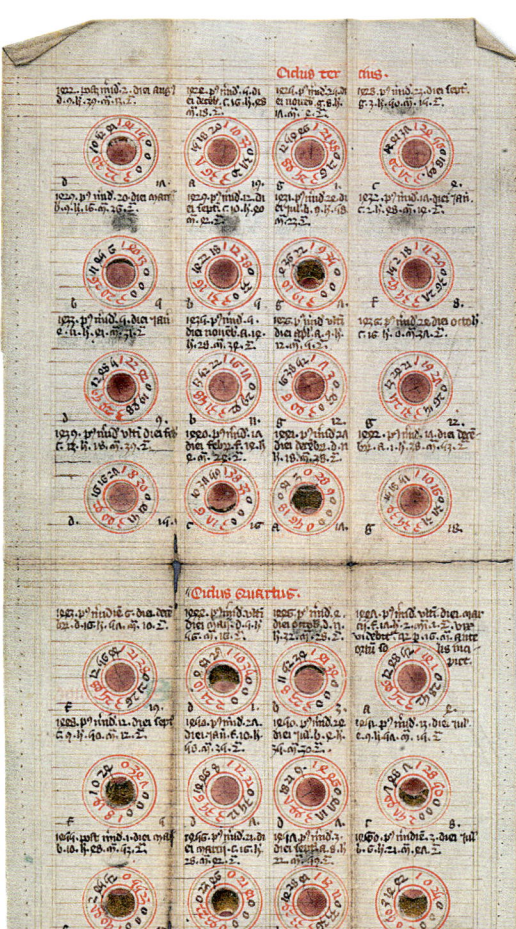

> "I shall here consider the condition and state of the ensuing year, and the accidents that therein are likely… according to the course of the stars, to attend mankind…"
>
> **JOHN GADBURY**, *EPHEMERIS, OR, A DIARY ASTRONOMICAL AND ASTROLOGICAL, FOR THE YEAR OF OUR LORD 1680*

Wall calendar
Some almanacs were designed to be pasted on the wall like a poster, such as this 1655 almanac for Utrecht, in the Netherlands. These almanacs usually focused on the calendrical aspects of astrology rather than prognostication.

Duchess of Brabant should be particularly wary, as her lands would be threatened and her people would become restless.

Predictions like Laet's proved valuable to political elites. For this reason, producing forecasts had long been a requirement for university professors of astronomy and astrology. Yet the advent of print in the 15th century meant that prognostications could now be disseminated to the masses in cheap almanacs. These were doubly useful for ordinary readers because they also provided advice for mitigating bad forecasts, from gathering enough firewood for cold winters to sourcing appropriate cures for incoming diseases. This concrete guidance rapidly helped almanacs to become the most widely read literature in Europe.

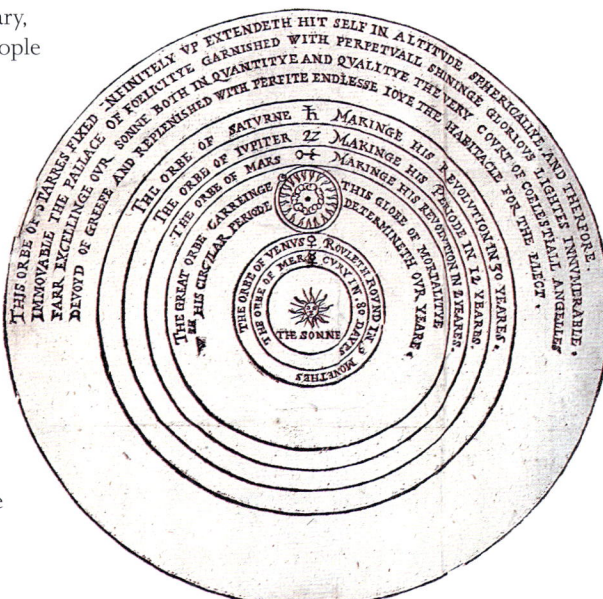

Eternal universe
Some almanacs were not written for a particular year, but instead contained "perpetual" prognostications. Leonard Digges' popular *Prognostication Everlasting*, published in 11 editions in England between 1555 and 1605, included astronomical diagrams and tables.

Above all, almanacs were valued for their medical advice, which included practical directions about when and how to engage in health-promoting practices, such as having a haircut or bathing, and healthcare treatments, such as blood-letting. They also featured remedies for common ailments, advice for pregnant and breast-feeding mothers, and guidance on balancing the four humours through the regulation of the six "non-naturals": food/drink; rest/exercise; sleep/waking; excretion; fresh air; and emotions (see pp. 164–67).

The public health forecasts in almanacs helped people to prepare for seasonal illnesses and major epidemics. Astrologers paid attention to mental as well as physical health in these forecasts, assessing the likelihood of afflictions such as melancholy. They also offered tips for avoiding the worst, including stocking the medical cabinet, steering clear of busy areas, and performing religious rites.

Operating times

Many almanacs were primarily written for doctors and surgeons, who could use the calendar to determine the best time for performing therapeutic procedures. The Zodiac Man (right) was especially useful, as it explained how different parts of the body were ruled by zodiac signs. This information was important because, according to medical astrology, it was dangerous to perform procedures when the Moon was in the sign that ruled the relevant body part. Physicians in some European countries were therefore required by law to have a copy of the current almanac on hand.

Control and mockery

Widespread though they were, almanacs were regulated and, in many countries, subject to pre-publication censorship. Authorities worried that predictions might fuel civic unrest. For this reason, the censors of the Mexican Inquisition deleted from the draft almanacs of 17th-century astrologer Carlos de Sigüenza y Góngora words like "riot", because they were "not convenient in present times". The Catholic Church also evaluated almanac drafts against the criteria of official decrees and the *Index of Prohibited Books*. Censors might edit forecasts to make them less deterministic, or remove predictions about the death of powerful people.

Perhaps inevitably, the ubiquity of almanacs made them a good subject for satire. Mock-almanacs parodied the vagueness of some prognostications with obvious predictions such as "the blind will see very little" (from a 16th-century French mock-almanac) and "the poor will face scarcity" (from a German one). Making fun of astrology was nothing new, and such ridicule was as likely to come from astrologers policing their own turf as from hardcore critics.

Celebrity writers

The popularity of almanacs made many astrologers into celebrities. This is what happened to 17th-century English astrologer William Lilly, whose almanacs sold tens of thousands of copies yearly. Lilly's charisma and relatability earned him a loyal audience. His almanacs began with heartfelt letters to his readers that made them feel they were his personal friends, and they wrote to him in return.

Something similar happened to Lilly's long-term rival John Gadbury, who decided to become an astrologer after reading an astrological book one evening in bed in 1650. Five years later, he produced his first almanac. Gadbury's almanacs became so popular that they were counterfeited. He received so much fan mail that he eventually announced that he would only respond to those who pre-paid postage.

Lilly's almanacs nearly always included a large portrait that highlighted his astrological learning.

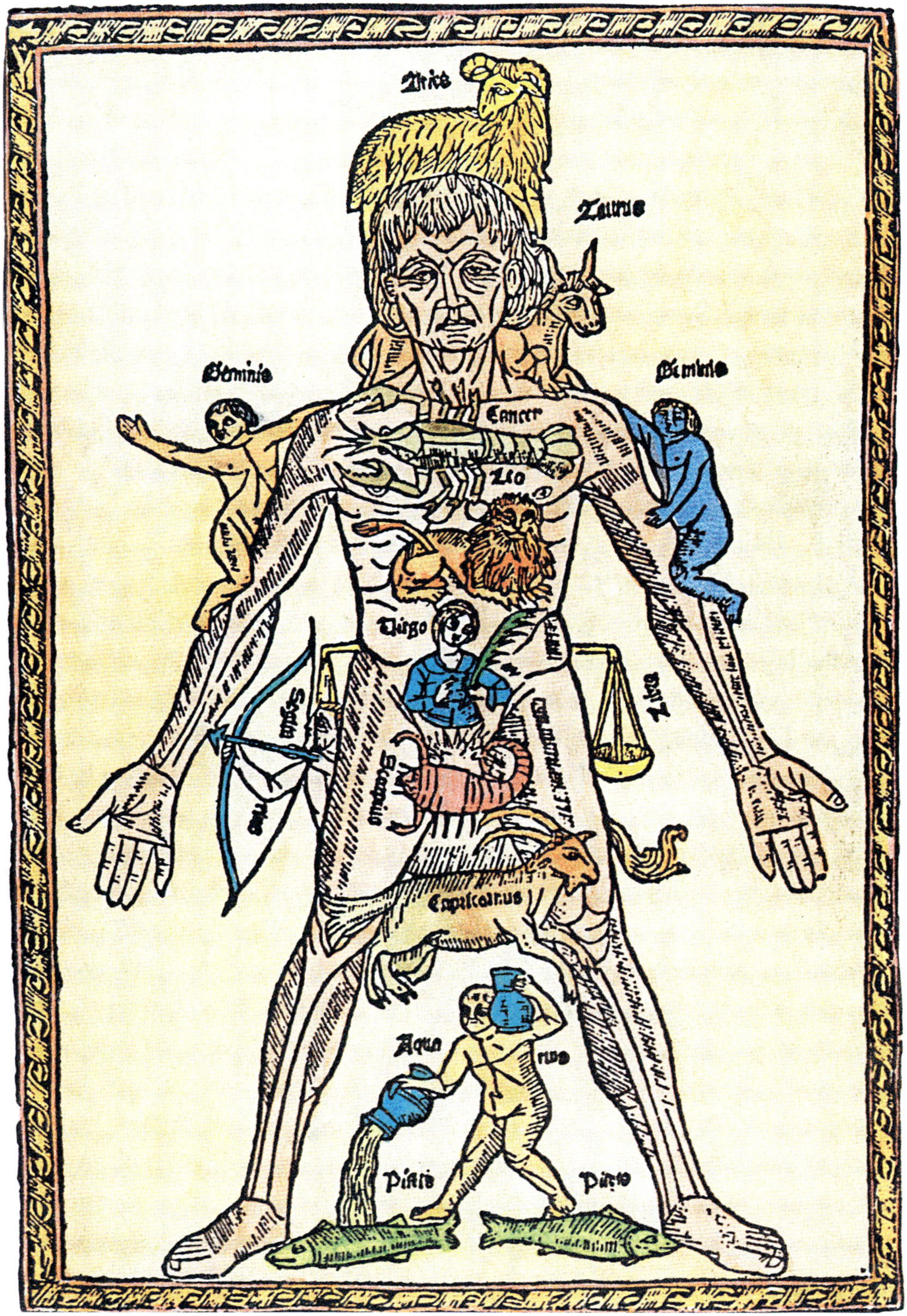

Astrological almanacs 179

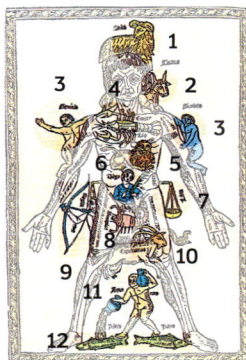

Key

1 The first zodiac sign, Aries, governs the head and brain.

2 Taurus rules over the neck.

3 Gemini is responsible for the arms and lungs.

4 Cancer governs the thorax.

5 Leo influences the heart.

6 Virgo rules over the intestines and the spleen.

7 Libra is connected to the kidneys and lumbar region.

8 Scorpio dominates the reproductive organs and bowels.

9 Sagittarius is linked to the hips, thighs, and sciatic nerves.

10 Capricorn governs the knees, joints, and skeleton.

11 Aquarius is in charge of the ankles and circulation.

12 Pisces dominates the feet.

Zodiac Man

A regular feature of almanacs, the Zodiac Man was one of the most recognizable illustrations in the early modern period. This 16th-century engraving was used in dozens of Renaissance medical and astrological texts.

> "…as though seated on a royal throne, the Sun governs the family of planets revolving around it."
>
> **NICOLAUS COPERNICUS**, *DE REVOLUTIONIBUS ORBIUM COELESTIUM*, 1543

Heliocentric vision
Earth and the other planets orbit the Sun in Andreas Cellarius's depiction of the Copernican cosmos from *Harmonia macrocosmica* (1660). The zodiac, lying on the same orbital plane as the planets, can be seen at the outer edge.

Circling the Sun
A heliocentric universe

For hundreds of years, astronomers had accepted Aristotle's vision of a geocentric cosmos, where a stationary Earth was orbited by planets moving in perfect circles (see pp. 84–85). Trying to reconcile this theory with observations of the heavens, however, proved difficult. In his 2nd-century CE astronomical treatise the *Almagest*, Claudius Ptolemy tried to explain the seemingly erratic movements of the planets with complicated yet somewhat unsatisfactory additional theories, such as that of epicycles – the idea that the planets make smaller loops along the main orbital path around Earth. In 1517, in an effort to resolve these issues, Polish astronomer Nicolaus Copernicus offered a solution: the theory of a heliocentric (Sun-centred) universe.

This theory occupied Copernicus for the rest of his life as he wrote his masterwork, *De revolutionibus orbium coelestium* ("On the Revolutions of the Heavenly Spheres"). However, it would take decades for his challenge to geocentrism to take root. The book was very technical and could only be understood by a small group of specialists. Another hurdle was that astronomy and mathematics were seen as theoretical disciplines: it was taken for granted that rather than describing the actual reality of nature, they simply came up with hypotheses. This situation slowly changed with the Scientific Revolution of the 16th and 17th centuries, and Copernicus's ideas were gradually accepted as descriptions of reality.

Impact on astrology

It is often assumed that Copernicanism undermined astrology. In fact, astrologers (many of them also astronomers) were among the first to advocate for the Copernican system, since it allowed them to make more accurate charts of planetary motion. As English astrologer Christopher Heydon wrote, "the astrologer careth not." What mattered for casting horoscopes was the positions of the planets relative to each other, and the zodiac, as seen from Earth.

Yet the new astronomy represented by Copernicus did affect astrology's fate. By raising the profile of astronomical theory and highlighting new challenges, Copernicus's findings distracted experts from astrological research. In the coming decades, discoveries – from new stars and comets to the rings of Jupiter – occupied specialists, and astrology was slowly marginalized in academic research.

Competing models
In this 1651 engraving, Astrea (the goddess of judgement) and Argus Panoptes (a mythological hundred-eyed giant) weigh the Copernican and Tychonic systems. The latter wins. On the floor is the geocentric model, discarded.

The geo-heliocentric model

Although Copernicus's model was preferable to geocentrism, it was far from perfect, and few astronomers were completely satisfied. Danish astronomer and astrologer Tycho Brahe (see pp. 182–83) developed an alternative model, in which the Sun and Moon orbit Earth, while other planets orbit the Sun. Keeping Earth stationary satisfied Aristotelian physics, according to which the planets revolved because they were made of ether, a substance not found on Earth. Tycho believed his model also fitted the description of Earth in Holy Scripture.

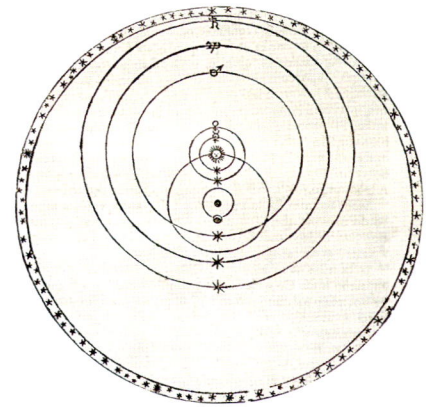

Tycho's planetary model, the "Hypothesis Tychonica", was depicted in Johannes Hevelius's *Selenographia*, published in 1647.

Changing heavens
Tycho Brahe's *nova stella*

In 1572, the impossible happened: a new star appeared in the sky. According to Aristotelian beliefs, the heavens were perfect and unchanging – a philosophy that came into question when Danish astronomer Tyge (Tycho) Brahe discovered his *nova stella*, Latin for "new star", in the constellation Cassiopeia. Tycho, usually referred to by the Latin name he took, was a noble who was passionate about astronomy and built a large observatory on the Danish island of Hven. There, he and his assistants, including his sister, used the best available instruments to observe the heavens.

A curious discovery
Tycho first spotted the "new and unusual star" in the sky on 11 November 1572, while he was at Herrevad Abbey (formerly in Denmark, but in present-day Sweden). Many thought the new object must be in the terrestrial realm – between Earth and the Moon – given that the heavens were believed to be unchanging. But the star did not have a tail, and it did not move, so it could not be a comet. Tycho showed that the star had no parallax, meaning it did not change position relative to the fixed stars. This meant it must be further away not only than the Moon, but also the planets.

Symbol shows position of the *nova stella*

Significant moment
Tycho cast this horoscope for the supernova of 1572. He dated its first appearance to 5 November 1572, during a conjunction of the Sun and Moon, recorded here to the right of the inner circle where the symbols overlap.

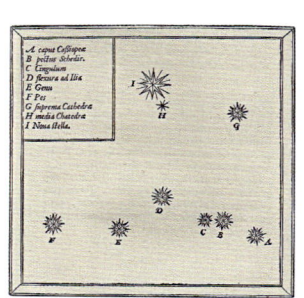

Locating the supernova
Tycho included this star map in *De nova stella* to show the position of the new star (labelled I, and shown larger than the rest) in the constellation Cassiopeia.

In his *De nova stella* ("On The New Star") of 1573, Tycho concluded the impossible: this was a new star. What Tycho actually observed was a supernova, the explosion of a dying star. Now known as SN 1572, this supernova was also documented by Chinese astrologers at the time. A few decades later, in 1604, Tycho's student Johannes Kepler (see pp. 204–07) made a similar discovery, and the 1572 *nova* could no longer be dismissed as an anomaly. Astronomers found themselves having to rethink the geocentric system (see pp. 84–85).

Diverging disciplines
Both Tycho and Kepler investigated the astrological significance of their "new stars". Kepler thought that his would affect not only humans on Earth, but also creatures that lived on Jupiter. Despite these musings, he and Tycho felt that astrology needed to be reformed. While a student, Tycho had seen a conjunction of Saturn and Jupiter that did not occur in the month the astronomical tables had predicted. He became convinced that improving astronomy would improve astrology. First, however, astrology needed to be purged of the many "superstitions" it had absorbed over time that were not originally part of the discipline, but were especially prevalent in 16th-century culture.

While Tycho never lost interest in astrology, he slowly sidelined it in his professional life, casting horoscopes in private settings but appearing in public as an observational astronomer. Tycho's shift reflects how astronomy and astrology began to diverge in the public arena, if not in the actual views of practitioners.

Tycho Brahe's *nova stella* 183

Key

1 The slit in the wall allowed the observer (in blue, on the far right) to see the heavens.

2 The cuadrant encircles a fresco depicting a cross-section of the observatory, including a basement with an alchemical laboratory, a library full of assistants, and scientific instruments on the roof.

3 The brass quadrant, with a radius of about 194 cm (76 in), is affixed to a wall built on the celestial meridian.

4 In the fresco, Tycho points with one hand to the heavens and the other to a text, highlighting the need for both theory and observation.

5 An assistant records the measurements.

6 Another assistant reads the time off a clock.

Wall chart

This illustration depicts Tycho Brahe's famous mural quadrant at his observatory. The instrument enabled an observer and their assistants to measure the altitude of celestial bodies.

The Great Comet

In 1577, a very bright comet was spotted by stargazers across the world, from Peru to Korea. Dubbed the "Great Comet" for its long tail and extreme brightness, its appearance was an ominous sign. Comets had long been seen as harbingers of doom, associated with plagues, earthquakes, and invasions. Indeed, Halley's Comet had appeared just before the Battle of Hastings in 1066.

A recorder of omens in Palestine noted the Great Comet, and while he did not offer an interpretation, it would have been common knowledge that earlier comets were linked to the destruction of Jerusalem. In Istanbul, Sultan Murad III's court astronomer Takiyüddin made detailed observations of the comet, but when the Black Death struck the city, Takiyüddin was blamed and his observatory destroyed.

In Europe, astrological pamphlets and poems were written about what the comet might portend. Scholars, including Danish astronomer Tycho Brahe, calculated the comet's position through systematic observations. Tycho demonstrated that it was a natural phenomenon that existed beyond the orbit of the Moon, and could therefore not be a "windy exhalation" of Earth, as ancient Greek thinker Aristotle had postulated many centuries earlier.

> "As the rainbow is a sign that the lands perished beneath the waters, so the fire [of the comet is a sign] that all things will perish in their own fires."
>
> **LAURENCE JOHNSON** DESCRIBING THE GREAT COMET, 1578

The comet of 1577 was depicted in Peter Codicillus's treatise *About a terrible and marvellous comet as appeared in the sky the Tuesday after St. Martin's Day*.

Astral advice
Court astrologers

Astrologers played important roles in Renaissance courts. In Europe, as in the Ottoman Empire (see p. 191), astrological manuals emphasized the importance of consulting the stars when managing populations. Rulers offered patronage to astrologers, employing them as powerful tools in constructing their public image and ensuring the security and success of their kingdom. Astrologers themselves also benefited, as a position in court gave them much-coveted social and financial security – at least for as long as they remained in their patron's favour.

Gauging the likelihood of incoming disasters is a necessary part of government. In the Renaissance, it was widely believed that celestial phenomena – comets, eclipses, and planetary conjunctions – were signs of what was to come. Astrologers were experts at reading these signs, so it is no surprise that almost every Renaissance court had an in-house astrologer. Court astrologers forecast events that would impact the people of a city or region – from earthquakes and floods, to famine, plague, and war. They were also expected to identify astrologically auspicious times for commencing important civic activities, such as military campaigns, royal weddings, major building projects, or launching new galleons – timing was crucial to the success of any venture.

The powerful Medici clan rarely made a political decision without first consulting the stars. In Florence, the family employed astrologers to advise on state as well as family matters. At the French court, Catherine de' Medici consulted Nostradamus, among other astrologers (see pp. 174–75).

Coronation horoscope
This horoscope was cast by Martin Bylica, astrologer to the king of Hungary, in 1464. Bylica's role included casting horoscopes for the king's family, kingdom, and even enemies, mostly for propaganda purposes.

Ordained by the stars
Political life can be fiercely competitive, and in the Renaissance, astrological propaganda was one way to stake a claim to power and undermine political opposition. When Maximilian I became Holy Roman Emperor in 1508, the Habsburgs had only recently claimed this office. Wanting to protect and advance the Habsburg dynasty, Maximilian commissioned astrologers like Sebastian Brant to create works that interpreted various phenomena as portents. Drawing on the astrological doctrine of great conjunctions (when Jupiter and Saturn appear to meet), Brant claimed that if Maximilian's subjects supported his reforms, Jupiter would treat them kindly.

Contrapasso
In the *Divine Comedy*, Dante placed astrologers in the eighth circle of hell. This 1587 illustration by Johannes Stradanus depicts them with their heads the wrong way round, doomed never again to look to the future.

Court astrologers 187

Printed instrument
This astrolabe dates to 1542. Made from wood and paper, with a brass dial, it was carefully crafted to help astrologers accurately locate celestial bodies in the heavens from a specific point.

Elements of astrolabe made from wood

Stars and zodiac signs printed onto paper

Royal horoscope
In 1503, William Parron presented Henry VII with this illustrated nativity of his son Henry, the future Henry VIII. It shows a world map, 12 "houses", and the positions of the zodiac signs on the dividing lines.

> "…if Mercury be in the tenth with the Part of Empire, fortunate and strong, [the questioner] shall undoubtedly obtain a Kingdom or supreme command…"
>
> **GUIDO BONATTI**, THE 125TH CONSIDERATION, *LIBER ASTRONOMIAE*, c. 1277

One of the most famous court astrologers of the Renaissance was John Dee, who for many years was advisor to Queen Elizabeth I of England. After studying at Cambridge, Dee quickly developed a Europe-wide reputation as a great mathematician and magician. Throughout his life, he was engaged in many different projects, from calendar reform to summoning and communicating with angels. Dee insisted on the practical uses of astrology, and made it clear to Elizabeth how useful and relevant it was to daily life, particularly as a ruler. Dee was appointed to choose Elizabeth's coronation date, and from then on played a significant role in her administration, advising on colonial projects and aiding in navigation.

After the ascension of King James I, however, Dee's fortunes changed. The new king was opposed to "superstition", including much of astrology. A scholar in his own right, James wrote *Dæmonologie* (1597), in which he condemned the use of astrology for claiming to predict things like "what common-weales [commonwealths] shall flourish or decay", or "what side shall winne in anie battel [win in any battle]". In these changed political circumstances, Dee fell out of royal favour and lived the rest of his life in poverty.

Privileged but precarious

In a competitive job market, the prospect of finding patronage in court was highly attractive to astrologers. As well as the privilege of influencing decision-making at the highest levels, patronage gave astrologers the time and resources they needed to focus on their craft. These prestigious posts attracted the period's leading astronomers, including Tycho Brahe (see pp. 182–83), who worked at the royal court of Denmark; Johannes Kepler (see pp. 204–07), who worked for the Habsburgs; and Galileo Galilei (see pp. 202–03), who for many years served the Medici.

Yet with patronage came the need to please one's patron. A record of bad counsel or incorrect predictions could ruin an astrologer's standing in court. Astrologers could also lose face when the regime they supported came to ruin. This is what happened to many Parliamentarian astrologers during the Restoration of the monarchy after the English Civil War (1642–51). Similarly, in late 17th-century Portugal, astrology declined in importance because the restoration of the Portuguese ruling dynasty, following a period of political turmoil, meant that there was little need for astrological propaganda.

Symbol of unity
This is the frontispiece to *Monas Hieroglyphica* (1564) by John Dee. It features an emblem he created using astrological signs for the Moon, Sun, and the four elements, representing unity.

Partners in prediction
John Dee and his assistant Edward Kelley experimented with scrying techniques in the hope of soliciting advice from angels and spirits. He described one of his crystal balls as "big as an egg: most bryght, clere, and glorious".

The Book of Felicity

The Ottoman sultan Murad III (r. 1574–95) commissioned *Matali' al-sa'ada wa manabi' al-siyada* ("Ascents of Happiness and Origins of Supremacy"), commonly known as the *Book of Felicity*, as a gift for his daughter, Fatima. It comprises a translation of the late 14th-century Arabic *Kitab al-bulhan* ("Book of Wonders") by Abd al-Hasan al-Isfahani with new illustrations, now regarded as masterpieces of Ottoman miniature art. The topics covered include the signs of the zodiac, the effects of celestial events on human affairs, and how to interpret dreams, fortune-telling, and supernatural phenomena. It also reflects Murad's fascination with astrology, not just as a divinatory tool but also as an instrument for governance.

During the reign of Murad III, astrology played a central role in the Ottoman court, with sultans taking advice from their *munejjim-bashi* (chief astrologer-astronomer) on the timing of important political, military, and personal events. The *Book of Felicity* is a testament to the high value placed on this guidance. Murad III's *munejjim-bashi*, Taqi al-Din al-Dimashqi, also supervised the establishment of the Istanbul Observatory in 1577.

> "The wise Abu Ma'shar said: 'A person born under this decan will be of bright colour, long nose, and lean flesh...'"
>
> **MUHAMMAD IBN 'AMIR AL-SU'UDI**, *BOOK OF FELICITY*

Exquisite miniatures in the *Book of Felicity* show the signs of the zodiac and their ruling planets in roundels, with their three ruling decans below.

Changing fortunes

1600–1900

Introduction

As the year 1600 dawned, astrology was practised in most cultures around the world. In China, it remained an adjunct to imperial power, while the cycle of the 12 animal years provided a popular guide to each year. For Hindus, astrology – known as *jyotihśāstra* (the "science of light") – was a Vedanga, one of the "pillars" necessary for understanding the Vedas, the sacred texts, and Hindu temples were often at the heart of astrological activity. In the Islamic world, the so-called "Golden Age" of learning was over, but some astrological traditions endured in Persia and the Turkish Ottoman Empire. Meanwhile, in Mesoamerica, the home-grown version of astrology no longer operated at a state level due to the Spanish conquest, but continued among the Indigenous population. Across Africa, the Americas, and Australia, Indigenous peoples saw the stars and planets as sources of mythical stories that could inform their calendars and social practices, such as the rites of passage that mark the transition from boy to man and girl to woman.

In 17th-century Europe, astrology was at its peak. It existed at both popular and elite levels, dealt with all sorts of personal questions, from lost property to marriage and business deals, and could provide personality descriptions, assist with medical diagnosis and treatment, advise on the most auspicious moments for political action, and offer a framework for long-range historical analysis. However, the discipline was not universally accepted in all its forms. Many people were sceptical of astrology's ability to give exact answers to precise questions, or to make accurate forecasts, but nevertheless accepted that the planets had a general role in material matters, such as health. This was easy to justify by reference to the Sun's indisputable role in the weather and the Moon's influence on the tides.

The first decisive moment in 17th-century astronomy took place in 1610, when Galileo Galilei published a report on his use of the telescope to observe the sky. He revealed that there are craters on the Moon, Venus has phases (like the

Indigenous American visions *see* p. 196

Forecasting fire in London *see* p. 211

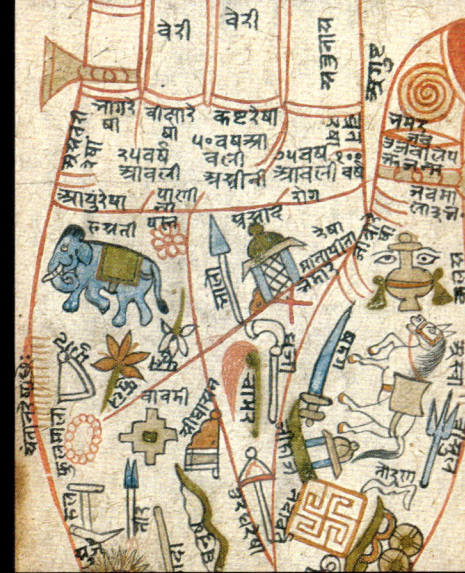

Destiny in the palm of the hand *see* p. 228

Moon, it appears to shrink and grow in size depending on its position in relation to the Sun), and Jupiter has its own moons. These observations led many people to decide that the old model of the universe that had sustained astrology – the geocentric model – no longer made sense. Then, in 1687, Isaac Newton published his *Philosophiæ Naturalis Principia Mathematica*, showing that all movement in the universe could be explained by gravity without planetary influences or consciousnesses. Both discoveries contributed significantly to astrology's loss of intellectual credibility by 1700.

For most of the 18th century, astrology survived in Europe in a popular form via annual almanacs. It thrived in a mass culture that also supported numerology and palm-reading (both of which often used astrological symbols), and among people who were not bothered about elite ideas. The 1780s saw the first attempts to republish astrology books, but it took nearly another century for astrology to find a fresh role in its alliance with theosophy – a spiritual movement that revolutionized Western society by drawing on esoteric traditions from the East, especially India, and the West.

> "The soul of the newly born baby is marked for life by the pattern of the stars at the moment it comes into the world."
>
> **JOHANNES KEPLER**, *HARMONICES MUNDI*, 1619

Mobile readings *see* p. 231

Call to arms *see* p. 243

Divining fortunes from dregs *see* p. 244

"[The Huron] think fasting renders their vision wonderfully piercing, and gives them eyes capable of seeing things absent and far removed…"

FATHER JEAN DE BRÉBEUF, FRENCH JESUIT MISSIONARY, *RELATIONS DES JÉSUITES*, 1636

Receiving visions
This painting by Métis artist Leah Marie Dorion depicts a vision quest ritual passed down to women from their grandmothers. The Métis people, who live in Canada, have both First Nations and European ancestry from the 17th-century fur trade.

Visions of power
Indigenous American vision quests

Diverse religious practices spanning Indigenous North America are referred to by the term "vision quest". Dreams and visions were (and remain) important sources of knowledge for Indigenous peoples. In the 17th and 18th centuries, European missionaries, traders, and government agents wrote about the supernatural encounters of the Indigenous peoples they came into contact with and their observations offer a rare glimpse into a world where people regularly sought help from guardian spirits. Through methods such as isolation, fasting, and prayer, people sought healing, guidance, and insights into their higher purpose in life.

Seeking spirit power
Although practices vary between nations, spirit power was widely considered to be essential for a successful life. Exceptional abilities were seen as the result of attracting guardian spirits. Children prepared early on for the rituals, learning practical skills and absorbing morality lessons taught by oral traditions. Upon reaching puberty, their vision quests began with purifying their mind, body, and spirit. Young people sought guidance from an elder, or spiritual leader, and engaged in fasting, prayer, and sweat-lodge ceremonies – in which steam purified them and opened their mind. Adolescents marked their transition to adulthood with the hope of receiving a vision about their life's purpose and a spirit helper to guide them.

Initiates isolated themselves in remote natural settings – places that were ripe with power, as they belonged to both the physical world and the spiritual realm. Without daily distractions, they prayed, fasted, and deprived themselves of sleep to heighten awareness and open themselves to power. Spirit helpers could appear in different forms: as animals (called totems), humans, weather, landforms, or even celestial bodies such as the Sun or Moon.

Different nations possessed distinct beliefs based on their unique circumstances. Among the peoples of the Great Basin, visions related to the demands of their challenging natural environment. Seeking spirit power reflected the subsistence needs of these small, egalitarian bands of foragers. On the other hand, among the resource-rich hierarchical societies of the Northwest Coast, the acquisition of spirit power was a mix of individual expression and hereditary rights. While a person's success was the result of their efforts, they also tended to have familial spirit helpers, as once a person died their guardians became available for others to acquire.

Modern challenges
US federal policies in the 19th and 20th centuries curtailed traditional beliefs by removing children from their communities, resulting in a loss of cultural knowledge. Today, Indigenous peoples continue to fight barriers to their religious expression, as reduced access to public lands and damage to the natural environment interfere with their quests for power and meaning.

Totem animal
This c. 1900 button blanket comes from the Haida people of Prince of Wales Island, Alaska. It depicts a two-headed eagle, a spirit animal indicating vision and leadership. The Haida frequently sought visions of animal spirit guides.

Blending beliefs

Divination in African syncretic religions

Adaptability – being able to incorporate new information or observances into existing beliefs and practices – is a defining characteristic of African belief systems. People in traditional African societies believe that living well means living in harmony with the family and wider community (usually including deities, spirits, and ancestors) and they welcome any new understanding of the world that can help to foster this harmony. Long before the transatlantic slave trade, Christianity and Islam (which had arrived earlier through migration and conquest) had already had a significant impact on traditional African beliefs.

The slave trade introduced a new dynamic. It took millions of Africans far from home to the Americas – a hostile environment where their

Dancing for spirits
Vodouisants gather in a *hounfour* (temple) to summon the *lwa* through music, drumming, and dance. At the temple's centre is the *potomitan*, a decorated wooden post where the *lwa* descend.

> "Whether the old man was a prophet, or the son of a prophet, I cannot say; but there is one thing certain, many of his predictions were verified."

WILLIAM WELLS BROWN, *NARRATIVE OF WILLIAM W. BROWN, AN AMERICAN SLAVE, WRITTEN BY HIMSELF*, 1849

beliefs were deemed inferior and threatening to the people holding them captive. Enslaved Africans adapted to create new ways to practise their religions, resulting in a mosaic of new syncretic religions that combined different belief systems.

African syncretic religions include Haitian Vodou and its variants – Cuban Santería, Brazilian Candomblé, Surinamese Winti, and others – which emerged from the 16th century onwards. These religions retained the fundamental cosmological and spiritual beliefs common to most African religions, while also incorporating Indigenous American practices – learned from their fellow oppressed peoples – and elements of Christianity, the religion of their captors.

Vodou guidance

Divination, the practice of consulting oracles to receive guidance from deities, spirits, ancestors, and other supernatural guides, continues to be a central practice in African syncretic religions. Divination practices include direct contact with spirits through trance or possession, contact mediated through consecrated objects, and ritual consultations.

In Haitian Vodou, which combines West and Central African, Indigenous Taíno, and Catholic beliefs, divination to communicate with the *lwa* (spirits) involves trance possession. There are thousands of *lwa*. Vodouisants (practitioners of Haitian Vodou) group them into 17 *nanchon* (pantheons), the two most important of which are the peaceful and benevolent Rada, and the forceful and dangerous Petwo. Each *lwa* has a particular song, dance, drum rhythm, and *vévé* (visual symbol) associated with it. The *lwas* of Haitian Vodou are also matched with Catholic saints, with the *lwa*'s role corresponding to the saint's spiritual power. For example, Saint Peter, who holds the keys to the kingdom of Heaven, corresponds with the *lwa* Papa Legba, the gatekeeper of the spirit world. Merging belief systems in this way enabled enslaved people to hide their beliefs in plain sight.

According to a common saying in Haiti: "The Catholic goes to church to speak about God, the Vodouisant dances… and becomes God." To summon a *lwa*, the presiding *ougan* (priest) or *mambo* (priestess) draws their *vévé* (symbol) on the ground using white cornmeal. Devotees sing, drum, and dance until the *lwa* possesses one or more of them to provide advice, prophecies, or healing. When the *lwa* possesses the devotee, it is said to have "mounted" the individual like a horse.

Calling card
This is the *vévé* of Papa Legba, the major *lwa* in Haitian and Louisiana vodou. As keeper of the crossroads between the human and spirit world, he must be invoked in all ceremonies.

Serpentine figure
Snake spirits such as Mami Wata (pictured) are important in Louisiana and New Orleans Voodoo – a variant of Haitian Vodou. Snakes are associated with Papa Legba and divination.

Spiritual presence
The Candomblé trinity of Yemaya, Oxala, and Oxum are summoned by drummers. Depicted carrying a mirror, Oxum (far right), is the *orixá* of love, water, and divination.

Powerful objects

African peoples use ritual objects such as dolls, figurines, amulets, and charms for protection and also for divination. In the American South, practitioners of Hoodoo – a syncretic religion that blends West and Central African religions with Indigenous American and European folkloric practices – are noted for making and using "conjure" or "mojo" bags and *minkisi* (statues and cloth bundles). These amulets are believed to house spirits, which can relay knowledge to their owners when "fed" with ingredients such as animal parts, herbs, and roots. Hoodoo practitioners also use bone throwing (a practice in which vertebrae, or other small bones, are scattered and their landing patterns analysed) and dream interpretation to understand and improve their fortunes.

Empowered figure
After spirits are summoned to inhabit *minkisi* figurines, the figurine is used to communicate with and channel the power and knowledge of the spirits and the ancestors.

Casting for fortunes

Among practitioners of Brazilian Candomblé and Cuban Santería (also known as Regla Ocha-Ifa, or Regla Lucumí), casting lots is a popular form of divination. These syncretic religions developed among enslaved Africans of Yoruba origin. Candomblé and Santería adherents recognize

Divination in African syncretic religions   201

Throwing shells

In Brazilian Candomblé, the divination practice of *jogo de búzios* typically uses 16 shells cut on one side. Diviners toss them on a plate and base readings on where they land and how – whether they are "open" or "closed". The shells are thought to convey spiritual messages, such as which *orixá* an adherent belongs to, which sacrifices and offerings should be made, and whether the *orixá* is pleased with the adherent's life. Non-adherents also use the practice, asking the shells everyday questions about success, health, and relationships.

This Candomblé *babalorixá*, or priest, is practising *jogo de búzios*, a form of cowrie-shell divination.

> "Divination mediates between earth (*aiye*) and heaven (*orun*). It proffers counsel and guidance to believers at all critical junctures... of the life cycle."
>
> **EUGENIO MATIBAG**, *IFÁ AND INTERPRETATION*, 1997

the Yoruba Supreme Being, Olodumare, and the *orixás* (spirits) with which each person is believed to be associated from birth. Like the Yoruba, they also use Ifá divination (see pp. 62–63) to establish which *orixá* or *orixás* a person belongs to. Adherents routinely consult an Ifá diviner to receive guidance and protection from their spirits.

The practice of casting lots in the syncretic religions echoes that of the Yoruba: priests or priestesses cast palm nuts or other objects, such as pieces of dried coconut shell, or practise cowrie shell divination – called *dilogún* in Santería or *jogo de búzios* in Brazilian Candomblé. Like the Yoruba *opele*, shells or nuts might be strung into a divining chain. After interpreting the configuration of the nuts or shells, the diviner consults the *odu*, a corpus of sacred verses that provide advice for the petitioner in time of crisis, illness, or when significant decisions need to be made. In the diasporic religions, divination is considered a spiritual diagnostic tool – comparable to physical examinations or scans in modern medicine.

Into the future

The accessories and associated oral traditions of divination practices were an important way for enslaved Africans in the Americas both to secure spiritual guidance and preserve their cultures and communities. As some Africans in the diaspora turn back to traditional practices, these divination methods continue to be used by practitioners of syncretic religions.

Trusty telescope
This 1858 fresco by Giuseppe Bertini shows Galileo (in grey) showing the doge of Venice, Leonardo Donato, how to use his telescope. Galileo demonstrated his first telescope to the doge in 1609, while teaching at the University of Padua.

Messenger of the stars
Galileo's astrological interests

Today, Italian astronomer Galileo Galilei is famous for the discoveries he made with his telescope, but in his own day, he was also known as a practising astrologer. He used both sides of the science of the stars to his professional advantage, even when his work got him into trouble with the Inquisition.

Galileo studied and then taught mathematics at the University of Pisa. In 1592, he moved to Padua, where he made the bulk of his scientific discoveries. From around 1608, he built an improved telescope, through which he was able to see craters on the Moon and four satellites orbiting Jupiter. These discoveries chipped away at the idea of a strict contrast between the terrestrial and celestial realms, because they showed that Jupiter and the Moon were much like Earth. Galileo published his findings in Sidereus nuncius ("Starry Messenger") in 1610, which he dedicated to the new grand duke of Tuscany, Cosimo II de' Medici.

Patronage and punishment
Before Galileo published Sidereus nuncius, he was struggling financially. The book changed everything, as it led Galileo directly to a place in the Medici court, a position he had been trying to gain for years. Yet it was not only Galileo's scientific success that earned him the job. The Sidereus nuncius, filled with flattery, was a strategic move in the patronage game. In the book, Galileo claimed that the timing of the discovery of Jupiter's moons, right after Cosimo's ascent to the throne, was no coincidence: they were a celestial monument to Cosimo's family.

Significantly, Galileo named Jupiter's moons after the Medici, following a long tradition among the family of connecting themselves to the planet. Galileo also echoed this with Cosimo's birth chart, in which Jupiter was prominently in the midheaven. He attributed to Cosimo several positive qualities associated with the planet, among them kindness, splendour, and power. Cosimo was charmed.

At court, Galileo's responsibilities included providing astrological advice to the Medici family. This was a role he was well equipped for, having long worked as an astrologer, casting and interpreting horoscopes for his family, patrons, students, and others. Practising astrology was not without peril, however: in 1604, he had narrowly escaped charges by the Inquisition after a neighbour accused him of making deterministic predictions. The neighbour alleged that Galileo was telling clients that his forecasts were certain – something banned by the Church.

A decade later, Galileo was less fortunate. As court astrologer, he no longer had to conform to the strict disciplinary separation between astronomy and philosophy. This enabled him to advocate more effectively for Copernicanism (see pp. 180–81) as reality rather than mere theory. However, Galileo took this too far by reinterpreting scripture to fit heliocentrism, a task that was reserved for theologians. Around 1615, he was called before the Inquisition, and was later convicted of heresy and put under house arrest. The Medici family withdrew their support.

Medici influence
This medallion commemorates the four Sidera Medicea ("Medicean stars") – Galileo's name for the moons of Jupiter – and Cosimo II. It was produced by goldsmith Gasparo Mola in around 1610.

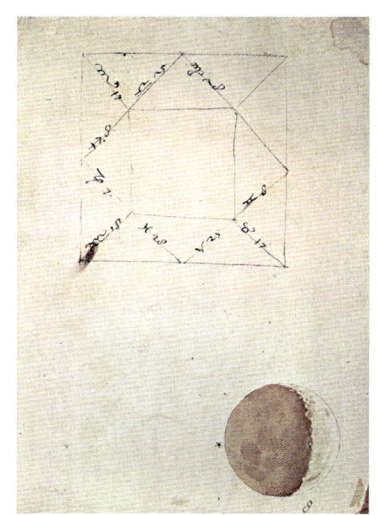

Astronomy and astrology
On this page, Galileo sketched the waxing Moon, seen through his telescope on 19 January 1609, as well as a first draft of his nativity for Cosimo II.

Discord and harmony
Explaining astrology

Fifty years after the death of Copernicus, another great mathematician, German-born Johannes Kepler, entered the astronomical scene. Kepler's interests in the heavens began as a six-year-old child when, with the help of his mother, he observed the Great Comet of 1577, followed by a lunar eclipse when he was nine. His education in Tübingen, Germany, also proved formative: it was here that he became a Copernican, promoting the idea of a heliocentric universe (see pp. 180–81), and began casting horoscopes.

After completing his studies, Kepler taught mathematics at Graz, in present-day Austria. One of his duties was to produce almanacs. The first of these, for the year 1595, was uncannily accurate in its prediction of a bitter winter, Turkish invasion, and peasant uprising. Kepler later forecast a fierce

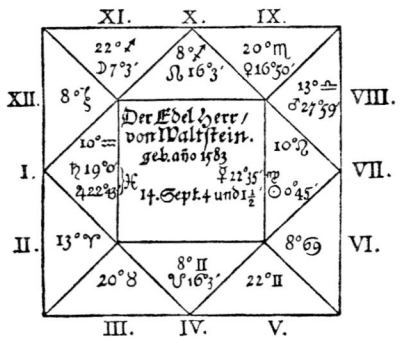

Forecasting difficulty
Kepler cast this horoscope for Albrecht von Wallenstein in 1608, foreseeing "difficult times" in March 1634. The general allegedly could not defend himself when he was assassinated in February that year.

thunderstorm, which arrived just at the time he had predicted it would. Such successes boosted his reputation, but Kepler was always clear that the complexity of causation meant that not all prognostications were certain.

Kepler tried to overcome some of the uncertainty with regards to weather prediction by systematically recording the weather in Graz alongside planetary configurations. After many years of observations, he noticed that bad weather seemed to correlate with certain planetary conjunctions. He kept these patterns in mind when making his forecasts.

As imperial mathematician, or "Imperial Mathematicus", a role in which he succeeded Tycho Brahe, Kepler advised the emperor, but was largely given free rein in his astronomical and astrological research. He only resumed making almanacs from 1617, apparently for financial reasons. Like many astronomers, Kepler supplemented his meagre income by practising astrology privately. During his lifetime, he cast horoscopes for at least 800 individuals. When interpreting nativities, Kepler believed it was important to be aware that the individual's free will was an unknown quantity. The same was true of the free will of the people in their life. Astrology, in other words, was a very uncertain art.

Kepler's supernova
In 1604, just a few decades after Tycho noticed his *nova stella* (see pp. 182–83), another supernova appeared. This one was so bright that it could even be seen with the naked eye during the day.

Rudolphine Tables

When Tycho Brahe died in 1601, he was in the midst of computing new planetary tables for Rudolph II. Kepler, Tycho's assistant at the time, was tasked with finishing the job, but lengthy legal disputes over access to Tycho's data and Kepler's financial hardship delayed his endeavours.

The work was tedious but Kepler finally published the tables in 1627. Not only were they the most accurate tables produced, but they allowed astronomers to calculate planetary positions far into the future.

The frontispiece to the *Rudolphine Tables* depicts astronomy's progress in Kepler's temple of Urania.

Kepler's observations of the star led to the publication of his *De Stella Nova* (1606), in which he reminded his readers that the heavens were not unchanging.

Having first seen the star while he was observing a conjunction of Mars, Jupiter, and Saturn, Kepler came to believe that its emergence at this time was significant. A conjunction of Saturn and Jupiter is fairly common, occurring roughly every 20 years. Far rarer are the moments when, after meeting in the same triplicity (group of three zodiac signs) for about 240 years, the planets begin to meet in a new triplicity. This is what happened in 1604, when Saturn and Jupiter left the water triplicity (Cancer, Scorpio, and Pisces) and moved to the fire triplicity (Aries, Leo, and Sagittarius). Such conjunctions had traditionally been linked with momentous transformations in society, including the birth of Christ. But although Kepler argued that the supernova was similar to the star the Magi had followed to find Jesus (see pp. 96–97), he was not willing to make specific predictions based on the new star.

A rising star
This star map from Kepler's *De Stella Nova* depicts the new star in the constellation Serpentarius (now Ophiuchus). The star N (*Nova*) can be seen on Serpentarius's right ankle, near the conjunction.

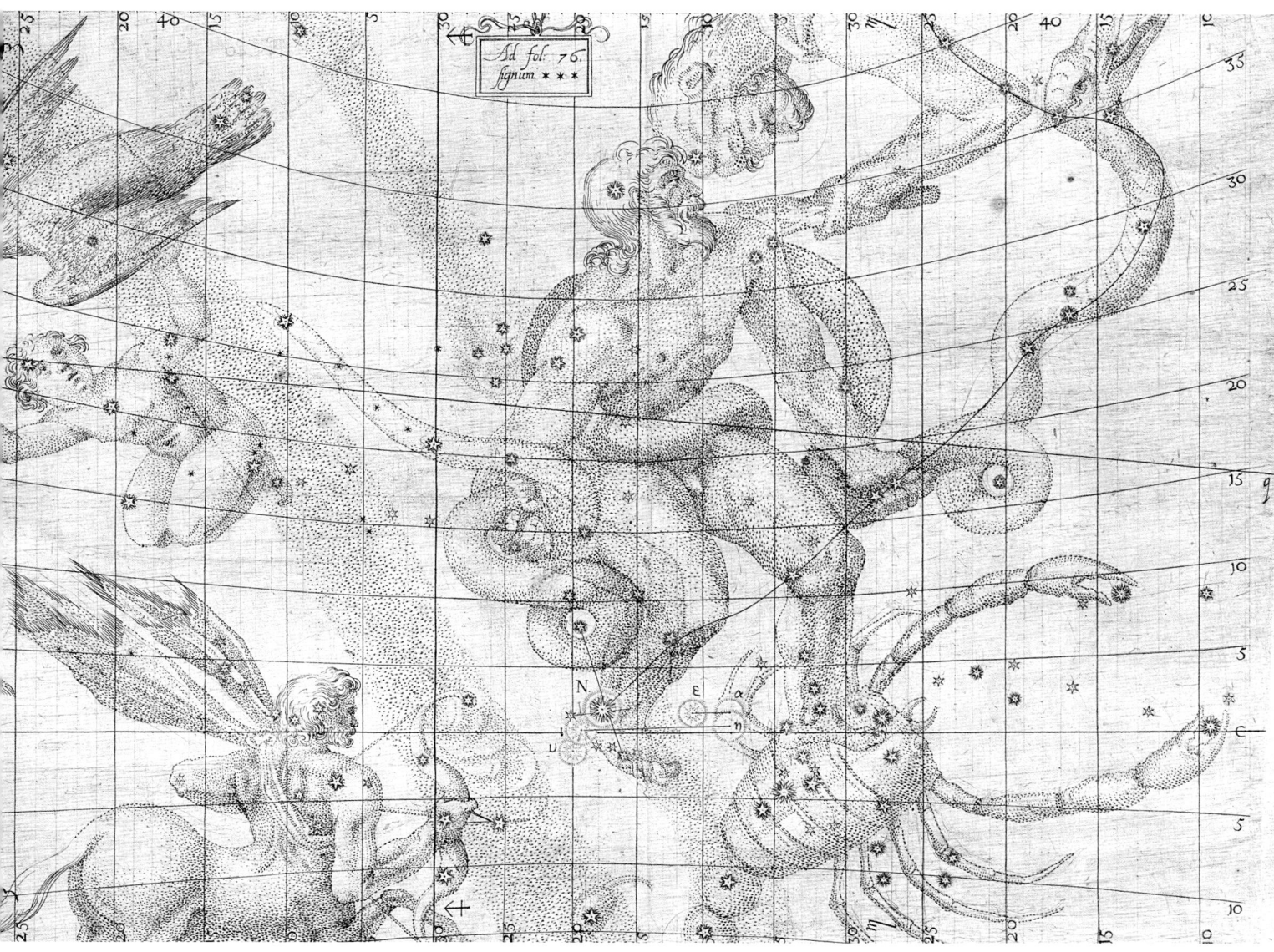

Cosmic knowledge
This depiction of a 17th-century gallery includes astronomical paraphernalia such as an armillary sphere, an astrolabe, a celestial globe, books, and a diagram of the Ptolemaic, Copernican, and Tychonic systems.

Kepler's attitude towards astrology was complicated. On the one hand, he dedicated much of his life to practising and improving it. On the other, he did not hold back on his critiques. In the 17th century, this was becoming increasingly common. For centuries, astrology had been subject to attacks by mathematicians, astronomers, and theologians. This led many to reject it, even if they continued to believe in the underlying theory of celestial influence. Kepler was one of several astronomers who chose to reform astrology, likening his work to Martin Luther's reformation of the Church.

During his life, Kepler's observations made him dissatisfied with traditional zodiacal astrology. He thought that the division of the ecliptic into 12 equal sections was arbitrary, as were the houses

of the horoscope. This view was similar to that expressed by Pico della Mirandola in his *Disputationes adversus astrologiam divinatricem* ("Disputations against Divinatory Astrology") of 1496. However, while Pico had rejected planetary aspects, Kepler believed these were the fundamental way in which the planets influenced life on Earth. According to Kepler, it was just the planets, not the stars, that emitted influence, and he was also convinced that the planets embodied warm–cold and dry–moist qualities.

Harmony of the spheres

Kepler's critical approach to astrology stemmed in part from his Copernicanism. One thing that heliocentrism changed for astrology was the number of planets, as the Moon was now a satellite rather than a planet. Why then, Kepler asked, did God create just six planets? His answer drew on his philosophical convictions about the links between astronomy, astrology, music, and theology. God was a geometer, he argued, and so the basis of the universe was geometrical. Kepler showed that the five Platonic solids (geometrical shapes), when nested within each other, produced layers that corresponded to the orbits of the six planets – but only if they were in the order established by Copernicus.

Music, traditionally one of the mathematical arts, was key to Kepler's theories. Following Pythagorean ideas about the harmony of the spheres (whereby celestial motion creates music), Kepler saw the planets as partaking in a kind of cosmic symphony. Raising the number of aspects (see p. 82) to 12, he found relationships between them and musical consonances (pleasing harmonies). Astrology, he said, was "silent music", as Earth's soul danced to the tune of the planetary aspects.

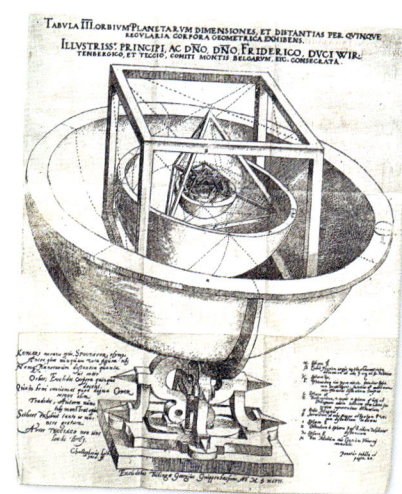

Platonic nest
Kepler's *Mysterium Cosmographicum* (1596) described a system of cosmic harmony, whereby the five Platonic solids were the geometrical basis of the universe.

"The human being… has such an affinity with the heavens… and this has been tested and proven in many ways, of which each is a noble pearl of astrology…"

JOHANNES KEPLER, THESIS 64, *TERTIUS INTERVENIENS*, 1610

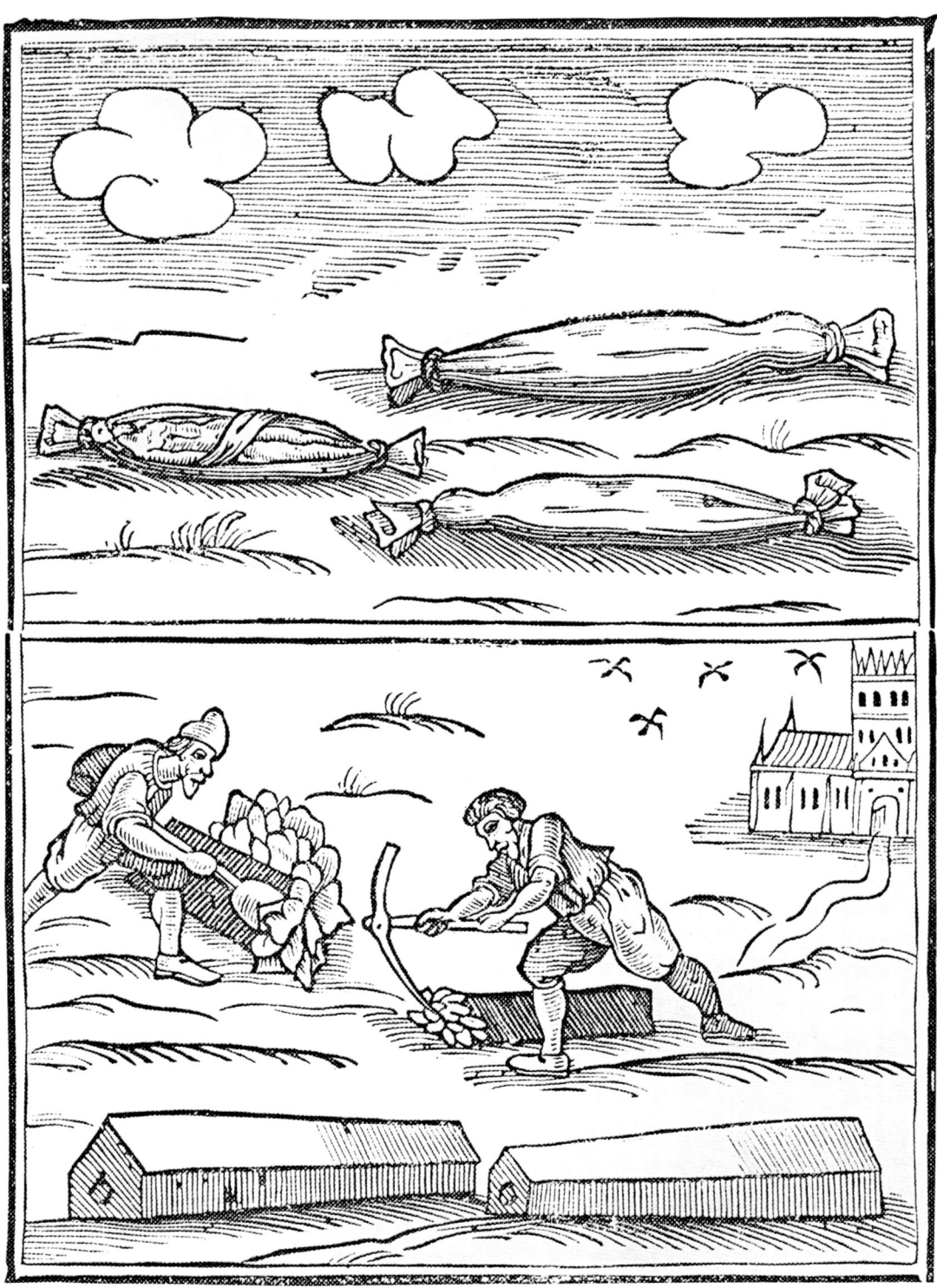

Plague and pestilence
William Lilly's readers interpreted this woodprint of corpses as a correct prediction of the Great Plague. Lilly moved out of London while the plague raged, but continued to cast horoscopes for wealthy clients with health concerns.

Answers for everything
Prophecy and horary astrology

In 17th-century England, astrologers were often seen as doomsayers, who always seemed to be predicting plagues and epidemics. But astrologers saw their public-health predictions as useful warnings for their town or city. London astrologer Richard Edlyn became famous when his prediction of "an approaching Plague, and that a very great one" in the city in 1665 came true. He had forecast the plague based on a great conjunction of Saturn and Jupiter, but the appearance of two comets in 1664 made his prophecy all the more compelling, and famous astrologers such as William Lilly (see p. 211) publicly endorsed it.

The prediction of plagues and large-scale misfortunes was part of general or judicial astrology, the type used in almanacs (see pp. 176–79). But early modern astrologers used all four traditional branches of astrology, each of which required a different kind of horoscope. Nativities (natal astrology), cast for the moment of birth, charted a person's destiny and characteristics. Elections (electional astrology) involved casting a horoscope for a specific moment in time to test whether that moment was good or bad for a particular action (such as a coronation; see pp. 186–89). Horary astrology was based on the idea that a horoscope cast at the moment at which a question was asked could help an astrologer to answer that question.

Seeking answers
Horary astrology was the type most used by English astrologer Simon Forman and his apprentice Richard Napier, who together left behind one of the biggest collections of case records in history. Their notes document the questions that troubled men and women in the decades around 1600. Many sought guidance in their personal lives, asking the astrologers, for example, whether they should stay in the city or move to the country, or if a person would make a good wife or husband. Some consulted them for business advice, while others wanted to know if their bad fortune was the result of being bewitched. Most people wanted to know about their health. In 1627, a man asked Napier for help with his "unsavoury breath". In 1632, a mother was concerned that she could not produce enough milk for her infant. Many years earlier, a 27-year-old called Joan Band asked Forman if she was pregnant. Forman cast a horoscope, and the positions of the planets, especially Venus, led him to believe that "she will be with child shortly". As it turned out, Joan was indeed already pregnant.

Digestive trouble
In May 1559, William Colles consulted Richard Napier about his gassy digestive system, after his physicians failed to help. He did not return: was he healed or did Napier also disappoint?

War effort
During the English Civil War (1642–51), almanacs became effective propaganda for both sides of the political divide. Many astrologers became famous for publicly supporting the Parliamentarian cause. But when Charles II regained the throne, they were accused of dangerous "radicalism". This was the case even for openly Royalist astrologers like John Heydon, who was imprisoned in 1667 for examining the new king's nativity.

Celebrity astrologer William Lilly publicly promoted the Parliamentarian cause in his 1645 pamphlet *The Starry Messenger*.

Destroyed by fire

In 1648, astrologer William Lilly predicted that London would soon be consumed by "sundry fires". A few years later, he illustrated his book *Monarchy or No Monarchy* (1651) with pictures showing the city on fire, along with other coded images, or "hieroglyphics", the meanings of which were designed to be understood by the wise but concealed from the "vulgar". When the Great Fire of London erupted in 1666, many took this as a successful prediction. However, it also led sceptics to believe that Lilly had started the fire to boost his reputation as a successful forecaster. He was arrested and questioned by a parliamentary committee. After defending himself by saying that God was the ultimate cause of the fire, he was acquitted.

Lilly was not the only astrologer to forecast 1666 as a bad year. According to the Book of Revelation, three sixes carry apocalyptic meaning, and this had led astrologers such as Nostradamus to muse on what might happen 100 years before the event. As Samuel Pepys recalled in his diary, in early 1667, Londoners were quite taken with the apparent success of such predictions.

> "…it will be ominous to London, unto her merchants at sea, to her traffique on land, to her poor, to all sorts of people… by reason of sundry fires and a consuming plague."
>
> **WILLIAM LILLY**, *ASTROLOGICALL PREDICTIONS FOR 1648*

This woodcut from *Monarchy or No Monarchy* conveyed Lilly's prediction that "sundry fires" would consume the city of London.

Integrating ideas
Japanese innovation

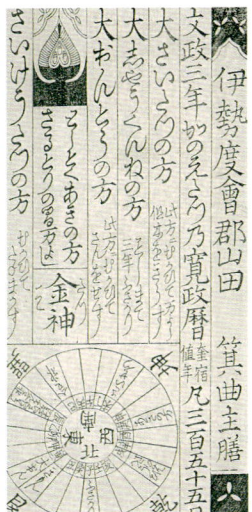

Jōkyō calendar
This 1729 printed calendar shows the more accurate lunisolar system developed by Shibukawa Harumi, using astronomical observations. Harumi's empirical approach led to the reformation of Japanese divination.

Divination in Japan had played a major role in government since at least the 6th century CE, when onmyōdō – a divinatory practice using astrology and calendars to discern which days were fortunate and to help guide decisions – was introduced from China (see pp. 120–21), along with the traditional Chinese calendar. From the mid-17th century, the flow of foreign ideas and practices into Japan was severely restricted by the isolationist policies of the Japanese government during the Sakoku period (1633–1853). Even so, some developments in astronomical science filtered into the country and these, combined with Japanese innovations, influenced how divination was performed.

The traditional Chinese calendar used by the Japanese court was reformed in the 17th century, after astronomer Shibukawa Harumi spotted inaccuracies in the astronomical data that made it impossible to predict eclipses correctly. In the 1670s, Harumi proposed a new calendar that drew on information from the Chinese book *Tianjing huowen* ("Queries on the Classics of Heaven"), which included ideas developed by European astronomers. His Jōkyō calendar was officially adopted in 1685, and Harumi became Japan's first court astronomer. His work marked a move towards the use of accurate observation in Japanese astrology and divination, rather than tradition.

Divination for the masses
Confucian scholar Nishikawa Joken also recognized the value of empirical scientific observation. In the early 18th century, he studied Chinese translations of European astronomical and astrological works and syncretized European science-based models with Japanese and Chinese cosmology. Instead of comets being a message from the divine – as was traditionally believed in Japan – he suggested that they were natural and explicable phenomena created by the flow of qi, the vital forces of the universe (see pp. 34–35).

Jesuit influence

A Catholic order of priests, the Jesuits were heavily involved in education and evangelization in Asia in the 1600s. Though banned from Japan, they were active in China, and brought European ideas with them. Some Jesuits, such as Ferdinand Verbiest, worked with the Chinese imperial court on matters of astronomy and the calendar, and court scholars incorporated European teachings into their work. These Chinese volumes were, in turn, read by Japanese thinkers. Verbiest built astronomical instruments for China's imperial observatory, and these were soon replicated across Asia.

Ferdinand Verbiest was commissioned by China's emperor to make European-style tools for the imperial observatory.

Japanese innovation

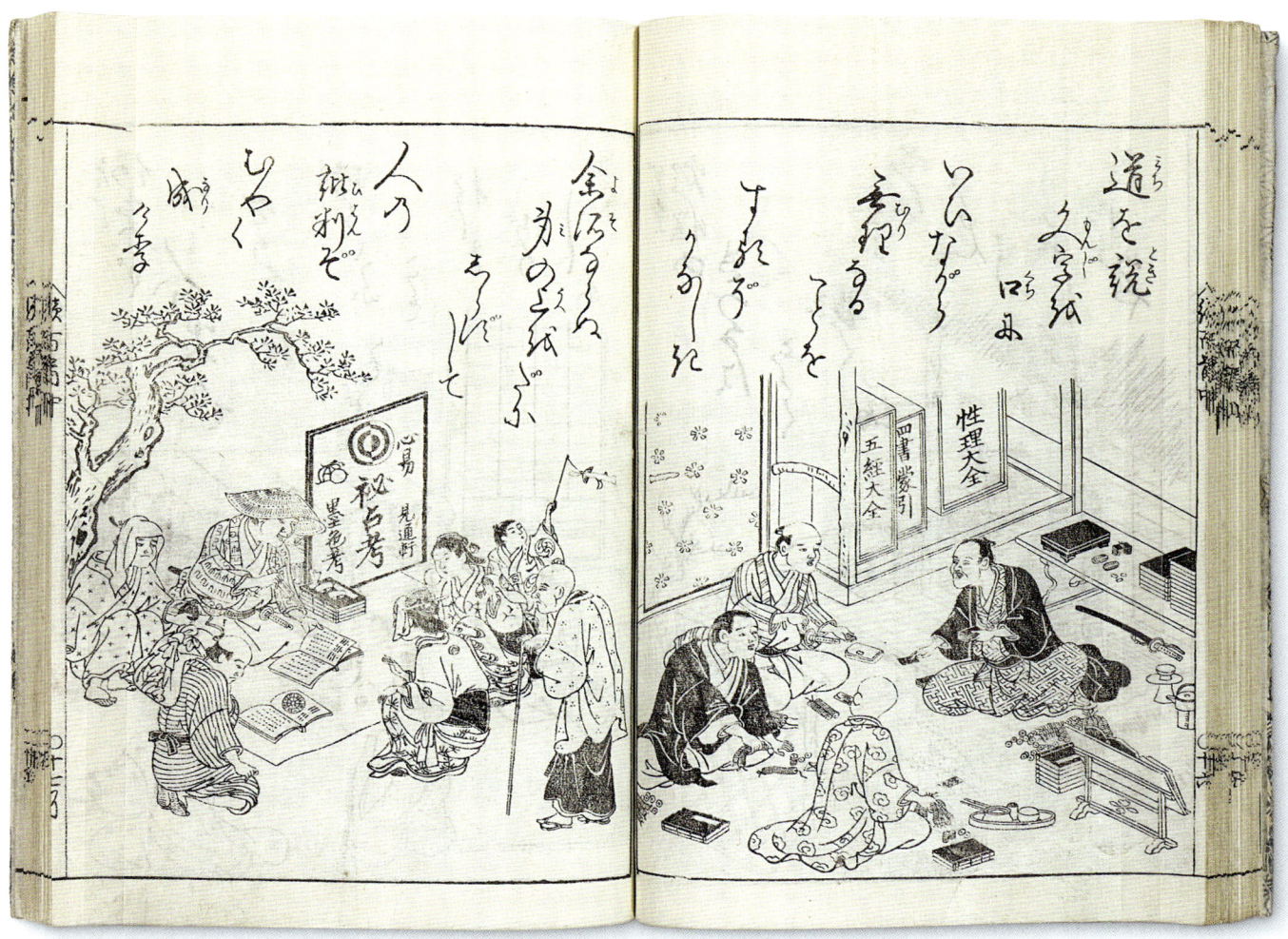

Divination was still largely the prerogative of court officials in the early 18th century, but the scholar Baba Nobutake began writing books that would bring the practice to the masses. His works drew on the Chinese *I Ching* (see pp. 20–23), but his translation of the hexagram meanings allowed for more certain answers than its Chinese precursor.

Nobutake also adapted the *I Ching* so that coins could be used instead of yarrow stalks, making it more practical as an everyday divinatory tool. Japan may have been isolated, but its intellectuals had access to enough foreign material to be able to create new, hybrid forms of knowledge, while maintaining a distinct Japanese cultural identity.

Diviner with books
This 1729 Japanese illustration shows (left) a diviner consulting his book of trigrams, symbols used in the *I Ching*, to offer advice and answers to questions.

"Learn the auspicious and the inauspicious from the sounds he hears, know the good and bad by looking at forms, and tell what is fortunate or unfortunate by carefully reflecting the principle."

BABA NOBUTAKE, *JURUI SANKŌ BAIKA SHIN'EKI SHŌCHU SHINAN*, 1697

Hawaiian *kahuna*
This drawing of a Hawaiian priest holding a divination tool is from *Encyclopédie des Voyages* (1792). While the book's illustrations provided a visual record of diverse cultures, the depictions reinforced stereotypical ideas of Polynesian peoples.

Guidance from the gods
Polynesian diviner priests

For the Polynesian peoples who lived on the islands of the Pacific Ocean in the 18th century, diviner priests played a crucial role in society. These priests – known as *kahuna* in Hawaii and *tahu'a* in Tahiti, meaning "one who sees" – provided the link between the spiritual and physical worlds. They conducted religious rituals, communicated with the gods, and performed divination to guide leaders and communities during times of conflict and exploration.

Divination in warfare

Before launching military campaigns, Hawaiian leaders would consult the *kahuna* to determine the right time to advance. Natural phenomena such as cloud formations, rainbows, lightning, bird behaviour, and celestial events – eclipses and the alignment of stars and planets, for example – would be observed and interpreted by the *kahuna* in order to discern an auspicious moment.

To ensure success in battle, the *kahuna* would perform rituals. These were likely to include offerings and prayers at *heiau* (sacred temples) to invoke the war god Kū. One Hawaiian legend suggests that it was a *kahuna* named Kapoukahi who advised Kamehameha I to build a sacrificial temple to secure divine favour in his wars of conquest. It was believed that the sacrifices made there, including animal and human offerings, were essential to Kamehameha's success in uniting the Hawaiian islands. In another story, Kamehameha's victories were attributed to playing the board game *konane* with his *kahuna*. The game – where stones were laid out on a chequerboard – was one of strategy, and the *kahuna* used it to plan out army movements, teach the patterns of constellations, and divine the future by scattering the stones and interpreting how they fell on the board.

Much like the *kahuna*, the *tahu'a* of Tahiti would perform rituals, make offerings, and read omens to ensure that the gods, particularly Oro (the god of war and fertility), were on their side. Oro was a

central deity in Tahitian religion, and the *tahu'a* would invoke his power through rituals and sacrifices, often carried out at *marae* (sacred sites).

While some priests specialized in warfare, others played key roles in navigation. Polynesians were exceptional navigators, and their voyages across the vast Pacific Ocean were feats of tremendous skill and knowledge. Those who specialized in navigation believed that the stars were a map provided by the gods, guiding them safely across the water.

Seafaring people
This engraving from 1784 shows a double canoe carrying Hawaiian warriors, one of whom is holding a carved idol, probably Kū, god of war, farming, and politics. Attacks were planned by diviner priests, whose astronomical knowledge was also used to navigate at sea.

Star compass

Polynesians successfully navigated the long distances between the scattered islands of the Pacific Ocean using a star compass – a mental construct based on the position of the Sun and stars as they rose and set on the eastern and western horizons.

The compass divides the full horizon into four houses – *akau* (north), *hikina* (east), *hema* (south), and *komohana* (west) – each with eight sections. Navigators would align the compass with a set point, such as the rising Sun, in order to stay on track.

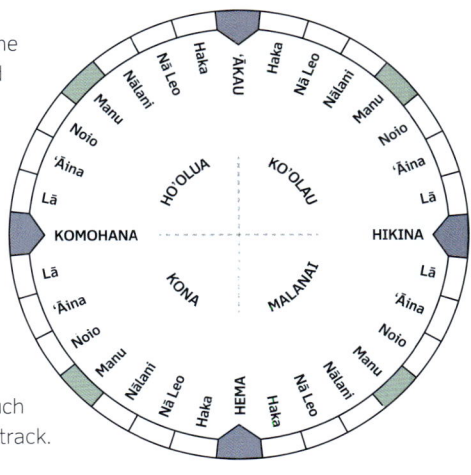

New beginnings
Indigenous African astrology

For many African societies, the vast dome of the sky is home to a Supreme Creator Being. It also houses powerful cosmic forces such as the Sun, Moon, and stars, the actions of which affect life on Earth. African cultures have long used their observations of the skies to inform their beliefs and ritual practices, and to chart the seasons for their agricultural and ritual calendars. These astrological traditions have been passed down orally from generation to generation, in folktales, songs, incantations, proverbs, and riddles, and have also been preserved in rituals and art.

Sun and Moon

The most powerful of celestial beings are the Sun and the Moon. Many southern African peoples traditionally divide their year according to when the Sun moves from its summer to its winter "house" (at the winter solstice) and back again (at the summer solstice). In some cultures, these beings are considered to be gods. To the Batammaliba people of Togo, Kuiye (the Sun) is the Supreme Being, referred to as Father and Mother of the people, and the architect of cosmic order. All aspects of Batammaliba life are orientated around Kuiye. Houses are built in alignment with Kuiye's daily course, with a hole in the roof to let Kuiye in as the Sun reaches its zenith. Entrances face west (towards Kuiye's home) so that the rays of sunset bathe the ancestral shrines positioned in their path, allowing Kuiye, it is believed, to talk to the departed ancestors.

By contrast, the Moon reigns supreme for the Sandawe people of Tanzania, who associate it with agricultural cycles and women's menstrual cycles, both essential for life. They believe that the Moon's phases determine the sex of newborn children – according to a Sandawe saying, "the Moon chooses the people". An "infant" (waxing) Moon points to the birth of a girl, while the full Moon (and its subsequent waning) is associated with boys. For the Sandawe, the gentle light of the Moon provides hope – as opposed to the dreaded heat of the Sun, which they associate with death.

Other African traditions also attribute positive characteristics to the Moon. The Luba people of the Democratic Republic of Congo associate the Moon's white light with heightened awareness and enlightenment; they therefore consider white to be a sacred colour. Meanwhile, to the Ngas of Nigeria, Tar (the Moon) is empowered by Mat Nen (the creator) as timekeeper and life-giver. The Ngas keep a lunar calendar and, at the end of every year, young men called *jep tar mwa* ("sons of the Moon"), painted in white, ritually shoot the old Moon to usher in the new one.

The Moon is generally depicted as feminine in African societies, but there are some exceptions. To the Wahungwe people of Zimbabwe, humanity is born of the male Moon, Mwedzi, and his second wife, Morongo (Venus, the Evening Star).

Holding up the heavens
This stool from the Dogon people of Mali depicts the cosmos – said to consist of two disks forming the sky and Earth. The supporting figures are founding ancestors who descended to Earth from the sky.

"In planting season we begin to watch the Moon closely, just as we watch the months before giving birth to the child. Without the Moon, there would be no life."

NGAS BARD JOHN A. KWASHI, 1974

Indigenous African astrology 217

Star, considered a "child of the sky" by the Akan

Crescent Moon, a feminine symbol for the Akan

Steady ruler
The juxtaposition of the star and crescent Moon on this 20th-century West African Akan chief's crown refers to the king's steadfastness: as a star, he is constant, unlike the ever-changing Moon.

Symbols made of wood with gold leaf

218 Changing fortunes

Key

1 In Namaqua folklore, the Pleiades are daughters of the sky god.

2 Aldebaran is the husband of the Pleiades.

3 Orion's Belt is three zebras; Orion's Sword is an arrow that missed them.

4 Betelgeuse is a lion watching the zebras.

5 The Southern Cross and its pointer stars are giraffes.

6 In southern Africa, the Pleiades are known as the digging stars.

7 In Tswana folklore, the Sun is eaten each night by a crocodile.

8 In Khoisan folklore, the Milky Way represents ashes thrown up by an upset girl.

9 In Sotho folklore, Canopus is Naka, the Horn.

Southern starlore
The vivid illustrations on this poster by South African artist Braam Botha depict star-related folklore from different southern African peoples. It was created in 1998 for South Africa's first Year of Science and Technology (YEAST).

As in many other astrological traditions, eclipses hold special significance for some African peoples. Solar and lunar eclipses have ominous meanings for the Zulu of southern Africa and Temne of Sierra Leone, while the Batammaliba believe that eclipses are a fight between the Sun and the Moon.

Following the stars

From the singular brilliance of Sirius, Canopus, and Polaris to the sprinkle of the Pleiades, stars have inspired rich folkloric beliefs on the African continent. In Mali, Dogon accounts feature Sigi Tolo or Sirius, the brightest star in the sky. In southern Africa, the appearance of Canopus, the second-brightest star, traditionally indicates the start of winter, the season for ants' eggs (food to some people), and the time to start breeding sheep. Among the Sotho people, anyone who first sights Canopus is rewarded with a cow. For the Venda and other nearby southern African peoples, the pointer stars and the Southern Cross are *dithutlwa* (giraffes), whose heads rise above the trees of October evening horizons to remind people to finish planting. Meanwhile, the |Xam hunter-gatherers consider these stars to be lions.

The Pleiades constellation is known by various names – as Kirimia to the Nyaturu of Tanzania, for example – but they all allude to the digging that starts off a new planting season. Among the Xhosa, the Pleiades (or isiLimela) also determine when certain male adulthood rites are held. Historical contact with Islam has influenced Indigenous beliefs about celestial bodies, especially in northern and western parts of Africa. The Barma of Chad believe that the Pleiades constellation (known as Nangkindjage) is the place where their Supreme Being created the first man and woman, who, in turn, gave birth to the 12 constellations of the zodiac.

The calendar

In many traditional African communities, ritual and agricultural calendars are based on a 13-month celestial cycle. In this system, each month begins or ends with the new Moon and years are calculated by observing constellations such as the Pleiades. It reflects the influence of lunar-based Islamic ritual calendars on Indigenous practices. As well as being important to agriculture and rituals, lunar cycles also traditionally guide daily life. The Chagga of Tanzania, for example, link the activities of each day of the week to the phases of the Moon, and associate the day and time of birth (and therefore the lunar phase) to a person's personality and fortune in life.

While modern astronomy and astrology have inevitably influenced Indigenous African beliefs, some traditions prevail. The Moon, for instance, with its predictable phases, still informs the timing of work, rituals, and social activities in many cultures.

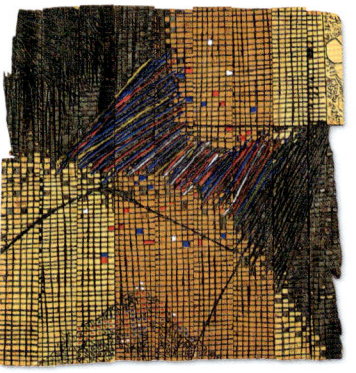

Mapping a relationship
The dots, lines, and colours of Ghanaian sculptor El Anatsui's *Earth Moon Connections* depict the movements of the lunar phases over the land and the connection to important seasonal calendars.

Cosmic power symbols

The British authorities who arrested and exiled Asante king Agyeman Prempeh (r. 1888–1931) may have missed the symbolism in the *adinkra* cloth he wore to meet them. The symbols decorating the cloth included stars, referring to the king's reliability; ram's horns, symbolizing leadership, strength, and humility; a Dono drum, played at royal processions to communicate authority; and both a castle and a wind house, emblems of the strength and resilience of the Asante nation. Altogether, they communicated the king's belief in his people's ability to endure and triumph.

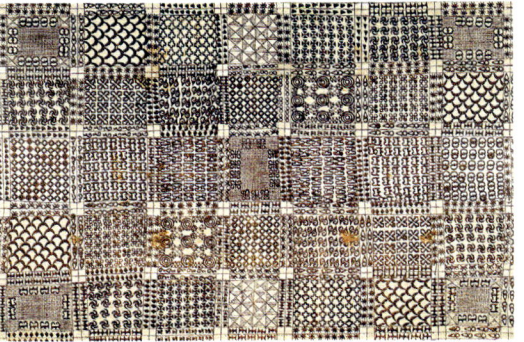

The *adinkra* cloth worn by the Asante king was adorned with clusters of crescent moons, stars, and terrestrial motifs.

Tied to fate

Knot divination

Knots are one of humanity's oldest tools, used to bind things together, and they have acquired a rich symbolism over millennia. The various meanings attributed to knots have given them a role in magical practice, religion, and divination in cultures around the world.

For the ancient Greeks, knots had both mystical and divinatory power. Greek writers told of the Gordian knot – an impenetrable knot that tied a holy chariot in place. According to a prophecy, the person who could untie it would rule all of Asia. Though many tried, they all failed, until Alexander the Great simply sliced the knot in half with his sword. Unbreakable knots also featured in Celtic art, where knot motifs were used as symbols both to ward off evil and represent the interwoven nature of the past, present, and future.

Knots were still being used in divination in early modern Europe, and in magic, as a way of trapping evil spirits. In the 17th century, British women tied their garters to their bedpost with nine knots to cause them to dream about who they would eventually marry, while tying multiple knots in a man's laces was said to have the power to remove his virility.

Nautical knots

Among the inhabitants of the Caroline Islands, in the Pacific Ocean, the use of knots in divination remains prevalent. The islanders have a long history of seafaring, with the skills to navigate their canoes between widely spread islands. One of the methods they use to ensure successful journeys involves the ritual tying of knots to predict the outcome of a voyage. Knot divination takes different names in the different dialects of the islands: it is often called *bwe*, but is also known as *ei* or *vei*, *be*, *bweng*, *bwä*, or *pue*. Europeans first recorded the practice in the 18th century, but various myths from the Carolines describing how the gods taught the method to humans suggest that it is much older.

Interpreting omens

Bwe varies from island to island, but it universally seems to involve a diviner harvesting fronds from a coconut tree and tying knots at random along them. Accounts of the practice from the island of Yap say that the frond is then placed between each of the fingers and thumb on the left hand, so the series of knots is showing. The diviner observes the number of knots on each frond by counting from one to four repeatedly; whichever number he ends his count on gives the answer for that frond. The process is repeated with each string of knots. Once counted, the diviner can interpret the combination of numbers generated. Each combination relates to a spirit said to paddle the "canoe of destiny"; some are lucky and some unlucky.

Every canoe house on the Caroline Islands has a coconut tree to provide material for *bwe*. Skilled diviners can use knots to predict the weather travellers will face, where the best fish can be found, and the correct direction of travel, as well as whether voyagers will return at all. Should the omens revealed be bad, a journey might be put on hold until a more propitious reading occurs. On the atolls of Woleai and Lamotrek, diviners also use *bwe* to identify malevolent spirits, called *yalius*, that are thought to be causing medical ailments.

Woven into fate
Ancient mosaics were often patterned with images of the Gordian knot (as seen on this 4th-century CE Roman mosaic panel from Syria), or other knotted designs, which represented the woven strands of fate that controlled human life.

Travel companion
This 19th-century *osonifei*, or effigy, from Onoun (Ulul) Island represents one of the spirits that guide travellers' journeys. It is decorated with woven and knotted coconut fibres.

"Do not be afraid; we are neither spirits nor men, we are destinies…"

THE GOD SUPUNEMEN, NAMOLUK MYTH DESCRIBING HOW HUMANS LEARNED *BWE*

Canoe community
This 19th-century European lithograph depicts a canoe house on the Caroline Islands. Used to store canoes and hold meetings, these special houses were built next to sacred coconut trees, the fronds of which were used in knot divination.

Revelations and ecstasies

Millenarianism and prophecy

Historians have observed that political upheavals, civil chaos, and social injustice often give rise to the emergence of millenarianism – religious movements proclaiming the imminent return of Christ and the establishment of a new Kingdom of God on Earth for a millennium. The persecution of religious minorities and dissidents following the Reformation in Europe provided fertile ground for such movements in the 17th and 18th centuries. Protestant beliefs emphasized personal faith and direct communication with God, intensifying the millenarian aspirations of the persecuted groups, and a number of "prophets" emerged. These self-proclaimed prophets were often labelled "enthusiasts" by mainstream clergy, a derogatory term describing religious fanatics and those claiming superior knowledge.

Huguenot refugees

Millenarianism took a dramatic turn in England when, in 1706, three French prophets – Durand Fage, Elie Marion, and Jean Cavalier – fled to England. They were members of the Camisards, a small denomination of the Protestant Huguenots who had revolted against brutal repression under King Louis XIV. Following their uprising in the Cévennes region of southern France, they sought refuge in London and an audience for their millenarian visions. On arrival in the city, the three men began delivering their prophetic predictions in ecstatic trances to fellow Huguenot exiles. However, as their movement gained momentum, their English followers – primarily Noncomformists such as Quakers and Baptists – soon outnumbered the French.

Prophetic hero
Jean Cavalier is the central figure in this painting by Pierre-Antoine Labouchère, 1864. Cavalier was one of the three Camisard prophets who arrived in England in 1706.

The prophets claimed to be possessed by the Holy Spirit and exhibited various signs of this possession during their ecstatic trances. These included intense convulsions, foaming at the mouth, swelling bellies, and speaking in tongues. The Spirit also allegedly bestowed upon them spiritual abilities, such as foretelling the future and performing miraculous cures (thaumaturgy).

Unfulfilled prophecies

Although the Camisard prophets invited audiences (usually in private meetings) to witness their ecstatic displays and claimed miracles, it was their circulation of printed books that disseminated their millenarian prophecies to a wider public. The spread of these prophecies aroused the suspicions of religious and secular authorities, who regarded the movement as a threat to social order. This culminated in the trial of Elie Marion and his condemnation to the pillory in November 1707.

The movement faced another setback when Thomas Emes, a prophet expected to serve in Christ's kingdom, suddenly died. In May 1708, prophet John Lacy attempted to resurrect Emes before a crowd of 20,000 at Bunhill Fields burial ground. His failure, together with numerous other unfulfilled prophecies by the group, led to the decline of the movement by the mid-18th century.

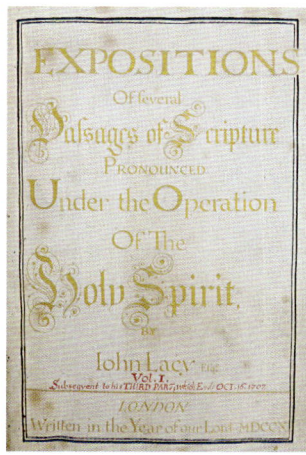

Printed pronouncements
English prophet John Lacy published *Expositions Of Several Passages of Scripture Pronounced Under the Operation Of The Holy Spirit* in c.1707–20, an example of printed material bringing prophecies to a wider public.

Scandalous and seditious
This contemporary news illustration shows Camisard prophet Elie Marion and his gentleman "scribes", Jean Daudé and Fatio de Duillier, who were all sentenced to stand in the pillory for two days for publishing false and blasphemous prophecies.

Cards containing secrets
The origins of tarot

Invented in China, playing cards reached Europe in the 1370s via the Mamluk Empire (an Islamic sultanate comprising modern Egypt, Türkiye, and Syria). Mamluk cards had four suits – cups, swords, coins, and polo sticks – each with ten pip (number) cards and three court cards consisting of a king and two deputies. The court cards were patterned, with the rank of the person given in letters. European decks added a queen to the court cards and illustrated each character.

In the 15th century, cards were commonly used for trick-taking games, in which one of the four suits functioned as a trump suit. By the 1440s, a fifth suit of trump cards (*carte da trionfi*), decorated with allegorical illustrations, was being used in card decks at the Italian courts of Milan, Ferrara, Bologna, and Florence. These decks were used to play a game called *tarocchi* in Italian – "tarot" is a French variant, adopted as the game spread across Europe. The inclusion of a fifth suit of 22 cards that served as a permanent set of trumps became tarot's defining feature, with most decks sharing the same card designs by the late 15th century.

The earliest tarot cards were hand-painted and only a small number of decks were created for wealthy patrons. Woodblock printed sets, initially produced in Germany, provided the first inexpensive decks and made tarot more widely available. By the early 16th century, printed tarots were widespread in Europe, and a large-scale card-manufacturing industry was established. The most popular pattern of these early printed decks, named for the city of their production, was the Tarot de Marseilles.

Tarot and the occult

During the 18th century, increasing interest in mysticism and the occult in France encouraged a new fascination with using cards for divination. Tarot cards acquired symbolic meanings and a system for laying them out developed. French occultist and professional card reader Jean-Baptiste Alliette was pivotal in this new craze for tarot. In 1770, under the pseudonym "Etteilla" (his name backwards), Alliette published a book providing divinatory meanings for a 32-card deck of regular playing cards (used in France for the game piquet), plus one non-traditional card (the "Etteilla card"), representing the person seeking the consultation. These explanations included interpretations for each card in its upright and reversed positions and, for the first time, narratives for spreads of cards – previously, card readers interpreted a single card taken from the top of the deck. Alliette's second book, *Manière de se récréer avec le jeu de cartes nommées tarots* ("Manner of Recreation with the Game of Cards

Woodblock prints
This uncut sheet of tarot cards from c. 1500, preserved as a makeshift endpaper for a book, is one of the earliest examples of printed cards.

French tarot
These cards belong to a Parisian tarot deck from the early 1600s – the earliest block-printed deck to survive in its entirety. The names and numbers on the trump cards are identical to the standard Tarot de Marseilles.

Named Tarots") published in 1783, suggested tarot was based on the writings of Hermes Trismegistus (see p. 71), appearing to confirm rumours that tarot encoded ancient wisdom. Alliette went on to establish a tarot school to promote his divinatory methods and, in 1789, issued his Grand Ettiella tarot deck, the first to give interpretations on the cards.

The notion that tarot cards embodied ancient esoteric knowledge had first been proposed by French scholar Antoine Court de Gébelin in his historical work the *Monde primitif* ("Primitive World"), published in 1781. De Gébelin argued that tarot symbols drew on an Egyptian book of wisdom, the *Book of Thoth*, and, while Egyptologists disputed this, the concept quickly gained currency.

Cartomancy

Separate to the development of dedicated tarot cards, ordinary playing cards have been used for divination since the late 14th century. Known as cartomancy, this informal card-reading practice was the most popular method of fortune-telling between the 18th and 20th centuries. Another form of cartomancy uses "oracle" cards. Published specifically for fortune-telling since the end of the 17th century, decks of this type have varying numbers of cards and designs and are sometimes called Sibella or Gypsy decks.

Allegory of Fortune, a 17th-century work by Lorenzo Lippi, depicts fortune as a woman and chance as a monkey.

Etteilla deck
With divinatory meanings on each trump card, this 18th-century Etteilla deck by Jean-Baptiste Alliette greatly influenced the occult tarot cards of the following centuries.

By the 19th century, the link between tarot and divination was well established and new strands were being added to the story of tarot's esoteric origins. In the 1860s, French occultist and magic aficionado Eliphas Lévi (real name Alphonse Louis Constant) published a series of influential books on magic, alchemy, and tarot. He argued that tarot was linked to the mystical traditions of Kabbalah (ancient Jewish mystical practices) and associated each of the 22 tarot trumps with one of the 22 letters in the Hebrew alphabet. Lévi provided an organizing principle for his esoteric system by arranging the 78 tarot cards as signposts on the Kabbalistic Tree of Life. This meant the cards functioned as steps on the journey to spiritual enlightenment.

Oswald Wirth deck
In 1926, Oswald Wirth revised his original tarot deck of 1889, reissuing it with more detailed images, decorative borders, and gold backgrounds, as on this card of The Empress.

Another French occultist, Jean-Baptiste Pitois, revived tarot's associations with ancient Egypt. Under the pen-name Paul Christian, he published *Histoire de la magie* ("The History of Magic") in 1870, in which he claimed tarot symbols originated in secrets, or "arcana", linked to Egyptian mystery cults. Significantly, he also divided the tarot cards into two groups – the Major Arcana (greater secrets), containing the 22 trump cards, each with its own meaning, and the Minor Arcana (lesser secrets), the 56 suit cards.

Towards modern tarot
Synthesizing the work of Lévi, Christian, and Alliette, Swiss occultist Oswald Wirth created the first tarot deck designed solely for divination. Published in 1889, it contained only the 22 cards of the Major Arcana and was the first to use Hebrew letters on the cards. Wirth was an important member of the Rosicrucians and Freemasons, esoteric societies that became important in popularizing tarot.

At the end of the 19th century, these societies became the means by which knowledge of occult tarot reached the English-speaking world. In 1888, followers of Eliphas Lévi founded the Hermetic Order of the Golden Dawn in England, with branches following in the US. One prominent member of this society, mystic and poet Arthur Edward Waite, published one of the first books in English on how to read tarot in 1889, and in 1909 created the Rider-Waite tarot deck with fellow member Pamela Colman Smith (see pp. 258–59). This would become one of the most widely used fortune-telling decks in the world. Inspiring many variants in the 20th century, including the Thoth deck by another Golden Dawn member, Aleister Crowley, it also popularized the idea of tarot cards as primarily a divinatory tool, despite their continuing use in Italy and France as a card game.

Esoteric societies

In the 18th and 19th centuries, esoteric societies such as the Freemasons and Rosicrucians achieved new popularity. Members believed that ancient mystical texts contained secrets or ultimate truths that could provide a path to spiritual enlightenment or societal reform. Occult groups such as the Hermetic Order of the Golden Dawn built on these beliefs, promoting the idea that tarot encoded these truths and that it could be used as a powerful and magical divination tool.

This Rosicrucian emblem was designed in 1888 for France's first occult Kabbalist society.

> "The symbolism of numbers and the allegory of figures easily gives the key to the poetry of the prophets."

ELIPHAS LÉVI, *HISTORY OF MAGIC*, 1860

In the hands of fate
The palm-reading revival

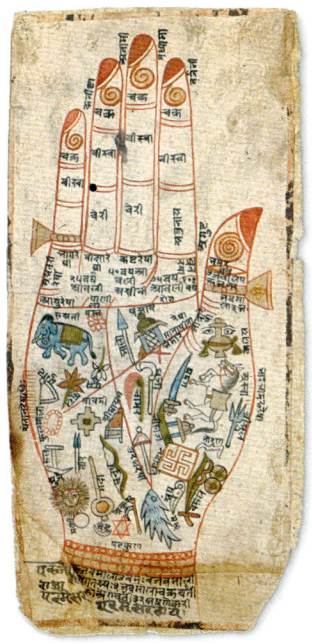

Eastern origins
This 19th-century South Asian manuscript depicts a right hand in red ink, with black inscriptions in Sanskrit. Vedic palmistry is known as *rekhashastra*, with *rekha* being the lines.

Also known as chiromancy or cheirology, palmistry is an ancient form of divination that involves studying features of the palm of the hand to determine an individual's personality and destiny. Some of the earliest records of palmistry come from India, where the Hindu sage Valmiki is thought to have written a book on palmistry more than 5,000 years ago. Palm-reading then spread to Egypt, Persia, Tibet, China, and Greece (see p. 46).

The practice did not spread across Europe until the 12th century CE. A series of treatises on the subject appeared around this time (see pp. 154–55), and numerous texts were published during the 16th and 17th centuries as palmistry reached unprecedented levels of popularity. Although fascination with this form of divination was condemned by the Catholic Church, which issued several edicts banning the practice, palmistry (along with astrology) remained part of the medical curriculum of many European universities until well into the 17th century.

Decline and rebirth
In England, France, and Italy, palmistry almost disappeared in the 18th century, although a few works appeared in Germany during this time. However, travelling fortune-tellers, often Roma (see pp. 230–31), continued to read palms. The traditional request of a practitioner – "cross my palm with silver" – was not simply a demand for payment; it also stemmed from the belief that using silver and making the sign of the cross would both ward off the devil and ensure no witchcraft was taking place.

Interest in palmistry grew with Casimir Stanislas D'Arpentigny's *La Chirognomie* (1839), which presented it in a scientific light and included the first systematic classification of hand types. However, the true rebirth of palmistry in Europe occurred in the late 19th century, along with an upsurge of interest in occult and Eastern traditions.

Palmistry attracted the interest of scientists and intellectuals, including Edward Heron-Allen, whose book *Palmistry – A Manual of Cheirosophy* (1883) sparked the palmistry craze of the 1880s and inspired Oscar Wilde's murder mystery *Lord Arthur Savile's Crime: a Story of Cheiromancy* (1887). Heron-Allen was also responsible for promoting the terms "chiromancy" or "cheiromancy" (divining the future by looking at the lines of the hand), "cheirognomy" (based on hand shapes), and "cheirosophy" (hand wisdom or knowledge).

In 1889, the Cheirological Society of Great Britain was founded by Katherine St Hill, and in 1897, Edgar de Valcourt-Vermont founded the American Cheirological Society. But it was the work of Irish-born William John Warner (later Louis Hamon), known as "Cheiro", that brought palmistry into mainstream culture. He first claimed to have learned palmistry from local gypsies, then to have studied it in India. Although neither story was true, he became instantly successful as a palmist from 1892 and ran a palmistry practice in London. His first book, *Cheiro's Book of the Hand*, was published in late 1892. He was hugely popular on both sides of the Atlantic after touring the US in 1893, and often featured in the press. Cheiro's books remain in print, and are still used by palm-readers today.

> "…it is only palmists who look deeper than mere others."
>
> **KATHARINE ST HILL**, *THE HANDS OF CELEBRITIES*, 1896

Face-reading

The art of physiognomy, or face-reading, originated in ancient India and Greece and is a method of assessing a person's character and prospects from their facial features. The oldest-known text on the subject is the *Physiognomonica* from the 3rd century BCE. Palmistry and physiognomy were seen as related, and many treatises dealt with both. Physiognomy became less popular from the 16th century, but was revived by Johann Kaspar Lavater in the late 18th century. It was used in criminology in the mid-19th century, when Cesare Lombroso suggested that potential criminals could be identified by their physical attributes. However, the discipline fell from favour due to its racist and sexist overtones.

A man's face is expressing a state of despair in this physiognomy drawing by W. Hebert (c. 1770).

Divination parlour
This illustration from *Cheiro's Language of the Hand* (1897) shows his London consulting room, which was probably based at 47 New Bond Street.

Roma fortune-telling

The Roma, thought to have migrated west from northern India around the 11th century, brought with them spiritual and mystic traditions as they travelled into Europe. By the 1600s, they had gained a reputation for their fortune-telling practices, which blended elements of their Indian origins with influences from the various cultures they had encountered. Fortune-telling suited the Roma's mobile way of life; it also became an important means of livelihood, especially as Roma communities faced marginalization in wider society. By the late 19th century, Roma fortune-tellers – nearly always women, known as *drabardi* – were often found at summer fairs and seaside resorts.

The most popular Roma fortune-telling method was palmistry (see pp. 232–33), but others included cartomancy with playing cards, tea-leaf reading (see pp. 244–45), dream interpretation, and scrying (see pp. 278–79). *Drabardi* also told fortunes using simplified forms of astrology, describing lucky and unlucky days and predicting marriage dates or the type of spouse a client would have. They sought to make a personal connection with clients, offering readings in a narrative style instead of simply giving facts or dates.

> "…fortune-telling… has deep roots in Romani culture and our development of human supernatural abilities."
>
> **GEORGE ELI**, *LOS ANGELES TIMES*, 2023

The Fortune Teller, a 19th-century oil painting by Oreste Cortazzo, depicts wealthy clients queuing to visit a Roma fortune-teller at a fair.

Reading palms

Most palmists read a person's dominant hand (the hand used to write with, or used the most). Although they consider several factors, the most common things to read into are the lines and marks on the palm. As well as giving character readings – assessing a person's personality traits – some palmists make predictions for the future based on breaks and marks on the lines. The lines can change slightly over time, reflecting changes a person makes in their life.

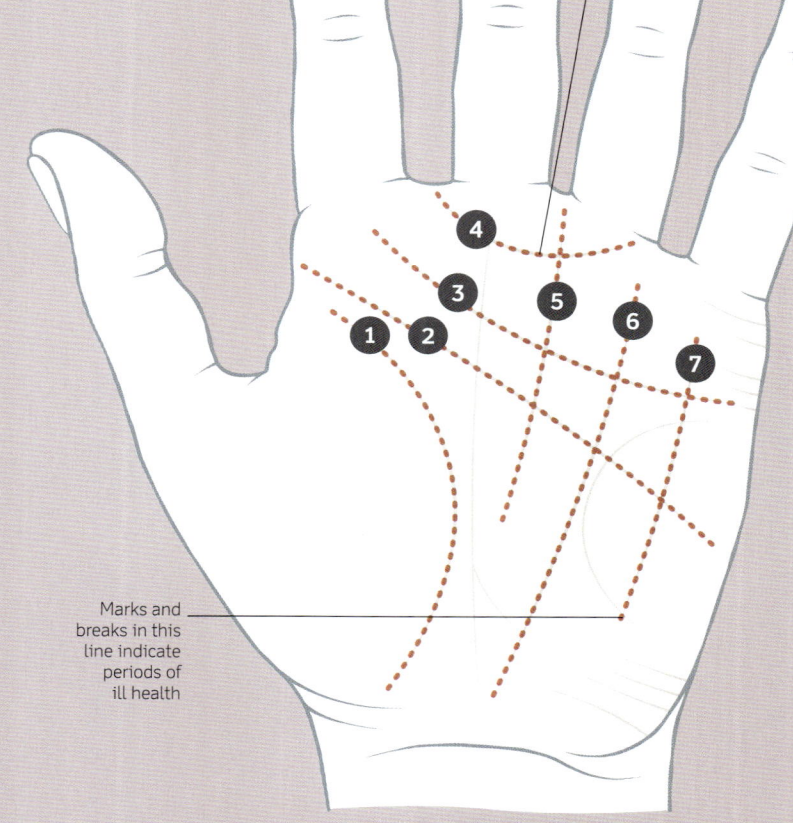

Only some people have this line

Marks and breaks in this line indicate periods of ill health

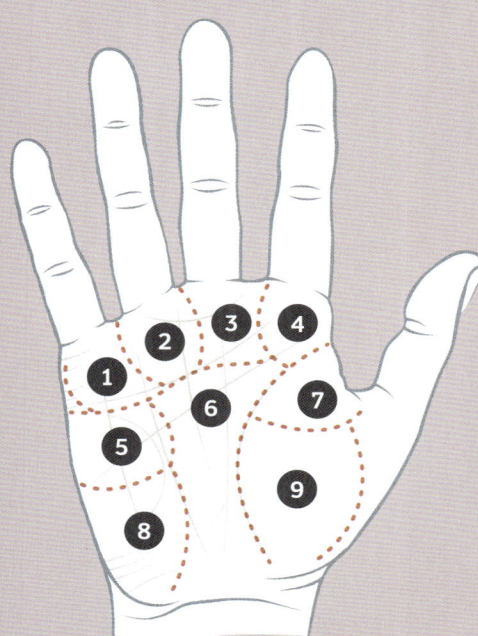

Mounts of the palm
Each mount denotes physical or emotional tendencies. Larger mounts reveal a person's interests, and the most dominant show what dominates their personality. Smaller mounts indicate issues to be overcome.

1 Mercury: mind, knowledge, resourcefulness, money
2 Sun/Apollo: creativity, optimism, enthusiasm
3 Saturn: duty, reliability, responsibility, integrity
4 Jupiter: ambition, purpose, leadership, honesty
5 Mars negative: anger, conflict, impulsiveness
6 Plain of Mars: the balance of Mars negative and positive
7 Mars positive: courage, daring, competitiveness
8 Moon: emotion, memory, imagination, intuition
9 Venus: love, romance, understanding, pleasure

Major lines
Each line reflects a form of energy. A prominent line means that issues relating to it are a priority. A short line suggests a limited range for its attributes, while breaks and marks show problems or events. A mark at the end of a line describes something happening in later life.

1 Life line: major life events, energy, general wellbeing
2 Head line: mind, reasoning, learning, self-reliance
3 Heart line: love, emotion, romance, relationships
4 Girdle of Venus: those with this are sensitive and highly emotional
5 Fate (Saturn) line: life path, destiny, stability
6 Sun (Apollo) line: popularity, success, talent, fame
7 Health line: physical wellbeing

Reading palms 233

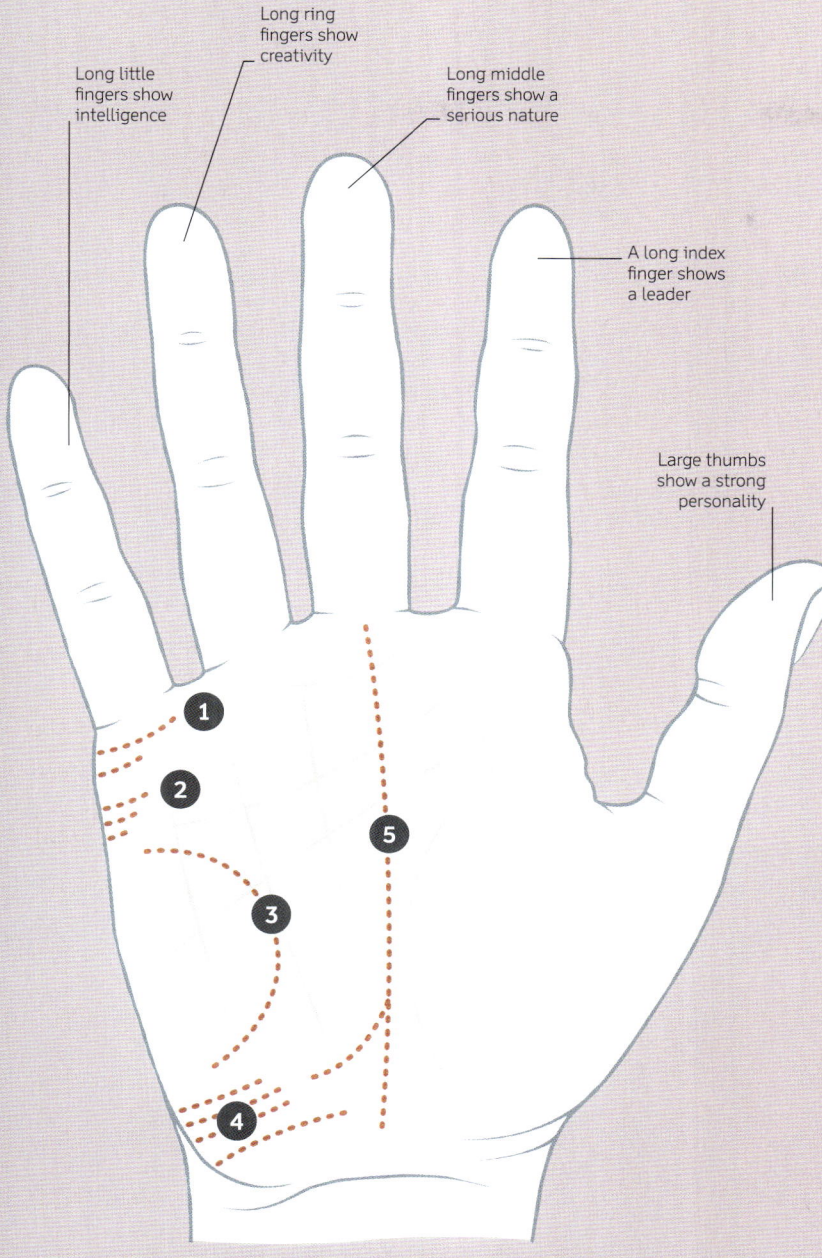

Long little fingers show intelligence

Long ring fingers show creativity

Long middle fingers show a serious nature

A long index finger shows a leader

Large thumbs show a strong personality

1 **Children lines**: indicate how many children the person will have
2 **Marriage lines**: show the number of important relationships in a person's life
3 **Intuition lines**: indicate a sensitive person
4 **Travel lines**: show a need for change and variety
5 **Lines of influence**: denote an important event related to the major line they merge with

Minor lines

Not everyone has the minor lines, and many palmists rely on the major lines alone. When they appear, the minor lines can add detail. Different schools of thought use different minor lines. Often, they confirm conclusions drawn from the rest of the hand.

Palmistry marks indicate different things, relating to which line they cross.

	Downward lines Loss, draining energy, and negative events. They reduce the strength of any line they descend from.
	Upward lines A positive attitude towards the issues indicated by the line they ascend from. They increase the strength of that line.
	Breaks A change or interruption to the aspect of a person's life the line relates to.
	Chains Obstacles, problems, or entanglements. A chain can indicate long-term issues.
	Cross Coming together of two forces. This is usually an unfavourable sign.
	Dot/point Wound or damage. It shows a temporary halt to the qualities of the line or mount where it appears.
	Grille An obstacle or difficulty. A grille can denote a lack of success in the aspect of life the mount it appears on symbolizes.
	Island A break in a line where it separates into two branches that rejoin. This indicates loss of energy, stress, or reduced promise in the line.
	Square Interruption, interference, or obstacle. The square is called the Mark of Preservation and shows escape from danger.
	Star Accentuates the qualities of any mount it is on and acts as a warning sign. This can be the sign of a revelation.
	Tassel Weakens the line on which it appears and suggests confusion or chaos. Can also show embarrassment.
	Transverse lines Reduce the positive qualities of any mount they are on.
	Triangle Scientific, intellectual, or commercial attainment. A triangle represents success and overcoming obstacles.
	Trident Very rare. If it rises from a line, it expands the qualities of that line. It promises influence and a position of power.
	Vertical lines Positive markings. When on a mount, they heighten its positive qualities.
	Circle An indication of success when found on a mount. However, a circle weakens the power of any line it is found on.

Seeing through smoke
Capnomancy and libanomancy

Predicting the future through examining the actions of fire (pyromancy) is an ancient form of divination with a number of variations. When practitioners observe how the smoke from a fire moves to foretell events, this is capnomancy, while libanomancy is when a diviner interprets smoke produced by incense thrown onto a flame.

Burning questions
Clay tablets recording the portents revealed by libanomancy have been found in Akkadian (an ancient Mesopotamian civilization) script, dating from the 2nd millennium BCE. The tablets tell priests how to interpret the direction, shapes, and movements of smoke from a *qutrēnu* (incense offering): for example, if the smoke travelled to the right, then the petitioner might defeat an adversary, but if it went left, they would be beaten.

Holy smoke
This 18th-century engraving shows a Roman soothsayer making a sacrifice at a temple fire. The smoke from sacrifices was considered to be particularly useful for divination.

From ancient Mesopotamia, the practice of pyromancy, as well as the art of reading smoke, spread around the Mediterranean world. Ancient Greek prophets, priests, and oracles (see pp. 44–49) from the 6th century BCE onwards were all said to look at the smoke of a burning sacrifice for signs sent by the gods. Temples maintained perpetual fires for such uses.

A perpetual fire produced by natural gas emerging from the Earth was used in divination in Illyria (in the western Balkan Peninsula) in the 3rd century CE. Practitioners would throw incense at the flames and interpret the smoke it gave off, believing this to be the gods' answer to questions. Ancient Celtic cultures predicted the future by setting specially chosen oak logs onto the fire at festivals to produce divinatory smoke.

Divination of all forms was condemned by the Catholic Church, but during the European Renaissance of the 14th–17th centuries, those interested in magic rediscovered libanomancy and capnomancy in classical texts and incorporated them into their work.

Modern diviners
Some cultures today still use fire and smoke for divination. The Semang people of Southeast Asia live a nomadic lifestyle in the rainforests and follow a complex animistic belief system. Each community relies on a *hala* (shaman). Before a new camp may be settled, the *hala* lights a fire and observes the smoke produced. Smoke divination is also used by the *hala* to determine the best way to treat illnesses. Similarly, many New Age practitioners of divination interpret the smoke produced from candles, oil lamps, and incense sticks in rituals.

Soot signals
This 21st-century photograph shows the tools of smoke-drawing: a piece of paper is passed through the smoke of a candle and the resulting soot patterns are then interpreted.

History of spiritualism
Spiritualist writer Emma Hardinge Britten's 1870 book recorded the history of spiritualism in the US, and defended the claims of mediums against what she called "scientific ignorance".

"Seeing" is believing
Spiritualism and clairvoyance

Proponents of spiritualism believe that the human consciousness persists after death and that the souls of the dead can be contacted by mediums. It became a popular practice in the 19th century in Europe and the US, having grown out of various religious, philosophical, and cultural movements.

Calling up the spirits of the deceased had a long history in European culture. In classical works such as the *Odyssey* and the *Aeneid*, heroes looked to the dead for guidance. The Witch of Endor summoned the spirit of the prophet Samuel in the Bible, and spiritualists pointed to her as evidence that mediumship was part of an ancient tradition.

The 18th-century Enlightenment created an environment where people were willing to posit new theories and put them to the test. In 1758, scientist and philosopher Emanuel Swedenborg published his book *Heaven and Hell*, which detailed how angels and spirits could communicate with the living. In the 1770s, Franz Mesmer created his theory of animal magnetism, claiming there was a flow of energy between the planets and all living things that could be used to heal illnesses. Mesmer was able to induce trances in his patients via a process that evolved into hypnosis. Practitioners of the technique (Mesmerism) soon began asking those in trances to try to communicate with spirits.

Rise of a movement
Modern spiritualism is said to have started in the US in the 1840s, when teenage sisters Kate and Maggie Fox of New York began to "communicate" with ghosts via rapping sounds. The story spread quickly, causing a public sensation, and the sisters (joined by their older sister, Leah) began charging a fee for audiences to attend large seances, where they would ask questions of the dead.

Spirit mediums soon began to appear across the US and Europe, fuelled by demand from bereaved families wishing to contact loved ones who had died in the American Civil War. Mediums used a variety of methods to contact the spirits, such as

Social spiritualism
This 1853 image of a Parisian spiritualist event shows a crowd using various methods for contacting spirits, including hat-turning, table-tipping, and the swinging of a pendulum.

automatic writing (in which, guided by a spirit, they would write without consciously controlling their hand) and table-tipping (where participants would place their hands on a table that appeared to move in response to a spirit). Public seances were popular evening events. Books and specialist journals, often printed by spiritualist societies, were published explaining spiritualist beliefs and teaching readers how to contact the dead. With the invention of photography, spiritualists also claimed to be able to capture images of spirits.

Although spiritualism gained many famous adherents, including author Arthur Conan Doyle and Mary Todd Lincoln, wife of President Abraham Lincoln, many doubted its veracity. Religious leaders associated the practice with magic, while sceptics such as Harry Houdini showed how seances could be faked. In 1888, the Fox sisters demonstrated how they had made their ghostly knocking sounds by cracking their toe joints.

Tricks of the trade
Some Victorian entertainers staged events to debunk the methods of mediums. This poster advertises a "Spiritualism Exposed" evening.

Clairvoyance, from the French meaning "clear vision", is the supposed ability to perceive things that are normally impossible for human senses to detect. While often this involves sensing the spirit world, it can also include a medium's ability to see distant things or events in the past or the future.

Seeing through time and space

Clairvoyants, or seers, with their claimed powers of "seeing" the past, have been called upon to solve crimes, either by distraught families or authorities. Some reports suggest that clairvoyants have been able to identify killers and locate their victims' bodies, but sceptics point to a number of times clairvoyance has led to mistaken arrests.

Forecasting the future is a skill that many clairvoyants claim to have, thanks to their extrasensory perceptions. These predictions can either be linked to specific people and events, or to more general trends, such as whether or not a war is imminent. One early spiritualist author, Andrew Jackson Davis, in his 1850 book *The Great Harmonia*, described seeing a large city burning to the ground. When the Great Chicago Fire of 1871 broke out, his supporters declared that this was proof of his clairvoyant powers.

Edgar Cayce, an American clairvoyant known as the "Sleeping Prophet", is said to have received thousands of visions while he reclined in a trance. These visions were transcribed and he is supposed

Foreseeing flames
This 1871 illustration shows the devastating fire that struck Chicago that year. Supporters of Andrew Jackson Davis, the "Poughkeepsie Seer", claimed he had predicted the event years before.

Icy visions
This painting imagines the fate of the 1845 team that disappeared while trying to discover the Northwest passage. Several mediums claimed to have "seen" the explorers lost in an icy wasteland.

to have twice predicted a severe fall in the stock market, just before the devastating Wall Street Crash of 1929. Like many clairvoyant predictions, however, Cayce's visions were deliberately vague, leading critics to assert that predicting such inevitable events required no special talent.

Known today as remote-viewing, the ability to "see" objects at a distance or hidden objects was one of the first skills to be claimed by mesmerists and spiritualists. The technique usually involved a male mesmerist who would put a seer (often an illiterate young woman) into a "mesmeric state" or trance and then instruct her to "visit" a location to find out information about it.

When the Franklin expedition to the Canadian Arctic disappeared after departing Britain in 1845, the search parties sent to look for the explorers found no trace of them. Jane Franklin, wife of the expedition leader Captain Sir John Franklin, employed unconventional methods in an effort to locate them – including using the services of clairvoyants, who claimed to have "travelled" to the Arctic while in a trance and "seen" members of the expedition trapped by ice.

The most famous clairvoyant to work on the Franklin case was known as Emma, "the Seeress of Bolton". On several occasions, the young woman was put into a mesmeric trance and had visions of the lost explorers. She saw them poorly nourished, but still alive and apparently in good spirits. Using the position of the Sun relative to Emma and the explorers in her visions raised hopes that an approximate longitude of their location could be calculated. These hopes were false, however – the Franklin expedition never returned.

Soul-searching

The 19th-century French educator Hippolyte Rivail, also known as Allan Kardec, founded a religious movement, Spiritism, based on his studies of spiritualist mediums. By posing questions to mediums, he claimed to have discovered the nature of the soul, reincarnation, and the existence of spirits.

Kardec's scientific approach to probing the spirit world appealed to intellectuals, and was instrumental in the development of psychical research, which investigates clairvoyance, telepathy, and other mystical experiences. His work also had an ethical dimension, which has contributed to Spiritism's wide following in modern times.

Allan Kardec sought to understand how mediums were able to convey messages from the spirit realm.

Fields of bl[ood]

In 1831, the deadliest revolt by enslaved [people]
took place in Southampton County, Virg[inia.] [Leading]
the rebellion was an enslaved Black man [named Nat Turner,]
who, from a young age, was noted for hi[s intelligence and]
pious Christian nature. He used to preac[h to other enslaved]
people, who began to refer to him as a p[rophet.]

Turner claimed to receive visions that [guided his actions.]
As a young man, he fled from his master [and hid in the]
woods until "the Spirit" appeared to him [and told him to]
return. He reported having visions of wh[ite and black spirits]
fighting in the sky, and his visions warne[d him that a day]
of judgement was approaching. While w[orking in the fields]
in 1825, Turner believed he saw blood ap[pearing on the corn]
"as though it were dew from heaven". He [took these visions]
to mean that there would have to be an u[prising of enslaved]
people – and that he was divinely appoin[ted to lead it.]

The first sign that it was time to rebel [came in February]
1831, when Turner saw a solar eclipse. T[his was followed in]
August by the sky turning blue-green du[e to an]
atmospheric disturbance. In a rebellion [that lasted two]
days, Turner and his followers killed arou[nd 60 white people]
before it was brutally suppressed, with 12[0 innocent]
Black people killed. Turner was captured [and executed.]

"...the Sun was darke[ned,]
thunder rolled in the [heavens,]
and blood flowed in [streams,]
and I heard a vo[ice..."]

NAT TURNER, *THE CONFESSIONS OF N[AT TURNER]*

Entitled "The Prophet", this 2016 quilted artwork [is]
one from a series that charts the life of Nat Turner.

Mouthpieces of the gods
African prophetism

A flurry of annexations occurred across the African continent in the period leading up to and after the Berlin Conference of 1884, which legitimized the colonization process. As European nations scrambled to secure pieces of the continent, communities turned to trusted spiritual intermediaries – diviners, mediums, and prophets – to make sense of the resulting turmoil. Prophets, in particular, were often insightful and charismatic individuals, and they became important in helping others to understand and resist the expanding threat of colonization.

Spiritual leaders

In eastern and southern Africa, prophets urged people to repair their relationships with ancestral spirits and deities. For some, ritual purification meant rejecting customs, paraphernalia, and anything else introduced or encouraged by the Europeans. For others, it meant abandoning antisocial activities like malevolent sorcery.

Ngundeng Bong, a Nuer prophet who led his people's resistance to British colonization in early 20th-century South Sudan, called for such purification. With guidance from the Nuer sky god Deng, he prophesied the defeat of the Anglo-Egyptian colonial powers if his followers heeded his call to relinquish any evil substances they possessed. He buried the items in a purpose-built *bieh* (ceremonial mound). Now purified, and unified in purpose, the Nuer were emboldened to resist the colonial authorities and continued to do so even after Ngundeng's death.

A widow named Mekatilili wa Menza led a similar movement on the Kenyan coast between 1912 and 1915. Encouraging the Giriama people to reject the British and embrace traditional customs, she initiated *kondo ya chembe*, the Giriama Uprising – a confrontation that failed to drive away the British and resulted in her arrest.

Prophets often performed rituals and gave their people protective talismans to aid their resistance. The combatants in the Tanzanian Maji Maji Rebellion, led by Kinjikitile Ngwale, mistakenly believed his *maji* (sacred water) would protect them from bullets. Similarly, Mlimo, who led the 1896–97 Ndebele Rebellion in Zimbabwe, was assassinated while performing an immunity dance.

The most significant achievement of African prophets was their ability to use the revelations and guidance they believed they received to unite people against their colonial oppressors. That these efforts nearly always resulted in defeat speaks of the desperation in their methods, their poorly informed strategies, and the sheer barbarism of the European response to the attempts of these individuals and their followers to protect their homelands.

Prophet silenced
This 1901 sketch depicts American military scout Frederick Russell Burnham's assassination of Mlimo, a Ndebele leader, as he dances in a cave.

Place of resistance
Ngundeng and his son Gwek constructed this 15 m- (50 ft-) high mound, or *bieh*. It became a spiritual centre for the Nuer people until it was destroyed by the British in 1928.

African prophetism 243

"It may be said that a prophet is a man who is possessed by one of the sky-spirits, or gods... Nuer have great respect for these spirits and fear, and readily follow, those whom they possess."

EDWARD E. EVANS-PRITCHARD, *THE NUER: A DESCRIPTION OF THE MODES OF LIVELIHOOD AND POLITICAL INSTITUTIONS OF A NILOTIC PEOPLE*, 1940

Widow, warrior, prophet
Kenyan artist and activist Zarina Patel's painting shows Giriama leader Mekatilili addressing a *baraza* (gathering), while others prepare for war with sacred drumming, making weapons, and taking oaths.

Fortune in a cup
Tasseography

Reading tea leaves, or tasseography – also known as tasseomancy – is a relatively modern, sociable style of divination. Its name comes from the French word *tasse* ("cup") and the Greek word *graphos* ("drawing"). Unlike many other divinatory methods, it is easy to learn and does not require special equipment, and coffee grounds or wine sediment can be used instead of tea leaves.

Tasseography originated in the 16th century, when coffee culture spread from Yemen to the Ottoman Empire, and the women of Sultan Suleyman the Magnificent's harem read coffee grounds as a way of exchanging news and stories. The practice soon spread across the Ottoman Empire, and it remains popular today in Türkiye, where fortune-tellers offer guidance in traditional coffee houses.

Serving a superior
Women of the Ottoman harem gather to serve coffee to the *valide sultan* (mother of the sultan and leader of the imperial harem) in this 1680s miniature by court painter Musavvir Hüseyin.

> "Tea-cup fortunes are only horary, or dealing with the events of the hour or the succeeding 24 hours at furthest."

"A HIGHLAND SEER", *TEA-CUP READING: HOW TO TELL FORTUNES BY TEA LEAVES*, 1881

Tea first arrived in Europe in the 17th century, when the British East India Company began shipping tea from China. At first it was expensive and drunk only by the upper classes. Tea became more popular in the 18th century, but it was not until the late 19th century that it was cheap enough for everyone to drink.

Reading tea leaves

As tea-drinking became a common practice in Europe, travelling Roma began to use tea leaves for divination, employing the same methods used by Ottoman women to read coffee grounds. During the Victorian era in Britain, fortune-tellers offered door-to-door services for a fee, while reading tea leaves became a popular activity at tea parties and charity bazaars.

By the early 20th century, tasseography was widespread. Tea rooms often offered free readings between World War I and World War II, and tea companies sent instruction booklets about tea-leaf reading to customers as promotional devices. When tea bags became popular from the 1950s, tasseography declined in popularity. However, it never completely disappeared and has undergone a revival in recent years with the rising popularity of herbal teas.

Seeing shapes

Tea-leaf readings may offer a quick response to a question or an outline of the near future. The ideal vessel is a white or pale-coloured tea cup with a wide rim and narrow base, which allows the leaves to spread around the cup. Any type of tea can be used, but a black loose-leaf tea is the most popular.

It takes practice to see the shapes in tea leaves and turning the cup to view them from a different direction is often helpful. Some shapes are easily recognizable, such as letters (suggesting a person with that initial), or are well known, such as a heart for love or a horseshoe for good luck. Others are common fortune-telling symbols, such as a bird representing news. The larger patterns are the most important to the reading, so practitioners will begin with the most obvious shape and then relate other symbols to it.

Seer's guide
The earliest-known book in English about reading tea leaves was published by an unnamed "Highland Seer", in 1881, during the heyday of Victorian fascination with divination and the occult.

A simple method

Once the tea is poured (without using a strainer), the person drinks their tea until only a spoonful of liquid remains. They then hold the cup by its handle in their left hand and swirl it anticlockwise three times. Finally, they carefully invert the cup over the saucer and let the liquid drain away.

Turning the cup over, the person can interpret the shapes and patterns of the tea leaves, starting from the cup's rim and working inwards. The nearer the pattern is to the top of the cup, the sooner what it describes will happen. As well as the symbols suggested by the tea leaves, any shapes in the empty spaces may be included in the reading.

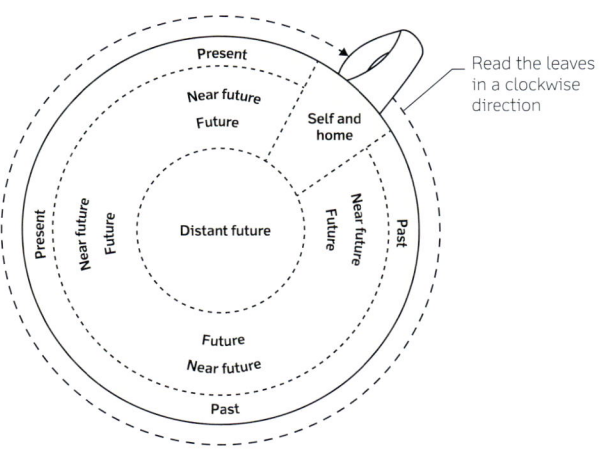

Reading the leaves

In Victorian Britain, many people were fascinated with occult methods of divining the future, especially those that could be practised at home. Tasseography, the art of reading tea leaves, coffee grounds, or the dregs of wine, had existed since at least the 16th century (see pp. 244–45), but became commonplace in 19th-century parlours and public tea rooms. Roma fortune-tellers travelled from house to house offering to "read the leaves", while tea rooms would invite fortune-tellers to divine the fates of their customers.

Around 1881, the mysterious *Tea-Cup Reading: How to Tell Fortunes by Tea Leaves*, written by an anonymous "Highland Seer", was published, apparently based on the work of Scottish spae-wives (fortune-tellers) who had long practised the art. It explained how to interpret the shapes formed by tea leaves left at the bottom of a cup, and made it possible for anyone to have a go at casting tea leaves.

With the development of psychoanalysis in the 1890s, self-analysis became fashionable among Europe's middle and upper classes. By offering tasseography at a social gathering, hosts were able to deliver a touch of sorcery to their guests that also supposedly revealed deeper truths.

> "In the early 1800s, a lady of the manor tossed the cups after breakfast and read fortunes for her servants."
>
> **BRITISH HISTORIAN ALEC GILL**

Tea-leaf reading became a popular and amusing activity among friends, as this early 20th-century British photograph shows.

Divine wisdom
Theosophy and astrology

In the late 19th century, the rise of the theosophy movement, promoted by Russian émigré Helena Blavatsky, had a profound effect on the practice of astrology. Meaning "divine wisdom", theosophy blends philosophical, mystical, and religious beliefs drawn from ancient Platonic, esoteric, Hindu, and Buddhist traditions. Core doctrines include the belief that all life is interconnected, and that there is a single absolute truth or higher spirit; the goal of life is to reunite the soul with this truth through spiritual enlightenment. The practice of astrology, which links human endeavour to the mechanisms of the cosmos, provides one means for pursuing this heightened spiritual awareness.

Influenced by theosophical theories, many astrologers began to adopt mystical ideas relating to spiritual goals and apply them to their practice. One of the most prominent was British theosophist and astrologer Alan Leo, who shifted the focus of astrology from predicting the future to improving self-awareness. In this more introspective approach, the birth chart was seen as a map of spiritual growth and used as a tool for self-discovery.

Incorporating ideas such as karma, reincarnation, and the evolution of the soul made astrology less fatalistic and more a means of grasping potential. This change in emphasis led to new schools of esoteric and psychological astrology (see pp. 268–71). It also led astrologers to consider how each person's spiritual journey related to astrological timeframes. At the individual level, theosophical theories on the cyclical nature of time suggested that planetary cycles might influence possibilities for personal growth. At a societal level, Blavatsky's claims that an era of spiritual enlightenment was imminent were interpreted to mean the arrival of a new astrological age (of Aquarius; see pp. 280–81).

Changing times
"Ezekiel's Wheel", from Helena Blavatsky's book *Isis Unveiled*, describes how eternity is divided into 12 transformational cycles, represented as astrological ages.

Starring the Sun
One of the biggest changes that theosophy brought to astrology was a new emphasis on the Sun. In her 1887 book *Isis Unveiled*, Blavatsky described the Sun as "the soul of all things". Alan Leo also argued that the Sun, as a life-giver, was the single most important factor in the zodiac. These assertions gave the Sun a new role as the focal point of a horoscope and spawned the concept of a simple astrology based on the zodiacal position of the Sun alone. The result was Sun-sign astrology and the development of the modern 12-sign horoscope column (see pp. 272–75).

Founding theosophist
After extensive travels, during which she allegedly studied with spiritual gurus in India, Russian-born Helena Blavatsky co-founded the Theosophical Society in New York in 1875. Blending ideas from East and West, the society quickly gained a strong following. Blavatsky claimed to have psychic powers and, although she was declared a fraud in 1885, her mystical theories remained influential.

Helena Blavatsky, photographed in New York around 1874, was often known as "Madame Blavatsky".

Understanding the self
This image from Alan Leo's *Modern Astrology* magazine, c. 1896–97, shows the new emphasis on astrology as a tool for self-awareness and personal empowerment.

Names and numbers
This diagram shows the 72 names of God from *Oedipus Aegyptiacus* (1652–54) by Athanasius Kircher. In the teachings of Kabbalah, these names are said to have enabled prophets to perform miracles.

The power of one
Numerology

According to numerology, numbers have a mystical significance, and human life, like everything else in the universe, is guided by numbers. The concept dates back thousands of years and has roots in teachings from ancient Babylon, Greece, Egypt, China, and India. It is also closely related to the invention of the alphabet, as some traditions assigned numerical values to letters and words. In some early Christian sects, for example, the number 888 was associated with the name Jesus.

Shaping destiny
There are two main schools of numerology – Chaldean and Pythagorean. Chaldean numerology has its roots in ancient Babylon and assigns a unique vibrational value, or energy, from 1 to 8 to a letter (9 is considered sacred and is usually omitted, unless it occurs as the result of the sum of vibrations). Pythagorean numerology is based on the work of the 6th-century BCE Greek philosopher Pythagoras (see p.70), who reasoned that the universe could be expressed numerically. Using the numbers 1–9, Pythagoras was said to be able to divine the fates of individuals, predict events, and even change a person's name to alter their destiny.

Kabbalah (see pp.158–59) integrated numerology into its teachings, but focused more on spiritual growth and esoteric knowledge than the practical insights of the Chaldean and Pythagorean systems. Each letter of the Hebrew alphabet corresponds to a number and a principle; for example, "A" (Aleph) is aligned to number 1 and represents the creation of life, breath, and power. Kabbalists used this method, called "gematria", to search for new layers of meaning in the Hebrew scriptures.

The 16th century witnessed a surge of interest in esoteric sciences, including numerology. German polymath Heinrich Cornelius Agrippa wrote about it in *De Occulta Philosophia* ("Occult Philosophy"), detailing many of the number meanings still in use today. A century later, Isaac Newton – scientist, alchemist, and strong believer in numerology – wrote extensively on the subject. In the late 18th century, a celebrity calling himself Cagliostro famously used numerology to predict lottery results in Paris. The practice gained further attention soon after, when French magician Eliphas Lévi (see p.226) synthesized occult knowledge – combining numerology with tarot, astrology, and Kabbalah.

Hidden forces
With new scientific discoveries relating to light, magnetism, and electricity, the theory that numbers correspond to energy patterns and vibrations gained prominence, especially among adherents of the New Thought movement. Originating in the US in the 19th century, this religious movement argued that numerology could be used as a way to understand God and ourselves. Works by L. Dow Balliett, Florence Campbell, and Julia Seton supported this view. Today, numerologists seek to obtain a holistic view of an individual by using their full birth name or birth date (see pp.252–53).

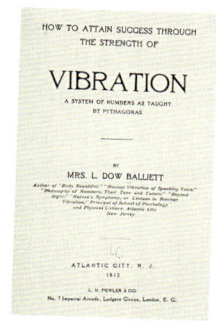

Good vibrations
This 1913 edition of L. Dow Balliett's book popularized the Pythagorean theory that everything in the universe has an intrinsic energy, or "spirit force", and vibrates at a different rate, which can be described in numerical terms.

Symbolic decisions
Napoleon Bonaparte was said to have consulted an "oraculum" – a system using numbers and symbols to answer questions – when making key decisions. Supposedly found in an Egyptian tomb during a French military expedition in 1801, the oraculum was translated on Napoleon's orders. Later called *Napoleon's Book of Fate*, it caused a sensation when it was published in 1822, and inspired many imitations. Though dismissed as a hoax, it remains in print.

The number and pattern of stars and their corresponding answers feature in *The Oraculum* or *Futurity's Mirror*, published in London in 1825.

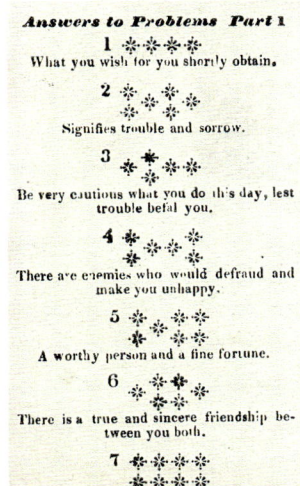

Practising numerology

The core tenet of numerology (see pp. 250–251) is the belief that the numbers associated with a person influence their character, behaviour, strengths, and weaknesses. These numbers can come from things such as a person's birth date, or numbers associated with the letters in their name. All numbers have both positive and negative characteristics. Numerology works by adding all digits until a single number is left. The exceptions are master numbers – 11, 22, or 33, intensified versions of 2 (1+1), 4 (2+2), and 6 (3+3).

Associations in numerology
Each letter is associated with a number, which is linked to particular qualities. Each number is also associated with planetary energies that provide added meaning (see p. 251).

Letters	Number	Planet	Positive qualities	Negative qualities
a j s	1	Sun	Assertive, high-achieving, pioneering, original, independent, courageous, charismatic, a leader	Stubborn, egotistical, blunt, dominant, wilful, selfish, melodramatic, impulsive, wastes talents
b k t	2	Moon	Protective, adaptable, cooperative, a peacemaker, considerate, tactful, insightful, sensitive, supportive	Self-conscious, grasping, over-protective, fears the unknown, hesitant, wasteful, lazy
c l u	3	Jupiter	Optimistic, fun, easy-going, humorous, friendly, energetic, spontaneous, creative, enthusiastic	Superficial, careless, pessimistic, foolhardy, lacks direction, indolent, restrictive, easily bored
d m v	4	North node	Organized, cautious, patient, logical, hard-working, loyal, steadfast, responsible, rational	Rigid, overly cautious, limited in viewpoint, fearful, insecure, a loner
e n w	5	Mercury	Curious, pragmatic, persuasive, shrewd, resourceful, motivated, analytical	Unreliable, inconsistent, critical, deceitful, restless, indecisive, a procrastinator, prone to boredom
f o x	6	Venus	Responsible, sympathetic, generous, caring, compromising, beautiful, charming, loving	Meddling, jealous, anxious, bitter, vengeful, unfaithful, opinionated
g p y	7	South node	Thoughtful, analytical, understanding, aware, reserved, eccentric, open-minded	Aloof, suppressed, distrustful, antisocial, impersonal, deceptive, argumentative
h q z	8	Saturn	Practical, self-disciplined, powerful, decisive, determined to succeed	Status-oriented, power-hungry, unscrupulous, judgemental, dogmatic, manipulative, belligerent
i r	9	Mars	Humanitarian, selfless, compassionate, generous, tolerant, intuitive	Impulsive, self-serving, resentful, unfocused, insensitive
	11		Wise, charismatic, psychic, inspirational, seeks to bring illumination	Insensitive, fanatical, unstable, impractical
	22		Idealistic, expansive, a visionary, seeks to build something to make dreams a reality	Fears loss, incites treachery from hidden enemies
	33		Compassionate, inspiring, honest, disciplined, brave, self-sacrificing, focused on the good of others	Lacks resources, love, or personal ambition

Personality number
The sum of the consonants in a person's name (known as their personality number) reflects the impression they make on the world and how others see them.

$$1+8+5+1+4+2+8 = 29$$
$$2+9 = 11$$

— Personality number or sum of the consonants (here, it is a master number)

Soul number
The sum of the vowels gives the soul number. This describes a person's inner self and private thoughts, including what is dear to their heart, likes and dislikes, and what they want in a partner.

$$6+9 = 15$$
$$1+5 = 6$$

— Soul number (sum of the vowels)

John Smith

$$1+6+8+5 \; + \; 1+4+9+2+8 = 44$$
$$4+4 = 8$$

— Expression number (sum of all letters)

Expression number
The sum of all letters, the expression number (or destiny number) represents what a person is destined to do and become in their lifetime. It reveals both inner goals and talents, and shortcomings.

Life path number
Based on a person's birth date, the life path number describes what that person is like deep down. It represents who they were at birth and the traits they carry with them.

14 December 1962 — **1.** Write down the person's date of birth.

14 12 1962

2. Convert the month to the number that represents its position in the year.

$$1+4+1+2+1+9+6+2 = 26$$
$$2+6 = 8$$ — Life path number (sum of all digits)

Modern futures

1900 onwards

Introduction

The turn of the 20th century saw a range of revolutionary technological developments that have since come to define the modern world, including the invention of motor cars and aeroplanes, the telephone, electric light, and the skyscraper. Genetics, space travel, the personal computer, the internet, the smartphone, and artificial intelligence followed as the century progressed. In the new discipline of psychology, the pioneering theories of Sigmund Freud and the foundation of psychoanalysis set the trend for a more introspective approach. Meanwhile, theosophy and its offshoots produced what is now known as New Age culture, in which followers can choose from a variety of age-old spiritualities and therapies from around the globe, as well as new ideas, to prepare for the much-anticipated dawn of a spiritual new world.

Western astrologers responded to these changes both by redefining their art as modern, and by developing new forms influenced by theosophy and psychology. The theosophical astrologer Alan Leo came up with a spiritualized form of personality study that aimed to give people a sense of how they could maximize their positive qualities in order to better contribute to the New Age. Later astrologers extended Leo's ideas to take reincarnation into account, seeking clues as to how a person could learn from past lives and prepare for future ones. In the early 20th century, psychological astrologers began to make their mark by expanding on the character descriptions of the planets and zodiac signs. By the 1970s, they were recasting birth charts as revealing not just what people are like, but also how they can change in order to release themselves from negative patterns. This led to a shift in the focus of astrology – and in the main forms of divination, such as tarot and palm-reading – away from the prediction of events and towards the promotion of self-awareness.

The effects of psychology and modernization on astrology gave rise to a new, simplified astrological language of birth (or "star") signs. Each zodiac sign was given a complete personality profile, with which everyone could identify

Tarot cards *see* p. 260

Mind of a warrior *see* p. 268

Astrology for everyone *see* p. 272

through their date of birth. Without consulting an astrologer, people could now establish whether they were an assertive Arien (born from 21 March to 21 April), a stable Taurean (born from 22 April to 21 May), and so on. Newspaper and magazine horoscopes, which first appeared in the 1920s, carried this new language across the Western world.

Globalization also introduced the 12 Chinese animal year signs to the West. Chinese New Year, celebrated at the new Moon between 21 January and 20 February (corresponding to the Western zodiac sign Aquarius), is now a huge global media event and a chance for people to find out if they are a brave but sometimes frightening Tiger, for example, or a faithful and industrious Ox. Alternatively, they can mix the Chinese and Western systems to determine whether they are an Arien or a Taurean Tiger, or a Geminian or a Cancerian Ox.

Thanks to the internet, the three major traditions of astrology – Chinese, Western, and Indian – and their associated divinatory practices are now available in every part of the planet, and can be taken apart and blended at will. As astrologers like to say, "We all live under one sky."

> "The journey through the planetary houses… signifies the overcoming of a psychic obstacle."
>
> **CARL JUNG**, *MYSTERIUM CONIUNCTIONIS*, VOL. 14, 1963

Age-old New Age practices *see* p. 283

Shamans and spirits *see* p. 287

Digital destinies *see* p. 297

A classic tarot
The Rider-Waite deck

During the 19th century, social, cultural, and scientific changes led to a growing fascination with magic and the occult. However, tarot was almost unknown in the English-speaking world when British linguist Kenneth Mackenzie visited French occultist Eliphas Lévi in Paris in 1861. Lévi had devised a system in which he associated the 78 tarot cards with the Kabbalistic Tree of Life (see pp. 226–27). When Mackenzie returned to England, he proposed the formation of an esoteric lodge based on revisions of Lévi's system, with a tarot deck as an integral part of its teachings.

Mackenzie's unpublished manuscript, known as *Book T*, described the meanings of tarot cards. He changed Lévi's work by assigning the first letter of the Hebrew alphabet to the Fool instead of the Magician and switched the meanings of the Strength and Justice cards. The numbers of the pip cards (suit cards numbered 1–10) were associated with the sephiroth on the Tree of Life and with the 36 decans (subdivisions) of the zodiac and the 72 Kabbalistic angels. The trumps (picture cards) were assigned to the paths on the Tree of Life.

Sketched symbols
These pages from a notebook belonging to Golden Dawn member W.B. Yeats show the "21st key" of the tarot (The World, or 21st trump in the Major Arcana), following a design devised by Eliphas Lévi.

Creating a masterpiece
After Mackenzie's death in 1886, his papers were acquired by William Westcott, Samuel Lidell MacGregor Mathers, and William Woodman, who used them to establish an occult society, the Hermetic Order of the Golden Dawn, in 1888. Dedicated to magical and mystical teachings, including alchemy, Kabbalah, and astrology, as well as tarot, the order attracted many prominent artists and intellectuals, including writers Arthur Conan Doyle and William Butler Yeats, and was the first secret society to admit women as well as men. Poet and mystic Arthur Edward Waite became a member in 1891 after studying the work of Eliphas Lévi. Although the Hermetic Order of the Golden Dawn broke apart in 1903, a number of other societies sprang up based on its teachings.

In 1909, Waite commissioned artist Pamela Colman Smith (see box, left) to design a deck of tarot cards that were published by Rider and so became known as the Rider-Waite deck. The following year, a guide written by Waite, *The Key to the Tarot*, was bundled with the cards.

Drawing the deck
Artist and illustrator Pamela Colman Smith was introduced to the Hermetic Order of the Golden Dawn by the poet William Butler Yeats in 1901. There, she met Arthur Edward Waite. In 1909, Waite commissioned her to illustrate a tarot deck. Although he gave detailed directions for the Major Arcana cards, he allowed Smith more freedom in illustrating the Minor Arcana, and some images strongly reflect her earlier work.

Smith was paid a flat rate for her work and her name was omitted from the deck, but she included her initials as a looping monogram on every card except the Fool. None of her original drawings have survived.

Pamela Colman Smith, painted in 1906 by Alphaeus Philemon Cole, championed women's rights.

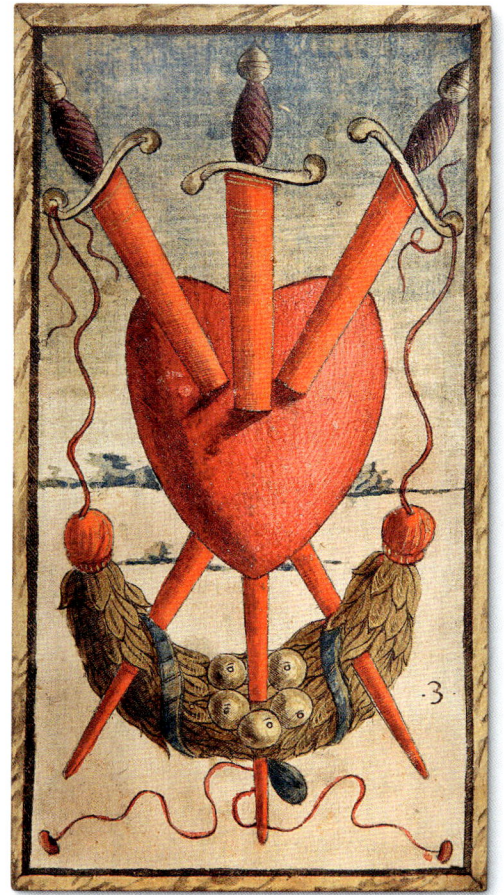 

Cards compared
The Three of Swords in the Rider-Waite deck (right) strongly resembles its Sola Busca counterpart (left), using the same proportions of imagery, albeit slightly simplified.

The Rider-Waite deck stayed true to the teachings of the Hermetic Order of the Golden Dawn, and the interpretation of tarot cards in Book T, and is replete with occult symbolism. However, it was different in that it featured pictures on the Minor Arcana cards – scenes appear on all cards except the four aces. In most tarot decks, the numbered suit cards had pips (a basic illustration of the card's number), like modern playing cards. In 1908, the British Museum exhibited photographs of the 15th-century Italian Sola Busca deck, which also included detailed scenes for the Minor Arcana. Smith's artwork drew inspiration from these early cards.

Lasting influence
Although US Games holds the copyright for a version of the deck published in 1971, the original Rider-Waite deck is now out of copyright. It is the most popular tarot deck in the English-speaking world today, and hundreds of other decks are based on its format.

In recent years, there has been a movement to rename the Rider-Waite deck the Rider-Waite-Smith deck in recognition of the role of Pamela Colman Smith. In 2009, US Games published "The Smith-Waite Centennial Deck", honouring Smith's contribution.

> "The true Tarot is symbolism; it speaks no other language and offers no other signs."
>
> **ARTHUR EDWARD WAITE**, *THE PICTORIAL KEY TO THE TAROT*, 1910

The Fool symbolizes a new beginning, embarking on a journey, and change.

The Magician stands for creativity and purposefulness, as well as realized potential.

The High Priestess is a symbol of intuition, looking beyond the obvious.

The Empress is a card of romance, nurture, and bringing ideas to fruition.

The Emperor denotes authority, setting things in order, and making plans.

The Lovers represent choice, and the need to make an important decision.

The Chariot indicates taking the reins, strength, focus, and willpower.

Strength stands for perseverance – seeing a situation through to its end.

The Hierophant reflects being bound by tradition and the need to conform. Rather than being stubborn, the questioner should examine their belief system to see if it still serves their needs.

The Hermit means solitude. It could indicate feelings of frustration and discontent.

Wheel of Fortune signifies a change in fortunes (for good or bad) or a new opportunity.

Justice indicates a time for decisions, fairness, and the consequences of actions.

The Major Arcana

The 22 Major Arcana cards contain distinctive images that have been used for hundreds of years and are easily recognizable. In modern contexts, the Major Arcana is said to represent the Fool's journey: a symbolic journey through life, during which the Fool overcomes obstacles and gains wisdom.

Death means major change. It is time to move on and let go of the past.

Temperance stands for moderation or making elements work together.

The Devil signifies feeling trapped, fear, lust, greed, and other dark thoughts.

The Hanged Man indicates that the questioner feels stuck in a rut. They must use their time wisely and rise above their problems. The best approach is not always the most obvious.

The Tower is a sign of sudden and unexpected change or crisis.

The Star is an optimistic card; it indicates positive action or unexpected help.

The Moon means facing fears, or a person being pushed against their will.

The Sun denotes confidence and success, with everything falling into place.

Judgement stands for making a decision and committing to change.

The World shows everything coming together. One chapter ends and another begins.

The Minor Arcana

In the 56 cards of the Minor Arcana, the number of the card combined with the suit forms the meaning of the cards. For example, the aces represent beginnings and the tens endings. The images on the cards further describe their meaning. Minor Arcana cards generally represent the more mundane, everyday aspects of events.

The Ace of Wands signifies good fortune beginning, but also a potential risk.

The Two of Wands means business success, and the time to make a bold move.

The Three of Wands relates to an offer of help and making long-term plans.

The Four of Wands means rest after labour and reaping what has been sown.

The Five of Wands stands for struggle and competition, or rising to a challenge.

The Six of Wands is good news. It means victory and success are within reach.

The Seven of Wands means a potential battle, or courage in the face of adversity.

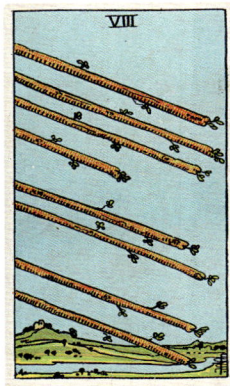

The Eight of Wands signifies swift action, a message, or an important discovery.

The Ten of Wands indicates heavy burdens, unwise use of power, or need for balance.

The Page of Wands is a messenger, standing for adaptability and opportunity.

The Knight of Wands stands for the start or end of an issue, and a surge of energy.

The Queen of Wands could signify a kind, adaptable person, ready to be involved.

The King of Wands is a man of authority, a fair leader ready to make major plans.

The Minor Arcana   263

Card number is signified both in the image and by a Roman numeral at the top of the card

Pentacles (or coins) represent earth and relate to practical or material matters, including money and health. The Eight of Pentacles may suggest a time to start again.

Swords are air cards, representing the mind and communication, as well as conflict. The Six of Swords represents transition and healing.

Cups are water cards, the element of the emotions. The Two of Cups suggests that it is time for the questioner to make a decision regarding relationships.

Wands are associated with fire – the element of energy, action, and creativity. Cards in this suit are often related to work situations. The Nine of Wands signifies overcoming obstacles.

Smith's monogram, a caduceus: the letters P, C, and S form snakes around a staff

Tarot-reading

A spread is a pattern for laying out tarot cards. To conduct a tarot reading, the first step is to shuffle the cards while focusing on an issue or question, then the cards are laid out in a spread. How a tarot card is interpreted is affected by its position in a spread. Sometimes pairs or sets of cards can also be interpreted together. For example, cards referring to the near and distant future are related, and both connect to a final outcome card. Some of the most common types of tarot spread are depicted here.

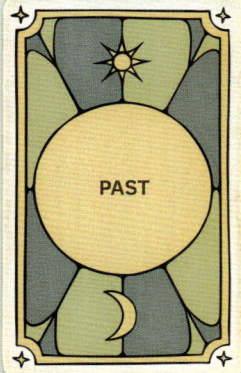  

Past–present–future is a three-card spread, which describes events and influences that affect a particular situation or problem. It allows a person to gain a fuller understanding of what is happening before making any changes.

In a yes/no spread, one card is drawn after shuffling: if it is upright, it means yes; if reversed, it means no. The card drawn will also explain the answer.

A five-card spread is used to determine a course of action. It offers a wider perspective of the person asking the question's situation, highlighting things that may not previously have been considered.

The most likely outcome

The Celtic Cross spread was popularized by Arthur Edward Waite (see pp. 258–59). It is the best-known tarot spread and can be used to answer specific questions or to make generalized readings.

1 The heart of the matter and how it affects the questioner
2 Challenges and obstacles they need to deal with
3 The root cause of what is happening
4 Events of the recent past affecting the issue
5 The near future (the next three months)
6 The more distant future (four months plus)
7 Attitude, or the role the questioner plays
8 Their environment and people around them
9 Their hopes and fears
10 The likely outcome

The first card drawn represents the questioner

As the second card crosses the first, it shows the obstacle crossing the person

The eighth card can signify resources that the person has to rely upon

The fourth card is beneath – it signifies what has already happened

Divining water
Dowsing

Also known as rhabdomancy, dowsing is a form of divination used to locate underground water sources, minerals, or hidden objects using a rod, stick, or pendulum. The origins of dowsing are unclear, but the practice was reportedly used as early as 2000 BCE in China, and later by the ancient Egyptians, Babylonians, and Greeks.

In medieval Europe, dowsing was used to identify criminals as well as to find metals and water, and it was around this time that the practice became more widely known. German miners used dowsing devices while seeking mineral ore, as described by scientist Georg Agricola in his text *De Re Metallica* (1556), and their apparent success led Cornish

Social dowsing
Dowsing became a social activity from the late 19th century, as depicted in this photograph of a group of British enthusiasts using hazel twigs to divine for water near Guildford.

miners in England to take up rods in their search for tin. By the end of the 17th century, dowsing was being used by farmers to locate water sources in parts of Europe, Australia, and the US (where it became associated with witchcraft and was known as "water-witching"). Despite this link, the US military later used dowsing to locate underground water, landmines, tunnels, and even submarines.

Search for supplies

During the Gallipoli Campaign (1915–16) of World War I, dowsing was used to search for sources of drinking water for the soldiers. The campaign, which took place on the Gallipoli peninsula in modern-day Türkiye, involved a joint British–French operation, supported by Australia and New Zealand, aimed at securing a sea route to Russia through the Dardanelles Strait. The area was infamous for its harsh conditions, including the lack of drinking water for troops, despite the military sinking several wells in search of a supply.

Stephen Kelley, an Australian sapper, gained the generals' attention with his effective use of a divining rod. According to reports, Kelley struck water within 180 m (590 ft) of the divisional HQ, opening up a well that produced enough to issue a gallon of drinkable water every day for each of the 100,000 soldiers. Soon after, Kelley apparently located a further 32 springs in the same way.

How to dowse

While it is not known how dowsing works, many of its supporters claim it is due to the individual dowser's sensitivity to geomagnetic phenomena. It is sometimes viewed as an inherited gift, since the ability to dowse often runs in families. Most scientists believe that the ideomotor effect is responsible: dowsers subconsciously move their hands slightly, which causes the tool to move.

To search for water, a dowser stands in the area where water is thought to be located. While tools and methods vary, many water diviners use a Y-shaped stick, traditionally made from hazel or willow — types of wood that, according to folklore and mysticism, have unique properties or energies. The diviner holds the two top ends in their hands, with the bottom of the Y pointing up, then walks over the ground. When the rod passes over a spot where water may be, the pointed end dips, or twists, often with considerable force.

Other popular tools are L-shaped rods, which are typically made from copper or brass, or from wire coat hangers. The shorter section of each of two rods is held in each hand, away from the body. As the diviner moves around the area, the rods appear to swing, point, or cross over each other to indicate the presence of water. Some dowsers report feeling strange sensations while dowsing, such as a pounding heart, muscle spasms, dizziness, and nausea.

Precious resource
This photograph shows members of the Australian 6th Battery pausing to rest while transporting filtered drinking water in cans at Gallipoli, c. 1915.

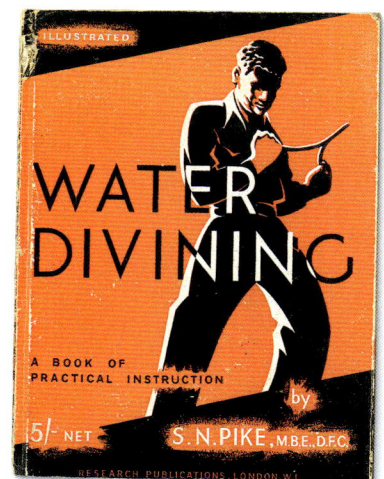

Divining guidebook
Dowsing techniques were often used in rural communities to find water for agricultural and domestic purposes. This book, published in 1945, is a practical guide to the method.

"If both wands swing to the right, turn and walk in that direction."

DOROTHY MCQUARY CALLAWAY, WRITING ABOUT HER HOME IN MILAM COUNTY, TEXAS, US, 2012

Stars and the psyche
Psychological astrology

Also known as astro-psychology, psychological astrology combines astrology with psychology to offer insights into a person's personality, behaviour, and life journey. Rejecting astrological ideas of a fixed character and unalterable fate, early 20th-century psychologists relied instead on their own observations of human behaviour to explain how personalities change and develop over time. By the 1960s, however, thanks largely to the theories of Swiss psychoanalyst Carl Jung, the two disciplines had became more closely aligned, and modern astrology turned away from predicting superficial traits and good and bad times to act, and instead focused on helping people to tackle their problems and clarify their goals.

Archetypes
While working with his clients, Jung noticed recurring universal ideas and mythical themes, or "archetypes". In 1916, he theorized that humans share a "collective unconscious" – a common psychic realm of thoughts, memories, and impulses, separate from an individual's "personal unconscious". Jung's archetypes aligned with the symbolic figures and myths represented by the planets and constellations of astrology, and he suggested that the zodiac mirrors images from the collective unconscious, projected onto the night sky.

In Jung's view, archetypes could provide insights into the human psyche, with astrological factors corresponding to facets of a person's character. In astrology, the Moon is often associated with the idea of motherhood, reflecting nurturing and emotional qualities. In psychology, the mother archetype represents maternal instinct and the mother–child relationship. Similarly, Jung's concept of the shadow, which refers to the hidden and repressed aspects of the psyche, is echoed by planetary placements in a birth chart that are traditionally considered challenging; for example, the Sun in the 12th house might indicate a tendency to avoid self-expression.

Synchronicity and individuation
Jung's theory of synchronicity, or "meaningful coincidence", is often invoked to explain how astrology works. Synchronicity refers to when two or more unrelated events are meaningfully intertwined, despite there being no causal relationship between them. In astrological terms, it describes how planetary movements correlate with an individual's character and psychic state (the microcosm; see below), as well as with the collective unconscious (the macrocosm, or wider universe). Synchronicity also explains how a dream or vision can later turn out to be a reflection of an event that takes place at a distance, or at a later date.

Drawing another parallel between psychology and astrology, Jung theorized that the process of individuation – self-realization and becoming an individual – is reflected in a person's birth chart.

Mystic misnomer
Many of the approaches in psychological astrology are based on the theories of Carl Jung, pictured here in 1960. Although he was a scientist, Jung's interest in mystical subjects meant he was often mistakenly seen as a mystic.

Mars archetype
In psychological astrology, each planet represents an archetype that reflects certain universal human traits and experiences. Mars, god of war and agriculture, is depicted in this 15th-century Lombard manuscript *De Sphaera*.

Perfect synchronicity
This 17th-century image depicts a figure (microcosm) encircled by the universe (macrocosm). The elements of mercury (Moon) and sulphur (Sun) provide the balance necessary for achieving wholeness on both cosmic and individual levels.

Cosmic movements are mirrored within the soul and body

Aries, one of the 12 zodiac signs in the macrocosm

He often drew up horoscopes of clients to gain a new perspective on their psychological make-up, and in a 1955 experiment he studied 800 birth charts. After examining the charts of married couples, he noted that Sun–Moon conjunctions and oppositions – traditional astrological indicators of compatibility – were common.

Building on Jung's theories, astrologers saw that a person's birth chart could help them to realize their potential by providing them with a plan for how they could integrate the various parts of their psyche to become "whole". This concept formed the basis of a new "humanistic" approach in astrology.

A new astrology

In *The Astrology of the Personality* (1936), French-American author Dane Rudhyar introduced the concept of humanistic astrology. Using Jung's theory of individuation, Rudhyar emphasized individual potential and self-actualization. This marked a shift from predictive to psychological and spiritual interpretations of astrological charts, reframing the role of the birth chart as a guide for personal transformation and growth. Further to this, Rudhyar developed the idea of "transpersonal astrology" – looking beyond the individual's "ego" to consider how they connect with the rest of society. Influenced by Rudhyar, Swiss astrologer Alexander Ruperti, who in the 1940s described himself as a psychological astrologer, promoted a positive, holistic approach to astrology in Europe.

Astrology was becoming increasingly popular by the late 1960s, especially in its new psychological guise with its therapeutic applications. When Liz Greene published *Saturn: A New Look at an Old Devil* in 1976, the notion of other methodologies came as a surprise to many new astrologers, who saw their discipline as an alternative language for discussing psychological concepts. Greene and fellow astrologer Howard Sasportas founded the Centre for Psychological Astrology in London in 1983.

In the US, astrologer Stephen Arroyo focused on the use of psychological astrology as a tool for psychological growth and spiritual development. He stressed the importance of free will and personal responsibility – encouraging individuals to view their astrological charts as a map of potential, rejecting what he perceived as the fatalism and negativity of old-fashioned astrology.

Although the 1980s and 1990s saw the revival of traditional forms of astrology, using pre-19th-century techniques and obscure astrological texts, psychological astrology is the most commonly practised form today. It integrates old and new ideas from Western and Eastern traditions, and the work of Jung and other psychologists.

The Huber method

Swiss astrologers and psychologists Bruno and Louise Huber developed their own approach to astrological psychology based on the theories of Italian psychiatrist Roberto Assagioli, creator of psychosynthesis – a form of psychology that emphasizes a person's unique life purpose.

The Hubers' "Life Clock" is a timing system that maps personal development stages over a lifetime onto an astrological chart. Twelve houses represent periods of six years from birth (1st house) to later life (12th house). The "Age Point" (the "hand") moves anticlockwise through the chart, activating the houses and planets it passes. It highlights focus areas and key experiences at each age that become steps towards a meaningful, integrated self.

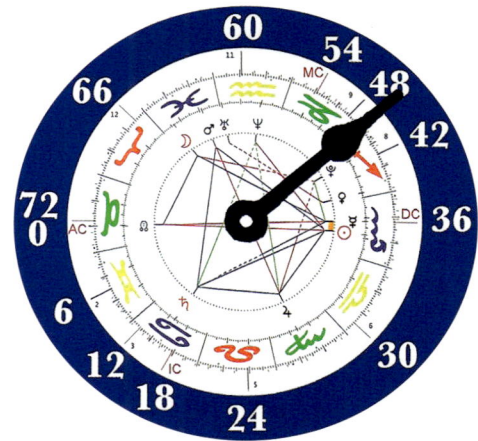

The Life Clock is a clock-like horoscope that charts a person's lifetime, with their current age appearing as the time.

Psychological astrology

Key

1 This mandala is made up of a large circle (the self) set within a square (conscious or physical experience).

2 The circle is divided into four quarters. This illustrates how all aspects of life (physical, emotional, mental, and spiritual) radiate from a central point, reflecting an ordered cosmos or psyche.

3 The central star symbolizes the origin of consciousness and life radiating outwards to energize the psyche, leading to wholeness.

The whole self

For Jung, a mandala was a symbol of wholeness and self-integration – an archetypal map of a person's psyche. This is Mandala number 107 from Jung's *The Red Book: Liber Novus*.

> "So far as I can judge, it would seem to me advantageous for astrology to take the existence of psychology into account, above all the psychology of the personality and of the unconscious."

CARL JUNG, LETTER TO ANDRÉ BARBAULT, 26 MAY 1954

Daily horoscopes
Sun-sign astrology

In the late 19th century, astrology began to change, moving away from specific predictions of individual fates towards an approach centred on general personality trends that were based on Sun-sign traits (a Sun sign being the zodiac sign occupied by the Sun when a person is born; see p. 95). This shift was driven, in part, by the popularity of regular astrology columns that made the subject more accessible to the general public.

In his 1887 book *Solar Biology*, Hiram Butler claimed he had invented a system making the Sun central to character analysis. But it was Alan Leo, often dubbed the "father of modern astrology", who is credited with transforming the practice to focus on character-based and psychological trends. In 1890, Leo (who was born William Allen, but later adopted the name of his Sun sign) and fellow astrologer F.W. Lacey founded *The Astrologers' Magazine* (later *Modern Astrology*). The magazine served as a platform to refine and modernize astrology's image. In 1909, Leo published *Everybody's Astrology*, which included interpretations of each zodiac sign when the Sun was positioned within it. His descriptions set the tone for future horoscopes.

Popularizing astrology

Astrology columns had begun to appear regularly in American newspapers after the *Boston Sunday Post* printed one in 1894. Such content was ideal for the newly formed national news syndicates, which sold the same column to multiple papers, allowing columnists to become celebrities. Some columnists

Not just fortune-telling
Alan Leo's magazine *Modern Astrology* formed part of his efforts to make astrology more accessible to the wider public and promote personal growth and self-understanding.

Star traits
In the early 20th century, booklets interpreting Sun signs were popular giveaways with women's magazines. This 1913 example is from American monthly publication *Woman's World*.

invited readers to write in to receive character delineations (what it meant to be born on a certain date), a few of which were printed. Other papers offered generalized astrological forecasts, with predictions for those born that day added at the end, but these rarely referred to zodiac signs.

Though astrology sometimes appeared in the British press in the late 19th century, it was usually in the form of articles giving characteristics of Sun signs or lists of lucky items. It featured more often from the early 20th century, when the first tabloids were printed. A 1911 column by George Bratley in Sheffield's *Picture Paper*, for example, offered birthday forecasts, a horoscope for a child born that day, and a list of lucky colours and flowers.

A royal horoscope

In 1930, the *Sunday Express* editor asked celebrity palmist and astrologer Cheiro to write an astrological article about the newborn Princess Margaret. Cheiro passed on the request to his assistant, R.H. Naylor. In his analysis of the princess's birth chart, Naylor declared she was a Leo and that "events of tremendous importance to the royal family and the nation will come about near her seventh year". At the end of the feature, he added political predictions and comments based on readers' birth dates.

Princess Margaret's horoscope was published on 24 August 1930. It was an instant hit.

The week ahead
By the 1950s, the 12-sign weekly horoscope column had become the most popular format for astrology features in newspapers and magazines across Europe and the US. This example was printed in the French magazine *Semaine du Monde* in October 1954.

By this time, astrology columns had appeared in women's magazines for several years. However, they did not become a mainstream feature until 1919, when the British girls' magazine *Peg's Paper* was launched. Early issues gave a simple character description for each zodiac sign, but soon, the magazine was printing daily predictions. These general forecasts were aimed at all readers, not split into zodiac-sign-based predictions. Another girls' magazine, *Pam's Paper*, printed the first-known regular 12-sign horoscope column in 1926.

In 1930, astrologer R.H. Naylor wrote a popular piece on Princess Margaret's natal chart in the *Sunday Express* (see p. 273). However, it was his prediction that British aircraft were in grave danger that secured his fame, since it was announced later that day that the R01 airship, on its maiden voyage to India, had crashed in northern France. Enthusiastic letters from readers led to Naylor producing a series of articles entitled "What the Stars Foretell". His simplified forecasts focused on general Sun-sign readings that could be broadly applied to large groups of people (unlike individual birth-chart analysis).

Familiar format

By the late 1930s, most national newspapers had their own horoscope column. Though Naylor is often credited with inventing the 12-sign format (with a description for each zodiac sign), he did not use it in the *Sunday Express* until 1939. Other astrologers also wrote about Sun signs – in a 1934 edition of the *People*, for example, Edward Lyndoe described the ideal holiday based on a person's Sun sign – but it is unclear who came up with the idea.

In the US, a 12-sign horoscope column featured in two magazines in 1932: *Your Destiny* and *Popular Astrology*. The latter publication was written by Canadian-American astrologer Paul Clancy, who went on to publish the best-selling *American Astrology* magazine the following year. From December 1935, astrologer Dane Rudhyar (see p. 270) took over from Clancy in writing its regular 12-sign column. Rudhyar, influenced by the teachings of the psychoanalyst Carl Jung, promoted the specific Sun sign–character type concept – with horoscopes offering useful general insights, rather than predictions. Regarding horoscopes as tools for personal growth and self-awareness aligned closely with the ethos of the later New Age movement of the 1960s and 1970s (see pp. 282–83).

Star signs

Most British newspapers dropped their horoscope columns for the duration of World War II – to save paper and alleviate concerns that predictions may affect people's morale – but women's magazines continued to publish them, offering escapism and hope at a time of uncertainty. After the war, the 12-sign format slowly became the most popular, and by the mid-1950s, the modern horoscope column was firmly established worldwide.

In the decades that followed, Sun-sign astrology pervaded other aspects of popular culture, as well as daily life. By the 1970s, everyone knew their "star sign" (a colloquial term for Sun sign), and astrology had become a common aspect of dating, with "What's your sign?" being a standard icebreaker.

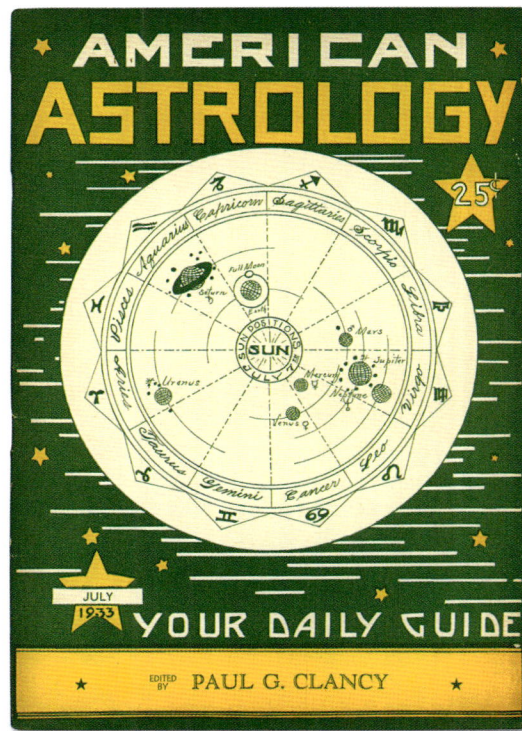

Ideas on astrology
American Astrology ran from 1933 to 2003. As well as its monthly 12-sign column, the magazine featured horoscopes of public figures and an astrological take on global events.

> "The stars incline, they do not compel."
>
> ASTROLOGICAL MAXIM

High-class horoscope
Astrology columns were a feature of cheap weekly magazines for younger women readers in the 1920s. After the success of Naylor's column, they began to appear in more aspirational monthly glossies, like *Vogue*.

Wartime magic
Occultism in World War II

In the aftermath of World War I (1914–18), social and economic instability in Europe and the US fuelled interest in astrology and the occult as people looked for answers. In Germany, the Nazi party, founded in 1919, was quick to harness this growing fascination with the supernatural and turn it to political advantage. Under the leadership of Adolf Hitler, the party machine became adept at using esoteric symbolism as a means to stir the masses. This included the adoption of the swastika, one of the most potent symbols of Nazi rule, which is a reverse image of a Hindu Sun-symbol. It is said that, by reversing the symbol, the Nazis hoped to evoke the spirit of darkness rather than light.

Success in the stars
The Nazis became associated with astrology after German astrologer Elsbeth Ebertin made a prediction for Hitler on the basis of his birth date in her yearbook for 1924, published in July 1923. While she did not mention Hitler by name, Ebertin described a "man of action", who was about to experience some danger but was destined to play a future "Führer-role". Ebertin hit the headlines after Hitler was injured in November 1923 during the Munich Beer Hall Putsch, when the Nazis attempted to overthrow the state government in Bavaria. Hitler's own attitude to astrology, however, seems to have been dismissive. Comments made in 1942 suggest he viewed the practice as a form of popular superstition that was risible.

Manifesting victory
An American propaganda film produced in 1941, *More about Nostradamus* shows Nostradamus predicting Hitler's rise to power and the outbreak of World War II, followed by his defeat by British forces.

Propaganda and prophecies
During the six years of World War II, the Nazis and the British (and later the Americans) used astrology for propaganda. The British ran a "black propaganda" operation, producing fake German astrological magazines that forecast German defeat. Meanwhile, Nazi propaganda chief Joseph Goebbels employed Swiss astrologer Karl Ernest Krafft to work out pro-German interpretations of Nostradamus's historic prophecies.

Other leading Nazis were also active users of astrology. These included Heinrich Himmler – head of the elite guard, the SS – and Rudolf Hess – Hitler's deputy. Himmler employed well-known German-Austrian astrologer Wilhelm Wulff, who performed tasks such as reporting on whether or not the British black propaganda was based on recognized astrological principles: he concluded that it was. Rudolf Hess's flight to Scotland on 10 May 1941, with the aim of negotiating peace, may well have been encouraged by astrological considerations. After Hess's flight, an enraged Hitler ordered the arrest of a number of prominent astrologers, including the previously favoured Karl Ernest Krafft.

Occult aspirations
Modifications to Wewelsburg castle in Westphalia imply it was to become the occult centre of Germany after the war. Its circular hall acquired a black Sun symbol inlaid on the floor, as well as 12 pillars symbolizing the leaders of the future German Empire.

Fake news
This hoax copy of German astrology magazine *Der Zenit*, produced by the British black propaganda unit, contained predictions of a Nazi defeat.

Gazing into the future
Crystal balls and scrying

High demand
This 1910 poster is an advertisement for Claude Alexander Conlin's crystal-ball act. Conlin became the highest-paid mind-reader in the world in the 1920s and earned millions of dollars during his career.

Scrying – the art of looking into a reflective surface to receive messages from the spirit world or to gain insight into the future – has been practised for thousands of years in cultures all over the world. It was often used by priests to communicate with gods and spirits. In ancient Greece, the Pythia of Delphi gazed into a bowl of liquid to receive prophecies from the god Apollo (see pp. 48–49). Celtic druids used crystals for divination in the form of scrying plates, and crystal balls have been found in graves dating back to the Iron Age. During the medieval period, scrying was condemned as a heretical practice by the Church, and associated with witchcraft. However, it continued to be performed by mystics, seers, and alchemists – often in secret.

Mystical sphere
From the late 19th century, the rising interest in spiritualism and the occult (see pp. 236–39) led to crystal balls becoming popular at seances as an aid to connecting with the spirit world. The ball soon became a symbol of mysticism and clairvoyance in literature, in art, and on the stage, and was also associated with Roma fortune-tellers (see pp. 230–31).

Crystal balls were common props in "crystal gazing" stage acts. One of the most famous of these was that of Claude Alexander Conlin, or "Alexander the Crystal Seer". Although Conlin exposed the techniques used by fraudulent mediums, he also never discounted the possibility that spiritualism might contain elements of truth, and he published his own spiritualist material, as well as performing readings for clients.

Psychic to the stars
Between the 1940s and 1970s, American psychic Jeane Dixon became celebrated for using a crystal ball that she claimed she had been given by a Roma fortune-teller. Dixon said she had begun receiving visions by the time she was nine. By the age of 14, she was making predictions for Hollywood stars.

Dixon's famous prophecies included the death of US President Franklin D. Roosevelt, the defeat and re-election of Winston Churchill, the 1947 partition of India, and the 1962 Cuban Missile Crisis. Her best-known prediction, made in 1956, foretold the election and assassination of President John F. Kennedy. Dixon acted as an adviser for President Richard Nixon after correctly predicting a terrorist attack, and later joined the coterie of astrologers consulted by Nancy Reagan, wife of President Ronald Reagan. Although many of her predictions did not come to pass, mass-media coverage of Dixon's prophecies led to an upsurge of interest in mystical and spiritual practices that fed into the New Age movement of the 1970s (see pp. 282–83).

Crystal clear
Jeane Dixon, pictured here in 1960, often used a crystal ball as a focal point to enter a trance-like state, facilitating her visions. In 2009, one of her crystal balls sold for almost $12,000 at auction.

Seeking answers
This watercolour painting by early 20th-century British illustrator Joseph Finnemore depicts a Roma fortune-teller with her crystal ball.

A new epoch dawns
The Age of Aquarius

Belief in the arrival of a spiritual Age of Aquarius was popularized by the 1967 hit musical *Hair*. Its iconic opening song "Aquarius", which spoke of the dawning of a new age of "harmony and understanding", came to summarize the spirit of the Sixties, a period of optimism in the West as prosperity returned after World War II (1939–45). It also captured the appetite for social, political, and cultural change, as many young people sought countercultural alternatives to what they saw as the conservatism of their parents' generation.

The mechanism underpinning belief in a new astrological age is known as the precession of the equinoxes. It was first recorded by Greek astronomer Hipparchus in his star catalogue, composed around 135 BCE (see pp. 76–77). Hipparchus noticed that

Celestial water carrier
This illustration from English astronomer John Flamsteed's influential *Atlas Coelestis* of 1729 shows Aquarius as a man with a jug of water, an iconography established by Greek astronomer Ptolemy in the 2nd century CE.

> "The history of the world since its formation to its end 'is written in the stars', i.e., is recorded in the zodiac."

HELENA BLAVATSKY, *THE SECRET DOCTRINE*, 1888

the positions of the constellations appeared to shift over time – a result of Earth "wobbling" (precessing) on its axis. This means that, as seen from Earth, the constellations make one complete revolution in relation to the tropical zodiac (a band of space that sits above and below the ecliptic, the apparent path of the Sun) every 25,722 years.

Astrologers measure this shift against the spring equinox (a point when day and night are of equal length), which is usually 21 March in the northern hemisphere. When Claudius Ptolemy fixed the tropical zodiac in the 2nd century CE (see p. 89), the Sun appeared to rise in the first zodiac sign, Aries, at the spring equinox. Due to precession, however, the Sun rises in a different constellation on 21 March every 2,144 years (one-twelfth of a full revolution). It currently rises in Pisces at the spring equinox, but most astrologers believe that in the near future, the Sun will rise in Aquarius, and the Age of Aquarius will begin. Since there is no consensus among astrologers as to the exact boundaries between constellations, there is no agreement on when one age ends and the next begins. Some argue that the Age of Aquarius is imminent, while others think the transition might not occur until around the year 2400.

Tying history to the stars

The notion of linking precession to the course of history was first proposed by English scientist Isaac Newton in his book *The Chronology of Ancient Kingdoms Amended*, published in 1728. Newton's work was expanded in 1775 by French scholar Jean Sylvain Bailly, who believed that changes to religious iconography since antiquity were the result of observed shifts in the position of the constellations. Swiss psychologist Carl Jung took up this concept in 1912. He argued that the beginning

of the Age of Pisces (the Fish) roughly coincided with the rise of Christianity, as reflected in Christ's reference to himself as the "fisher of men".

In her 1944 book *Towards Aquarius*, Vera Reid made a clear link between astrological ages and history, describing the Age of Pisces as one of instability and confusion, and the preceding Age of Aries as one of war and great empires. She thought that the Age of Aquarius would begin in the year 2160, and that people should prepare for it. Theories about what to expect vary – for example, theosophist Alice Bailey suggested that physical matter would literally begin to dissolve – but most astrologers agree that the Aquarian age will herald a worldwide period of peace, love, and harmony.

Fisher of men
In this 14th-century Italian painting, Jesus calls on the fishermen Peter and Andrew to join him in "fishing for men" (or Christians). Carl Jung saw this description as evidence of a correlation between the foundation of Christianity and the start of the Piscean age.

Song of the Sixties
Following the success of the musical *Hair*, US group 5th Dimension released a medley containing its most popular song, "Aquarius" (advertised in this poster). The track became one of the best-selling singles of 1969.

282 Modern futures

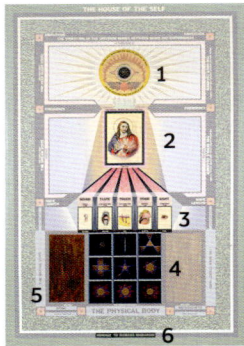

Key

1 The Eye of Transcendence, pictured above a lotus leaf (a symbol of spiritual development), can only be awakened by destiny.

2 This Jesus-like figure represents the soul's arrival into life on Earth as a physical body, or the becoming of the ego.

3 The five senses are associated with the five elements, and the five "Lams" (sounds) of the chakras.

4 This grid of abstract patterns represents the mind's ability to think mathematically (the Number Intellect).

5 The Number Intellect grows out of the Soil of Sisu (the perseverance of the rational mind).

6 This art pays homage to Ramana Maharshi, the Great Seer – an Indian guru who lived from 1879 to 1950.

First house

This New Age artwork, *The House of the Self* by Paul Laffoley (1971), depicts the arrival of the soul on Earth in a physical body. It refers to the belief in astrology that the first house is the house of the self.

Manifesting the future
New Age divination

The concept of the New Age – or Age of Aquarius (see pp. 280–81) – stemmed from the 1960s counterculture movement, as Westerners sought alternatives to the materialism and inequality they saw dominating society. After an era of war, they hoped for a new age of peace, during which people could find harmony and spiritual enlightenment.

Many of the New Age beliefs of the 1970s had earlier origins in late 19th-century ideas about religion and personal transformation. They were particularly inspired by theosophy, which included beliefs in mystical experiences and a deep spiritual state (see pp. 248–49) and New Thought, with its beliefs in affecting the physical world through thinking. These philosophies were blended with ideas originating in Eastern spirituality, Western esotericism (including the work of Rudolf Steiner, George Gurdjieff, and P.D. Ouspensky), Indigenous traditions, and modern psychology, in particular the work of Carl Jung (see pp. 268–71).

Spirit and self
New Age spirituality centres around love, harmony, holism (the interconnectedness of all things), and self-awareness. It asserts that the divine exists within each person, rather than being external, and that a human being is essentially spiritual. It emphasizes inner development (psychological or spiritual) and the individual's pursuit of knowledge and enlightenment. Belief in spiritual awakening has led to New Age followers adopting traditional tools to deepen their self-knowledge, access ancient wisdom, and communicate with divine forces. This includes practices such as yoga, meditation, and other mindfulness techniques that focus on uniting mind, body, and spirit. Such practices are sometimes linked to a belief in past lives, or spirit guides that practitioners might communicate with and learn from.

New Age thinkers often believe in destiny – an understanding that humans all follow a predetermined path. Divinatory practices, many from ancient traditions, have been revived as key tools for achieving the guidance, knowledge, and personal growth needed to usher in a new, enlightened age. Practices such as astrology, tarot-reading (see pp. 264–65), palmistry (see pp. 232–33), and numerology (see pp. 252–53) have become popular ways for people to understand themselves and their place in the wider universe. The use of such methods by New Age adherents has also garnered them wider attention, bringing many ancient practices back into mainstream culture.

Captured energies
In New Age thought, crystals are believed to harbour energies that can help to manifest specific outcomes. Serpentine is believed to channel divine guidance from spirits and gods.

Body and soul
Traditionally a way of uniting spiritually with the divine, yoga became popular with New Age followers. This 19th-century image shows a yogi in the lotus pose, often used for meditating.

Agitated animals
This Roman fresco from Pompeii is thought to depict the god Bacchus surrounded by highly active creatures prior to an eruption of Mount Vesuvius.

Animal instincts
Interpreting animal behaviour

For thousands of years, humans have observed animal behaviour in the hope of predicting the future – and they continue to do so. In part, this is because some traditionally believed animals acted as messengers from the divine, while others think that animals possess a "sixth sense" – an innate ability to detect impending natural disasters.

The Roman writer Aelian was certain that animals were able to perceive everything from coming famines and plagues to earthquakes and floods. In 373 BCE, the city of Helike in Greece was completely destroyed by an earthquake and then submerged by the tsunami that followed. According to Aelian (writing in the 3rd century CE), in the five days leading up to these catastrophic events, all manner of animals had fled the city, yet the citizens had failed to recognize the significance of this behaviour.

Fact or folklore?
In Japanese folk belief, the appearance of an oarfish is a harbinger of an earthquake. These fish can grow to 11 m (36 ft) long and are rarely seen as they live more than 200 m (650 ft) below the surface of the ocean. When an oarfish does appear, it is known as a *ryugu no tsukai* ("messenger from the sea god's palace"). In 2011, around 20 oarfish washed up along Japan's northern coast just days before a devastating earthquake and tsunami.

Predicting natural disasters is difficult for scientists, and strange animal behaviour that may precede such phenomena has long been considered anecdotal. But there are examples that have led to greater empirical research.

Back in the 1960s, the Chinese government had started to explore whether traditional knowledge could be used alongside modern science in order to influence policy. In the winter of 1975, when snakes were seen emerging prematurely from hibernation and freezing to death on the roads near the city of Haicheng, among various reports of unusual animal activity, an evacuation order was issued in the nick of time: the following day, a large earthquake destroyed vast areas of the city.

In Tennessee, US, in 2014, a colony of golden-winged warblers was being tracked by scientists studying migrations. Less than 24 hours before a series of tornadoes struck the area, the birds flew 700 km (435 miles) from their nesting sites. After the storm, the birds returned to their nests.

It is not clear how animals detect such events. They may be sensitive to the small tremors, changes in air pressure, and electromagnetic disturbances that occur beforehand. In the case of the birds, scientists hypothesized that they may have sensed the low-frequency vibrations produced by the weather conditions that spawn tornadoes. Today, researchers in China continue to monitor snake activity as a tool to help predict earthquakes.

Omen of the deep
Japanese mythology associates sightings of the usually deep-sea-dwelling oarfish with impending earthquakes. Seismic activity may disorientate the oarfish, driving them to the surface.

Early warning system
This government-issued leaflet, distributed to some rural communities in China, offers guidance on how to report unusual animal behaviour, such as jumping fish, chickens refusing to roost, and rearing horses.

Journeying to spirit realms
Shamanism and neoshamanism

Encompassing a range of spiritual practices that originated among hunter-gatherer communities in the Central Asian steppes and Siberia, shamanism is thought to date back to c. 30,000 BCE. There are difficulties in defining shamanism as beliefs and worship differ between groups, but in general, shamanic faiths perceive the world as full of spirits that interact with humans and can influence events.

Shamans are believed to be able to communicate with spirits and ask for their aid or control them. The term shaman means "one who knows, or heals", and shamans were traditionally important members of their communities, called upon to predict natural disasters, determine the outcomes of hunts, battles, or harvests, and heal the sick.

In order to divine knowledge from the spirit realm, a shaman may enter a trance state induced by drumming, chanting, fasting, or taking psychoactive substances. Some, such as Mongolian shamans, believe that the soul leaves the physical body, going on a visionary journey to talk to the spirits. It may be accompanied and protected by an animal or ancestral spirit guide. By questioning the spirits, a shaman is able to gain knowledge of the future and offer advice to those seeking answers, or act as a medium through which the spirits can communicate directly.

Other shamanic rituals may involve divinatory practices such as casting lots – as in the Siberian tradition of using reindeer bones to seek guidance from the animal spirits – or scrying, used on the Korean peninsula to divine the future by gazing into a reflective surface.

Shamanic faiths have long faced suppression. The Sámi of Scandinavia were persecuted by Christian authorities for centuries, while the atheist Soviet government banned shamans from public life and confiscated their ritual instruments. After years of being practised in secret, shamanism in Mongolia was revived and awarded protected status in 1992, following the dissolution of the Soviet Union.

A shamanic revival
The 1990s saw a growing interest in shamanism, particularly in Western societies, as a result of greater access to shamanic communities and the popularity of anthropological works such as Michael Harner's *The Way of the Shaman* (1980). At this time, the New Age movement (see pp. 282–83), which embraced personal transformation, holistic spirituality, and Indigenous and ancient traditions, gave rise to "neoshamanism".

The notion of being connected to the spirits of the natural world chimed with environmental concerns and offered a more personal connection to the divine. Practitioners sought knowledge of themselves and the future through ritual dancing, drumming, and sometimes hallucinogens. However, critics of neoshamanism believe the eclectic choice of rituals removes shamanic practices from their cultural context and appropriates Indigenous beliefs.

Shamanic shaker
This instrument, featuring a carving of an octopus, was used by west coast North American shamans during healing rituals; the sound induced a trance state.

Beating a connection
A shaman in Khentii province, Mongolia, beats a ceremonial drum in front of a sacred *ovoo* (cairn), where offerings of gratitude are left for the spirits of ancestors and local nature.

> "Talk to the rivers, to the lakes, to the winds, as to our relatives."
>
> **JOHN FIRE LAME DEER**, LAKOTA SHAMAN

Calls to the other side
Psychic hotlines

The early 1990s were marked by uncertainty – the Gulf War, combined with economic instability and recession, left many people seeking reassurance. As with the New Age movement of the 1970s (see pp. 282–83), these circumstances spawned a wave of interest in the spiritual and paranormal, including the work of psychics. Business and the media were quick to cater to this market, producing television, radio, and print content focused on astrology, and promoting psychic hotlines – personalized guidance given over the telephone. Made possible by advances in telecommunications and the deregulation of the television industries in the UK and US, these hotlines launched the careers of celebrity psychics, and made millions of dollars as people sought psychic advice from the comfort of their homes.

Spiritual connections
New Age beliefs from the 1960s and 70s, which fostered spiritual and psychic practices, regained popularity in the 1990s. They were promoted by festivals such as this Moondance gathering at Snoqualmie Pass, Washington, US, in 1993.

Premium-rate phone numbers that charged higher prices for select services, with the profits split between the service provider and business owner, first appeared in the early 1980s. Within a decade, these numbers had burgeoned, as technological improvements increased the number of lines available and made it possible for callers to select different options by pressing chosen numbers on touch-tone phones. Astrological phone lines began to appear, including a Dial-a-Horoscope service, launched by British Telecom in the UK in 1986. These early services, while hugely popular, relied on recorded information. In 1987, however, the American telecommunications company AT&T started a scheme that allowed content creators to earn money from their premium-rate numbers; many began to offer a broader range of more interactive and personalized astrological and psychic services.

Predicting a fortune
Television played a key role in promoting psychic phone services. Deregulation of the US broadcasting industry in the 1980s resulted in the launch of numerous new cable television channels desperate to attract audiences. One of these, the Psychic Friends Network, which launched in the US in 1991, began broadcasting late-night infomercials for hotlines. These followed a talk-show format, with members of a studio audience explaining how they had benefited from their psychic readings. Hosted by singer Dionne Warwick

> "All it takes is a telephone and an open mind."
>
> **TV PSYCHIC LINDA GEORGIAN**

and psychic Linda Georgian, each instalment featured a number for viewers to call at a rate of $3.99 per minute. By 1994, the network was making around $125 million a year in profits.

Imitators soon followed. The Psychic Readers Network promoted its own psychic – "Miss Cleo" (real name Youree Dell Harris) – in infomercials that aired from 1997 to 2003. Using a fake Jamaican accent and the memorable catchphrase "Call me now!", Miss Cleo became the most famous psychic in the US in the late 1990s.

While Miss Cleo answered a number of calls during her programme, most callers were directed to a network of psychics tasked with keeping them on the line for as long as possible, aiming to build personal relationships that would encourage repeat calls. Though some of these psychics were genuine, others worked from scripts and claimed no psychic ability at all. By the early 2000s, allegations of fraud had prompted increasing regulation of the hotline industry, with crackdowns on content and hidden charges. This, along with the rise of the internet, encouraged services to move online. While seeking psychic advice remained as popular as ever, hotlines were largely replaced by instant messaging, social media, and web chat.

Telephone advice
Psychic Angelina performs a tarot reading over the phone at the Psychic Eye Bookstore, California, US, in 2001. Phone consultations fed a growing desire for more personalized astrology services.

Services boom
Traditional outlets for psychic services, such as fairs, books, magazines, and high-street fortune-tellers, thrived in the 1990s alongside the boom in psychic hotlines.

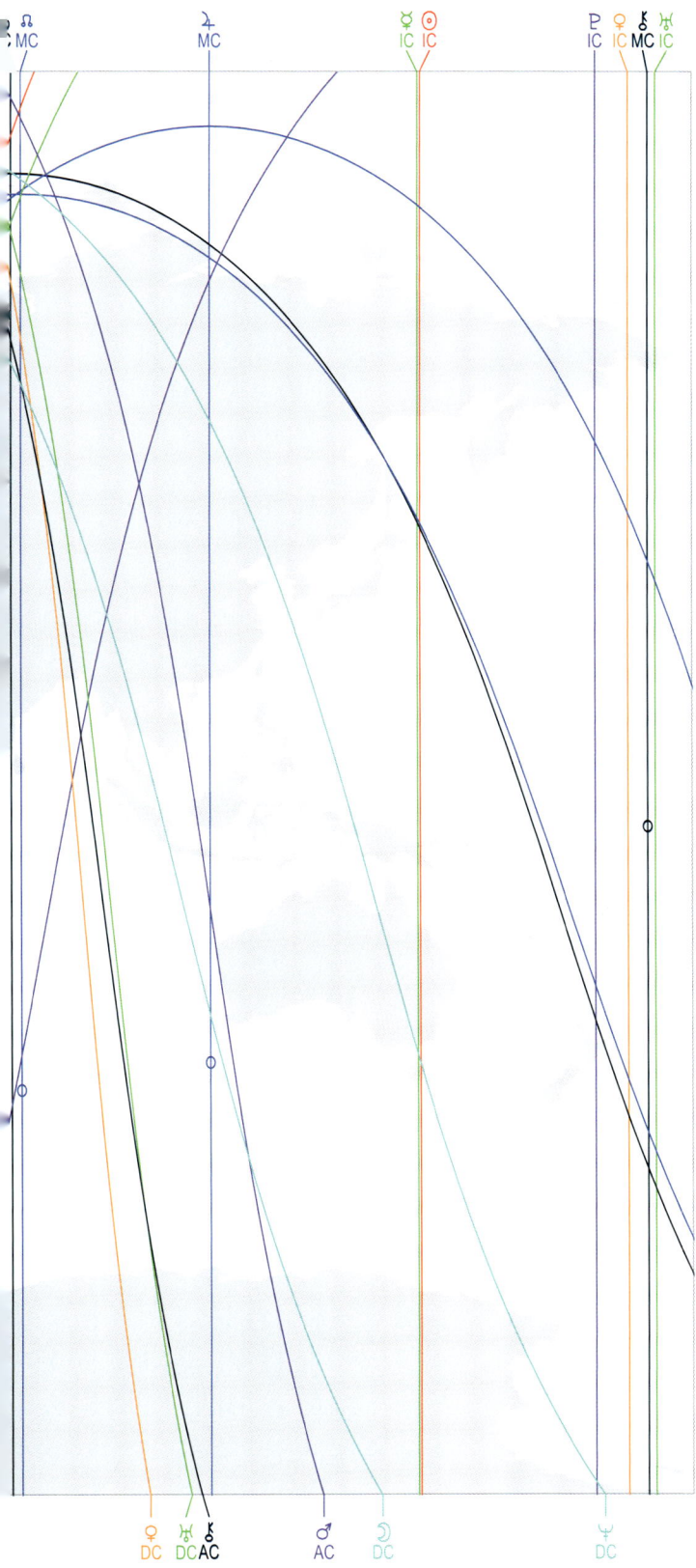

Astrocartography

Also known as locational astrology, astrocartography is a branch of astrology that pinpoints locations on the globe that have the potential to exert a strong influence on a person in various aspects of their life. Pioneered by US astrologer Jim Lewis in the 1970s, it uses a person's natal chart to map the paths of the Sun, Moon, planets, and other celestial bodies, such as Pluto and Chiron, from the angle of rising at the time of birth (ascendant; AC) to the angle of setting (descendant; DC). The places where these lines cross the angles of the midheaven (MC; highest point) and imum coeli (IC; lowest point) are also marked.

Depending on where a person is located in relation to these lines and angles, they may experience transformative changes, such as in relationships for the Venus line, business or career for Mercury, or education and travel for Jupiter. Levels of influence are particularly marked at points where two or more lines intersect. People might use an astrocartographic map to determine where they should live or work, and where they should travel to, or perhaps avoid.

> "We now had a tool to describe
> the significance of Earth
> directions in our lives,
> be it for our natal planets
> or any other object placed
> on Earth or in the sky."

MARTIN DAVIS, *FROM HERE TO THERE: AN ASTROLOGER'S GUIDE TO ASTROMAPPING*, 2007

The lines are marked with planetary symbols, with four angles (AC, MC, DC, IC) for each, which modify the influence of the celestial body.

Supernatural abilities
Reflecting the era's fascination with psychic powers, the 1935 film *The Clairvoyant* tells the story of a fake psychic (played by Claude Rains) who finds he really can predict the future when he makes eye contact with one young woman (played by Fay Wray).

The magic of cinema
Divination on film

Ever since the early days of Hollywood, films have included references to the occult. In part this reflects cultural trends, mirroring spikes of interest in the supernatural, but also the role of cinema in exposing hidden realities or new perspectives. One of the first silent film series, *The Mysteries of Myra* (1916), played on curiosity about the secret activities of esoteric societies, such as the Hermetic Order of the Golden Dawn, which were gaining popularity at the time (see pp. 258–59). Assuming that film audiences were interested in divinatory practices, newsreels before the main feature in these first years of cinema also offered guides to palmistry and astrology.

Prophetic plotlines

Corresponding with the rise of daily horoscope columns in the 1930s (see pp. 272–75), several films used astrology as a plot device. Among these were *Thirteen Women* (1932), in which astrological predictions come true when a series of characters die, and *When's Your Birthday?* (1937), a romantic comedy in which a boxer predicts events using astrology. Another film, *When Were You Born?* (1938), features an astrologer who helps the police to solve a murder involving 12 suspects, each of whom is represented by a zodiac sign.

Fascination with clairvoyants and psychics was also depicted on screen, particularly in the 1940s. Seances are staged in *The Uninvited* (1944) and *Blithe Spirit* (1945), with the latter also featuring a crystal-ball-gazing medium, Madame Arcati. Other fortune-telling methods shown included tarot and palmistry; for example, *The Wolf Man* (1941) is about a Romani palmist who sees a pentagram on the palm of his client.

By the 1960s, popular interest in the occult was reflected on television as well as in the cinema. Shows such as *The Addams Family* (1964) and *The Twilight Zone* (1959–64) blended magical worlds with reality and often included some form of divination. In contrast to television portrayals, which usually set occult practices in a light-hearted context, occult themes have always featured heavily in the horror film genre, where they are used to darker effect. Horror films play on audience fears of supernatural forces, as in *The Curse of the Moon Child* (1972), which featured demonic compulsion among children born under the sign of Cancer.

The concept of an "ordinary" person who has inherited prophetic abilities is an enduring theme. In one example, the eponymous teenager in the TV series *That's So Raven* (2003) has hidden psychic abilities and tries to prevent her visions coming true. Another approach allows the audience to glimpse what lies ahead, while the protagonists remain oblivious to their fate. Some films also feature self-fulfilling prophecies, which only come true because those they concern believe in them.

Screen psychic
In the James Bond film *Live and Let Die* (1973), Jane Seymour plays Solitaire, a character with psychic powers who uses tarot cards to foretell the future.

Chosen one
The concept of the predestined hero creates a prophetic plotline in many films, including *The Matrix* trilogy. Here, Keanu Reeves plays Neo, the "chosen one" destined to save humanity.

Searching for hidden truths

In the first book of Philip Pullman's trilogy *His Dark Materials* (1995–2000), the young protagonist, Lyra Belacqua, is given a divinatory device called an alethiometer (derived from the Greek word *aletheia*, meaning "truth") to help her fulful her destiny. She is joined on her quest by her daemon Pantalaimon, a manifestation of her soul in the form of an animal and an integral, yet separate, part of her.

Lyra's alethiometer, a golden compass, resembles an astrolabe or an ornate pocket watch, with four hands and 36 icons around its face. Each icon has several symbolic meanings; for example, an anchor signifies hope, steadfastness, prevention, and the sea (and its dangers). Lyra consults the alethiometer by setting three of its hands to specific symbols representing her question; she then waits for a fourth hand to move on its own. As it moves, it pauses at various symbols in a sequence, producing a response that she intuitively understands. Many of the symbols are similar to those found in dream dictionaries. Other divinatory elements in the novels include a box of yarrow sticks and a copy of the *I Ching* (see pp. 20–23), which physicist Dr Mary Malone uses to communicate with "Dust" – the elementary particle in the story responsible for consciousness, that is itself conscious.

> "We are all subject to the fates. But we must all act as if we are not…"
>
> **PHILIP PULLMAN**, *NORTHERN LIGHTS*, 1995

Lyra Belacqua, watched by her daemon Pantalaimon, consults her alethiometer in the HBO TV series of *His Dark Materials*.

Advice from algorithms
Digital divination

Since the late 1990s, digital technology has transformed the art of divination. The process began in the early 90s, with changes in the media and telecommunications industries that brought psychics and their services to a new audience (see pp. 288–89). The rise of the internet, increasing use of smartphones, and the launch of social media platforms brought further changes that have turned divination into a global industry.

Digital platforms now allow people to access divinatory services remotely, ranging from tarot readings to dream interpretation. They offer more variety than traditional face-to-face consultations, often for free or at a low cost, and they also have the advantage of convenience, with advice available in real time from a diverse, global pool of practitioners. Large online divination communities have formed, allowing people to discuss predictions with others and to learn techniques themselves. Social media platforms have also led to the proliferation of influencers and spirit guides with huge followings.

The power of data
Historically, data-driven forecasting has been used in a variety of areas, including predicting the weather and anticipating stock market trends. The same approach is now being used for digital divination. Divination typically draws on established systems and texts, including that of the *I Ching* and standard tarot-card interpretations. Using machine-learning, artificial intelligence (AI) combines these systems with algorithms based on huge data sets, such as birth charts and personality tests, to find patterns that can provide instant and personalized readings. Random number generators can simulate drawing tarot cards or casting runes, emulating the "chance" factor of traditional physical methods, while AI chatbots can mimic in-person fortune-telling. Many online services also feature interactive options. For example, users can choose their preferred style of tarot deck or select from a range of questions. Readings from a human practitioner may even be offered for an additional fee, for those who want a more personal experience.

Challenges or opportunities?
Although digital divination has improved choice and accessibility, concerns have been raised about the authenticity and true spirituality of this new form of practice. Some people maintain that digital sessions and AI-generated content cannot replicate the ritual aspects and personal connection of face-to-face consultations. There is also criticism that spiritual practices have become over-commercialized, since many astrological and divinatory platforms have business models that include in-app purchases, subscription services, or paywalls.

Digital oracle
In 2023, Chinese artist Cai Guo-Qiang used digital technology such as blockchain (a digital ledger) to create an oracle called EET ("Exchange with Extraterrestrials"), which answers users' questions with a randomly generated reading.

> "If you can know your future destiny anytime and anywhere with just 100 HKD ($13), why not?"
>
> **26-YEAR-OLD WONG FUNG,** HONG KONG

Blending old and new
Consulting her smartphone, this fortune-teller in Hong Kong epitomizes the rapid take-up of digital practices in the Asia-Pacific region, where an advanced technology infrastructure coexists with ancient traditions of fortune-telling.

Other fears relate to quality control and security, including worries that online practitioners might not be skilled or genuine and that personal data might not be adequately protected. Despite these qualms, and some practitioners' preference for traditional tools such as tarot cards over software, digital divination services continue to evolve and the number of users continues to increase. The global online psychic-reading market alone is expected to be worth at least US$1.16 billion within the next decade, making digital divination one of the most profitable growth industries.

Digital scrying

In traditional scrying, practitioners use a reflective surface, such as a crystal ball or pool of water, to induce a trance state that allows insights or predictions. New digital approaches include the creation of virtual reality environments, where users interact with virtual reflective surfaces, augmented reality apps that overlay digital images on the real world, and crystal ball simulators, where users tap a screen to initiate visual effects. Digital technology has also created completely new forms of scrying in which computer-generated imagery, noise, or data streams are studied for meaningful patterns or are used to induce a meditative state.

Even the smartphone screen itself is used by some practitioners as a black, reflective scrying "mirror".

Cosmic tools for self-care
Astrology and wellness culture

Manifesting success
American astrologer Aliza Kelly has many thousands of followers on social media. Her book *This is Your Destiny* promises to explain how to use astrology to gain a greater level of personal understanding and success.

Newspapers have published daily horoscopes to offer readers a glimpse into their future since the 1930s (see pp. 272–75). In recent decades, however, the practice of popular astrology has evolved, with followers using it to evaluate their personalities, as well as for self-care and personal growth. In this guise, astrology has become part of a broader "wellness" movement, along with New Age practices such as yoga, meditation, and mindfulness (see pp. 282–83).

In today's uncertain times, when political, economic, and environmental disasters are beyond individual control, these approaches seem to offer a degree of empowerment (see pp. 300–01). They tap into the idea of wellness as a personal journey, involving mental, physical, and spiritual growth. Astrology can provide a road map for understanding and navigating this journey, setting out a starting point (the birth chart), and highlighting potential pitfalls or opportunities along the way, depending on the motion and influence of celestial bodies. It also suggests that – if hazards can be predicted and avoided – it is possible to manifest success.

Taking control of destiny

The notion that astrology can unlock potential and foster wellbeing, as well as more concrete forms of success, has been popularized by social media. Influencers have built vast followings by describing how astrology has benefited their lives and by posting guidance on how others can improve their outcomes, too. This focus on personal development in line with the stars has also been aided by advances in technology. New apps allow a level of personalization and astrological detail previously unavailable, and can also provide advice in real time.

They make it possible for anyone to track planetary movements, and then to use this information to guide their daily lives. This is significant in terms of wellness rituals, because some practices are thought to be particularly beneficial at specific times. Certain planetary events, for example, may indicate a good time for setting goals, meditating, or letting go of negative emotions. They may also offer psychological insights, when used to analyse and interpret changes in behaviour and feelings.

Integrating astrology

While astrology is now an established mechanism for self-care in its own right, it has also been absorbed into other wellness practices. Lunar yoga, which uses the cycles of the Moon to guide a sequence of poses, is one of the practices that is increasing in popularity. Crystal healing has also gained new followers through its astrological connections. In this practice, each type of crystal has planetary or solar conditions when it is believed to be more powerful. Depending on these timings, and their own astrological traits, people can choose an appropriate crystal to promote harmony or healing. The use of sound for healing, known as sound-bathing, can also be timed by astrological events. Sound waves are thought to align the body with celestial energy frequencies, which are more powerful at certain times in the planetary cycle. In this, as well as other therapeutic fields, astrology has become a gateway to wellness and self-improvement.

Beneficial vibrations
Used in healing sound baths, singing bowls like this brass example are struck to produce a sustained note that induces harmony.

> "Astrology has helped me accept my past, present, and future potential more radically and with greater certainty than anything else has."
>
> CANADIAN ASTROLOGER AND SOCIAL MEDIA INFLUENCER CHANI NICHOLAS

Lunar energy
A full Moon occurring around the autumn equinox is believed to relieve tension and negative emotions. Here, Japanese yoga practitioners take advantage of this lunar cycle by practising outdoors in September 2013.

Answers in the stars

Astrology in the age of uncertainty

Interest in astrology tends to spike during periods of political and economic instability and social crisis. There is comfort in the promise of being able to predict what might happen when the future feels mired in uncertainty, and people have always looked to the stars for guidance. This long-running search for answers has driven a vast resurgence of interest in astrology since the turn of the millennium, particularly among younger generations.

While people who grew up in the post-war period of the 1950s and 60s could look forward to a cheap education, stable jobs, and home ownership, those aged under 40 now face more precarious lives. Lack of job security, a volatile political landscape, international instability, and concerns over climate change have all contributed to feelings of anxiety and a lack of control. These anxieties were exacerbated during the Covid-19 pandemic, when many turned to astrology to make sense of what was happening, and in the hope of knowing when normality would return.

Romantic guidance
In 2022, a reality dating show looked to the stars to guide romantic pairings. It involved three astrologers matching 12 people born under different signs of the zodiac using only their birth charts.

Because astrology ties each individual to cosmic cycles and events, it provides a useful framework for explaining uncontrollable outcomes, while also offering assurance that there is a pattern to life. Working at both the individual and societal level, it validates each person's characteristics and life journey, as dictated by planetary positions at the time of birth, and contextualizes their existence within the wider universe. In this respect, astrology can also provide answers for those looking for spiritual meaning. As organized religion continues to decline in popularity in the West, many people are turning to astrology as a means of finding deeper spiritual connections and understanding.

Mercury in retrograde
When the planet Mercury appears to reverse its motion in the sky, astrologers say that it is "in retrograde". This happens three or four times a year, for about three weeks at a time, and is an optical illusion created by Mercury orbiting the Sun at a faster rate than Earth. Astrologers believe that this planetary event causes chaos and provokes negative emotions. Social media has popularized the notion, circulating thousands of jokes and memes that blame everything from failing relationships to computer glitches and burnt dinners on Mercury in retrograde.

Mercury orbits the Sun 60 per cent faster than Earth does, creating the illusion of moving backwards at times.

Business is booming
Providing answers has proved extremely profitable, with businesses cashing in on the new astrological renaissance. Apps that analyse horoscopes and offer detailed readings to users are receiving large investments and being downloaded by millions. Even decisions about the purchase of clothing or household items are gaining an astrological aspect, with some companies providing "shopping horoscopes" or investing in partnership deals with astrology influencers in order to guide buyers. As life will always involve uncertainty, it seems likely that astrology will continue to be big business.

Astrology in the age of uncertainty

On trend
New York department store Saks Fifth Avenue chose an astrological theme for its 2023 holiday season display. Christian Dior's huge wheel of fortune, with a central zodiac and celestial bodies, lit up the building's facade each night.

Glossary and Index

Glossary

Almanac An annual calendar containing important dates and astronomical information. Especially popular in the 16th–17th centuries, almanacs also included astrological predictions about the weather, crops, and politics.

Angle/cardinal point The four points (see *Ascendant*, *Descendant*, *Imum coeli*, and *Midheaven*) are the cusps of the first, fourth, seventh, and tenth astrological houses, where planets and stars change direction in the sky. Of great significance in astrological charts.

Angular distance The angle, or distance, between celestial bodies on a star chart, which determines the strength of their interaction.

Archetype In psychological astrology, the universal human traits that are associated with a celestial body and over which that body has influence, such as nurturing for the Moon.

Ascendant (AC) The zodiac sign rising on the eastern horizon at birth. The cusp of the first house, it offers insight into a person's nature and interactions. Also known as the rising sign.

Aspect The angular distances between celestial bodies on a birth chart that show how the planets interact. Some aspects are positive (such as the sextile, formed by a 60 degree distance); others are negative.

Asterism A pattern of stars, smaller than a constellation, distinctly visible in the night sky; prominent in Indian and Chinese astrology.

Astral magic The belief that emanations from celestial bodies can be channelled by magical means to influence people and events on Earth.

Astrocartography The superimposition of the celestial data from a birth chart onto a terrestrial map to show places and lines of particular astrological significance in a person's life.

Astrolabe An instrument that can be used for astrological observations composed of a flat metal disk inscribed with a map of the night sky and a rotating disc to measure the altitude above the horizon of celestial bodies.

Astrology The practice of studying and interpreting the movements of the stars and planets in the belief that they can influence or predict human lives and events on Earth.

Astronomy The study of objects and forces beyond Earth. In pre-modern times, astrology was regarded as a subdivision of this.

Augury Reading omens in natural phenomena, such as weather patterns, the flight of birds, or the entrails of sacrificial animals.

Benefic A celestial body that has a positive astrological influence, such as Venus or Jupiter.

Bibliomancy The use of books to tell the future, by turning to a passage at random.

Calendar round A 52-year cycle in the Maya or Mexica calendars, after which the combinations of day name and day number of the ritual calendar and day number and months of the solar calendar repeat.

Cardinal sign A zodiac sign into which the Sun appears to move at the start of a season: Aries for spring; Cancer for summer; Libra for autumn; and Capricorn for winter.

Celestial bodies Objects that move through the sky, such as planets, stars, and the Sun and Moon, the relative positions of which, according to astrology, can influence life on Earth.

Celestial sphere An imaginary sphere around Earth that contains the celestial bodies. The celestial meridian is a line that passes through the north and south poles of this sphere.

Chiromancy See *Palmistry*.

Clairvoyance The ability to perceive objects and events that are outside the normal range of sensory perception.

Cleromancy The ancient Chinese divinatory practice of casting yarrow stalks and interpreting how they fall as solid or broken lines. Casting six times results in a hexagram with six rows whose meaning can be found in the *I Ching*.

Comet A small celestial body composed of ice and gas that orbits around the Sun in a long elliptical orbit; often seen as a bad omen.

Conjunction An event when two or more celestial bodies are in the same zodiac sign and are at or near the same degree, which causes their astrological energies to mingle and strengthen.

Constellation A group of stars that form a discernible pattern, 12 of which, the signs of the zodiac, form a belt in the sky through which the Sun appears to move during the year.

Decan One-third of a 30-degree zodiac section; each decan covers 10 degrees of the celestial sphere.

Descendant (DC) The zodiac sign rising on the western horizon at birth, which is at the cusp of the seventh astrological house.

Determinism The belief that events are determined in advance by forces, including astrological ones, beyond a person's control, and cannot be altered.

Dowsing (rhabdomancy) Divination using a rod, wand, or staff to find hidden objects, including water sources.

Eclipse An event when the aligning of celestial bodies causes the light of one to be partly or totally blocked by the other, such as a solar eclipse, when the Moon blocks the Sun.

Ecliptic The apparent path of the Sun across the sky as viewed from Earth.

Equinox Either of the two occasions in the year (spring or autumn) when the centre of the Sun appears to be directly above the equator, and day and night are of equal length.

Esotericism A tradition of mystical, specialized (esoteric) knowledge held only by a privileged few, such as Rosicrucianism and Kabbalah. Esoteric astrology regards individuals as spiritual beings, who may carry influences from their past lives.

Expression (destiny) number In numerology, the number that indicates a person's innate personality, talents, and weaknesses, calculated as the sum of all letters in a name.

Extispicy A type of divination carried out in ancient Mesopotamia and Greece by examining the entrails of a sacrificial animal.

Feng shui The practice, originating in China, of orienting buildings and their interior arrangement to harmonize with *qi*, the force of energy that flows through everything.

Fixed sign A zodiac sign that the Sun enters in the middle of a season: Taurus for spring; Leo for summer; Scorpio for autumn; and Aquarius for winter. It denotes permanence and stability.

Fuji (spirit-writing) A form of divination in which messages from spirits or deities are written with a wooden or metal stylus guided by human spirit mediums.

General astrology The application of astrology to larger groups than the individual, such as families, nations, or even the whole of humanity.

Geocentric A model of the universe that places Earth at the centre of the solar system, with the Sun and the planets orbiting it. Most astrological systems have a geocentric model as their basis. Often called Ptolemaic from the ancient Greek astronomer Claudius Ptolemy, who first described it.

Geomancy A method of divination that involves interpreting either markings on the ground or the patterns formed by tossed handfuls of soil, rocks, or sand.

Gregorian calendar A solar, 365-day calendar with additional leap days added every fourth year. It was originally introduced in 1582 and is now used almost universally.

Heliocentric A model of the solar system that places the Sun at the centre, with Earth and the planets orbiting it. First suggested by ancient Greek astronomers, it was described scientifically by Nicolaus Copernicus in 1543.

Hexagram A diagram made up of six solid or broken lines that represents how yarrow stalks or coins fall when they are cast. Its meaning can be looked up in the *I Ching*. See *Cleromancy*.

Horary astrology A form of astrology used to answer a specific question by consulting a chart based on the precise time it is asked.

Horoscope A map of the heavens for a particular time and place indicating planetary positions and relationships, used to make predictions about personality, fate, events, or the best times to take actions.

House In astrology, one of the sectors of an astrological chart, which is based on the division of the celestial sphere into 12 parts.

Humanistic astrology A branch of astrology, partly deriving from the work of psychologist Carl Jung, that views astrological charts as a means for people to understand their natures and personalities and to use this understanding to achieve spiritual growth.

Hydromancy Divination by observing bodies of water and related phenomena such as ripples or waves.

Ifá A form of divination among the Yoruba people of West Africa, in which diviners cast lots with cowrie shells or pine nuts, which indicate the form of lines to be drawn on a divining tray. These lines are in turn interpreted to provide the answers to questions.

Imum coeli (IC) Corresponding to the fourth house and also called the Lower Heaven, it is one of the cardinal points and is associated with a person's ancestral family and home.

Judicial astrology The form of astrology dealing with predictions about an individual.

Jyotiśāstra The system of Indian astrology, originating in Vedic texts from 3,000 years ago.

Kabbalah The ancient Jewish practice of mystical interpretation of the *Tanakh* (Hebrew Bible), first by word of mouth and then by secret codes. Its understanding of powers that emanated from God was translated into an astrological system.

Kundali In Indian astrology, a chart showing the position of the *navagrahas* (celestial bodies) at a specific time, such as a person's birth.

Lecanomancy A form of hydromancy that looks for patterns in a dish of water or observes the ripples created by a stone dropped into the water to predict the future. See *Hydromancy*.

Life path number In numerology, the number based on a person's birth date that indicates the challenges they will face in life and the strengths and strategies they can use to overcome them.

Luminaries The Sun and the Moon, so-called because they provide light.

Lunar calendar A system based on complete cycles of phases of the Moon, producing a 354-day year with 12 months of 29 or 30 days.

Lunar mansion A division of the ecliptic that uses the lunar month as its basis, creating 28 sectors or mansions.

Lunisolar calendar A calendrical system based on both the Moon and the Sun that generally has lunar months of 29 or 30 days, and an extra month every second or third year, to make an average of 365 days per year. The Jewish and Buddhist calendars are lunisolar.

Macrocosm The whole of a large and complex structure, such as the universe, in contrast to a small part of it (see *Microcosm*), such as humankind or an individual person. Astrology is based on the idea that changes in the macrocosm can have a direct effect on the microcosm.

Mahayana A form of Buddhism that teaches that enlightenment can be obtained in a single lifetime. While Buddhism generally condemns astrology, Mahayana, focusing on cosmological principles, is the branch most open to it.

Maize divination (*boleomancia*) A form of divination practised by Indigenous peoples of Mesoamerica that involves the interpretation of patterns made by throwing maize kernels.

Major Arcana In a pack of tarot cards, the 22 named cards that are regarded as particularly influential in a reading.

Medium A person who acts as an intermediary between the living and the spirits of the dead.

Melothesia The idea, prevalent in Mesopotamian and Greek astrology, that parts of the body are associated with and influenced by particular celestial bodies.

Microcosm A small thing with the traits of a larger counterpart (see *Macrocosm*). In astrology, the microcosm (individuals) is influenced by events or changes in the macrocosm (universe).

Midheaven (MC) The highest point of a planet on the ecliptic, it is directly opposite the imum coeli, and at the cusp of the 10th astrological house. It represents status, ambition, and career.

Millenarianism The belief that the end of the world is close at hand, sometimes with a specific date predicted. It gave rise to many religious movements in the 17th and 18th centuries.

Minor Arcana The 56 non-named cards in a tarot pack, which are divided into the four suits of wands, swords, cups, and pentacles.

Mundane astrology The application of astrological principles to larger groups of people, such as cities or nations, or to natural phenomena such as earthquakes.

Mutable sign The zodiac sign the Sun enters at the end of a season: Gemini for spring; Virgo for summer; Sagittarius for autumn; and Pisces for winter. It denotes inconsistency and change.

Nakṣatra One of the 27 lunar mansions in Hindu astrology (see *Lunar mansion*), each occupying a sector of the ecliptic and associated with a significant star or asterism.

Natal astrology The branch of astrology that predicts the life course of an individual, based on the position of celestial bodies at the time of their birth.

Nativity The birth chart of a particular person is their nativity, and the person associated with a particular birth chart is its native. The term "native" can also describe someone born under a particular sign.

Natural astrology The branch of astrology concerned with universal principles and general trends rather than an individual.

Navagrahas In Hindu astrology, the nine heavenly bodies (the seven planets and the Sun and Moon).

Necromancy The branch of magic concerning communication with the dead, originally as a way of acquiring knowledge from them. In the late medieval era it came to mean the conjuring of demons to harness their magical powers.

Neoshamanism "New" forms of shamanism, or ways of seeking visions or healing from spirits.

New Age A movement beginning in the 1970s that encompasses a range of spiritual beliefs and practices, as an alternative to capitalism. It includes belief in the "Age of Aquarius", a new astrological era in which the Sun will rise in the constellation of Aquarius, heralding a future of peace and harmony with nature.

Nodes The two points on the ecliptic where the path of the Sun intersects with that of the Moon. The north node is where the Moon passes into the northern hemisphere and the south node is where it moves into the southern hemisphere.

Numerology Using numbers to understand past events and predict the future.

Occult Hidden mystical, supernatural, or magical powers, practices, or phenomena.

Omen An event regarded as a portent (sign) of good or evil.

Oneiromancy A form of magic which uses the interpretation of dreams to suggest actions to be taken to resolve a problem.

Onmyodo The main form of Japanese divination, concerned with the cosmic balance of yin and yang and the five elements, to determine auspicious times for offerings to the deities of the planets, zodiac, and hours.

Onomancy A form of Islamic numerology that considers there are hidden esoteric meanings in names and phrases that can be revealed by deriving numbers from them.

Oracle A soothsayer who answers questions by delivering advice from a god, often in a cryptic form, or the place where they deliver responses.

Ornithomancy Ancient Greek divination carried out by observing the flight of birds.

Palmistry An ancient form of divination that interprets a person's character or life by studying the lines and mounds on the palm of their hand. Also called ch(e)iromancy or palm-reading.

Personality number In numerology, a number derived from the consonants in a person's name that describes their outward personality as perceived by others.

Physiognomy The practice of divination using the facial characteristics of a person. First recorded in Hellenistic times, it was revived by 19th-century criminologists.

Pip card One of the 10 cards in each of the four suits of a tarot deck that bear symbols (wands, swords, pentacles, or cups).

Planchette A small, flat board (often made of wood) on castors, which is employed in seances or spirit communication. In Chinese spirit-writing, mediums use a writing tool to trace out messages on the planchette.

Platonic Relating to the ancient philosopher Plato, who believed each human soul has a companion star that guides it in life and to which it returns in death. Also refers to the platonic solids – the five regular polyhedra, associated in astrology with the five elements and the first five planets.

Pointer stars Dubhe and Merak, two bright stars in the Big Dipper constellation that "point" towards Polaris, the Pole Star, and can be used to locate it in the night sky.

Polarities Pairs of zodiac signs that sit opposite each other on the ecliptic (such as Cancer and Capricorn) and that share other opposite qualities (yin/yang, earth/water, feminine/masculine).

Precession The phenomenon caused by Earth's axial rotation, by which the stars appear to move backwards along the ecliptic over a long cycle of 26,000 years, meaning the equinoxes and the astrological zodiac months become misaligned with the constellations.

Prophet A person with the power to speak messages that come from divine beings.

Psychic A person such as a medium who has the ability to perceive things beyond the normal senses, including reading others' minds.

Psychological astrology A branch of astrology derived from the work of the psychologist Carl Jung that combines the study of birth charts and psychological archetypes to understand someone's personality and the choices they should make.

Ptolemaic model See *Geocentric*.

Pyromancy The use of fire for divinatory purposes. See *Scapulimancy*.

Qi In Chinese philosophy, the force that flows through the universe, whose different manifestations as yin/yang and the five elements play a key role in Chinese astrology.

Quadrant A division of the ecliptic into four equal parts, formed by the angles between the cardinal points. Each of these is then further divided into three to form 12 houses.

Retrograde The apparent backwards motion of a planet through a zodiac sign, which is caused by Earth's period of orbit around the Sun being different from that of the other planets.

Rising sign See *Ascendant*.

Rune Any of the letters of an ancient alphabet cut into stone or wood in the past by the peoples of Northern Europe, or any similar mark with an esoteric or magical meaning. In runic astrology, each of the 24 runes in the Norse Elder Futhark alphabet is associated with half a zodiac month.

Scapulimancy A form of pyromancy used in ancient China by heating the shoulder blade (scapula) of an ox or the shell of a turtle and interpreting the resulting cracks.

Scrying Divination by gazing into water, mirrors, or other reflective surfaces for signs.

Seance A demonstration during which a medium channels spirits, acting as an intermediary between those spirits and the people present.

Seer A person who claims to be able to predict what will happen in the future.

Seiðr A form of Norse divinatory magic, in which seeresses entered a trance to contact spirits for information about the future.

Shamanism The spiritual practices of people in the steppe lands of Central Asia and Siberia, dating back around 40,000 years; the term is sometimes used more generally (and controversially) to refer to wider spiritual and magical traditions, especially those communicating with a spirit world. Prehistoric peoples are sometimes described as having "shamanic" practices.

Sidereal zodiac A system that calculates the zodiac signs by reference to fixed stars, avoiding the problem of the precession of the equinoxes by keeping the constellations and the zodiac months aligned. It is the most commonly used system in India.

Solar calendar A calendar based on the period of the rotation of Earth around the Sun (roughly 365.25 days).

Soul number In numerology, a number derived from the vowels in a person's name that indicates their innermost desires.

Spiritualism A movement dating from the 19th century, based on the belief that people who have died can communicate with the living, typically through a medium; also the religious belief that all reality is spiritual, rather than material.

Star sign See *Sun sign*.

Stoics A group of ancient Greek philosophers who believed that all people's fates were fixed and inevitable, and that living things were connected by "sympathies" to celestial bodies whose movements influenced their destinies.

Sun sign The sign of the zodiac that the Sun appears in at the moment of a person's birth.

Supernova A luminescence in the sky caused by the explosion of a dying star. The first recorded observation of one, in 1572, caused astrologers to question the idea of an unchanging pattern of stars.

Synchronicity The idea, derived from the psychologist Carl Jung, that there may be a meaningful correlation between two apparently unrelated phenomena, such as planetary movements and the personality of an individual.

Syncretism The combining of different religions, cultures, or ideas. Syncretic belief systems are formed when two cultures come together; for example, Brazilian Candomblé is a syncretization of African traditional religion and Catholic beliefs.

Tarot A system of divination using a deck of 78 specially designed cards, made up of 22 Major Arcana, each of which carries special significance, and 56 Minor Arcana assigned to one of four suits – wands, pentacles, swords, and cups.

Tasseomancy/Tasseography A form of divination by reading coffee grounds or tea leaves that originated in the Ottoman Empire in the 17th century.

Teratoscopy Divination based on interpreting extraordinary events, such as the appearance of ghostly apparitions, monsters, or the birth of animals with a deformity (such as two heads).

Theosophy A philosophy based on the idea that a knowledge of God may be achieved through spiritual ecstasy, direct intuition, and intense study of the occult.

Triplicities Divisions of the zodiac into four groups of three signs, each associated with one of the cardinal directions or the four elements.

Tropical zodiac A system that calculates the zodiac signs by reference to the date of the equinoxes and solstices and is subject to the problem of the precession of the equinoxes (see *Precession*). The tropical zodiac is the most commonly used system in European astrology.

Zodiac Man An illustration of a human body, common in medieval and Renaissance works, showing which zodiac signs were believed to influence particular organs.

Index

Page numbers in **bold** indicate main entries

A

Abbasid dynasty 129, 132, 135
Abe no Seimei **121**
abjad (letter-number system) 142
Abu Ma'shar al-Balkhi **130–31**, 132, 147, 149, 191
Adelard of Bath **149**
Aelian 285
Aeschylus 55
aettir 98, 99, 102
Africa
    divination in syncretic religions 198–201
    Indigenous astrology 194, 216–19
    prophetism 242–43
Age of Aquarius 248, **280–81**, 283
Age of Aries 281
Age of Pisces 281
Agni 32, 33
Agricola, Georg 266–67
agriculture 32, 56, 58, 176, 216, 219, 267
Agrippa, Heinrich Cornelius 139, 170
Agrippina 106
Agyeman Prempeh of Asante **219**
air pressure 285
air signs 89
Akan people 217
Akbar, Emperor 115
Akkadians 15, 234
al-Andalus 149
al-Barbari, Khalaf 139
al-Battani 132
al-Biruni 129, 132
al-Buni, Ahmad 142
al-Dimashqi, Taqi al-Din 191
al-Hamawi 129
al-Hindi, Tumtum 139
al-Isfahani, Abd al-Hasan 191
al-Jajarmi 135
al-Kashi, Mahmud ibn Yahya ibn al-Hasan 136–37
al-Khwarizmi 149
al-Kindi 130, 148, 149, 151
al-Mansur, Caliph 129
al-Qazwini 134
al-Sabti, Ahmad 142
al-Sufi 132, 135
al-Su'udi, Muhammad ibn 'Amir 191
al-Tusi, Nasir al-Din 139
al-Ya'qubi 129
al-Zanati, Abu 'Abdullah Muhammad ibn 'Uthman 139
alchemists 278
alethiometers 294
aleuromancy 47
Alexander the Great 25, 45, 53, 68, 220
Alexandria 68, 69, 124
Alfonsine Tables 159
Alfonso X of Castile 148
algorithms 296
Allen, William *see* Leo, Alan
Alliette, Jean-Baptiste 224–25, 226
Almagest (Ptolemy) 77, 84, 89, 134, 135, 173, 181
almanacs
    as propaganda **209**
    astrology 146, **176–79**, 195, 209
    celebrity writers **178**
    Chinese 40
    Kepler's 204
    medieval European 166
    satire and mock- 178
alpha Scorpio 27
alpha Taurus 27
American Astrology 274
American Civil War 237
Amoghavajra 127
amulets 111, 159, 200
ancestral shrines 216
ancestral spirits 242, 286, 287
Angelina (psychic) 289
angels
    communicating with 189
    fallen 161
    orders of 161
Anglo Saxons, runes 100
anima mundi (world soul) 68, 170
animals
    Chinese zodiac 40, **42–43**
    interpreting behaviour of **284–85**
    spirits 286
Anselmi, Giorgio 161
Anthologiae (Valens) 81, 82, 83, 87, 92
Antikythera mechanism 77
Aphrodite 60, 71
apocalypse 58, 172, 278
Apollo **45**, 46, 49, 53, 109
apps 298, 300
Aquarius 24, 89, **91**, 95, 116, 179
Aquinas, Thomas 151, 161
Arabs
    geomancy **138–39**, 153
    horoscopic astrology 75
    translations of Arabic texts 46, **148–49**, 151, 155, 159, 161, 166
archangels 161
archetypes 269
Ares 71, 81
Aries 25, 77, 89, **90**, 95, 116, 179
Aristander of Telmessos 45
Aristophanes 60
Aristotle 70, 84, 87, 130, 146, 148, 161, 171, 181
Arroyo, Stephen 270
art
    astrology in **171**
    Indigenous African 216
    mysticism and clairvoyance in 278
Artemidoros 45
artificial intelligence (AI) 256, 296
Asante people 219
ascendant 78, 81, 87, 94, 95, 117, 136, 291
Asclepius 46
Ashurbanipal of Assyria 51
aspects, birth charts 94
Assagioli, Roberto 270
Assyria/Assyrians 25, 52, 60
asterisms 122
astragalomancy 47
astral omenology, Chinese **38–39**
astro-medicine **164–67**
astro-psychology *see* psychological astrology
astrocartography **290–91**
astrolabes 131, 154, 187, 294
astrological manuals 16
astrology
    17th- and 18th-century European 194–95
    Abu Ma'shar's treatises **130–31**
    in the age of uncertainty **300–01**
    almanacs **176–79**
    ancient 12
    in art **171**
    astrocartography 290–91
    and astronomy 182, 191
    attacks on 206
    Ayurvedic 32–33, 111
    Chinese 74, 124, 194, 257
    Christian practice and 151
    and Copernicanism 181
    court astrologers **186–87**
    Hellenistic **68–71**, 74, 76–89
    humanistic approach to 270
    Indian 32–33, 74–75, 89, 111, **112–17**, 257
    Indigenous African **216–19**
    Islamic Golden Age **132–35**, 146
    Japanese 212
    Jewish and Kabbalistic **158–59**
    Kepler's explanation of **204–07**
    medieval European 146
    Mesoamerican **56–59**
    newsreel guides 293
    Persian 129
    phone services 288
    and politics in imperial Rome **106–07**
    prophecy and horary **208–09**
    psychological **268–71**
    Renaissance European 146–47, **170–73**, 186–89
    Stoic **78–79**

Sun-sign **272–75**
theosophy and **248–49**
translation of Arabic texts 146,
   148–49
and wellness culture **298–99**
Western 74, 256, 257
in World War II **276–77**
Astronomica (Manilius) 71, 78, 79,
   87
astronomical diaries 25
astronomical timekeeping **32–33**
astronomy
   and astrology 181, 182
   first star catalogue **76–77**
   Indian observational 32–33, 113
augury **52–53**, 151
   Roman augurs 53
Augustine of Hippo 151
Augustus, Emperor 71, 82, 106
auspicious/inauspicious times 32,
   40, 56, 57, 82, 114, 120, 127, 176,
   186, 212, 230
   days 40, 59, 121, 157
   hours 30, 121
Australia, Indigenous astrology 194
automatic writing 237
Ayurvedic medicine **110–11**
Aztecs see Mexica

B

Babylonians
   astro-medicine 164
   astrology 71, 74, 106
   astronomy 77, 87
   dowsing 266
   lecanomancy 60
   numerology 251
   omenology 12, 16, 17, 52
   zodiac **24–27**, 68, 89, 124
Baghdad 130, 132
   founding of **128–29**
bagua 36, 37
Bailey, Alice 281
Bailly, Jean Sylvain 281
balance, health and 111, 164, 171, 178
Balliett, L. Dow 251
Band, Joan 209
Baptists 223
Barma people 219

Barton, Elizabeth (The Holy Maid
   of Kent) 168–69
Bārûtu (Art of the Diviner) 15
Batammaliba people 216, 219
Bayt al-hikma (House of Wisdom)
   132
bee nymphs 45
Berlin Conference 242
Bible
   Hebrew 159
   random consultations 153
bibliomancy 153
bindrunes 100
birds, behaviour of 13, 33, 45,
   52–53, 66, 67, 215, 285
birth charts 26, 82, 83, 87, 111,
   124, 136–37, 172, 203, 248, 256,
   269, 270, 274, 296, 298
   reading Western **94–95**
   reading Indian **116–17**
birthday forecasts 273
Black Death 166
Blavatsky, Helena **248**, 281
blockchain 296
bloodletting 164, 165, 166
board games 215
Bologna 149, 151, 161
Bonaparte, Napoleon 251
bone throwing 200
Book of Felicity, The **190–91**
Brahe, Tycho 189, 204
   geo-heliocentric universe **181**
   nova stella **182–83**, 204
Branchidai 45
Brant, Sebastian 186
Bratley, George 273
Brown, William Wells 199
Buddhism 113, 121, 124–27, 248
buildings
   feng shui 37
   siting of 35
burial sites, position of 35
Butler, Hiram 273
bwe (knot divination) 220

C

Caesar, Julius 55, 66, 67, 106
Cagliostro 251
Cairo 132

Calchas 45, 53
calendars
   African ritual and agricultural
      216, 219
   ancient Indian 33
   Babylonian 17
   Chinese **40–41**, 43, 212
   Christian liturgical 156–57
   Egyptian **28–29**, 30
   Gregorian 40
   Islamic lunar 132, 219
   Japanese *Jōkyō* 212
   Maya **56–58**, 147
Calvinism 172
Camisards 223
Campbell, Florence 251
Cancer 25, 89, **91**, 95, 116, 179
Candomblé 199, 200–01
canoe houses 220, 221
Canopus 219
capnomancy 47, **234**
Capricorn 25, 26, 89, **91**, 95, 106,
   116, 179
Cardano, Girolamo 172
cardinal directions 37, 161
Carmen Astrologicum (Dorotheus
   of Sidon) 87
Caroline Islands 220, 221
cartomancy **225**, 230
Cathbad 67
Catherine of Aragon 168
Catholic Church 168, 172, 178,
   199, 203, 234, 278
Cavalier, Jean 222, 223
Cayce, Edgar (Sleeping Prophet)
   238–39
Cecco d'Ascoli 161
celestial bodies
   and health 111
   and human destinies 78, 87,
      298
   as signs of things to come 186
   astrocartography 291
   Chinese astral omenology **38–39**
   distance between 82
   Hellenistic astrology 70–71
   position and movement of 132
celestial coordinates 77
celestial divination **16–17**
   Babylonian zodiac **24–25**
celestial globes 132

Celts
   capnomancy 234
   druidic seers 66–67, 278
   knots 220
censorship 172, 178
Centeotl 105
Chagga people 219
Chaldean numerology 251
character analysis 273, 274
Charaka's Compendium 111
Charles II of England 209
Charles V of France 153
charms 200
chatbots 296
Chaucer, Geoffrey 157
Cheiro see Hamon, Louis
cheirognomy 228
cheirology 46, 228
Cheng Tang 19
Cherubim 161
Chichén Itzá 58
chickens, sacred 53
China
   astral omenology **38–39**
   astronomy 74, 124
   Buddhism and astrology **127**
   calendar **40–41**
   cleromancy and the *I Ching* 13,
      20–23, 213
   constellations **122–23**
   cosmic balance 74, 120
   dowsing 266
   feng shui **34–37**
   horoscopy 124, 126–27
   interpreting animal behaviour 285
   Jesuit influence **212**
   numerology 251
   oracle bone divination **18–19**
   spirit-writing **118–19**
Chinese New Year 257
chiromancy 46, 151, 155, **228–29**
chresmologoi 45
Christ, Jesus 96, 106, 205, 281
   millenarianism 223
Christian, Paul 226
Christianity
   African syncretic religions 198, 199
   attitude to divination 151–53,
      155, 234
   ecstatic visions **168–69**
   and heliocentrism 203

and medieval European cosmos 161
numerology 251
Reformation and Counter-Reformation **168**
rise of 75, 89, 106
Star of Bethlehem **96–97**
Churchill, Winston 278
Cicero 66, 106
cinema **292–93**
civil calendar 29, 30
civil unrest 178
clairvoyance **236–39**, 278, 293
Clancy, Paul 274
Claudius, Emperor 106
cleromancy 13, 19, **20–23**, 47
climate change 300
cloud-diviners (*néladoir*) 67, 215
Codex Borbonicus 104
Codex Borgia 163
Codex Magliabechiano 105
Codex Tepetlaoztoc 162
coffee grounds 244, 245
coins, in *I Ching* 13, 22, 213
collective unconscious 269
Colles, William 209
colonization 189, 242
colours, lucky 273
Columba, St 67
comets 19, 38, 96, 106, 124, 181, 186, 204, 209
compasses
  magnetic 35
  star **215**
computer-generated imagery 297
concentric spheres 134, 142, 161, 171
Confucius 21
Conlin, Claude Alexander 278
conquistadors 163
Constantine I (the Great), Emperor 106, 107
  vision of **108–09**
constellations
  celestial divination 16, 25
  Chinese **122–23**
  geocentric universe 84
  Hellenistic horoscopes 81
  zodiacal 89, 90, 135
Copernicus, Nicolaus/Copernicanism 146–47, 180, 181, 203, 204, 207

Córdoba 132
coronations, dates of 189
Corpus Hermeticum 71
corruption 161
cosmic sympathy 70, 78
cosmos
  Buddhist 127
  Chinese 20, 212
  Hellenistic 68, 70, 84
  Islamic 134
  Japanese 212
  medieval European 92, 160, 161
  Mesoamerican 56
  Ptolemaic 88
  Renaissance European 170, 171
  soul of the 171
  Yoruba 63
Counter-Reformation **168**
counterculture movement, 1960s 280, 283
court astrologers **186–87**
court cards 224
Covid-19 pandemic 300
cowrie shells 63, 201
Crassus 106
crimes, solving 238
criminals, dowsing 266
Crowley, Aleister 227
crystal balls **278–79**, 293, 297
crystal healing 298
crystals 278, 283
Cuban Missile Crisis 278
Culpeper, Nicholas 166–67
cuneiform tablets 26

D

Dæmonologie (James I) 189
Daishōgun 121
dancing, ritual 286
Dante Alighieri 186
Daoism 21, 118, 127
D'Arpentigny, Casimir Stanislas 228
data protection 297
Davis, Andrew Jackson (Poughkeepsie Seer) 238
dead, consulting the 46, **54–55**, 237
decans 29, 30, 68, 81, 191

decumbitures 166
Dee, John 163, 189
deep spiritual state 283
Delphi 45, 46, **48–49**, 61, 278
demons
  planetary **160–61**
  possession 50
descendant 94, 95, 291
destiny 65, 71, 74, 78, 98, 100, 113, 127, 209, 228, 283
  taking control of 78, 251, 298
destiny numbers 253
Di 19
dice divination 46, 47, **153**
diet 111
Digges, Leonard 177
digital divination **296–97**
Diodorus Siculus 66
direct vision (*imbas forosnai*) 67
divination
  African syncretic religions **198–201**
  ancient 12, 13
  Arabic geomancy **138–39**
  capnomancy and libanomancy **234–35**
  cartomancy **225**
  celestial **16–17**
  Chinese astral omenology **38–39**
  Chinese spirit-writing **118–19**
  cleromancy **20–21**
  dice **153**
  digital **296–97**
  dowsing **266–67**
  dream **50–51**
  earliest condemnations of 153
  early practices **14–15**
  feng shui **34–35**
  on film **292–93**
  hydromancy 60
  Ifá **62–63**
  Islamic onomancy **142–43**
  Japanese **212–13**
  knot **220–21**
  and magic 151
  medieval European **154–55**
  Mesoamerican maize **104–05**
  Mexica obsidian mirrors **162–63**
  New Age **282–83**
  old Norse *seiðr* and **64–65**

onmyōdō in Japan **120–21**
oracle bone **18–19**
palmistry **228–29**
Polynesian diviner priests **214–15**
provoked and unprovoked 15
reviving ancient practices **150–53**
scrying 162, **278**
shamans 286
tarot **224–27**
tasseography **244–47**
Dixon, Jeane 278
Dodona 46
Dogon people 216, 219
dolls 200
Domitian, Emperor 106
Donnolo, Shabbetai 159
Dorotheus of Sidon 87
doshas 110, 111
double hours 40
dowsing **266–67**
Doyle, Arthur Conan 237, 258
drabardi 230
dragon bones 19
dream dictionaries 294
Dream of Dumuzid, The 51
dreams
  dream divination **50–51**, 67
  dream states 45, 46
  Indigenous Americans 197
  interpretation of 45, 50, 51, 200, 230
  manuals 51
  waking 50
Dresden Codex 57
druids **66–67**, 278
drumming 286, 287
Du Mu 127
Dunhuang Star Atlas **122–23**

E

Ea 17
Eadwine Psalter **155**
Earth
  axial rotation 77, 81, 281
  geocentric universe 70, **84–85**, 181
  heliocentric universe 180, 181

earth signs 89
earthly branches **40**, 43
earthquakes 186, 285
East Asian horoscopy **124–27**
Eastern Han dynasty 118
Ebertin, Elsbeth 276
eclipses 16, 38, 132, 176, 186, 215
   in Indigenous African traditions 219
   lunar 17, 26, 204, 219
   solar 19, 219, 241
ecliptic, the 25, 27, 81, 113, 206, 281
economic instability 298, 300
Edlyn, Richard 209
Egyptian days **157**
Egyptians
   astronomy 87
   augury 53
   calendar **28–29**, 30
   dowsing 266
   Hellenistic astrology 68
   horoscopes 124
   inauspicious days 157
   numerology 251
   star charts **30–31**, 68
Elder Futhark 98, 99
electional astrology 129, 209
electromagnetic disturbances 285
Elizabeth I of England 163, 189
Emes, Thomas 223
Emma, the Seeress of Bolton 239
emotions, negative 298, 299, 300
empowerment 298
English Civil War 189, **209**
Enlightenment 237
enlightenment, spiritual 216, 248
enslaved people, revolts **240–41**
entrails
   animal 13, 15, 45, 66
   human 66
Enūma Anu Enlil 17, 24, 25
environment, influence of 87
environmental disasters 298
Epic of Gilgamesh 50, 51
epicycles 181
epidemics 24, 178, 209, 300
equal houses 81
equinoxes 26, 27, 40, 58, 176, 281, 299
   precession of **77**, 281
esoteric astrology 248, 249

esoteric societies **227**, 258, 293
ether 88
Euclid 149
Euripides 13
Eusebius of Caesarea 109
evil spirits, knots to trap 220
exorcists 50, 121
expression and soul numbers 253
extispicy 15, 16, 45
Ezra, Abraham bin 149, 159

F

face-reading **229**
Fage, Durand 223
familial spirit helpers 197
famine 24, 186, 285
fasting 197, 286
fate 26, 46, 55, 59, 65, 67, 71, 78, 81, 127, 159
Fates 78
feng shui **34–37**, 121
Ficino, Marsilio 171, 172
field allocation 38
Figulus, Publius Nigidius 106
figurines 200
Filelfo, Francesco 172
film, divination on **292–93**
fire (pyromancy) 13, 234
fire signs 89
five elements 37, 40, 120, 124
fixed stars 132, 135
Flamsteed, John 280
floods 186, 285
Florentine Codex 163
flowers, lucky 273
Fludd, Robert 170
foaming at the mouth 223
folklore
   dowsing 267
   European 200
   Indigenous African 216, 218, 219
Forbidden City (Beijing) 34, 35
Forman, Simon 209
fortune-tellers
   card-reading 225
   Chinese 40
   crystal balls and scrying **278–79**
   digital 297
   on film 293

palm-reading 228
   Roma 228, **230–31**, 247
   tasseography **244–47**
four elements 68, 70, 88, 130, 139, 142, 161, 164
four states 164
Fox, Kate, Maggie, and Leah 237
Franklin, Jane 239
Franklin, Sir John 239
fraud 289
free will
   and fate 78
   and psychological astrology 270
   astrology as threat to 172
   divination against doctrines of 151
Freemasons 226, 227
Freud, Sigmund 256
Freyja 65, 98, 102
fuji see spirit-writing
futhark 98
Fy Xi, Emperor 20, 21

G

Gabirol, Solomon ibn 159
Gabriel, the Angel 139
Gadbury, John 176, 178
Galen of Pergamon 164, 166
Galilei, Galileo 189, 194–95, **202–03**
Gallipoli Campaign 267
games of chance 47, 215
Ganivet, Jean 166
Gaugamela, Battle of 45
Gaurico, Luca 172
Gébelin, Antoine Court de 225
gematria 251
Gemini 25, 89, **90**, 95, 116, 179
genethlialogy 26
geo-heliocentric universe **181**
geocentric universe 70, **84–85**, 134, 146–47, 181, 182, 195
geomagnetic phenomena, sensitivity to 267
geomancy 153
   Arabic **138–41**
   feng shui **34–35**
   geomantic figures **140–41**
geometry 207
Georgian, Linda 288, 289

Gerard of Cremona 149, 153
Gerbert of Aurillac 148–49
Gershon, Levi ben (Gersonides) 159
ghosts
   in Greek literature 55
   knocking 237
Giriama people 242, 243
globalization 257
gods and goddesses
   African 242
   ancient Greek 45–49
   animals as messengers of 285
   augury 52–53
   celestial divination 16–17, 24
   Chinese spirit-writing **118**
   and dreams 50–51
   early divination 15
   and human destiny 78
   Indigenous African 216
   lecanomancy 60
   Moon, Sun, and planets as incarnations of 16, 70–71, 81
   Norse 65, 98, 100
   and seven-day week **127**
Goebbels, Joseph 276
Gordian knot 220
gravity 195
Great Basin, peoples of the 197
Great Chain of Being 171
Great Chicago Fire 238
Great Comet 204
Great Fire of London **210–11**
Great Plague 208
Greece, ancient
   astronomy 87
   augury 53
   capnomancy and libanomancy 234
   chiromancy and onomancy 155
   divination **44–49**
   dowsing 266
   geomancy 153
   knots 220
   lecanomancy **60–61**
   medicine 164
   necromancy 54–55
   numerology 251
   see also Hellenistic astrology
Greek Magical Papyri 45, 60
Greene, Liz 271
Gregorian calendar 40

guardian spirits 197
Gudea of Lagash 51
Gulf War 288
Gundissalinus, Dominicus 149
Guo Pu 35
Gurdjieff, George 283
Gwalleuk 120

H

Habsburg dynasty 189
Hades 55
hadith 138
Hagall 98, 102
hagiography 151
Haida people 197
Halévi, Judah 159
hallucinogens 286
Hamon, Louis (Cheiro) 228, 229, 273
Han dynasty 21, 39, 43
Han Yu 127
hands
　dominant 232
　types/shapes 228
Harappan civilization 32
Hardinge Britten, Emma 236
harmony
　cosmic 70, 74, 207
　wellness 298
Harner, Michael 286
Harumi, Shibukawa 212
Harun al-Rashid, Caliph 132
Hávamál 98, 100
Hawaii 214, 215
Hecate 55
Heian period 121
heightened awareness 197, 216, 248
heliocentric universe 146–47, **180–81**, 203, 204, 207
Hellenistic astrology 26, 27, 74
　first star catalogue **76–77**
　formalizing **86–89**
　geocentric universe **84–85**
　horoscopes 74, **80–83**, 113
　origins of **68–71**
　Stoic astrology **78–79**
　see also Greece, ancient
henbane 65
Henri II of France 175

Henry VII of England 188
Henry VIII of England 168, 188
herbal medicine 111
heredity 87
Hermann of Carinthia 149
Hermes 71
Hermes Agoraios 46
Hermes Trismegistus 71, 139, 225
Hermetic literature 71
Hermetic Order of the Golden Dawn 159, 227, 258, 259, 293
Herodotus 28
Heron-Allen, Edward 228
Hess, Rudolf 276
Heydon, Christopher 181
Heydon, John 209
hieroglyphics 211
higher purpose in life, insights into 197
Highland Seer 245, 247
Himmler, Heinrich 276
Hinduism 111, 113, 124, 194, 248, 276
Hipparchus of Nicaea **76–77**, 280–81
Hippocrates 68, 164, 166
His Dark Materials (Pullman) 294
Hitler, Adolf 276
Hittites 60
holism 111, 283
holistic spirituality 286
Hollywood 293
Homer 45, 53, 55, 78, 237
Hoodoo 200
horary astrology **208–09**
horoscopes
　12-sign format 248, 274
　apps 300
　astro-medicine 166
　Babylonian 26
　early 26
　East Asian **124–27**
　Egyptian 124
　for the revolution of the year 176
　and four traditional branches of astrology 209
　Hellenistic 74, **80–83**
　Indian 113–15
　Islamic 136–37
　Maya 58
　newspaper columns 257, 273, 274, 293, 298

reading a birth chart **94–95**
　royal 273
　Stoic 78
　Sun-sign astrology 248, **272–75**
　telephone 288
horror films 293
hotlines, psychic **288–89**
Houdini, Harry 237
houses 81–82, 114, 140, 206–07
　birth charts 94, 111, 116, 117
　house division **81**
Huber, Bruno and Louise **270**
Hugo of Santalla 138, 153
Huguenots 223
human behaviour 269
human consciousness, after death 237
humanistic astrology 270
humours, four 164, 171, 178
Hun Hunahpu 105
Huron people 196
hydromancy 46, 60
hypnosis 237

I

I Ching 13, **20–23**, 213, 294, 296
ibn al-Faqih 129
ibn al-Haytham 132
ibn al-Nadim 135
ibn 'Arabi, Muhammad 142
ibn Khaldun, Abd al-Rahman 138, 139, 142, 143
ibn Mahfuf, Abdulla 139
ibn Qurra, Thabit 149
Ibn Sina 132
ideomotor effect 267
Idris 139
Ifá divination **62–63**, 201
ilm al-rami (science of the sand) 138, 153
incantations 216
incense 234
incubation 45, 51, 55, 67
Index of Prohibited Books 178
India
　astrology 74–75, 89, **112–15**, 257
　astronomical timekeeping **32–33**
　Ayurvedic medicine **110–11**

horoscopy 113, 124, 125, 127
numerology 251
palmistry 228
reading Indian birth charts **116–17**
Indigenous Americans
　astrology 194
　religion 197, 199, 200
　vision quests **196–97**
individuation 269
Indus Valley civilization 32
influencers 296, 298, 299, 300
initiation ceremonies 197, 219
Inquisition 172, 178, 203
instant messaging 289
Intelligences, angelic 161
intensified versions of numbers 252
interconnectivity 12, 13
internet 289, 296
Ireland, druidic seers 66, 67
Ishtar 51
Iskandar, Jalal al-Din, nativity chart **136–37**
Islam
　African syncretic religions 198
　Golden Age astrology 75, **132–35**, 194
　and Hellenistic astrology 89
　onomancy **142–43**
　polemics challenging astrology 135
　translation of Arabic astrological texts 148, 166
isolation 197
isolationism, Japanese 212
Istanbul 132, 191

J

Jade Emperor 43
James I of England (James VI of Scotland) 189
Japan
　divination innovation **212–13**
　feng shui 35
　horoscopy 127
　interpreting animal behaviour 285
　onmyōdō **120–21**
Jericho 55

Jesuit missionaries 21, 38, 196, **212**
Jews
    astrological knowledge 149
    Jewish and Kabbalistic astrology **158–59**
Jin dynasties 35
John of Sacrobosco 157
Joken, Nishikawa 212
Judaism 149, **158–59**
judicial astrology 87, 209
Jung, Carl 257, 269–71, 274, 281, 283
Jupiter 71, 81, 82, 89, **92**, 124, 130, 161, 181, 182, 291
    moons 195, 203
Justinian I, Emperor 107
jyotiḥśāstra 111, 113, 194

K

Kabbalah **155**, 226, 227, 250, 251, 258
kahuna 214, 215
Kamehameha I of Hawaii 215
Kardec, Allan **239**
karma 74–75, 113–14, 248
Kazan, Emperor 121
Kelley, Edward 189
Kelley, Stephen 267
Kelly, Aliza 298
Kennedy, John F. 278
Kepler, Johannes 182, 189, 195, **204–07**
Khoisan people 218
Khosa people 219
Kircher, Athanasius 250
Kitab al-Shu'a'at (Book of the Rays; al-Kindi) **151**
knocking, ghostly 237
knot divination **220–21**
knowledge, spread of 132, 148, 172
knucklebones 46
Kos 68
Krafft, Karl Ernest 276
Kronos 70, 71
Kū 215
Kuai-Xiang 34
Kuiye 216
Kūkai 127

L

Lacey, F.W. 273
Lactantius 109
Lacy, John 223
Laet, Gaspard 176–77
Laffoley, Paul 282
landmines 267
latitude 77
Lavater, Johann Kaspar 229
leap months 33, 40
leap years 77
leaves, rustling of 45, 46
lecanomancy 46, **60–61**
Leo 25, 27, 82, 89, **91**, 95, 116, 179
Leo, Alan 248, 249, 256, 273
letters, esoteric meaning of 142, 143
Lévi, Eliphas (Alphonse Louis Constant) 226, 227, 251, 258
Lewis, Jim 291
libanomancy **234–35**
Libo, Drusus 106
Libra 25, 89, **91**, 95, 116, 179
Life Clock **270**
life path numbers 253
lightning 215
Lilly, William **178**, 208, 209, 211
Lincoln, Mary Todd 237
Lindow Man 67
lines, palm 232–33
literature
    mysticism and clairvoyance in 278
    spirits of the dead in 237
livers, reading 15
Llull, Ramon 142
locational astrology **290–91**
lodestones 35
logic 12
Lollia Paulina, Empress 106
Lombroso, Cesare 229
Long Count calendar 58, 147
longitude 77
Lorges, Gabriel de 175
lots, casting 150, 200, 201, 286
Louis XIV of France 223
Lü Dongbin 118
Lu Jia 75

Luba people 216
Lucan 55
lunar calendar 29, 40, 43, 132
lunar yoga 298
lunisolar calendar 17, 40
Luther, Martin/Lutheranism 168, 172, 206
lwa 198, 199
Lyndoe, Edward 274

M

machine-learning 296
Mackenzie, Kenneth 258
macrocosm-microcosm 32, 167, 171, 269
Madrid Codex 58–59
magazines, astrology columns 257, 274, 275
Magi **96–97**, 205
magic
    divination linked to 151
    runic 100
maize 58
    readings **104–05**
Maji Maji Rebellion 242
Major Arcana 226, 258, **260–61**
Makir, Jacob ben 159
Mami Wata 199
Mamluk Empire 224
mandalas 127, 271
Mandate of Heaven 38
Manilius, Marcus 71, 78, 79, 87
manteis 45–46
mantic alphabets 151, 153
maps, astrocartographic **290–91**
Marcus Aurelius, Emperor 106
Marduk 25
Margaret, Princess 273, 274
Marion, Elie 223
Mars 71, 81, 82, 89, **92**, 111, 124, 135, 161, 268–69
Masha'allah ibn Athari 128, 129
master numbers 252
matchmaking 172
Maternus, Julius Firmicus 71, 106, 107
mathematics
    astrological models 132
    Islamic onomancy 142–43

    sacred 70
    trigonometry 76
Mathers, Samuel Lidell MacGregor 258
Matthew, Gospel of 96
Matthias Corvinus of Hungary 172
Maxentius, Emperor 109
Maximilian I, Emperor 186
Maya
    astrology **56–59**, 147
    Calendar Round **56**
    maize 105
media, changes to 296
Medici, Catherine de' 186
Medici, Cosimo II de' 203
Medici family 171, 186, 189, 203
medicine
    almanacs 178
    astral **25**
    astro-medicine 139, **164–67**
    birth of Ayurvedic **110–11**
    divination and 201
    four humours 68, 70
    geomancy and prognosis 153
    miraculous cures 223
    shamans 286
meditation 111, 283, 298
mediums, spirit 237, 238, 239, 286
Meiji restoration 121
Mekatilili wa Menza 242, 243
Melampodidai 45
melothesia 25
memes 300
Mercury 71, 79, 81, 89, **93**, 124, 291
    in retrograde **300**
Mesmer, Franz/Mesmerism 237, 239
Mesoamerica
    astrology **56–59**, 194
    maize readings **104–05**
Mesopotamia 12, 15, 16, 25, 50, 51, 68, 74, 106, 164, 234
metals, dowsing 266–67
Métis people 196
Mexica
    astrology 56, 59, 147
    maize readings **104–05**
    obsidian mirrors **162–63**
Mexican Inquisition 178
micro-zodiac 26
Milan, Edict of 109

military campaigns 186, 215
Milky Way 38, 218
millenarianism, and prophecy **222–23**
Milvian Bridge, Battle of 109
mindfulness 283, 298
Ming dynasty 34, 118
Minor Arcana 226, 258, 259, **262–63**
mirrors
  feng shui 37
  Mexica obsidian **162–63**
  scrying 151
Miss Cleo (Youree Dell Harris) 289
Mixe people 105
Mlimo 242
Moctezuma II 163
Mohenjo-daro 32
moira 78
Monmu, Emperor 120
months 29, 33, 40, 56
Moon 194, 207
  in ancient India 32, 113
  and astro-medicine 164
  celestial divination 16, 17, 24, 25
  in classical astrology 93
  god 71
  in Hellenistic astrology 81, 89
  in Indigenous African traditions 216–17, 219
  in Islamic Golden Age astrology 132
  lunar calendar 29, 40, 43
  lunar mansions 32, 116, 117, 121, 122, 124, 127, 142
  lunar yoga 298
  Sun–Moon conjunctions/oppositions 270
  and yin 124
More, Sir Thomas 168
mounts of the palm 232
mundane astrology 24, 26, 113
Munich Beer Hall Putsch 276
Muqaddima (ibn Khaldun) 138, 139, 142, 143
Murad III, Sultan 191
music 74, 207
mysticism/mystics 224, 278, 283
  Kabbalah 159
  theosophy 248

mythology
  Caroline Islands 220
  Chinese 21
  maize and **105**
  Norse 98, 100

N

Nahua people 105
nakṣatras 32, 113, 116, 124, 127
Namaqua people 218
namburbû 12, 17, 51
names, esoteric value of 142
Napier, Richard 209
Naram-Sin of Akkad 15
natal astrology 26, 43, 59, 68, 74, 87, 111, 124, 136–37, 172, 209, 273, 274, 291
nativities 166, 209
natural astrology 87
natural disasters 186, 284, 285, 286
natural philosophy 87, 92
natural world 286
Naubakht 129
nautical knots 220
navigation
  astrolabes 154
  astrology and 189
  nautical knots 220
  Polynesians 215
Naylor, R.H. 273, 274
Nazi regime 276, 277
Ndebele Rebellion 242
Nechepso 71
necromancy 46, **54–55**
Neo-Assyria 16
neo-Platonism 171
neoshamanism **286–87**
Neptune 93
Nero, Emperor 71, 106
New Age movement 147, 234, 256, 274, 278, 288, 298
  Age of Aquarius **280–81**
  divination **282–83**
  and *I Ching* 21
  and shamanism 286
New Thought movement 251, 283
newspapers, astrology columns 257, 273, 274, 293, 298

Newton, Isaac 195, 251, 281
Ngas people 216
Ngundeng Bong 242
Ngwale, Kinjikitile 242
nightmares 50
Nile, flooding of 29
Nixon, Richard 278
Nobutake, Baba 213
non naturals, six 164
Nonconformism 223
Norns 64, 65, 98, 101
Norse divination **64–65**
North Star 122
Nostradamus (Michel de Nostredame) **174–75**, 186, 211, 276
Nuer people 242, 243
numerology 195, **250–53**, 283
Nut 29
Nyaturu people 219

O

oarfish 285
obsidian mirrors **162–63**
occult/occultism 159, 163, 224, 226, 227, 251, 258, 259, 278, 293
  on film 293
  in World War II **276–77**
Odin 65, 98, 99, 100
Odu Ifá 63
offerings 63, 121, 215
olive oil 60
Olmecs, astrology 56
Olodumare 63, 201
omens/omenology
  ancient Indian 113
  augury 53
  Babylonian 12, **16–17**
  celestial **16–17**
  Chinese astral omenology **38–39**
  compendia 17, 24, 45, 52
  dream 51
  East Asian horoscopy 124
  reading 215
On Critical Days (Galen) 166
oneiromancy 50
online divination **296–97**
onmyōdō **120–21**

onomancy 155
  Islamic **142–43**
opposing qualities 89
oracles
  ancient Greek 45–46, 48–49
  oracle bone divination **18–19**, 20
Oraculum 251
oral tradition 197, 201
ornithomancy 45, **52–53**
Oro 215
Orpheus and Eurydice 54, 55
Orunmila 63
Osiris 60
Ottoman Empire 186, 191, 194, 244, 245
Ouija boards 118
Ouspensky, P.D. 283
owls 53

P

palm-reading (palmistry) 46, 63, 151, 155, 195, 201, 230, 256, 283, 293
  newsreel guides 293
  reading palms **232–33**
  revival **228–29**
palmomancy 47
Pan 45, 46, 79
Papa Legba 199
papermaking 132
parallax 182
paranormal 288
Paris Magical Codex 60
Paris, Matthew 155
Parliamentarians 209
Parron, William 188
patronage, court astrologers 186, 189
Pausanias 47
Pepys, Samuel 211
persecution
  religious minorities 223
  shamans 286
Persian Empire
  Abu Ma'shar's treatises **130–31**
  astrology 75, 129, **132–35**, 194
  founding of Baghdad **128–29**
  horoscopy 124, 127
  Islamic Golden Age **132–35**

personal growth 298
personal transformation 286, 291
personality 74, 116, 232, 256, 269, 273
personality numbers 253
personality tests 296
Petosiris 71
photography, and spiritualism 237
physiognomy **229**
Picatrix 148, 149, 161
Pico della Mirandola, Giovanni 207
Pisces 26, 89, **91**, 95, 116, 179
Pitenius, Titus 83
Pitois, Jean-Baptiste 226
places *see* houses
plague 166, 176, 186, 208, 209, 285
planchettes 118
planetary demons **160–61**
Planetary Hypotheses (Ptolemy) 84
planets **92–93**
　alignment of 215
　anthropomorphization of 134, 135, 136
　astrocartography 291
　Ayurvedic medicine 111
　birth charts 94
　celestial divination 16, 17
　conjunctions and cycles 32, 38, 39, 96, 114, 130, 134, 135, 166, 186, 204, 205, 209
　and demons **160–61**
　four qualities 87–89
　geocentric universe 70, **84–85**, 134, 181, 182
　and good/evil behaviour 161
　heliocentric universe **180–81**, 207
　Hellenistic astrology 70–71, 81, 82
　horoscopes 124
　Indian astrology 113–14, 116, 117
　Kepler's view of 207
　linked to five elements 124
　opposing qualities 89
　outer **93**
　psychological astrology 269
　and seven-day week **127**
　signs of the zodiac 90–91

planispheres 25
plants
　feng shui 37
　medicinal 166–67
plastromancy 19
Plato 68–70, 71, 84, 171, 248
Platonic solids, five 207
playing cards 224, 225
Pleiades 32, 46, 218, 219
plotlines, prophetic film 293
Pluto 93
Polaris/Pole Star 77, 219
political astrology 24
political instability 298, 300
politics, astrology and 186, 189, 203
Polynesians, diviner priests **214–15**
Pompeii 60, 284
Pompey 106
popular astrology 298
possession
　demonic 50
　by Holy Spirit 223
　by spirits 199
prayer 197
precession **77**, 281
predestination 293
priests, Polynesian diviner **214–15**
printing 146, 172
Procheiroi kanones (Handy Tables; Ptolemy) 89
prodigies, study of 46
prognostications
　in almanacs 176–77, 204
　Indian astrology 113
propaganda
　astrological 189
　World War I 276
prophecy
　African prophetism **242–43**
　clairvoyance 238–39
　crystal balls and scrying **278–79**
　in film plotlines 293
　and millenarianism **222–23**
　World War II 276
prophets, millenarian 223
Protestant Reformation **168**, 172, 223
proverbs 216

Psalters
　Eadwine Psalter **155**
　random consultations 153
psychics **288–89**, 293, 296, 297
psychoactive substances 286
psychoanalysis 247, 256
psychological astrology 248, **268–71**
psychology 256
Ptolemaic dynasty 68
Ptolemy, Claudius 68, 76, 77, 81, 82, 84, 86–89, 92, 130, 134, 135, 148, 149, 171, 173, 181, 280, 281
public health 178, 209
pujas 75
Pulcher, Publius Clodius 53
Pullman, Philip 294
puns 51
pyromancy 19, 234
Pythagoras **70**, 74, 207, 251
Pythagorean numerology 251
Pythia 46, **48–49**, 278

Q

qi 35, 37, 38, 75, 124, 212
Qiang people 18
Qin dynasty 38
Qing dynasty 118
quadrants 130, 183
Quakers 223

R

Ra 30
Ragnarok 65
rainbows 215
random number generation 296
ravens 53, 67
Reagan, Nancy 278
Regiomontanus, Johannes 173
Reid, Vera 281
reincarnation 70, 74, 239, 248
reindeer bones 286
religion
　African syncretic **198–201**
　decline in organized 300
　see also Buddhism; Christianity; Hinduism; Islam; Judaism

religious minorities 223
remote-viewing 239
Renaissance, European astrology **170–73**, 186–89
Revelation, Book of 211
rhabdomancy *see* dowsing
Richard II of England 153
riddles 216
Rider-Waite deck 227, **258–59**
Ríg (Heimdall) 98
ripples, interpreting 46, 60
Rivail, Hippolyte **239**
Rochberg, Francesca 12
Roma
　crystal balls 278–79
　fortune-telling 228, **230–31**, 278
　tea leaf readings 245, 247
Romans
　astrology and politics in imperial Rome **106–07**
　augury 53
　capnomancy 234
　Christianity 106, 107, 108–09
　collapse of Western Empire 148
　and druidic seers 66
　foundation of Rome **53**
　Hellenistic astrology 71
　inauspicious days 157
　interpreting animal behaviour 284, 285
　lecanomancy 60
　necromancy 55
Romulus and Remus **53**
Roosevelt, Franklin D. 278
Rosicrucianism 159, 226, 227
royal weddings 186
Rudhyar, Dane 270, 274
Rudolph II, Emperor 204
Rudolphine Tables **204**
Ruiz de Alarcón, Hernando 104, 105
rulers
　court astrologers **186–87**
　importance of astrology to 106–07, 109, 122, 219
　importance of divination to 15, 16–17, 19, 24, 38, 53, 212
runes 67, **98–101**, 296
　reading **102–03**
　rune casters 100
Ruperti, Alexander 270

S

sacrifices
   animal 15, 45, 49, 66, 67, 215
   blood 58
   human 66–67, 215
   Polynesian 215
   smoke from 234
   Vedic 32, 33
   Yoruba 63
Saga of Egill 100
sagas, Norse 65, 100
Sagittarius 25, 89, **91**, 95, 116, 179
Sahagún, Bernardino de 162, 163
Sakoku period 212
Salamis, Battle of 49, 53
Samarkand 132
Sámi 286
sand divination 138, 153
Sandawe people 216
Santería 199, 200, 201
Sasportas, Howard 270
satire 178
Saturn 70, 71, 81, 82, 89, **92**, 111, 114, 124, 130, 171, 182
scapulimancy 19, 67, 151
Scientific Revolution 181
Scorpio 25, 89, **91**, 95, 116, 179
Scramble for Africa 242
scrying 60, 151, 162, **278**, 286
   digital **297**
Seal of God (*sigillum Dei*) 161
seances 237, 293
seasons 29, 30, 32, 33, 40, 77, 81, 89
seers/seeresses 13, 15, 45, 52, 65, 278
   clairvoyance 238
   druidic **66–67**
   Mesmerism and spiritualism 239
sefirot 159
seiðr **65**
seismic activity 285
Seleucid dynasty 26
self-analysis 247
self-awareness 248, 249, 256
self-care 298
self-discovery 248
self-knowledge 283
Semang people 234

Semeru, Mount 127
Septimius Severus, Emperor 106
Seton, Julia 251
sexagenary cycle 40
shamanism/shamans 234, **286–87**
Shamash 16, 17
Shamsi-Adad V of Assyria 16
Shang dynasty 19, 40
shells, throwing **201**
shield chart, geomantic **141**
Shinto 121
ships, launching 186
shrines
   dream interpretation 51
   oracular 45, 46
Sicily 149, 155
Sidereus nuncius (Galileo) 203
signs of the zodiac *see* zodiac
Sigüenza y Góngora, Carlos de 178
Silk Road 75, 124
Sîn 16, 17, 24
singing bowls 298
Sirius 29, 219
sixes, three 211
sixth sense 285
slave trade 63, 198–99, 201
sleep
   deprivation 197
   dream divination **50–51**
smartphones 256, 296, 297
Smith, Pamela Colman 227, **258**, 259
smoke-drawing 234
smoke, reading 234
Smoking Mirror 162, 163
snakes 284, 285
social crisis 300
social media 289, 296, 298, 299, 300
Sol Invictus **106**
solar calendar 29, 40
solstices 26, 40, 216
Song dynasty 21, 118
songs 63, 199, 216, 280, 281
Sopdet 29
Sortes Sanctorum **153**
Sotho people 218, 219
soul
   assigned to a star 68

evolution of 248
nature of 239
reincarnation 70
soul numbers 253
sound-bathing 298
Southern Cross 218, 219
Spain, translation of Arabic texts 148–49, 153
Sphere of Life and Death/Sphere of Pythagoras 154, 155
Spica 77
spirit-writing, Chinese **118–19**
spirits
   shamanism and neoshamanism **286–87**
   spirit guides 296
   spirit helpers 197
spiritual awakening 283
spiritualism **236–39**, 278, 288
spring (vernal) equinox 27, 58, 77, 176, 281
St Hill, Katherine 228
Stabili, Francesco 161
star catalogues, first **76–77**
star charts, Egyptian **30–31**
star compasses **215**
star maps, Chinese 122–23
Star of Bethlehem **96–97**, 205
star signs 274
stars
   alignment of 215
   in Indigenous African folklore 219
Steiner, Rudolf 283
Stoic astrology 70, **78–79**, 84
Strabo 49
Śubhakarasiṃha 127
Suetonius 106
suits, card 224
Suleyman the Magnificent, Sultan 244
Sumerians 16, 51
Sun
   in ancient India 32
   in classical astrology 93
   god 16, 30, 71, 106
   heliocentric universe **180–81**
   Hellenistic astrology 71, 81
   movement of 132
   Sun-sign astrology 248, **272–75**

Sun–Moon conjunctions/oppositions 270
and theosophy 248
and yang 124
sundials 29
supernatural 293
supernovae 182, 204–05
superstition 47, 105, 172, 182, 189, 276
Supreme Creator Being 216, 219
surgeons 178
Sushruta's Compendium 111
swastikas 276
sweat-lodge ceremonies 197
Swedenborg, Emmanuel 237
Sylvester II, Pope 149
sympathetic resonances 38
synchronicity 269
syncretic religions, divination in African **198–201**

T

table-tipping 237
Tacitus 66, 100
Tahiti 215
tahu'a 215
Taíno people 199
talismans
   angelic Intelligences 161
   astrological 82, 149
   and celestial rays 151, 159
   geomantic 139
   protective 121, 135, 171
Tang dynasty 127
tarot 251, 256, 283, 293, 296, 297
   Major Arcana **260–61**
   Minor Arcana **262–63**
   origins of **224–27**
   reading **264–65**
   Rider-Waite deck 227, **258–59**
tasseography/tasseomancy **244–47**
Taurus 25, 89, **90**, 95, 116, 179
tea leaves **244–47**
technological developments 256, 288
telecommunications, advances in 288, 296
telepathy 239

Index 317

telephone services, astrological 288–89
telescopes 194, 202, 203
television
    occult themes 293
    psychics 288–89
Telliadai 45
Temne people 219
temples, oracular 46
Tenochtitlán 162
teratoscopy 46
Teresa of Avila, St 168
Tetrabiblos (Ptolemy) 68, 87, 89, 92, 130, 149
Tezcatlipoca 162, 163
thaumaturgy 223
Themistocles 49
theosophy 195, **248–49**, 256
Thoth 29, 71
Thrones 161
Thumim 159
Tianshidao school of Daoism 118
Tiberius, Emperor 71, 106
time
    astronomical timekeeping in India **32–33**
    cyclical nature of 248
    measuring 29, 40, 56
Timocharis of Alexandria 77
Timur Lenk 115, 136
Timurid dynasty 136
Tiresias 45, 53, 55
Tokugawa shoguns 121
Toledo 149, 155
tongues, speaking in 223
tornadoes 285
totems 197
trances
    African syncretic religions 199
    clairvoyance 238
    ecstatic 46, 223
    Mesmerism 237, 239
    scrying 297
    shamans 286
    völur 65
transpersonal astrology 270
Tree of Life (Kabbalistic) 226, 258
trick-taking games 224
trigonometry 76
triplicities 89, 130, 205
Trojan War 45, 47, 53

Trophonios 45
trump cards 224
truth
    hidden 294
    single absolute 248
Tsuchimikado family 121
tsunamis 285
Tswana people 218
Turner, Nat **240–41**
Tyr 98, 100, 102

U

uncertainty, times of 298, **300–01**
Underworld 26, 51, 54, 55, 56, 60
upbringing 87
Urania 79
Uranus 93
Urban VIII, Pope 172
Urim 159

V

Valcourt-Vermont, Edgar de 228
Valens, Vettius 81, 82, 83, 87, 89, 90, 91, 92, 93
Valmiki 228
Varāhamihira 112, 113, 114
Varro 153
Vedas 32, 111, 112, 113, 194
Vedic people 32–33, 111
Venda people 219
Venus 16, 17, 57, 58, 71, 81, 82, 89, **93**, 114, 124, 127, 135, 147, 149, 161, 171, 194–95, 291
Verbiest, Ferdinand 212
Vesuvius, Mount 284
vibrations, low-frequency 285
Victorious and Vanquished 155
Vikings 65
Virgo 25, 89, **91**, 95, 116, 179
virtual reality 297
visions
    clairvoyance 238–39
    druidic seers 67
    ecstatic 46, 168–69
    Indigenous American vision quests 196–97
    Nat Turner 241

Vodou 198, **199**
volcanic eruptions 284
völur 65
volvelles 164
vultures 53

W

Wahungwe people 216
Waite, Arthur Edward 227, 258, 259, 265
waking dreams 50
Wall Street Crash 239
Wang Yirong 19
war 15, 19, 24, 25, 52, 53, 57, 124, 186, 209, 237, 238, 267, 274, 276–77
Warner, William John 228
Warring States period 38
Warwick, Dionne 288
water
    dowsing **266–67**
    lecanomancy **60–61**
water clocks 29
water signs 89
weather, predicting 24, 26, 204, 296
web chat 289
weeks 29, 30, 40, 109
    deities and the seven-day **127**
wellness culture, astrology and **298–99**
Wen, Emperor 21
Wenceslaus IV of Bohemia 153
Westcott, William 258
Western astrology 74, 256, 257
Wewelsburg castle 276
whole-sign houses 81
Wilde, Oscar 228
William of Auvergne 161
Winti 199
Wirth, Oswald 226
witchcraft 267, 278
Woodman, William 258
wordplay 51
World War I 267, 276
World War II 274
    occultism **276–77**
Wu, Emperor 21
Wulff, Wilhelm 276

X

|Xam hunter-gatherers 219
Xhosa people 219

Y

yarrow-stalk divination 13, 20–21
years, sexagenary cycles 40
Yeats, William Butler 258
Yellow Emperor (Huangdi) 40
yes/no questions 19, 46, 142, 155
Yggdrasil 65, 98
yin and yang 21, 35, 40, 74, 118, **120–21**, 124
Yixing 127
yoga 283, 298, 299
Yoruba people 62–63, 200–01
Younger Futhark 98

Z

Zeno of Citium 70, 78
Zeus 46, 53, 71
Zhou dynasty 19, 20, 21
Zigu (the Purple Maiden) 118
zodiac
    Babylonian **24–27**, 68, 74, 81, 89, 124
    and body parts 178, 179
    Buddhist 125
    Chinese 40, **42–43**, 257
    four qualities of signs 89, 130
    Hellenistic 81
    Indian astrology 112, 113, 116, 125
    natal astrology 26
    reading a birth chart **94–95**
    sidereal 77, 89
    signs of the Western **90–91**, 256
    Sun-sign astrology **272–75**
    tropical 77, 81, 89, 281
Zodiac Man 25, 164, 178, 179
Zoroastrianism 96
Zulu people 219

Acknowledgments

DK would like to thank the following: Christine Stroyan, Joy Evatt, and Ann Kay for editorial assistance, Gregory McCarthy for design assistance, Diana Vowles for proofreading, Helen Peters for indexing, Senior Jacket Designer Suhita Dharamjit.

The publisher would also like to thank the following for their kind permission to reproduce their photographs:

Key: a-above; b-below/bottom; c-centre; f-far; l-left; r-right; t-top

3 Bibliotheque de Bordeaux. 4 ChinaFotoPress: (tr). NRF|SAAO: (l). 5 Getty Images: De Agostini / DEA / A. Dagli Orti (tl). Library of Congress, Washington, D.C.: Ficino, Marsilio, Author. Three Books on Life (tr). 6 Alamy Stock Photo: EMU history (tr). 7 Alamy Stock Photo: Florilegius. 8 Library of Congress, Washington, D.C.: Alfonso I D'Este, Duke of Ferrara, Patron, and Cristoforo. 12 Alamy Stock Photo: World History Archive (bc). Photo Scala, Florence: (br). 13 Alamy Stock Photo: Album (br); Florilegius (bc). © The Trustees of the British Museum. All rights reserved. 14 © The Trustees of the British Museum. All rights reserved. 15 © The Trustees of the British Museum. All rights reserved. 16 © The Trustees of the British Museum. All rights reserved. 16-17 The Metropolitan Museum of Art: Rogers Fund, 1985 (c). 17 © The Trustees of the British Museum. All rights reserved. 18 Shutterstock.com: Granger. 19 Alamy Stock Photo: CPA Media Pte Ltd / Pictures from History. 20 Bibliothèque nationale de France, Paris. 21 Alamy Stock Photo: Yogi Black (t). The New York Public Library: The Miriam and Ira D. Wallach Division of Art (b). 24 Photo Scala, Florence: The Morgan Library & Museum / Art Resource, NY. 25 © The Trustees of the British Museum. All rights reserved. 26 © The Trustees of the British Museum. All rights reserved. 27 Photo Scala, Florence: bpk, Bildagentur fuer Kunst, Kultur und Geschichte, Berlin (t). 28-29 Getty Images: Hulton Archive / Ann Ronan Pictures / Print Collector. 29 Getty Images: SSPL (br). 30-31 Tübingen Unversity: Ägyptische Sammlung der Universität Tübingen, H. Jensen. 32 Anupam Kumar Suman: The Asiatic Society of Mumbai (b). Bridgeman Images: (t). 33 Wellcome Collection 34 Alamy Stock Photo: Album. 35 Getty Images: Royal Geographical Society (with IBG) (b). 38 Getty Images: Pictures From History / Universal Images Group (b). Library of Congress, Washington, D.C.: Chinese Rare Book Collection (c). 39 ChinaFotoPress. 40 British Library: (cl). Wikipedia: Li Ung Bin, Outlines of Chinese History, Shanghai 1914 (tc). 41 Bridgeman Images. 42-43 Alamy Stock Photo: World History Archive. 44 Photo Scala, Florence. 45 Bridgeman Images. © The Trustees of the British Museum. All rights reserved. 46 © The Trustees of the British Museum. All rights reserved. Science Photo Library: David Parker (b). 47 Photo Scala, Florence. 48-49 Getty Images: Sepia Times / Universal Images Group. 50-51 © The Trustees of the British Museum. All rights reserved. 51 © The Trustees of the British Museum. All rights reserved. 52 © The Trustees of the British Museum. All rights reserved. 53 Alamy Stock Photo: Florilegius (t). Bridgeman Images: © Look and Learn (b). 54 Bridgeman Images. 55 Alamy Stock Photo: funkyfood London - Paul Williams (b). Bridgeman Images: Prismatic Pictures (t). 56 The Metropolitan Museum of Art: The Michael C. Rockefeller Memorial Collection, Gift of Nelson A. Rockefeller, 1963 (t). Patricia Martin Morales: (b). 57 Alamy Stock Photo: World History Archive. 58 © The Trustees of the British Museum. All rights reserved. 58-59 Alamy Stock Photo: Album. 60 © The Trustees of the British Museum. All rights reserved. Getty Images: De Agostini / DEA / Archivio J. Lange (b). 61 Photo Scala, Florence: bpk, Bildagentur fuer Kunst, Kultur und Geschichte, Berlin. 62 Bridgeman Images: Saint Louis Art Museum / Funds given by Thomas Alexander, Emily Rauh Pulitzer, Anabeth Calkins and John Weil, Susan and David Mesker, Ted and Sissy Thomas, and other donors in memory of Dr. Alvin R. Frank. 63 Bridgeman Images: Courtesy of the Museum of Fine Arts, Houston / Gift of Frank Carroll in memory of Clytie Allen (tr). The Metropolitan Museum of Art: Gift of Mr. and Mrs. Klaus G. Perls, 1991 (tc). 64 Alamy Stock Photo: Album. 65 Bridgeman Images: Photo © The Holbarn Archive (b). Naionalmuseet, Denmark: CC-BY-SA / Roberto Fortuna og Kira Ursem (tr). 66 Getty Images: Fine Art Images / Heritage Images. 67 Alamy Stock Photo: Ashmolean Museum of Art and Archaeology / Heritage Images (t). Courtesy Of The Board Of Trinity College, Dublin: (br). 68 © The Trustees of the British Museum. All rights reserved. Getty Images: De Agostini / DEA / S. Vannini (b). 69 Bridgeman Images: Photo © The Holbarn Archive. 70 Bridgeman Images: © Giancarlo Costa (bc). © J. Paul Getty Trust / Open Content Program: (tl). 70-71 Science Photo Library: Middle Temple Librarby. 74 Alamy Stock Photo: Smith Archive (bl). 75 Alamy Stock Photo: Lanmas (br). Bridgeman Images: From the British Library archive (bl). 76 Getty Images: Hulton Archive / Culture Club / Bridgeman. 77 Images First Ltd / Tony Freeth PhD: (br). 78 Alamy Stock Photo: Adam McLean. 79 Alamy Stock Photo: Historic Images. 80 Photo Scala, Florence: RMN-Grand Palais / Gerard Blot / RMN-GP. 81 Alamy Stock Photo: Charles Walker Collection (t). 82 Bridgeman Images: Ancient Art and Architecture Collection Ltd (t). Volnoe Delo Oleg Deripaska Foundation: (br). 83 Bridgeman Images: From the British Library archive. 84-85 Getty Images: De Agostini / DEA / A. Dagli Orti. 86 Getty Images: Corbis Historical / Photo Josse / Leemage. 87 Bridgeman Images: From the British Library archive (t); From the British Library archive (b). 88 Bridgeman Images: © Giancarlo Costa. 89 Alamy Stock Photo: Smith Archive (b). Harvard Art Museums: Fogg Museum, Arthur K. and Mariot F. Solomon Collection (t). 90 Getty Images: Pictures From History / Universal Images Group (tl); Pictures From History / Universal Images Group (cl); Pictures From History / Universal Images Group (r). 91 Getty Images: Pictures From History / Universal Images Group (tl); Pictures From History / Universal Images Group (tc); Pictures From History / Universal Images Group (tr); Pictures From History / Universal Images Group (cl); Pictures From History / Universal Images Group (c); Pictures From History / Universal Images Group (cr); Pictures From History / Universal Images Group (bl); Pictures From History / Universal Images Group (bc); Pictures From History / Universal Images Group (br). 92 Library of Congress, Washington, D.C.: Alfonso I D'Este, Duke of Ferrara, Patron, and Cristoforo De Predis (x3). 93 Bridgeman Images: Photo © CCI (tr). Library of Congress, Washington, D.C.: Alfonso I D'Este, Duke of Ferrara, Patron, and Cristoforo De Predis (x4). 96-97 Getty Images: Heritage Art / Heritage Images. 98 Alamy Stock Photo: Lars Hallstrom. 99 State Historical Museums, Sweden: Bruxe, Ulf, Historiska museet / CC BY 4.0. 100 Getty Images: Fine Art Images / Heritage Images (b). Naionalmuseet, Denmark: CC-BY-SA / Arnold Mikkelsen (tl). 101 Statens Museum For Kunst, Copenhagen. 104 Bridgeman Images. 105 Alamy Stock Photo: Historic Collection (b). © The Trustees of the British Museum. All rights reserved. 106 © The Trustees of the British Museum. All rights reserved. Wikipedia: Mark Landon / CC BY 4.0 (b). 107 Getty Images / iStock: Tolga TEZCAN. 108-109 Bibliothèque nationale de France, Paris. 110 Wellcome Collection. 111 Los Angeles County Museum of Art: Gift of Emeritus Professor and Mrs. Thomas O. Ballinger (M.87.271a-g) / South and Southeast Asian Art (b). Wellcome Collection. 112 Chris Ilsley. 113 Anupam Kumar Suman: (t). 114 Anupam Kumar Suman. 115 Bridgeman Images: From the British Library archive. 118 Getty Images: SSPL (b). Philadelphia Museum of Art: (tl). 119 AF Fotografie. 120 Kyoto University Library. 121 © The Trustees of the British Museum. All rights reserved. The Metropolitan Museum of Art: Rogers Fund, 1917 (t). 122-123 Bridgeman Images: From the British Library archive. 124 Wikipedia: Jinxianguan. 125 Wikipedia: kaladarshan.arts.ohio-state.edu. 126 © The Trustees of the British Museum. All rights reserved. 127 The Metropolitan Museum of Art: The Harry G. C. Packard Collection of Asian Art, Gift of Harry G. C. Packard, and Purchase, Fletcher, Rogers, Harris Brisbane Dick, and Louis V. Bell Funds, Joseph Pulitzer Bequest, and The Annenberg Fund Inc. Gift, 1975 (b). Wikipedia: Tokushima Prefectural Museum (tc). 128 Alamy Stock Photo: Lanmas. 129 University of Edinburgh. 130 Bridgeman Images. © The Trustees of the British Museum. All rights reserved. 131 Alamy Stock Photo: CPA Media Pte Ltd / Pictures From History. 132 Alamy Stock Photo: Science History Images / Photo Researchers (t). The Metropolitan Museum of Art: (bc). 133 The Metropolitan Museum of Art: Rogers Fund, 1913. 134 Bibliotheque de Bordeaux. 135 The Metropolitan Museum of Art: Rogers Fund, 1944 (t); Rogers Fund, 1919 (b). 136-137 Wellcome Collection: MS Persian 474. 138 © The Trustees of the British Museum. All rights reserved. 139 AF Fotografie. Bibliothèque nationale de France, Paris. 142 AF Fotografie. U.S. National Library of Medicine, History of Medicine Division. 143 The Metropolitan Museum of Art: Edward C. Moore Collection, Bequest of Edward C. Moore, 1891. 146 Alamy Stock Photo: Adam McLean (br). Bridgeman Images. 147 Bridgeman Images: From the British Library archive (bc). Getty Images: De Agostini (bl). Shutterstock.com: The Art Archive (br). 148-149 Bridgeman Images. 149

Jagiellonian University, Kraków: (br). Leiden University Library, The Netherlands: (cr). **150** Bridgeman Images. **151** © The Trustees of the British Museum. All rights reserved. **152** The Bodleian Library, University of Oxford. **153** Berlin, Staatsbibliothek zu Berlin - Pressischer Kulturbesitz - Handschriftenabteilung: (tc). The Bodleian Library, University of Oxford. **154** The Bodleian Library, University of Oxford. **155** Bridgeman Images: From the British Library archive (t). Courtesy of The Board of Trinity College, Dublin. **156-157** National Library of Poland (Biblioteka Narodowa, Warszawa). **158** Bibliothèque nationale de France, Paris. **159** © The Trustees of the British Museum. All rights reserved. **160** Bridgeman Images. **161** Biblioteca Medicea Laurenziana: (tr). Bridgeman Images: British Library Archive (b). **162** © The Trustees of the British Museum. All rights reserved. **163** Bridgeman Images. © J. Paul Getty Trust / Open Content Program. **164** Bridgeman Images: Granger. Llyfrgell Genedlaethol Cymru – The National Library of Wales: (br). **165** Jeremy Norman Collection. **166** Biblioteca nazionale centrale di Firenze: (tl). Bridgeman Images. **167** Alamy Stock Photo: Florilegius. **168** Bridgeman Images: Lebrecht History (t); Photo © The Holbarn Archive (b). **169** Alamy Stock Photo: Gallery of Art. **170** Alamy Stock Photo: Adam McLean. **171** © The Trustees of the British Museum. All rights reserved. Getty Images / iStock: Tashka (b). **172** Getty Images: De Agostini (t). Library of Congress, Washington, D.C.: Ficino, Marsilio, Author. Three Books on Life. (cl). **173** Library of Congress, Washington, D.C. **174-175** Bridgeman Images: Photo © Photo Josse. **176-177** Wellcome Collection. **176** Wellcome Collection. **177** Wellcome Collection. **178** © The Trustees of the British Museum. All rights reserved. **179** Alamy Stock Photo: Science History Images / Photo Researchers. **180** Getty Images: De Agostini. **181** The Metropolitan Museum of Art: The Elisha Whittelsey Collection, The Elisha Whittelsey Fund, 1959 (t). Science Photo Library: Library Of Congress (b). **182** Wikipedia: (tc). **183** Getty Images: De Agostini / DEA / G. Dagli Orti. **184-185** Bridgeman Images: © Giancarlo Costa. **186** Alamy Stock Photo: The Picture Art Collection (b). Wikipedia: Biblioteka Jagielloska (tr). **187** History of Science Museum, University of Oxford. **188** Bridgeman Images: From the British Library archive. **189** Science Photo Library: Library of Congress (t); Sheila Terry (b). **190** Shutterstock.com: The Art Archive (tl); The Art Archive (tc); The Art Archive (tr); The Art Archive (bl); The Art Archive (bc); The Art Archive (br). **191** Shutterstock.com: The Art Archive (tl); The Art Archive (tc); The Art Archive (bl); The Art Archive (bc). **194** akg-images: André Held (br). Alamy Stock Photo: Charles Walker Collection (bc). Leah Marie Dorion: (bl). **195** Bibliothèque nationale de France, Paris. Photo Scala, Florence: Christie's Images, London / Oreste Cortazzo (bl). The AwaaZ Samosa Festival: Zarina Patel (bc). **196** Leah Marie Dorion. **197** Getty Images: Universal Images Group / Werner Forman. **198** Bridgeman Images: © Archives Charmet. **199** National Museum of African Art, Smithsonian Institution: National Museum of African Art (br). Wikipedia: chris (ca). **200** The Art Institute of Chicago: Ada Turnbull Hertle Endowment (bl). **200-201** Instituto Pintora Djanira. **201** Getty Images: Bruna Prado / Stringer (tr). **202** ESO: Giuseppe Bertini. **203** Bridgeman Images: Photo © Raffaello Bencini (b). Wikipedia: sailko (tc). **204** Bridgeman Images: From the British Library archive (b); Lebrecht History (t). **205** Bridgeman Images: Christie's Images. **206-207** Bridgeman Images: Christie's Images. **207** Bridgeman Images: Granger (tr). **208** Bridgeman Images. **209** Bridgeman Images: From the British Library archive (b). Reproduced by kind permission of the Syndics of Cambridge University Library: (c). **210-211** Alamy Stock Photo: Charles Walker Collection. **212** Bridgeman Images. National Diet Library, Japan: (cla). **213** National Museum of Asian Art, Smithsonian. **214** Getty Images: Universal Images Group / Florilegius. **215** Alamy Stock Photo: EMU History (ca). **216** National Museum of African Art, Smithsonian Institution. **217** Bridgeman Images: Museum of Fine Arts, Houston / Gift of Alfred C. Glassell, Jr. / Akan School. **218** NRF|SAAO. **219** National Museum of African Art, Smithsonian Institution. **220** Australian War Memorial: (tl). Fine Arts Museums of San Francisco: (bc). **221** Bridgeman Images: Look and Learn / European School. **222** Alamy Stock Photo: The Picture Art Collection. **223** Alamy Stock Photo: FLHC K (bc). Chethams Library: (tr). **224** Bibliothèque nationale de France, Paris. Yale University Library: (bl). **225** Alamy Stock Photo: Vidimages (br). Bibliothèque nationale de France, Paris. **226** Alamy Stock Photo: Charles Walker Collection (bc). **226-227** Wikipedia. **227** Alamy Stock Photo: Charles Walker Collection (crb). **228** akg-images: André Held (cl). **229** Bridgeman Images: Look and Learn (b). Getty Images: Hulton Archive / Heritage Images (tc). **230-231** Photo Scala, Florence: Christie's Images, London / Oreste Cortazzo. **234** Bridgeman Images: Jacques Grasset de Saint-Sauveur (bc). **235** Rissa Miller. **236** Alamy Stock Photo: Chronicle. **237** Bridgeman Images: The British Library Archive (br). Getty Images: Hulton Archive / Print Collector (ca). **238** Alamy Stock Photo: Science History Images / Photo Researchers. **239** Alamy Stock Photo: GRANGER - Historical Picture Archive / W. Thomas Smith. (tl). Bridgeman Images: Tallandier / Hippolyte Leymarie (br). **240-241** Stephen Towns: www.stephentowns.com. **242** Bridgeman Images: Illustrated Papers Collection / Look and Learn / Joseph Nash (cla). Pitt Rivers Museum, Oxford: (br). **243** The AwaaZ Samosa Festival: Zarina Patel. **244** Bibliothèque nationale de France, Paris. **245** Bridgeman Images: The British Library Archive (cra). **246-247** Bridgeman Images: Valerie Jackson Harris Collection / Look and Learn. **248** Getty Images: Universal Images Group (bc). National Digital Library of India: (tc). **249** AF Fotografie. **250** Bridgeman Images: Christie's Images. **251** Library of Congress, Washington, D.C.: Balliett, L. Dow (cra). The Rosenbach of the Free Library of Philadelphia Foundation: (br). **256** Science Photo Library: New York Public Library (bc). **257** Alamy Stock Photo: Imaginechina Limited (br). Bridgeman Images: The British Library Archive. Getty Images: The Image Bank / Tuul & Bruno Morandi (bc). **258** DOYLE: (bc). National Library Of Ireland: (tc). **259** Alamy Stock Photo: Carolyn Jenkins (tc). Wikipedia. **260-261** Wikipedia: Arthur Edward Waite. **262-263** Wikipedia: Arthur Edward Waite. **266** Mary Evans Picture Library. **267** Getty Images: Fairfax Media (tr). Mary Evans Picture Library: Water Divining - A Book of Practical Instruction by S. N. Pike MBE. (crb). **268** Science Photo Library: New York Public Library. **269** Bridgeman Images: Universal History Archive / UIG (br). Getty Images: Paul Popper / Popperfoto (tr). **270** Bruno and Louise Huber. **271** W.W. Norton. **272** Roland Smithies / luped.com: Modern Astrology. **273** John Aster Archive: Womans World (ca). Mirrorpix: Sunday Express (br). **274** Alamy Stock Photo: BooksR (tl). American Astrology: (br). **275** Getty Images: Conde Nast Collection / Zeilinger. **276** Getty Images: AFP / John Macdougall (bc). TV Tropes. **277** Imperial War Museum. **278** Bridgeman Images: Everett Collection (cla). Getty Images: Bettmann (br). **279** Bridgeman Images: Mallett Gallery, London / Joseph Finnemore. **280** Alamy Stock Photo: EMU history. **281** Courtesy National Gallery of Art, Washington: (cra). Wikipedia: Soul City (bc). **282** Kent Fine Art: Courtesy of Paul Laffoley. **283** Alamy Stock Photo: Steve Sant (cra). Bridgeman Images: The British Library Archive (bc). **284** Alamy Stock Photo: Adam Eastland. **285** Alamy Stock Photo: Penta Springs Limited / Artokoloro (cra). U.S. National Library of Medicine, History of Medicine Division. **286** Getty Images: Universal Images Group / Werner Forman (bl). **287** Getty Images: The Image Bank / Tuul & Bruno Morandi. **288** Wikipedia: Joe Mabel. **289** Alamy Stock Photo: Associated Press / Liz Hafalia (t); imageBROKER.com / Jochen Tack (bc). **292** BFA Imaging. **293** Alamy Stock Photo: AJ Pics (br). Getty Images: Moviepix / Screen Archives (cra). **294-295** Alamy Stock Photo: Landmark Media. **296** Dreamstime.com: Alexey Boldin (bc). **297** Alamy Stock Photo: Imaginechina Limited (t). Getty Images: Bloomberg (br). **298** Getty Images / iStock: Guenterguni (br). Getty Images: Cindy Ord (cla). **299** Getty Images: The Asahi Shimbun. **300** Alamy Stock Photo: Buradaki (bc). BFA Imaging. **301** Alamy Stock Photo: Patti McConville. **302** Wellcome Collection: MS Persian 474

Senior Editor Kathryn Hennessy
Editors Anna Cheifetz, Kath Hill,
Abigail Mitchell, Victoria Pyke
Senior Art Editor Helen Spencer
Project Art Editor Katie Cavanagh
Designer Judy Caley
Managing Editor Gareth Jones
Managing Art Editor Luke Griffin
Production Editor Andy Hilliard
Production Controller Nancy-Jane Maun
Picture Researcher Sarah Smithies
Assistant Picture Researcher Manpreet Kaur
Jacket Designers Juhi Sheth, Surabhi Wadhwa
Senior DTP Designer Harish Aggarwal
DTP Designer Vikram Singh
Senior Jackets Coordinator Priyanka Sharma Saddi
Publishing Director Georgina Dee
Managing Director Liz Gough
Art Director Maxine Pedliham
Design Director Phil Ormerod

First published in Great Britain in 2025 by
Dorling Kindersley Limited
20 Vauxhall Bridge Road,
London SW1V 2SA

The authorised representative in the EEA is
Dorling Kindersley Verlag GmbH. Arnulfstr. 124,
80636 Munich, Germany

Copyright © 2025 Dorling Kindersley Limited
A Penguin Random House Company
10 9 8 7 6 5 4 3 2 1
001–341851–Aug/2025

All rights reserved.
No part of this publication may be reproduced, stored
in or introduced into a retrieval system, or transmitted,
in any form, or by any means (electronic, mechanical,
photocopying, recording, or otherwise), without the
prior written permission of the copyright owner.
DK values and supports copyright. Thank you for respecting
intellectual property laws by not reproducing, scanning or
distributing any part of this publication by any means without
permission. By purchasing an authorised edition, you are
supporting writers and artists and enabling DK to continue
to publish books that inform and inspire readers.
No part of this publication may be used or reproduced in
any manner for the purpose of training artificial intelligence
technologies or systems. In accordance with Article 4⑶
of the DSM Directive 2019/790, DK expressly reserves this
work from the text and data mining exception.

A CIP catalogue record for this book
is available from the British Library.
ISBN: 978-0-2416-8280-7

Printed and bound in UAE

www.dk.com

This book was made with Forest
Stewardship Council™ certified
paper – one small step in DK's
commitment to a sustainable future.
Learn more at www.dk.com/uk/
information/sustainability